The Japanese Economy
in the Tokugawa Era, 1600–1868

Edited with introductions by

Michael Smitka
Washington and Lee University

GARLAND PUBLISHING, INC.
A MEMBER OF THE TAYLOR & FRANCIS GROUP
New York & London
1998

Library of Congress Cataloging-in-Publication Data

The Japanese economy in the Tokugawa era, 1600–1868 / edited with introductions by Michael Smitka.
    p. cm. — (Japanese economic history, 1600–1960 ; 6)
    Includes bibliographical references.
    ISBN 0-8153-2710-2 (vol. 6 : alk. paper). — ISBN 0-8153-2704-8
(7 vol. set : alk. paper)
    1. Japan—Economic conditions—To 1868. I. Smitka, Michael.
II. Series.
HC462.6.J36 1998
330.952'025—dc21   98-9411
                                     CIP

Printed on acid-free, 250-year-life paper
Manufactured in the United States of America

Contents

Introduction

Japan evolved from a closed society in 1850 to a budding Asian power by 1900, with an accompanying evolution of her political system. Change proceeded more slowly for the common man, but by the onset of World War II Japan's agrarian-centered society gave way to an urban and increasing industrial structure that transformed the pattern of daily life for much of the population. That is now a half century behind us, and even the Cold War is past. That older history in itself may not stir interest, but Japan's rise in a single generation from the ashes of defeat in 1945 to the world's second largest economy caught the attention of the rest of the world and promulgated Asian studies programs in universities everywhere.

This series collects a select set of papers from the now vast outpouring of writings on Japan, tracing her economic development during the past three centuries. It is aimed at the historian seeking to place political and cultural events in their economic context and at the economist looking for comparative material to help illuminate the wider process of economic growth. It focuses thus on an array of topics that contribute to a wider picture of Japan—the antecedents to modern growth in the Tokugawa era (1603–1868), studies of the development process and the role of trade, the interplay of agriculture and demographics, the textile industry as the leading sector of industrialization, Japan's experience in the 1930s, and the post-World War II reconstruction process.

Economic History

History interprets other times and other places through today's eyes. It is an inherently comparative undertaking, and to do it well requires interpreting the perspectives of multiple disciplines to bring a subject into better focus. Economic history is a useful, and indeed often essential, element of that process. As Tom Rawski phrases it, "Even if man does not live by bread alone, economics lurks beneath the surface of any historical inquiry."[1] The economist's analytic models highlight how living conditions and opportunities vary, and they illuminate the way in which the environment of times past has constrained behavior. It is thus complementary to understanding political choices, social conditions, family roles, and even the intellectual milieu.

The essence of a model, the economist's tool of trade, is the deliberate simplification of what is known of the world. As such, models may strike the historian as unduly simplistic (and, perhaps, as unnecessarily formal). But no historian writes without systematic simplification, or without a framework of some sort in which to locate the story. If anything, economists do this in a more transparent manner than other practitioners of history. The explicit comparisons of economic models make clear where the stories begin, and where they leave off. Such simplicity seldom is as pleasing to read as the polished prose of a historian, but it does force economists to state what they believe really matters. This in turn facilitates adding nuance to the core argument in a systematic manner.

But history and comparative studies are also crucial to the economist. Sociologists and other social scientists can generate their own data through surveys and experimentation. The economist, though, has little ability to use such approaches and must turn instead to the historical record in search for data. Economists, then, are at the mercy of Clio for data that reflect the impact of variations in institutions, culture, and the living environment.

Japanese History

Studying Japan's economic and social history is appropriate for various and sundry academic purposes. But it is also full of high drama, and for all its potential drudgery, doing history can be downright interesting. Japan in 1500 was a lightly populated group of islands governed by a small elite in a society little removed from slash-and-burn subsistence. During the 1500s, new crops and irrigation technology were imported from China, and the musket became known through the Portuguese. Scattered domains were unified in a series of wars in the second half of the sixteenth century, culminating with the founding of the Tokugawa bakufu in 1603.

Peace brought population growth during the succeeding century of perhaps one percent per year, while local governments fostered irrigation projects and (indirectly) domestic trade. (International trade, however, was severely restricted from the 1630s on.) In 1720, the majority of the population still followed agricultural pursuits. Farm productivity, however, was high enough to support an urban network as large as that found anywhere in Europe outside of the Netherlands. During the course of the seventeenth century the new capital of Edo grew from a fishing village into the world's largest city, with a population of over one million and a vibrant urban culture. The eighteenth century saw a stagnation of overall population growth, but a continued, albeit gradual, increase in production and domestic trade. By the early 1800s, the majority of the output of the more prosperous regions was industrial in character, even if the workers themselves remained on the farm, and the products—cotton textiles, sugar, paper, silk—relied on agricultural inputs. This growth, however, took place largely in isolation from the industrial revolution taking place in England, and made little use of machinery.

In 1854 the American Matthew Perry's "Black Ships" brought two centuries of isolation to an end. The political drama that ensued—the Meiji Restoration of 1868 and the founding of a modern state—is well known. So is the rapid improvement in military capability that not only kept Japan from being colonized, but led to the start of her own colonial empire with the acquisition of Taiwan in 1895. Here economic history provides a surprise, for it finds no economic transformation in the nineteenth century, only a gradual continuation of an upswing in growth that dated from the 1820s. This growth, in turn, followed patterns apparent in a piecemeal manner from early in the Edo period (under the Tokugawa bakufu, 1603–1868).

By the end of the nineteenth century, the industrial revolution began to make its power felt. Railroads transformed overland transport, while steamships lowered the cost of coastal and international shipping. Newly incorporated banks proffered financing, while the telegraph and newspapers began to tie even remote areas to the trends of the capital, now renamed Tokyo. Clocks changed the rhythm of daily life, as did the slow extension of compulsory education.

Parts of this were financed through the export of primary products, coal and tea, and above all, silk. But as in Britain, and later in America and parts of continental Europe, the leading industry was cotton textiles. Mills turned to female labor, girls and young women off the farm, who worked for a few years to supplement family resources—a pattern similar to that found in New England. Within two decades Japanese mills had supplanted Western imports as a source of yarn for the domestic weaving industry. By the end of World War I it was the Japanese and not the British who were beginning to clothe China with machine-woven materials.

By the interwar years, the industrial structure was beginning to deepen. One route was textile machinery, including the Toyoda Automatic Loom works, whose profits financed entry into manufacturing motor vehicles in the late 1930s. But shipbuilding was more important for the capital goods industry, supplemented by military procurement. Electrical products also stand out. Textile mills turned to electric lighting by the 1890s, permitting them to run two shifts with less danger of fire. Rural electrification in the 1920s—earlier than in the United States—let farmers use electric pumps for irrigation. By the 1930s heavy industry was developing—fertilizer, chemicals, steel, and electrical generators. Yet the early availability of electric motors, combined with fluid labor markets, meant that much of production was carried out not in factories operated by immovable steam engines, but in small urban workshops. The market was large enough to attract foreign investors (Ford set up an assembly plant in 1925) particularly as it encompassed Japan's growing Asian empire, which included not only Taiwan (1895) and Korea (1910) but also Manchuria (from 1931) and later a portion of northern China.

The interwar years closed with the Great Depression—at least in much of the world. In Japan as well, 1929 saw the start of an economic downturn. This was sparked by a change in governments that led to Japan returning to the gold standard—just as others were leaving—and the maintenance of a "strong" yen at the pre-World War I parity. But in comparison to the rest of the world, the decline was mild; it is not even clear that output actually fell. The recession was also brief, ending in 1932. That turnaround is due almost certainly to one man, Korekiyo Takahashi, who implemented a "loose" monetary policy, stimulative budgets, and currency devaluation when he became prime minister in December 1931. These "Keynesian" policies, which went against the reigning economic orthodoxy, were implemented five years before the publication of the General Theory of Employment, Interest and Money.

The turnaround is underappreciated by economists, whose focus on the Great Depression has been on the traumatic events transpiring in Europe and in the United States. But it is also poorly understood by historians of Japan, since received wisdom presumes that the depression must have been severe, given the slide into war that followed. Both (Western) economists and (Japanese) historians have much to learn from a careful reexamination of these years.

The Pacific War broke out in earnest in 1937, when Japan invaded China. This quickly led to the imposition of trade sanctions and the formation of a "yen bloc." The Japanese government sought to incorporate her colonies more directly into the economy. Foreign ventures (such as Ford and General Motors) were forced to close, while controls were gradually expanded over domestic firms. But rationing was implemented on an *ad hoc* basis, and plans were poorly coordinated. The result was chaos. At the same time, many institutional changes were implemented. The banking system was consolidated and reorganized, the nascent labor movement was folded into the "sanpo" patriotic associations, and the government-business relationship was transformed. The details, however, are hard to sort out; there has been little interest in delving into that era.

The war ended in economic collapse. Domestic agriculture, for example, was in shambles—fertilizer production had ceased, and able-bodied workers had been drafted. This was compounded by the loss of Japan's colonies, the source of food and many raw materials, and by the disruption of transportation. The U.S. Occupation sought to "democratize" Japan, but initially had little direct interest in the economy; indeed, official policy was that Japan should remain permanently poor. Along with restructuring the political system, the emphasis was thus on assorted institutional reforms—breaking up industrial concerns (zaibatsu dissolution), land reform, and the fostering of labor unions. Widespread rationing and other economic controls remained in place; the U.S. Army, for example, ran Japan's trade.

The need to stave off further economic collapse, including overcoming hyperinflation, forced some change. This shift was reinforced by the onset of the Cold War and the impending collapse of the nationalist government in China. An American banker, Joseph Dodge, was sent from Germany to Japan in 1949. He instituted reforms that brought an end to an array of subsidies and controls, balanced the budget, and normalized trade under a unified exchange rate. A Columbia University economist, Carl Shoup, restructured the tax system. The reforms and the immediate consequences are quite similar to those of subsequent restructuring programs in many other countries. Inflation was brought in check, but the reforms also caused a steep recession.

The Korean War broke out in June of 1950, leading to an immediate turnaround of the economy—an export boom financed in large part by American "special procurements" for the war effort. There was thus no need for a Marshall Plan in Japan. By 1955 the economy reached prewar levels of output, and as exports increased and trade and other controls eased, rapid growth commenced. This was reinforced by Prime Minister Ikeda's "Income Doubling" plan of 1960, and for the next decade growth continued at an unprecedented average nine percent per year. In 1968 Japan surpassed the German economy in size, and by 1970 income levels were on a par with Europe. Japan's era as a developing country came to a close.

In a little over a century, then, Japan went from a society closed off to the West and its industrial revolution (without a centralized government or significant international trade) to achieving parity with England. Part of this success is found in the legacy of the Tokugawa era, which saw the rise of a commercialized economy and widespread proto-industrialization. The following section addresses the parts of that story covered by the papers in this reprint series.

Theme of the Series

Japan has been a source of fascination for many Western social scientists, who have produced a rich variety of research. In addition, Japan's leading economic historians have been active internationally, and major parts of their work are available in English.[2] One consequence is an excess of riches; even with seven volumes, many arbitrary cuts had to be made. The series, for example, excludes material from monographs, since book chapters are seldom able to stand by themselves, though they are the preferred form of exposition for many historians. Likewise, papers of a highly technical or mathematical nature were excluded, since they would be accessible to only a narrow range of readers.

Similar limitations were made in the periods of coverage. This series makes no attempt to cover the period before the Tokugawa period, which began circa 1600. While the sixteenth century is clearly an era where political unification and Chinese and other foreign technology sowed the seeds of change, these sprouts took root and grew only in the two and one-half centuries of peace that followed. Likewise, the series ends with the onset of the high-growth era of the early 1960s. A vast and growing literature is available on the period of Japan's "economic miracle," but little of it is historical in perspective. Instead, it is better to look at the 1960s and beyond as part of Japan's modern economy, better analyzed with standard microeconomic and macroeconomic tools than with those of the economic historian.

Even with these limitations, the papers in this series quickly filled seven volumes. To help bring order to the wealth of available material, these volumes are organized on a thematic basis. Papers were selected accordingly, resulting in the exclusion of otherwise worthwhile items that did not fit. Several topics were excluded because they have been covered in other, recent collections of material. For example, in general this series does not include works in business history. Readers wanting to pursue this area can turn to two annuals, the *Japanese Yearbook of Business History* and the *International Conference on Business History*, as well as the overviews of Wray and Fruin.[3] Topics in finance can be found in two volumes co-edited by Hugh Patrick of Columbia University.[4] Treatment of a variety of law and economics issues can be found in books by Ramseyer, Ooms, Haley and Upham.[5] Transportation sector developments are covered by Ericson and Wray.[6] Other potential topics might include labor history, histories of specific industries, and studies of political economy and industrial policy.[7] Finally, no attempt is made to cover the history of economic thought, albeit that is in part because relatively little is available in English.[8] There is too much available to even attempt an introductory bibliography—for that see Wray's book-length compilation.[9] Nevertheless, this series provides a useful introduction to the themes that dominated the last three decades' work in economic history.

Volume 1: Japanese Prewar Growth: Lessons for Development Theory?

Japan has been, and continues to be, a testing ground for theories of economic development. This volume combines papers that grapple with the large issue: How did Japan grow? (Much harder, of course, is the related question: Why did Japan grow?) As the only non-Western economy to "develop," Japan was long seen as unique. That is starting to change, and it is likely that Japan will henceforth be seen as the archetype of the rapidly industrializing economies, including its neighbors, China, Korea, and Taiwan.

Japan's growth caught the eye of a number of economists in the prewar era. Joseph Schumpeter's personal library, for example, resides at Hitotsubashi University in Tokyo, and his wife Edith Schumpeter led a team of economists in the first large-scale study of the country, *The Economic Development of Japan and Manchukuo* (New York: The Macmillan Company, 1940). Similarly, E.F. Penrose wrote on demographics, using Japan as a base, as did Irene Taueber. In the postwar era, the new techniques of econometrics were soon applied to Japan by Lawrence Klein and his disciples.

Other than a few items of Marxist analysis, little of the early analysis by Japanese scholars survived to influence others (see the paper by Yasuba). The main exception is the Akamatsu paper, which gives his "flying geese" model of technological development and foreign direct investment. This was later expanded by Kiyoshi Kojima,[10] and is similar in flavor to parts of the analysis of Alexander Gerschenkron and to Raymond Vernon's model of the international product cycle.

It remained for a wave of postwar economists to attack issues with a new vigor. These scholars were influenced by Simon Kuznets, and more generally by Gerschenkron and Ragnar Nurkse, and later by W. Arthur Lewis. The core of this group was under Kazushi Ohkawa at Hitotsubashi University and involved in the LTES (Long Term Economic Statistics) project. The 14-volume set of historical data that was eventually published (described in the paper by Ohkawa and Shinohara) has provided the gristmill for two generations of economists. Indeed, the LTES data are used by other papers included in this volume to test ideas of capital accumulation, technical change, and the linkage between agriculture and industry. The latter issue led to a particularly lively interchange over two sector "labor surplus" models between Minami, Fei and Ranis, and others, and included alternate models such as that of Williamson and De Bever. Other papers examine the data themselves, calling into question, for example, the plausibility of the original data on agricultural output (Rosovsky) or noting other data sources (Matsuda). Finally, these debates in development economics informed research on agriculture, demography, labor markets and the Tokugawa legacy. It is thus a useful starting point for understanding the themes that economic historians of Japan have examined.

Volume 2: The Interwar Economy of Japan:
Colonialism, Depression, and Recovery, 1910–1940

Many Japanese historians look to the period between World War I and the outbreak of the Pacific War in 1937 in an attempt to understand the roots of Japanese militarism.

Here the assumption is that the era was one of poor economic performance which led to social conflict and ultimately the collapse of the nascent "Taisho" democracy. Certainly Japan was not immune to the forces that swept the global economy. But it is not at all clear that the agricultural sector was a locus of unusual misery in the 1920s. It is clear, though, that Japan effectively side-stepped the onslaught of the Great Depression. Several papers in this volume analyze the period leading up to the Great Depression, as well as the sharp recession of 1929–1931 and the rapid growth that ensued thereafter. (See also papers in volume seven on agriculture during that era.) At the same time, any analysis of this era leads directly into an analysis of Japan's management of its colonies and their impact on the mother country. Such studies comprise the remainder of the volume.

World War I induced a boom in Japan—and inflation. Rice riots broke out in 1918 and led Japan to open its markets to agricultural imports. This led in turn to a shift in colonial policy, which ultimately turned Taiwan (a colony from 1895) and Korea (annexed in 1910) into an agricultural hinterland to feed the growing urban populace of Japan proper. In contrast, the northern part of Korea, together with Manchukuo, an independent state–*cum*–colony from 1931, became a source of raw materials and a locus of heavy industry.

Lower agricultural prices fit into the goal of Japan's return to the gold standard. Delayed by the aftermath of the Tokyo earthquake of 1923, and a financial panic in 1927, Japan only managed to do so in December 1929, just as the onset of the Great Depression was forcing the rest of the world off the gold standard. A sharp recession ensued, the government fell, and the new government that came to power in December 1931 immediately left the gold standard, devaluing the yen by 50 percent. At the same time, tight monetary policies were eased and the government engaged in deficit spending. Within the year the economy was growing again, and overall the decade of the 1930s proved one of strong growth and rapid industrialization.

Obvious questions ensue. First, how did Japan manage to recover so quickly? Second, how much of the growth in the 1930s was due to militarism, and how much to rising consumption and improvements in technology unconnected to the military? In neither case are clear answers at hand. Much also remains to be done in the careful comparison of Japanese colonial policy with that of other colonial powers, particularly given the rapid growth of Japan's former colonies during the past 20 years (including Manchuria, the seat of China's heavy industry). With much of Asia embroiled in exchange rate and other economic crises in 1997–98, a better understanding of Japan's 1930s experience could help improve policy today.

Volume 3: Historical Demography and Labor Markets in Prewar Japan

Over the long run in a pre-modern society, even optimists anticipate that improvements in productivity will be reflected in population growth; pessimists expect that in addition, Malthusian pressures will prevent any sustained improvement in living standards. For many societies there is insufficient data to explore such issues, but thanks to the requirement to register at Buddhist temples that accompanied the seventeenth-century ban on Christianity, Japan is endowed with large amounts of primary data. The Tokugawa government also collected population statistics from the late seventeenth through the start of the nineteenth century. Demographics thus offers the possibility of developing an understanding of the evolution of the economy during a time period when a decentralized political system left few measures of overall output.

The broad trends in population now appear clear. There was rapid growth in the seventeenth century, but this was followed by a century of stagnation from 1720–1820. Finally, an upturn began in 1820, and continued through the post-WWII baby boom (after which population growth again plummeted). This would suggest that economic growth stagnated in the eighteenth century, too. Volume six presents evidence that shows otherwise: agricultural productivity continued to increase, suggesting rising incomes, and this was matched by improvements in housing, clothing, and other areas of consumption.[11] How, then, can these findings be reconciled?

Studies of village population registers for a variety of villages have produced several different answers. One early and controversial claim of T.C. Smith and others is that rural Japanese practiced systematic infanticide, limiting family size ex post facto so as to maintain their increased level of income.[12] But subsequent studies of other villages failed to find the same sharp patterns of nonrandom gender sequences and timing of births. One alternate explanation is regional variation: several parts of Japan were hit by repeated crop failures, and saw their populations decline, while other regions enjoyed continued growth. Another alternative is that diet and other factors resulted in very low fecundity. The urban "mortality sinkhole" found in Europe, however, does not appear to be a strong factor. Despite a large urban population, water supplies and waste removal were unusually good in Japan – nightsoil, for example, had commercial value. Research continues, but the debate is unlikely to be settled soon, because of the labor required to ferret out and compile village registers.

A second set of issues are those of migration and labor behavior. How did Japan's big urban complexes become populated? What were rural and urban labor markets like? These tie into the two-sector models included in volume one, because labor flows were one link between agriculture and industry. Such flows date back to the "dekasegi" (seasonal migration) of the Tokugawa era, which could see entire farming and fishing villages integrated into distant labor markets. Later flows included the temporary migration of girls and young women to work in textile mills (see volume four), as well as permanent movement off the farm. As in England, the latter included substantial parts of the population working as personal servants. (Unlike India and China, women had employment opportunities outside the household.) In general, Japanese labor markets developed quite early, and were sensitive to macroeconomic fluctuations. Likewise, migration proceeded by short hops, and was as much "pull" as "push." While data are often scarce for the prewar period, Japan's experience nevertheless provides interesting parallels with the experience of nineteenth century Europe, and with the developing countries of today.

Volume 4: The Textile Industry and the Rise of the Japanese Economy

The cotton textile industry was the first major "modern" industry in Japan, and it remained the single largest manufacturing sector from the late 1800s through the 1950s. Silk also was important. Development of both industries dates to the seventeenth century, when cotton cultivation diffused, and when domestic silk replaced imports from China. Both came to be organized on a "protoindustrial" basis, with fiber production, spinning, and weaving often separated geographically. This ultimately facilitated the modernization of industry, for change could be introduced at one stage of production (such as the substitution of imported for domestic cotton fiber in the 1890s) without disrupting the overall industry. Subsequent development also built upon a tradition of tinkering and handicraft production.[13]

Silk was the major export when Japan's trade with the outside world expanded in the late 1850s, after the forced signing of commercial treaties with the West. This was of tremendous importance in raising farm incomes, often in previously poor regions such as the mountainous area around Nagano (see also volume seven). In addition, most spinning took place in nearby rural areas. Silk exports declined precipitously in the 1930s, never to recover. Little has appeared in English, however, on the impact of this shift upon rural Japan.

In any event, by the end of the nineteenth century Japan was a rising force in cotton textiles, becoming a net exporter of yarn in 1897 and of cloth in 1910. At first, domestic spinning merely substituted for the coarser grades of imports, but particularly after the protection to domestic cotton growers was eliminated in the 1890s, Japan was also able to export coarse counts of yarn. Most domestic cloth consumption was of narrow widths, which provided a measure of natural protection from imports for domestic weavers. Spinners later integrated vertically for the production of export cloth, though the domestic weaving industry continued to develop and eventually included districts specialized in export goods.

Cotton textiles subsequently dominated exports and factory employment and were important for the development of management and mass manufacturing technology. Cotton spinning was also the first sector to engage in direct foreign investment. Furthermore, a mass of data survive from the early part of this century, permitting an unusually detailed analysis of many facets of the industry. Such studies encompass labor, technical change, product strategy, and industrial organization. In addition, many of these studies are explicitly comparative in their framework, and so are particularly useful to those whose primary interest is in a country other than Japan.

Japan, like New England, relied upon young farm girls as a labor source, housing them in dormitories. Turnover was very high, but labor productivity was enhanced by a core of experienced workers who stayed on for several years, while capital productivity was improved by the adoption of double shifts. (Electric lighting, installed from 1896, facilitated productivity while lessening the risk of fire.) Technology diffused rapidly, both through the activities of the Japan Cotton Spinners Association and through a common reliance upon the Platt Brothers and their engineers for machinery and technical consulting. In addition, rivalry remained fierce; no firm dominated the domestic market, while imports kept pressure upon the domestic producers.

How did the industry not only survive but prosper? One aspect was the adoption of "ring" technology, which permitted greater operating speeds. This was complemented by more intense use of labor and by corporate strategies that concentrated on coarse counts. This lessened direct competition from British and Indian producers, who made finer grades; it also left Japan well situated to supply the Chinese market. Indeed, in the 1930s the Japanese were the largest foreign investors in Shanghai and Tianjin and accounted for the bulk of output. Ironically, these ventures ultimately failed, destroyed in the course of the Japanese imperialist enterprise of the late 1930s.

Volume 5: Japan's Economic Ascent: International Trade, Growth, and Postwar Reconstruction

This volume reflects two intertwining themes: the role of trade in Japan's development, and Japan's postwar reconstruction and growth. One set of papers examines exports and growth. Japan had a large and relatively prosperous population, and so it is not surprising that the domestic market remained the dominant source of demand in both the prewar and postwar periods; the one major exception was during WWI. Exports did expand gradually from around 10 percent of GDP in the 1890s to 20 percent in the 1930s, but imports grew just as rapidly, and so trade did not increase domestic demand. Indeed, chronic balance of payments deficits were a significant problem, as with many of today's developing countries. These problems extended almost unbroken from the opening of Japan to trade in the 1850s, until the late 1960s. A large stock of domestic gold in the mid-1800s, large reparations from the Sino-Japanese War in 1895, and then export earnings during WWI provided some respite. Nevertheless, the need to borrow abroad to finance these deficits was a source of period crises.

Export growth was nonetheless important in that it financed imports; these imports shifted from machinery and consumer goods in the mid-1800s to food and industrial materials by the 1930s. Large shifts can also be observed in the structure of exports, going from tea and raw silk to cotton goods and other light manufactures, and finally to shipbuilding and heavy industry by the outbreak of WWII. Similar sharp shifts occurred in the post-WWII era. The Japanese economy thus appears to have maintained a strong export orientation during most of the period after the 1850s, with rapid changes in economic and trade structure in line with shifting comparative advantage.

The second set of papers examine Japan's transition from defeat into the high-growth era of the 1960s. (Japan's wartime experience has received little attention, though this may be changing.)[14] The U.S. Occupation sought to "democratize" Japan, carrying out a series of political and economic reforms. These included labor reform, land reform, and the breaking up of the large prewar family holding companies—the *zaibatsu*. A second set of issues was macroeconomic stabilization, for Japan ended the war with a large monetary overhang, which produced an immediate hyperinflation. Production was in disarray, and a complex web of subsidies sought to stimulate output, though at the same time these contributed to continued high inflation. Japan thus serves as an interesting example of stabilization policies, culminating eventually in the Dodge reforms of 1949 that eliminated subsidies, reformed the tax system, balanced the budget, and regularized international trade under a unified exchange rate.

Finally, several papers examine the transition from wartime reconstruction to the high-growth era. One set of issues was the debate over the "Income Doubling Plan" issued by Prime Minister Ikeda in 1960. Second, what were the sources of growth? One approach is to set up a careful accounting framework, and separate out change in inputs and outputs in various industries. This highlights the interrelationship of the reallocation of labor from agriculture to industry, improvements in skills, investment, and technical change in the context of an evolving industrial structure. A second, diametric approach examines growth in a "Keynesian" framework that emphasizes the structure of demand, and in particular urbanization and family formation. These echo the debates of volume one on the overall process of economic growth.

Volume 6: The Japanese Economy in the Tokugawa Era, 1600–1868

In the early 1600s, Tokugawa Ieyasu, the third of a series of national unifiers, led a coalition of local lords to victory in battle and established a dynasty that lasted through 1868. This was the culmination of a century of change, including the introduction of civil works technology from China, and new crops and the musket from the West. The 1600s saw large-scale riparian works that significantly extended land subject to irrigation. After a century of almost continuous civil war, the seventeenth century also brought peace. Population expanded accordingly. Cities grew as well, for the Tokugawa family both directly and indirectly used the flow of tax revenue to build up the new capital of Edo (modern Tokyo). The 250-odd local domains, while bowing to Edo in foreign policy and other areas, retained a measure of independence, and likewise built up their castle towns.

All of this fostered a rise in commerce, and commerce in turn fostered specialization. The systematic improvement of ports and overland transport contributed to the expansion of long-distance domestic trade, even while foreign trade diminished during the course of the 1600s as supplies of silver dwindled, and as foreign policy concerns led official trade to be limited to Nagasaki (and, for Korea, Tsushima). The growth of domestic commerce enabled Edo's population to surpass one million by the end of the century; the population of three other cities topped 100,000. This commerce grew in sophistication as well; formal institutions arose to support this trade, including, from 1720, a rice futures market in Osaka.

Growth appears to have slowed during the 1700s, in that population stagnated. However, architecture, diet, and clothing all evolved in a direction that suggests a real increase in the level of consumption in the more prosperous regions of the country. Markets were not limited to big cities; the hinterland of Osaka, for example, engaged in commercial farming of vegetables and cotton. By the end of the 1700s, such specialization appeared in a variety of outlying domains as well, and the overall economy was growing again from the 1820s, a trend that continued largely unabated through today.

Decentralized political administration, combined with the destruction from WWII, leave only a limited range of data for the country as a whole. However, the population was highly literate (perhaps 40 percent of men could read and write) and they maintained copious records. These records survive for a range of villages and even entire domains, and permit the piecemeal reconstruction of the structure of the economy. Various researchers have compiled wage and price indices, monetary statistics, and "national" accounts of local production and consumption; in addition, several generations of Japanese scholars have amassed large amounts of data on agriculture, and written a host of local histories.

Two debates are of considerable interest. One is over the nature of (rural) industrialization, paralleling the protoindustrialization debate for Europe. As elsewhere, farmers engaged in a range of production activities, including industrial production and off-season wage labor. By the end of the Tokugawa era these were tied into local capital markets, with commodity prices, wages, and interest rates all affected by trends in Osaka and other commercial districts. The other is over the impact of this industrialization. How much, if any, did average incomes rise? Was industrialization local, or (as seems likely) did it lead to improvements throughout most of the country, in what was effectively a national economy? In the aggregate these studies provide a picture of a dynamic economy, indeed of an "industrious" revolution, that was able to incorporate smoothly and rapidly the new technologies and business organizations of the nineteenth-century Western industrial revolution.

Volume 7: Agricultural Growth and Japanese Economic Development

Japan was until the 1930s an agrarian economy, and was again so briefly following World War II. It is thus important to understand agriculture itself, for the pace of change in agriculture determined not only rural incomes but the pace of change elsewhere. Even foreign trade was affected; silk featured prominently in exports, while the slow growth of domestic food production led to imports following WWI. One theme has thus been that of technical change, tracing the diffusion of cultivars and technology that led to a remarkable increase in agricultural productivity in the 1920s and 1930s, which continued into the early postwar period. The perception of the importance of cultivars and local adaptations, in turn, helped inform thinking on agricultural change among development economists at the International Rice Research Institute and elsewhere, and hence influenced the extension of the "green revolution" to today's developing countries.

Returning to linkages, the improvement in agricultural productivity enabled the outflow of workers into industry and urban services, facilitating overall economic growth. At the same time, the outflow was encouraged by stable agricultural prices, held down from the early 1920s by imports from Japan's colonies. The presumption in much of Japanese historiography has been that these twin forces produced widespread suffering, which fomented rural unrest in the 1920s and 1930s that helped destabilize the political system on the eve of the Pacific War. As such, agriculture has been one focus of Marxist studies of Japan's economic development, though unfortunately much of this effort was sidetracked into sterile debates over the stage of Japan's development — was Japan feudal, and hence needing a period of capitalism, or capitalistic, and hence ripe for a socialist revolution?

One research direction thus focused on tenancy and rural social structure. Here the presumption was that tenancy was exploitative and immiserating. However, economic studies of developing economies show the welfare implications of tenancy to be far more complex than commonly realized, and exploitative only under very specific conditions. A modest start has now been made to use the raw data culled from the historical record by generations of Marxists to develop an empirically grounded revisionism. It suggests a much more complex interweaving of rural nonagricultural production with agriculture, and of an intertwining of landlords and tenants via rural capital markets.

These concerns vanished with the postwar land reform that effectively ended both tenancy and precluded the growth of large farms. In retrospect, this may have been one of the greatest errors in postwar policy, for it set a precedent for controls on land that not only stifled the subsequent growth of agriculture, but that in their urban parallels have prevented the development of affordable housing and efficient city services. The immediate impact of land reform was modest, and given the rapid pace of industrialization, the "problem" of tenancy would in any case have soon disappeared. But the enduring legacy is the inability to consolidate land, and given the application of mechanization, this resulted in a highly capital-intensive farming sector with high land productivity and also high labor productivity. This in turn necessitated large government subsidies if farmers were to be able to make a living from their meager allotments of land. To date, however, the modest short-run impact of the postwar reforms (and their deleterious long-run impact) have not been integrated into the debates over tenancy in early periods.

Conclusion

A careful examination of the economic history of Japan offers much food for thought for those interested in the history of Japan, as well as the development of the European economies, and of the contemporary developing world. The wealth of data generated by Japan's literate populace and bureaucratic governments permit research that often cannot be duplicated for other countries. At the same time, the variation in culture and politics that Japan represents helps balance the search for "unique" factors that are often used by economic historians to explain Europe's success. Hopefully the careful application to Japan of models used to analyze other economies can help counter a similar trend to view Japan as unique.

Many open questions remain. The piecemeal nature of our understanding of developments in the Tokugawa era means that new research could lead to considerable refinement in our understanding of overall trends. The transition from the end of the Tokugawa period in the 1840s through the 1880s, when the Meiji government began to compile reliable statistics, is murky and needs much work. Too much attention has been devoted to trade, too little to international finance. The wealth of research in business history has only been partially integrated into economic history, e.g., for the study of technical change and of the role of financial markets in development. Japan's escape from the Great Depression cries out for further study, from the reworking of the underlying data (did output even decrease?) to a more careful dissection of policy. The era from the mid-1930s through the end of WWII has been a virtual taboo, yet many postwar institutions appear to have their roots in that era. The management of firms during the war, and of the war effort itself, have been even more of a taboo. Industry has received much attention, urban services and rural labor much less. It is time for revisionism in the study of rural society, of a more careful attempt to cast off the blinders of ideology and analyze who benefited how from the many changes in agriculture in the pre-WWII era. In short, while a lot has been learned, much fascinating work remains to be done. The papers in this series, at any rate, provide a good overview of the achievements to date.[15]

Notes

[1]*Economics and the Historian*, ed. Tom Rawski et al. (Berkeley: University of California Press, 1996), p.1.

[2]A good entry point for the Japanese-language literature is the eight-volume series, *Nihon Keizai Shi*. Tokyo: Iwanami Shoten, 1988–1990. *See also* the lengthy review of the series by Kozo Yamamura in the *Journal of Japanese Studies* 17:1 (winter 1991): 127–43.

[3]These items are (i) *Japanese Yearbook on Business History*. Japan Business History Institute, annual from 1984; (ii) the *International Conference on Business History* ("Fuji Conference"), published annually by the University of Tokyo Press, 1975–1994, and subsequently by Oxford University Press; (iii) William D. Wray, editor, *Managing Industrial Enterprise: Cases from Japan's Prewar Experience*. Cambridge, Mass.: Council on East Asian Studies, Harvard University, distributed by the Harvard University Press, 1989; and (iv) W. Mark Fruin, *The Japanese Enterprise System: Competitive Strategies and Cooperative Structures*. Oxford, U.K.: Clarendon Press; New York: Oxford University Press, 1992.

[4]These two volumes are (i) Hugh Patrick and Yung Chul Park, editors, *The Financial Development of Japan, Korea, and Taiwan: Growth, Repression, and Liberalization*. New York: Oxford University Press, 1994 and (ii) Masahiko Aoki and Hugh Patrick, editors, *The Japanese Main Bank System: Its Relevance for Developing and Transforming Economies*. New York: Oxford University Press, 1994. *See also* J. Mark Ramseyer and Frances M. Rosenbluth, *The Politics of Oligarchy: Institutional Choice in Imperial Japan*. New York: Cambridge University Press, 1995.

[5]On law, economics and history *see* (i) J. Mark Ramseyer, *Odd Markets in Japanese History: Law and Economic Growth*. New York: Cambridge University Press, 1996; (ii) Herman Ooms, *Tokugawa Village Practice: Class, Status, Power, Law*. Berkeley: University of California Press, 1996; (iii) John Owen Haley, *Authority Without Power: Law and the Japanese Paradox*. New York: Oxford University Press, 1991; and (iv) Frank K. Upham, *Law and Social Change in Postwar Japan*. Cambridge: Harvard University Press, 1987.

[6]On transportation *see* (i) Steven J. Ericson, *The Sound of the Whistle: Railroads and the State in Meiji Japan*. Cambridge, Mass.: Council on East Asian Studies, Harvard University, distributed by Harvard University Press, 1996 and (ii) William D. Wray, *Mitsubishi and the N.Y.K., 1870–1914: Business Strategy in the Japanese Shipping Industry*. Cambridge, Mass.: Council on East Asian Studies, Harvard University, distributed by Harvard University Press, 1984.

[7]For labor history, a good introduction is Andrew Gordon, *The Evolution of Labor Relations in Japan: Heavy Industry, 1853–1955*. Cambridge: Harvard University Press, 1985. The classic on industrial policy study of Japan as a "developmental state" is Chalmers Johnson, *MITI and the Japanese Miracle: The Growth of Industrial Policy, 1925–1975*. Stanford: Stanford University Press, 1982. Economic analysis of the role of industrial policy, as well as a fine set of industry studies, can be found in Ryutaro Komiya, Masahiro Okuno, and Kotaro Suzumura, editors, *Industrial Policy of Japan*. San Diego: Academic Press, 1988.

[8]*See* (i) Tessa Morris-Suzuki, *A History of Japanese Economic Thought*. New York: Routledge Press for Nissan Institute of Japanese Studies, Oxford, 1989, and (ii) Bai Gao, *Economic Ideology and Japanese Industrial Policy: Developmentalism from 1931 to 1965*. New York: Cambridge University Press, 1997.

[9]William D. Wray, *Japan's Economy: A Bibliography of Its Past and Present*. New York: Markus Wiener Publications, 1989.

[10]On these models *see* Kiyoshi Kojima, *Direct Foreign Investment: A Japanese Model of Multinational Business Operations*. London: Croom Helm, c1978. His seminal Japanese-language book on this topic was published in 1958.

[11]Susan Hanley, *Everyday Things in Premodern Japan: The Hidden Legacy of Material Culture*, Berkeley: University of California Press, 1997.

[12]*See* Thomas C. Smith, *Nakahara: Family Farming and Population in a Japanese Village, 1717–1830*. Stanford: Stanford University Press, 1977.

[13]Tessa Morris-Suzuki, *The Technological Transformation of Japan: From the Seventeenth to the Twenty-first Century*, New York: Cambridge University Press, 1994.

[14]For the wartime period, the best work remains the classic of Jerome B. Cohen, *Japan's Economy in War and Reconstruction*. Minneapolis: University of Minnesota Press, 1949. A recent work is Jun Sakudo and Takao Shiba, editors, *World War II and the Transformation of Business Systems*, The International Conference on Business History 20 [Proceedings of the Fuji Conference]. Tokyo: University of Tokyo Press, 1994. *See also* a book by Yukio Noguchi, *1940-nen Taisei* (The 1940 System). Tokyo: Toyo Keizai, 1995, as well as ongoing work by Takafusa Nakamura.

[15]There are also several texts and surveys of Japanese economic history. A development-economics oriented study is Ryoshin Minami, *The Economic Development of Japan: A Quantitative Study*. New York: St. Martin's Press, 1994. The translation of the Japanese-language text by Takafusa Nakamura, *The Postwar Japanese Economy: Its Development and Structure, 1937–1994*, 2nd edition. Tokyo: University of Tokyo Press, 1995. A classic but still useful survey of the Meiji and Taisho eras is William W. Lockwood, *The Economic Development of Japan: Growth and Structural Change, 1868–1938*. Ann Arbor: Michigan Classics in Japanese Studies, No. 10, reprint edition of 1993. Finally, a survey of the older Marxist literature is Mikio Sumiya and Koji Taira, *An Outline of Japanese Economic History, 1603–1940: Major Works and Research Findings*. Tokyo: University of Tokyo Press, 1979.

The Tokugawa Monetary System: 1787–1868*

E. S. Crawcour
Australian National University
Kozo Yamamura
Boston College

I. Introduction

The collapse of the Tokugawa regime, which paved the way for Japan's modernization, is linked, insofar as it was due to internal causes, to the growth of a commercial economy and the rising economic power of the merchant class. This article is an attempt to examine this general proposition and to throw light on the particular mechanisms by which this came about through a quantitative examination of the late Tokugawa monetary system.

Most modern discussions of the Tokugawa monetary system content themselves with a description of the coinage. The banking institutions of Osaka or the financial or price policies of the Bakufu (Tokugawa government) are commonly treated as though they had almost no relation to the monetary system as a whole beyond the fact that the Bakufu tended to try to solve its financial problems by debasing the coinage. Despite the fact that compilations like the Ministry of Finance's *Dai Nihon Kahei Shi* have preserved a great many odds and ends of information, there is very little direct evidence of how the system worked and, so far as we know, there has been no serious attempt to present a coherent reconstruction. According to one Japanese scholar, "Works written by numismatists and monetary historians tell us what types of money were issued, but not the amounts or their effects. We get only a static picture and not the more important one of the system in action."[1]

This paper puts forward some hypotheses about the operation of the

* This article is a preliminary report of work being done under a grant from the Harvard East Asian Research Center. We are indebted to Professors H. Rosovsky, K. Ohkawa, H. Patrick, and J. Nakamura for criticisms and comments on the earlier drafts of this paper.

[1] Takagaki Torajirō, *Kindai Nihon Kinyūshi* [Financial history of modern Japan], *Ginkō Sōsho* (Tokyo: Zenkoku Chihō Ginkō Kyōkai, 1955), 20: 31.

1

monetary system in the last third of the Tokugawa period which challenge in some respects the conventional wisdom on the subject. After providing some essential background information on the institutional context, we suggest some hypotheses about the working of the monetary system and test them against a rather large body of hitherto unanalyzed quantitative data. We then apply our findings to some features of the economic history of the period to see whether they suggest any useful insights. Finally, we attempt to incorporate our findings into a tentative interpretation of the monetary history of the period. Our discussion is based throughout on a quantity theory of money.[2]

II. Background
A. The Monetary System

Before attempting to explain the behavior of the monetary system in the period covered by our data, let us briefly review the history of the currency in the seventeenth and eighteenth centuries. When the Tokugawa monetary system originated in the early seventeenth century, its gold coin, the *koban* or 1-*ryō* gold piece, became the standard of value in the shogun's own capital of Edo and its environs, but in Osaka and most other areas the Tokugawa *koban* was treated in the same way as any other coin—and there were over 100 types of gold coin in circulation at the beginning of the seventeenth century. These coins were valued in terms of a numeraire consisting of standard unit of silver in the same way as the many types of coins in circulation were handled in premodern Europe.[3] Silver currency (*chōgin, mameita-gin*) circulated by weight and had to be weighed, and sometimes cut, for each transaction. This was not only inconvenient but also expensive, since a charge was made for weighing. At that time the value of the numeraire was linked to the commodity value of its silver content, and since trading in precious metals was not strictly controlled, the value of gold coins was related to the commodity value of their gold content. As long as import and export of bullion or specie were permitted,

---

[2] A classical quantity theory of money was current in Tokugawa Japan. "Commodity prices are high because the quantity of money is large. The annual production of commodities is fixed, while the quantity of currency minted each year is not. The greater the quantity of money the more acute the rise in prices. The principle is exactly the same as trying to feed more people by cutting the cake into smaller portions" (Satō Jizaemon, *Kahei hiroku* [The secret of currency] ca. 1840, in *Nihon keizai sōsho* [Bibliotheca Japonica oeconomiae politicae], ed. Takimoto Seiichi [Tokyo, 1917], 32: 320).

[3] For the way this operated in Europe, see L. Einaudi, "The Theory of Imaginary Money from Charlemagne to the French Revolution," in *Enterprise and Secular Change*, ed. F. C. Lane and J. C. Riemersma (London: Allen & Unwin, 1953), pp. 229–61; C. M. Cipolla, *Money, Prices and Civilization in the Mediterranean world* (Princeton, N.J.: Gordian Press, 1956), p. 45.

E. S. Crawcour and Kozo Yamamura

the relative value of gold and silver was close to that in Europe and, as in Europe, attempts to maintain gold coins at a ratio that varied much from that current in other countries would lead to disturbing outflows of either gold or silver.[4] Throughout the seventeenth century the rise in the Japanese gold/silver ratio roughly paralleled that in Europe.[5] Within Japan, however, maintenance of this rate in the face of large and continuous deficits in both the Bakufu's budgets and Edo's balance of payments with Osaka led to virtual exhaustion of the Bakufu treasury's gold reserves.

The Bakufu attacked this problem on three fronts. First, it isolated the coinage from overseas gold/silver ratios by measures designed to restrict foreign transactions in precious metals to a minimum. From the 1690s, foreign trade was conducted on a barter basis with any balances carried over to the following trading season.[6] Second, it isolated the relative values of gold and silver coinage from their commodity values by effectively banning private transactions in precious metals[7] and prescribing very severe penalties for counterfeiting. It was thus able to take the third step of declaring its gold *koban* legal tender for one *ryō* of gold irrespective of its actual gold content. The Bakufu had been able to have its gold coinage accepted on this basis in Edo following the debasements of 1695, but in 1700 the same treatment was required, and accorded, in Osaka.[8] At about the same time the awkward silver currency-by-weight began to go out of use for everyday transactions and to be replaced by credit instruments of various kinds expressed in units of silver.[9]

Between 1714 and 1736 the quantity of monetary silver (*chōgin*) in circulation fell by nearly 60 percent, and in the period under study it does not seem to have circulated at all. According to one source, "When the *ryō* is quoted at 60 *momme* of silver this does not refer to the weight of

[4] See K. Glamann, *Dutch-Asiatic Trade, 1620–1740* (Copenhagen: Danish Science Press, 1958).

[5] Ōkurashō [Ministry of Finance], ed., *Meiji zenki zaisei keizai shiryō shūsei* [Collected materials on the history of finance in the early Meiji period] (Tokyo: Kaizōsha, 1931–33), 12: 19–20, 31–36.

[6] Honjō and Yoshida, eds., *Dainihon kaheishi* [History of the Japanese currency] (Tokyo: Ōkurashō, 1925–26), 6: 552–53.

[7] Ōkurashō [Ministry of Finance], ed., *Nihon zaisei keizai shiryō* [Materials on the history of Japanese finance] (Tokyo: Zaisei Keizai Gakkai, 1922–25), 2: 739–44.

[8] Mitsui Takasumi, *Ryōgae nendaiki kanken* [Key to the annals of the moneychangers] (Tokyo: Iwanami, 1933), 2: 329.

[9] See Crawcour, "The Development of a Credit System in Seventeenth-Century Japan," *Journal of Economic History* 21 (September 1961): 342–60. Silver made up in parcels of 500 *me* continued to be used for certain purposes. The fineness of silver in these parcels was not specified (see *Ryōgae nendaiki kanken*, 2: 188).

chōgin but is simply the exchange rate at which gold units are converted into silver units. From about 1700 the gold 1-*ryō* piece, or *koban*, was fixed at 60 *momme* [for day-to-day purposes in Edo] but in Osaka where silver was the unit of account the rate fluctuated. 'Silver' (*gimme*) meant not a weight of metal but merely a unit of account, represented in Osaka by bills (*tegata*) expressed in that unit."[10] Not that real silver actually became extinct—there were still some 800 tons of it at the time of the Restoration[11]—but it does not seem to have circulated as normal currency. What role it played is not clear, but the most likely explanation is that it was held by the banking system as a reserve of some kind.[12]

Zeni, or copper cash, seems to have been originally intended to circulate as petty coinage at 4,000 to the gold *ryō*, but large issues reduced its value and only sporadic attempts were made to peg it for most of the Tokugawa period. In the eighteenth century its value fluctuated considerably. As in Europe: "When a debasement was put into effect, the maneuver gave to the mint farmers . . . a good chance of gain through speculation upon the difference between the current face value of the petty coins and their newly debased metallic content. Consequently the issues of petty coins entered a period of boom. Quite generally the quantity of petty coins in circulation quickly reached a point at which their current value was forced down till it reached the commodity value of the coins. At this point nobody had an interest in striking petty coins. Issues contracted until a new debasement was decreed."[13] In the eighteenth century, debasement sometimes took the form of minting *zeni* from iron or brass. The market for *zeni* was far from unified, and even while its value was declining in the major cities it was sometimes in acutely short supply in other parts of Japan. Although its value shows a declining trend over the Tokugawa period as a whole, in our period it was very stable in Edo and Osaka at about 6,700 to the *ryō* until the last few years, when its price fell considerably in terms of gold coinage.

[10] Miyamoto Mataji, ed., *Kinsei Ōsaka no bukka to rishi* [Prices and interest rates in Tokugawa Osaka] (Osaka: Nihon Kinsei Bukkashi Kenkyūkai, 1963), p. 35.

[11] Yamaguchi Kazuo, "Edo jidai ni okeru kinginka no aridaka" [The volume of gold and silver currency in circulation in the Tokugawa period] in (Tōdai) *Keizaigaku Ronshū* 28, no. 4 (March 1963): 79. The *chōgin* silver of the 1860s, however, contained only about one-sixth the silver content of the original *chōgin* of the early seventeenth century (see *Meiji zenki zaisei keizai shiryō shūsei*, 12:31, 45).

[12] Sakudō, based on earlier studies, suggests that silver was known to have been used in some cases as a reserve with a ratio of 1:6 or 1:7 against outstanding credit (Sakudō Yotarō, *Nihon kahei kinyūshi no kenkyū* [A study on the history of Japanese currencies and finance] [Tokyo: Mirai-sha, 1961], pp. 287–88).

[13] Cipolla, n. 3 above, p. 32.

With the virtual disappearance of silver currency-by-weight, the cash supply in our period consisted of gold and copper coins all over Japan, including Osaka. In practice the gold cash supply included subsidiary coins—one-quarter *ryō* pieces, one-eighth *ryō* pieces, one-sixteenth *ryō* pieces—which were actually made of a silver alloy, but these had no connection whatsoever with either *chōgin* or the silver unit of account. They played the same role as quarters and dimes do now. In Osaka, however, and for that matter over most of Japan and even to some extent in Edo, accounts for credit purposes continued to be kept in the now-imaginary silver units. This may have been partly because of the convenience of their divisibility by a decimal system, but more importantly because this procedure greatly simplified the accounting of currency whose value fluctuated from day to day, and made it possible to state long-term assets and liabilities in a stable unit. The alternative, actually adopted in 1868, of abandoning silver altogether and using the *ryō* (renamed *yen* in 1871) as the unit of account, was rejected because, although officially legal tender, it was subject to debasement, and in fact several qualities of *koban* were in simultaneous circulation at various discounts. In these circumstances a change in the value of cash in terms of the silver unit of account affected the cash value of instruments whose face value was expressed in the accounting unit.

B. Edo-Osaka Trade and Payments

Osaka was the great entrepôt of Tokugawa Japan. As summarized in figure 1, it acted as a collection point for goods (food, sake, fuel, building materials, household utensils, etc.) from most of Japan, and a large part of these goods was shipped to Edo. It should be remembered that although Osaka had a very large surplus in its balance of trade and usually a substantially favorable balance of payments with Edo, its situation was reversed vis-à-vis the rest of Japan so that in fact Edo ran a deficit with the rest of Japan via Osaka.[14] Most of Osaka's exports were in fact reexports and in addition she, like Edo, had to import most of her consumption requirements. The earnings of her processing industries and commercial services were probably not very much more than sufficient to support her approximately 400,000 inhabitants. These imports into Edo were paid for principally with the tax revenues of the Bakufu and the services provided to daimyo and their retinues in Edo. If these were insufficient, as they were for much of our period, they were supplemented by Bakufu deficits. Edo never ran out of means of payment because, although its production of precious metals decreased, it could increase the supply of coinage through

[14] Some data on the quantity, value and composition of imports into Osaka and Edo are given in Yamaguchi Kazuo, *Nihon keizaishi kōgi* [Lectures on Japanese economic history] (Tokyo: Tōkyō Daigaku Shuppan Kai, 1960), pp. 46, 48.

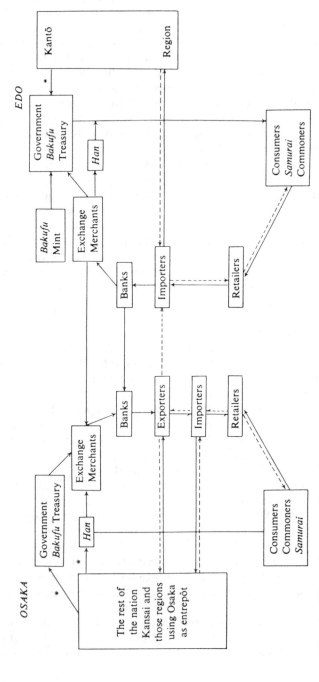

Fig. 1.—Flows of money and goods. —— indicate money; – – – indicate goods; * indicate tax payments. *Han* are administrative districts, controlled by *daimyō*.

6

debasement; a procedure limited only by increasing difficulty in recovering older coins and by the increasing temptation it presented to the counterfeiter. Most of the revenues of both Bakufu and daimyo came to Edo through Osaka, where their tax rice was marketed and settlement between the two cities was normally effected by means of bills of exchange.

C. The Exchange Bill Market

Osaka merchants who sold goods to Edo drew bills of exchange on their Edo customers or their own branches in Edo. These bills were bought by Osaka exchange dealers who used them to remit Bakufu or daimyo tax proceeds that they had accepted for forwarding to Edo. These transactions were effected in the Osaka exchange bill market where the exchange dealers (on-kawasegata) were the buyers and the export merchants (torikuminin) were the sellers, with the banks (ryōgaeya) acting as brokers (see fig. 1). The banks acting as brokers charged a brokerage commission (uchibu) which was paid by the seller. Depending on the state of the market, Edo exchange bills might be at a premium (gyakuuchi) paid by the buyer or discount (hon-uchi) charged to the seller. When the premium balanced the normal commission the bills were quoted at par (mu-uchi).[15]

When, because of heavy remittances of tax proceeds or forced loans (goyōkin), an austerity drive in Edo, or possibly speculative or arbitrage operations, Osaka had an unfavorable balance of payments with Edo, demand for Edo bills exceeded the supply and the premium on them rose. If, however, it rose above the cost of shipping cash (including possible losses on exchange if the gold cash price were lower in Edo than in Osaka) the exchange dealers shipped cash to Edo (shōkudashi). This reduced the premium on Edo exchange bills in two stages. First, it immediately reduced the demand for the bills. Second, since it was cash that had to be sent to Edo, it produced a demand for gold cash in exchange for credit instruments expressed in silver units, thus tending to raise the spot cash price and therefore reduce the premium on bills over cash. If the excess of demand for Edo exchange bills was so strong as to raise the Osaka gold price in this way, arbitrage remittances from Edo would supplement the supply of Edo exchange bills, again tending toward equilibrium. In the more frequent case of a favorable balance of trade with Edo, this mechanism worked precisely in reverse. When the discount on Edo exchange bills exceeded the cost of shipping cash (again including exchange), Osaka exporters brought their sales receipts from Edo in cash (gyaku-shōkudashi), which they normally deposited in the bank probably to repay an advance (expressed in silver units) against their original consignment of goods to Edo. This tended to depress the gold price with results similar to those already described.

[15] Matsuyoshi Sadao, Nihon ryōgae kinyūshi ron [History of money-changing and finance in Japan] (Tokyo: Kashiwa Shobō, 1965), pp. 246–47; Ryōgae nendaiki kanken, 2: 230.

The price of spot cash in Osaka could vary temporarily from that in Edo and the nature of this gap affected the exchange bill market. For example, if the gold *ryō* was quoted at 65 *momme* in Edo and 64 *momme* in Osaka, the price of an Edo exchange bill in Osaka would include an exchange discount (*hon-uchi*) of one *momme* per *ryō*. If the gap were sufficiently wide, the gain from arbitrage could make it profitable to adopt the alternative of shipping cash.[16] In practice the gap was normally very small.

D. The Osaka Gold Cash Market

In the early Tokugawa period, when Edo used gold coin and Osaka used silver by weight and the credit market was still undeveloped, the gold market was the market between gold coin and *chōgin*, and transactions between Edo and Osaka were probably a major factor in it. Despite official pegging, fluctuations appear to have been fairly wide. In our period, however, when gold coin was as acceptable in Osaka as in Edo and *chōgin* had been replaced as a means of payment in Osaka by silver notes or other credit instruments expressed in silver, the Osaka gold market was the market between gold cash and a unit of credit expressed in terms of silver accounting units.

In these circumstances, the balance of payments with Edo was only one factor in the Osaka gold market which was also influenced by the state of payments between Osaka and the rest of Japan and the supply and demand for credit and cash in Osaka, as well as by expectations and the general state of business confidence. The Osaka gold cash price itself was set by the banking system, or more specifically by the *Jūnin ryōgae*, or Big Ten, who held the reserves of the Osaka banking system and in some respects acted like a kind of central bank.[17] Since the Osaka banks operated on a correspondent system through a pyramid culminating in the Big Ten, this small group—not always consisting of exactly ten members—was highly sensitive to the state of the credit/cash market, and also exercised control over credit policy. They were, moreover, the major lenders to daimyo. In this situation they could, if they wished, influence the gold price through credit policy. If an inflow of gold were the result of a rise in exports to Edo, it was largely offset by a correspondingly increased outflow for purchases of goods from other parts of the country, but if the gold inflow were caused by a drop in tax revenues, it would tend to be offset by an increase in loans to daimyo or the Bakufu (*goyōkin*). There is

---

[16] Mitsui-ke Hensanshitsu, ed. (*Temmei 7-nen–Meiji 4-nen*) *Ōsaka kingin beisen narabi ni kawase hibi sōba hyō* [Daily Osaka market quotations for gold, silver, rice, copper coins and exchange: 1787–1871], *Mitsui-ke kawasegyō shi* [History of the banking and exchange business of the Mitsui family], *Shiryō hen* [Data section], part 5 (privately printed), 1: 16–17.

[17] See Crawcour, n. 9 above, p. 354.

ample evidence that loans of this kind as well as advances to merchants and producers outside of Osaka increased substantially over our period.[18]

E. Rural Developments

The period with which we are dealing was a period of rapid rural commercial development. This was not a new development. The commercialization of rual economic life seems to have been rapid during the first century of the Tokugawa period, and although it may have slowed during the eighteenth century, Andō, Smith, and others[19] have shown that the tempo increased again from around the start of the nineteenth century. For most of this time increases in production of commercial crops and the growth of rural industry were primarily in response to rising urban demand.

Technical progress in industry was very slow and the output of urban industry was approaching its limit before the middle of the eighteenth century. Thereafter city merchants sought increased supplies by utilizing part-time and off-season rural labor, at first in the Kinki region but progressively over more and more remote areas of the country.[20] Rising demand for industrial goods stimulated increases in the production of industrial crops. Almost all of this increased output was channeled to the cities, especially to Osaka, through monopsonistic merchant associations backed up by the political power of the Bakufu. In return, the countryside was supplied with increased amounts of fertilizer but with very few consumption goods, and the balance was settled by a flow of cash to the rural areas. This does not seem to have raised prices of rural products to the cities until around the 1830s (see fig. 2 and table A4) because of a strongly rising rural transactions demand for cash with the monetization of the rural economy. As subsistence agriculture gave way to a monetary economy, goods which had once been self-consumed or bartered were sold for cash, so the supply of goods available for sale for a time increased faster than production. In this situation the volume of monetary transactions could increase faster than output without inflationary results. By the 1830s, however, the monetization process had reached a plateau, and from then on continued rises in rural income were accompanied by rising

[18] Of the many sources, Horie Yasuzō, *Nihon shihon shugi no seiritsu* [The establishment of Japanese capitalism] (Tokyo: Daidō Shoin, 1939), pp. 39–53, is detailed and lucid.

[19] Andō Seiichi, *Kinsei zaikata shōgyō no kenkyū* [A study of rural commerce in the Tokugawa period] (Tokyo: Yūhikaku, 1958); Thomas C. Smith, *The Agrarian Origins of Modern Japan* (Stanford, Calif.: Stanford University Press, 1959).

[20] This process provides an interesting comparison with that in Europe as described by P. Mantoux, *The Industrial Revolution in the Eighteenth Century*, rev. ed. (New York: Harper & Row, 1965), pp. 181–84.

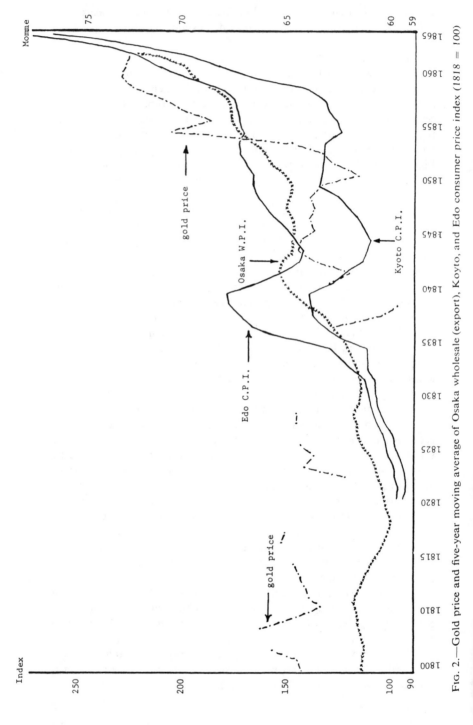

Fig. 2.—Gold price and five-year moving average of Osaka wholesale (export), Koyto, and Edo consumer price index (1818 = 100)

prices. Also, rural inflation and rising rural demand began to cut into the supply of goods to the cities, and even a determined effort by the Bakufu to reform the system of marketing in the early 1840s had only a temporary effect. Thereafter, control of distribution drifted beyond the waning power of the Bakufu, especially when alternative sales routes by-passing the official system were sponsored by daimyo. By the 1850s the mechanism by which the cities had been able to run a large trade deficit with the countryside without raising import prices against themselves was no longer operating effectively.

F. The Role of the Bakufu
Behind the efforts to maintain adequate supplies of goods to Edo and to keep prices down lay the political power of the Bakufu, applied with varying degrees of effectiveness at almost all points of the system. By exhortation and regulation; this power attempted to restrict rural consumption and to encourage agricultural production. When goods were in short supply in Edo, it sent people out of Edo and back to the country. It backed up the monopoly marketing institutions that compelled shipment of goods to Osaka and Edo and prevented their sale to rural areas. When Edo prices rose, from time to time it brought pressure to bear on merchant associations to reduce them. When the gold price showed a tendency to fall, it set a floor price and occasionally tried to maintain it by buying gold from the banking system in return for silver.[21] Whether on these occasions it sold real *chōgin* or not is not clear, but most likely the "silver" consisted of silver certificates which perhaps played a role analogous to treasury bills.

The Bakufu could influence the money market in other ways also. Although salaries of samurai were in principle payable in rice, the Bakufu adopted the practice of paying a proportion in cash at a conversion rate which could vary from the current rice price. By varying the proportion paid in cash and the rate at which rice was converted, it could exercise some influence over the Edo money market. The extent to which this was done at the expense of the samurai will be clearer when we have analyzed the data on these payments and compared it with rice and gold price series. Further, the Bakufu was itself a substantial lender, particularly to daimyo but also to some extent to Edo bankers and merchants. In our period these loans were running at the level of about 3.5 million *ryō*, which was a very considerable sum.[22] Through these loans it could exert

---

[21] *On-kaiage kin, On-haraigin.* See, e.g., *Ōsaka kingin beisen*, 1: 545.

[22] Takeuchi Makoto, "Bakufu keizai no hembō to kinyū seisaku no tenkai" [Changes in the Bakufu economy and the development of financial policy], in *Nihon keizaishi taikei* [Japanese economic history series], no. 4, *Kinsei no ge* [Tokugawa period 2], ed. Furushima Toshio (Tokyo: Tōkyō Daigaku Shuppan Kai, 1965), pp. 177–224.

some influence on the credit market. They seem also to have been a means of gaining acceptance for issues of debased coinage by issuing them in the form of loans at low interest. When all else failed and the Osaka banking system was so glutted with gold cash that the gold price was in serious danger, it could relieve the pressure by requiring a cash loan from the Osaka banking system which might or might not be repaid.[23]

The Osaka rice market seems to have been largely beyond the control of the Bakufu. Only one attempt was made to peg the price of rice in our period (and this was not a floor price but a ceiling), namely, for the three winter months of 1811 following a poor harvest. When the rice price was unusually low as it was in the early 1800s, the Bakufu simply ordered Osaka bankers and merchants to buy up rice. Sometimes, as in 1806,[24] it offered low-interest loans, or ordered the Osaka bankers to make loans, for this purpose. On the whole these operations do not seem to have been very effective. The Osaka rice market was very large and contained a considerable speculative element which was thought to be destabilizing by the Bakufu. Rice brokers and speculators, however, operated on very small margins and they were financed by specialized institutions, the *komegata ryōgae*. It seems strange, therefore, that the Bakufu did not attempt to influence the market more directly through these credit institutions.

In summary, though the effectiveness of official policy varied, it played an important role in the operation of the economic system, and the Bakufu, at least in the short run, was by no means simply a passive victim of economic forces. The relationship between the economic disruption of the end of the period and the decline of the political power of the Bakufu can scarcely have been a simple one-way one.

III. Quantitative Appraisal of the System

The purposes of this section are to examine two generally accepted hypotheses against a large body of hitherto unanalyzed data and to report some statistical results, obtained from the data, which contribute to an understanding of the workings of the Tokugawa monetary system. The data examined are *daily* series of the relative prices of gold, silver, and copper currency, the price of rice, and the margins (discount or premium) on gold bills of exchange drawn on Edo for the period from 1787 to 1868—with a few gaps.[25] We have also calculated wholesale (export) price index for Osaka and consumer price indexes for Edo and *Kamigata*

---

[23] These forced loans were resorted to occasionally throughout the period but with much greater frequency from the 1850s.

[24] Takeuchi, p. 211.

[25] *Ōsaka kingin beisen.* The missing years are 1788, 1790–92, 1796–97, 1802–3, 1815, 1818–19, 1821, 1829, 1831, 1833–35, 1839.

(Kyoto-Osaka region) from existing price data on selected commodities for the period between 1751 and 1868.[26]

The first hypothesis to be examined is the long-accepted view that changes in the relative values of gold and silver currency performed the function of a flexible rate of exchange in trade between Edo and Osaka, "in a fashion quite analogous to that observed between two nations nowadays."[27] This hypothesis implies that when Edo had adverse balance of payments the gold price fell, making her imports dearer and her exports (tax receipts?) cheaper until equilibrium was restored.

An examination of the data, however, clearly refutes this hypothesis. As is evident in figure 2 and table A1, despite great variation in Osaka–Edo economic relations, the gold price was stable for over half a century until 1854, when Perry arrived and the whole monetary system entered a period of rapid change, as will be noted shortly. In fact, the standard deviation of gold price for the period between 1800 and 1849 was 2.266 *momme* about a mean of 63.772 *momme*, or a coefficient of variation of 0.036. It should be noted also in table A1 that the gold price shows no falling trend, and actually rises when the financial condition of the Bakufu is at its worst.

To examine the above result further and to ascertain the possible mechanism which enabled such secular stability of the gold price in the face of the known constant adverse balance of trade for Edo vis-à-vis Osaka, we have calculated annual means and standard deviations for the difference between the gold exchange bill price and the gold price (i.e. the margin on exchange bills) as shown in table A2. As this difference is either the discount (*hon-uchi*) or premium (*gyaku-uchi*) on gold exchange bills, it represents the relative strength of demand and supply in the Osaka exchange bill market. Standard deviations are included to provide an indication of the variability of discount or premium around the par (*mu-uchi*) value (at which the difference between the gold exchange bill and spot gold prices is zero).

In calculating these means and standard deviations we added proxy values of +200 *momme* per 100 *ryō* for gold shipment from Osaka to Edo and −200 *momme* per 100 *ryō* for reverse gold shipment from Edo to Osaka. By doing so we attempted to include in our calculations the impact of these shipments on the bill market. It will be recalled that continued excess demand or supply conditions for bills resulted in gold shipment which tended to restore the market to equilibrium. The values plus or minus 200 *momme* per 100 *ryō* were chosen as, in our judgment, the values which on one hand are sufficiently above the highest discount or premium figures observed and on the other hand are not so high as to

[26] For the sources, see notes to tables A3 and A4.

[27] Sakudō, n. 12 above, p. 340. Sakudō regards this as accepted theory and cites a number of earlier authorities, all of whom give the same interpretation.

exaggerate the effect of these shipments. We believe these values are acceptable proxies for the impact of gold shipments, and although not presented in this paper, monthly means and standard deviations calculated with these proxies show, when examined against the raw data, that the use of these proxies reflected the actual market conditions quite realistically.[28]

The results of calculations seen in table A2 provide striking findings. First we discover that the annual means of the margins (premiums or discounts on exchange bills) are extremely small throughout the period covered by the data. Before 1854, when the situation changed profoundly as will be noted shortly, the largest absolute value of this annual mean was only 2.12 *fun* (0.212 *momme*) for 1838. This is less than 0.04 percent of the mean gold price for that year (59.84 *momme*). Even for the turbulent years following 1854, the maximum annual mean of the margin reached only about 0.13 percent (1860). In more general terms, the mean margin for the entire period, namely for the 13,209 days for which this data is available, was − 0.1094 *momme* per *ryō*, or about 0.16 percent of the mean gold price for the entire period (68.75 *momme*).[29] This is very close to the cost of

[28] The cost of shipping cash from Osaka for delivery in ten days in Edo is shown in the following table.

COST OF SHIPPING CASH: OSAKA–EDO

Year	*Momme* per 100 *Ryō*	%
1800......	8	0.13
1806......	11	0.17
1838......	8.5	0.14
1858......	10	0.14

SOURCE.—*Ryōgae nendaiki kanken* (n. 10 above), 1: 736–45.

The standard handling charge for exchange bills is said to have been two *momme* per 100 *ryō*, or approximately 0.03 percent according to Sekiyama Naotarō, *Nihon kahei kinyūshi kenkyū* (Tokyo: Shinkeizai Sha, 1943), p. 53. Nevertheless, the margin on bills could be much higher than the cost of transporting cash if there was a substantial gap between the Edo and Osaka gold prices.

[29] Confirming this observation, when a regression equation is calculated in the form gold price = *a* + *b* (gold bill price), we obtain an intercept of − 0.1338 *fun* and a regression coefficient of virtually 1 (the first seven figures after the point were 9s). Given the smallness of the difference between the gold bill and gold prices, this is a result to be expected. That is to say, the unexplained error term is so small that the ratio of explained error divided by total error is bound to be extremely high.

14

shipping cash (see n. 28), which indicates that the gap between the Osaka and Edo gold cash prices was not systematically biased in either direction. The second significant observation, closely connected with the comments just made, is that the standard deviation of the exchange bill margins for any given year were large *relative to their annual means for that year.* The ratio of standard deviation to the mean, that is, the coefficient of variation, fluctuated widely and often exceeded 5.0. For the entire period the ratio was as high as 3.7. On inspection, this wide band of fluctuation is found to apply equally to monthly data and to the raw data themselves.

The high coefficient of variation coupled with the very small absolute value of the means of the margins indicate that the market was highly sensitive and functioned very smoothly. The extreme smallness of the means of the margins was not an inevitable result—they could well have been much larger than observed had the market not worked so efficiently. For example, if a particular month had experienced fifteen days of gold shipment and fifteen days of equilibrium (*mu-uchi*), the mean of the margin for that month would have been 1.5 percent of the gold price, assuming the latter to have been 60 *momme* to the *ryō*. Our monthly data contain no such magnitude, but behave very much like the annual data shown in table A2. This indicates that any gap between the Edo and Osaka gold prices was quickly adjusted.

These findings indicate that the gold bill market was highly sensitive to the balance of payments between Edo and Osaka and functioned with an efficiency comparable with that of the international exchange market, with premia and discounts fluctuating narrowly around the stable gold price without involving a mechanism analogous to flexible exchange rates. The fluctuations of the margins seem large when evaluated in terms of coefficient of variation only because they are seen in relation to the extremely small means of these fluctuations.

The persistent negative signs of the annual means of the exchange bill margins indicate net shipment of gold cash from Edo to Osaka, although we are unable to determine the quantities involved. Nevertheless, since the mean margin was negative in forty-nine out of fifty-five years for which we have data between 1800 and 1868, the total flow of cash from Edo to Osaka over this period was presumably substantial. Such a flow of gold might have been expected to have depressed the Osaka gold price, but as noted earlier, the gold price displays no obvious trend before 1854 and thereafter moves sharply up rather than down (fig. 2).

In view of the above findings, our second question concerns relative price movements. If Edo's persistent balance-of-payments deficit vis-à-vis Osaka was settled by gold shipment as described above, did this raise the price level in Osaka more visibly than in Edo? On the analogy of international trade with stable exchange rates we would expect that it did.

The answer suggested by the available data, however, is negative. That is, as seen in figure 2 and table A4, the price level in Osaka—both wholesale (export) and consumer goods—was consistently below that of Edo during the period for which we have the data. More importantly, we find that when prices began to rise sharply during the early 1830s, the Edo price index rose faster and it maintained approximately 30 points differential from the *Kamigata* (Kyoto–Osaka) indexes until 1854, when *Kamigata* prices, too, began to rise very steeply.

Our results indicate that Edo–Osaka payments were balanced by an effectively functioning exchange bill market and by shipment of gold currency to Osaka, and not by a mechanism analogous to that of a flexible exchange rate which required the price of gold to fall under the constant excess import condition of Edo. It is also clear that, in spite of the gold shipment to Osaka, Osaka export prices did not rise until the 1830s (see table A3), remained stable at this higher level during the 1840s, and then rose sharply again from 1850 to the end of the period. We have very little information on the volume of Osaka exports to Edo, but there are some indications that it did fall in response to the rise in Osaka export prices in 1840–42.[30]

At this point, however, it will be useful to add some results of our empirical findings, as they not only provide quantitative answers to long-standing questions of the Tokugawa economy but also provide additional evidence which helps clarify the explanations to be offered in the following section.

First, although the Bakufu attempted to stabilize the rice price, as the data in table A1 show, yearly means fluctuate significantly with large standard deviations. In fact, for the entire period, 1787–1868, the co-efficient of variation was a large 0.422.[31] As we examine the monthly means of the rice price, which have been calculated though not presented

[30] See a report by Abe Tōtōmi-no-kami printed in *Ōsaka shishi* [History of Osaka City], ed. Ōsaka Shiyakusho [Osaka Municipal Government], 2d ed. (Osaka: Ōsaka Shiyakusho, 1927), 5: 679. The Osaka city officials were required to report the volume of exports to Edo of eleven commodities at three-month intervals from the 1720s, but· these records do not seem to have survived (see *Ōsaka shishi,* 1: 312).

[31] The mean price of rice for the entire period was 83.405 *momme* per *koku* and the standard deviation was 36.88 *momme*. The rice price has been adjusted to take account of differences which occurred in actual quantity of rice per nominal *koku*. In the raw data the daily quotation for rice was given in terms of six different types of rice, each expressed in *koku* of differing real content. To eliminate apparent price fluctuation due to changes in the standard rice, we divided each price by the actual amount of rice contained. For example, *Kaga* rice which contained 1.036 *koku* per unit was divided by 1.036 to obtain the price per standard *koku*. Higo rice which contained 0.967 standard *koku* per unit was adjusted similarly. All calculations in table 1A were in terms of these adjusted rice prices.

in this paper, it is evident that the price was a function of seasonal variation and harvest conditions. When the daily price of rice was regressed against the stable gold price, the results obtained, whether for the entire period or per year, yield correlation coefficients which are consistently small vis-à-vis sample sizes, and 22 percent of the monthly correlation coefficients calculated (168 months out of 727 months) were negative. We conclude that the rice price reflected general monetary conditions only weakly, and was relatively unresponsive to monetary policy.[32]

IV. Gold and Commodity Prices, 1787-1868

The aim of this section is to explain the movement of the gold price from 1787 to 1868 in the light of our statistical findings and historical events, and to suggest an interpretation of the monetary history of the period.

The exceptionally low gold price from 1787 to 1793 was associated with the disastrous Temmei famine of 1786. The price of rice soared to an annual mean not reached again for fifty years, and Bakufu tax income in 1787 fell to 22 percent below the average of the five years on either side of that year. Moreover, this drop in revenue followed a period of chronic deficits[33] that resulted in a fall in Bakufu reserves from 3,004,100 ryō in 1770 to 817,207 ryō in 1788.[34] In normal times the Osaka banking system might have absorbed this and still maintained the relative value of gold cash, for example by expanding silver credit, but in the famine conditions of the late 1780s this was not possible.

In the summer of 1787, Matsudaira Sadanobu took office as Senior Councillor (rōjū) and head of the government, and immediately announced an economy drive which ushered in the period of the Kansei reforms. With the help of forced contributions from daimyo and the Osaka banks, the Bakufu achieved a net cash surplus over the following decade of some 263,000 ryō, which may well have contributed to the improvement in the gold price. Between 1798 and 1816, however, the cash reserves of the Bakufu again fell by 428,000 ryō[35] despite some forced loans. Nevertheless, the effect of this deficit on the gold price was very small. This does not seem to have been because the Osaka banking system expanded silver-unit credit to match the increase in holdings of gold cash, since if this had been

---

[32] Only exception is the Tempō kaikaku (Reforms of Tempō) during the early 1840s, as will be discussed in the next section.

[33] Nihon zaisei keizai shiryō (n. 7 above), 10: 483.

[34] Mukōyama Gendayu (Seisai), Edo jitsujō Seisai zakki [Seisai's miscellany of conditions in Edo], Edo sōsho [Edo series] (Tokyo: Edo Sōsho Kankō Kai, 1917), 9: 36-37.

[35] This information is from Furushima Toshio, "Bakufu zaisei shūnyū no dōkō to nōmin shūdatsu no kakki" [Trends in Bakufu income and the periodization of peasant exploitation], Nihon keizaishi taikei, 4:37. This article provides an excellent summary of sources available on Bakufu finance.

the case we should expect the value of gold and copper cash to move together relative to silver, whereas in fact the relationship is very weak ($R = .007$ for $n = 2,396$ for the decade 1800–1809).[36] We believe that what kept the Osaka gold price from falling at this time was a flow of cash from Osaka to rural areas, a flow that had been going on for many years and which was now resumed after an interruption caused by the 1786 famine.

The increase in the rural money supply did not raise the prices at which rural products were supplied to the cities. In fact, the Osaka wholesale price index fell by about 10 percent between 1800 and 1818 (see table A3). As already stated, we believe that the increase in the rural cash supply was absorbed by a rapidly rising volume of rural cash transactions associated with commercialization of agriculture and monetization of the rural economy at this time. In addition, increasing production for the market and a monopoly procurement system (the Osaka *kabunakama*) that had still not lost its effectiveness combined to reduce procurement prices.

Toward the end of 1819 the coinage was debased. Unfortunately we do not have data for this year; in fact the data are missing for several of the most interesting years in which fluctuations could be expected to have been higher than usual, and this may exaggerate somewhat the impression of stability conveyed by the tables and other statistical results. When the data starts again, only two months after the debasement, the gold cash market was still unsettled and low with a mean of 56.51 *momme* in January. Copper and rice were also cheap and the Osaka wholesale price index fell, suggesting appreciation of silver rather than depreciation of gold. Since *chōgin* was debased even more than gold coin, the net effect of the debasement was to raise the intrinsic value of gold relative to *chōgin*, but this fact seems to have had little significance. This confirms our speculation that the standard against which gold currency was measured was not *chōgin* but the unit of silver credit, which therefore appreciated with the debasement of gold currency in much the same way as a fall in the price of gold is now equivalent to appreciation of the dollar. In fact, although the debasement was of the order of 13 percent, the fall in the gold cash price was less than 9 percent. The Edo exchange bill market seems to have worked smoothly through this period with margins and standard deviations not noticeably higher than usual. By 1823 all series returned to normal levels, although the debased coinage continued to be issued in large quantities into the 1830s.

What kept the gold price stable during the 1820s seems to have been primarily an increase in silver-unit credit in Osaka. For the decade 1820–29, all price series expressed in silver move much more closely together than

[36] Here and below, where coefficients of correlation are given for decades, they have been checked against annual and monthly correlations, and in each case the decade figure reasonably accurately reflects the relationship within years and months.

usual (Gold and copper: $R = .603$ for $n = 2,367$; gold and rice: $R = .517$ for $n = 1,646$). This could be explained by a trend from the side of silver itself, and this explanation is confirmed by the marked trend of commodity prices expressed in silver (see fig. 2 and table A4). Expansion of the cash supply and the supply of silver credit reversed the downward trend of commodity prices despite a run of good rice harvests, but the rise in commodity prices was still mild because of the continued capacity of rural areas to absorb cash.

It was in the 1830s that commodity prices first rose steeply with the Edo consumer price index, reaching twice the 1830 level in 1837. Osaka wholesale prices also began a pronounced upward trend at this time. The rise in consumer prices is clearly due to a very sharp increase in the cash supply. The issue of one-eighth-*ryō* gold pieces (*nishukin*) in 1832 added 7.4 million *ryō* to the cash supply, in 1835 a new debased copper coin (*Tempō sen*) was issued, and by 1870 no less than 38.78 billion *mon* of this new copper coinage was put into circulation. This sum is roughly equivalent in value to 6 million *ryō* or ₍ne-third of the gold currency in circulation in 1818.[37] This was followed in 1837 by a debasement of the gold coinage that increased the amount in circulation by 3.45 million *ryō*,[38] and in the same year the first quarter-*ryō* silver pieces were issued—the first of some 80 million issued between that year and 1854. Although made of silver, they in fact added to the supply of gold-unit cash. This large issue of small-denomination subsidiary coins in gold units, added to the large issue of copper, probably contributed to the fall in the value of copper cash in 1838, which prompted the Bakufu to attempt to maintain its price at 5,700–6,000 to the *ryō*, apparently with little success.

The volume of silver-unit credit also seems to have expanded during the 1830s. Depreciation of *chōgin* by almost 20 percent in 1837 added 80,000 *kamme* to the supply and if this was, as we have surmised, some sort of reserve, it is likely that the volume of credit based on it expanded by much more. The steep rise in commodity prices expressed in silver suggests the same conclusion.[39] Despite this, however, the gold price fell steeply from an annual mean of 64.53 *momme* in 1830 to an annual mean of 59.84 *momme* in 1838. We attribute both the steep price rises and the fall in the value of gold cash to a kind of saturation of rural demand for cash. Monetization of the rural economy had reached a plateau, and the

---

[37] Yamaguchi, "Edo jidai ni okeru kinginka no aridaka," p. 79.

[38] *Ryōgae nendaiki kanken* (n. 8 above), 1: 782.

[39] No inference about the movement of silver can be made from the fact that the coefficient of correlation between gold and copper is low in this decade ($R = .057$ for $n = 1,558$) since, because of independent movements in the volume of gold and copper in circulation, we would expect a weak relationship, even though there were some trends in the volume of silver-unit money.

volume of monetary transactions could no longer increase faster than the volume of production without inflationary effects. Two factors intensified the effect of this change in the 1830s. First, the increase in the cash supply was greater than in any previous decade covered by our data. Second, rural output was increasing at a slower rate, partly because of poor harvests in the late 1930s and partly because the geographical spread of rural industry was approaching a temporary limit. These conditions are reflected in the widespread rural unrest that characterized the decade.

It was to deal with these problems that the Tempō reforms were announced in mid-1841, inaugurating a change in Bakufu economic policy. Control through official procurement and distribution agencies was clearly becoming ineffective in the face of rising rural cash demand, and the Bakufu was forced to consider controlling the sources of inflation—namely high wages, rising costs of raw materials, and high costs of production in general. The official urban trade organizations (*kabunakama*) were dissolved and attempts were made to find a more comprehensive form of control closer to sources of supply. As in earlier periods of reform, the Bakufu instituted strict budget economy. In 1842, price and wage controls were imposed and interest rates were ordered to be lowered from 15 percent to 12 percent,[40] and in the following year a loan of 855,000 *ryō* was raised from the merchant community of Osaka and its environs. Even though the amount raised was less than half the amount "requested," it was still by far the largest amount raised up to that time.[41] At the same time the Bakufu called in its own loans on a large scale.[42] Edo's imports from Osaka were reduced not only by fiscal economy but by two other factors. First, efforts were made, beginning in 1843, to reduce Edo's demand for consumption goods by ordering the evacuation of all unauthorized Edo residents to their native villages. Second, a tendency for imports from Osaka to be replaced by purchases from the hinterland of Edo was strengthened by the dissolution of the Edo–Osaka trading monopolies.[43]

By these and other related measures, aided by good harvests, consumer prices were sharply reduced and the gold price strengthened. The improvement was, however, shortlived. In particular the Osaka wholesale price index, which reflects the prices at which goods were supplied from rural areas, failed to fall in the 1840s, but fluctuated around a level 36 percent above the average of the 1820s. Attempts to control rural prices

[40] Tsuda Hideo, "Tempō kaikaku no keizaiteki igi" [The economic significance of the Tempō reform], *Nihon keizaishi taikei* 4: 301–57.

[41] Honjō Eijirō, ed., *Nihon keizaishi jiten* [Encyclopedia of Japanese economic history] (Tokyo: Nihon Hyōron Sha, 1940), 1: 597.

[42] Furushima, 4: 43.

[43] See Itō Kōichi, *Edo jimawari keizai no tenkai* [Development of the Edo hinterland economy) (Tokyo: Kashiwa Shobō, 1966), chap. 3.

having met with little success, the *kabunakama* were restored in modified form in 1851, but they were no more effective than they had been in the 1830s. The rural economy was no longer able to absorb rapid increases in its money supply without inflationary results, and the Bakufu was no longer able to prevent rural cash demand from effectively competing with the cities for supplies of goods. In more general terms, the cities could no longer run a deficit with rural Japan with impunity. Thus the expedient by which the Bakufu had long been able to supplement the resources available to it by running a cash deficit with rural Japan was now denied to it—and just at a time when demands on its resources were enormously increased. Defense commitments which had begun to rise in the 1840s soared with the arrival of Perry in 1853, and these increased commitments made it impracticable to follow the kind of deflationary fiscal policy that the monetary and price situation called for. Continued deficits financed by further increases in currency issue sent prices far above the peaks of the 1830s.

On the analogy of previous periods of heavy deficit financing, we might have expected the gold price to fall, but on the contrary, it rose at an accelerating rate for the rest of the period. Several factors account for this. The first and by far the most important was depreciation of the silver unit. Again the strength of the trend in silver is illustrated by a very high relationship between gold and copper, both expressed in terms of silver ($R = .782$ for $n = 1,857$ for the period 1860–68) despite a marked change in the value of copper in terms of gold. Depreciation of silver was the result of an unprecedented increase in loans by the Osaka market to daimyo to cover increasing burdens of expenditure, especially for military purposes. Between 1844 and 1867 (the bulk probably after 1850), loans to diamyo amounted to 11,220,841 *yen* in the currency of the 1870s.[44] This figure understates the amount of these loans since the loans were converted to the new currency at a low rate. Loans contracted in Edo were converted at 1 *yen* = 60 *momme*; those contracted in Kyoto were converted at the annual average price of the *ryō* in the year the loan was contracted; and those contracted in Osaka were converted at the price of the *ryō* on the day the Osaka gold market closed (1 *yen* = 219 *momme*). On the conservative assumptions that half the amount was contracted in Osaka, one quarter in Kyoto and one quarter at Edo at an average gold price of 1 *ryō* = 80 *momme* (the average rate for the period), the amount of the loans would have been 1.7 million *kamme* in silver units or 21 million *ryō*. This huge sum is roughly comparable with the total debts of the daimiates outstanding in 1844. To this must be added loans to the Imperial Court.

Among other reasons for the strength of the gold price were large forced loans from the Osaka merchant community to the Bakufu. Whether

[44] *Hansai shūroku* [Account of *han* debts], in *Meiji zenki zaisei keizai shiryō shūsei*, 9: 138.

21

these loans were made in gold cash or silver credit is not clear, but either way the effect on the gold price would be the same. Edo's imports from Osaka also probably continued to decrease as Edo imported more from its own hinterland and as daimyo and their large retinues moved out of Edo to Kyoto or to their home provinces. The effect of this move is clearly reflected in the relative movements of Kyoto and Edo consumer prices after the relaxation of the requirements of *sankin kōtai* by which daimyo were required to maintain establishments in Edo.

With the opening of foreign trade in 1859 under the Ansei treaties we might have expected very large movements in the gold price to adjust to the international ratio between gold and silver metal. In fact the rise in gold price could hardly have been due to this cause. The sudden outflow of gold following the opening of trade in 1859 has been estimated at 500,000 *ryō*[45] but it is not reflected in any way in the Osaka gold cash price. The reason is that the outflow of gold was largely balanced by an inflow of Mexican silver dollars which circulated in Japan, not as silver (*gimme*),but as three-quarter *ryō* pieces and so formed part of the gold-unit currency.

The higher overseas gold/silver ratio was reflected in the relative value of gold coins vis-à-vis silver coins expressed in gold units but it was not reflected in the Osaka gold price, which confirms our assumption that the latter had very little to do with the metallic content of either gold coin or *chōgin*. This does not rule out the possibility that expectations generated by the overseas ratio may have contributed to loss of confidence in silver in the closing years of the period.

By the 1860s the Bakufu's needs had completely outrun the resources available to it and, apparently in desperation, it ran unprecedented budget deficits financed by depreciation. This resulted in an increase in the supply of gold-unit currency from 48.8 million *ryō* in 1854 to 127.2 million *ryō* at the time of the Restoration.[46] Although the volume of *chōgin* actually fell by 10 percent over this period, this fact was of no significance whatever compared with the precipitous depreciation of the silver credit unit, the extent of which is reflected in the soaring relative price of gold despite such an increase in its volume. Even without the added financial commitments associated with the opening of the country and the disturbances that preceded it, deficits could have been expected to rise at an accelerating rate. With the rural "transactions trap" filled, each deficit raised prices, and since revenue was price-inelastic the deficit became greater each year. This accounts for the exponential appearance of the price series in figure 2. The similar upward trend of the gold price is an indication that the daimyo were, if anything, in an even more serious financial condition.

[45] See Okada Shumpei, *Bakumatsu ishin no kahei seisaku* [Monetary policy in the late Tokugawa and Restoration periods] (Tokyo: Moriyama Shoten, 1955), chap. 3.

[46] Yamaguchi, "Edo jidai ni okeru kinginka no aridaka," p. 79.

V. Conclusions

Looking at our period as a whole, we are impressed with the general stability of the gold price and the apparently smooth working of the exchange bill market. Our data suggest that the Osaka gold cash price was very unresponsive to changes in the balance of payments between Edo and Osaka, and what data we have suggest that although urban commodity prices fluctuated, particularly in Edo, they do not show a marked tendency to rise until the 1830s, and the rise becomes very marked after 1854. We find strong evidence to suggest that silver was a unit of credit with very little if any relation to the composition of metallic silver currency (chōgin).

Our findings suggest that there was a strong tendency for increases in the gold-unit cash supply to be balanced not by movements in the gold price—the ratio between gold cash and silver credit—but either to be dispersed into rural areas or to be balanced by increases in the supply of silver-unit credit money. Since Osaka commodity prices began to rise consistently only in the late 1820s and 1830s, we conclude that increases in the cash supply moved out of Osaka into rural areas up to that time, and that this increase in rural cash supply was not reflected in higher procurement prices for rural goods until then because of a combination of political control, elastic supply conditions, and the process of monetization of the rural economy.

Beginning around 1830, however, this situation no longer obtained. The flow of cash to rural areas now began to raise the general level of rural prices, and with the elasticity of supply (at least to the cities) probably falling, the Bakufu and the commercial agencies it sponsored could no longer keep procurement prices down. The Bakufu, which had long relied on the ability of the rural economy to absorb its deficits—and indeed the deficit of urban vis-à-vis rural Japan—was deprived of this resource just when its needs were greatest. Thus we conclude that the process of commercialization in a sense aided the Tokugawa regime, and that it was the leveling off of the process before other sources of revenue could be found that precipitated the financial crisis associated with its fall.

Appendix

Monetary units reference to are: gold, 1 ryō = 4 bu = 16 shu; silver, 1 kamme = 1,000 momme = 10,000 fun = 100,000 rin = 1,000,000 mō; copper, 1 kammon = 1,000 mon; rice, 1 koku = 2.5 hyō = 10 to = 100 shō.

TABLE A1
ANNUAL MEANS AND SDs OF GOLD, COPPER, AND RICE PRICES
(1787–1868)

	GOLD*		COPPER†		RICE‡	
YEAR	Mean	SD	Mean	SD	Mean	SD
1787.....	55.518	0.868	9.407	2.728	103.241	24.365
1789.....	55.613	0.504	9.709	0.104	60.483	3.814
1793.....	58.415	0.549	9.522	0.070	77.078	6.538
1794.....	62.347	2.458	9.425	0.289	74.968	18.625
1795.....	63.452	1.713	9.527	0.110	59.014	3.002
1798.....	61.400	0.389	9.269	0.218	66.020	2.447
1799.....	62.540	4.644	9.108	0.189	60.862	3.680
1800.....	63.030	0.462	9.385	0.158	69.789	5.465
1801.....	61.640	2.421	9.328	0.308	65.589	6.131
1804.....	64.377	3.808	9.464	0.419	51.893	4.131
1805.....	64.571	0.633	8.900	0.438	54.636	3.501
1806.....	65.730	0.505	9.304	0.492	58.144	14.921
1808.....	66.437	0.217	9.252	0.084	66.848	4.947
1809.....	66.624	1.237	9.248	0.065	63.055	7.413
1810.....	63.513	0.336	9.275	0.039	55.277	14.270
1811.....	64.080	0.195	9.261	0.063	65.340	11.604
1812.....	64.330	0.138	9.229	0.055	55.729	6.758
1813.....	64.548	0.322	9.175	0.078	61.371	7.017
1814.....	64.759	0.188	9.012	0.862	67.290	3.279
1816.....	65.388	0.221	9.001	0.037	60.221	6.753
1817.....	65.293	0.171	8.913	0.064	64.079	3.334
1820.....	59.524	1.287	8.879	0.178	48.391	5.359
1822.....	62.417	0.619	8.880	0.060	54.219	2.961
1823.....	64.355	0.870	8.937	0.072	57.351	3.192
1824.....	63.859	0.912	9.166	0.207	58.821	3.018
1825.....	64.501	0.398	9.805	0.269	61.277	6.484
1827.....	64.654	0.127	9.540	0.072	55.492	2.983
1828.....	64.662	0.308	9.439	0.053	64.653	10.927
1830.....	64.532	0.160	9.361	0.144	73.799	8.480
1832.....	63.770	7.696	9.247	0.062	67.963	4.257
1836.....	62.896	1.232	8.971	0.134	102.632	26.996
1837.....	60.597	0.906	9.003	0.220	162.709	52.205
1838.....	59.839	1.263	8.895	0.081	102.210	15.698
1840.....	63.060	6.523	9.040	0.093	65.541	8.026
1841.....	62.181	0.257	9.539	0.644	64.579	4.917
1842.....	63.905	0.941	9.523	0.535	66.971	9.042
1843.....	64.616	0.403	9.884	0.205	67.475	6.742

TABLE A1 (*continued*)

	GOLD*		COPPER†		RICE‡	
YEAR	Mean	SD	Mean	SD	Mean	SD
1844.....	64.517	0.372	10.000	0.000	72.150	5.363
1845.....	63.891	0.612	9.704	1.601	78.903	8.140
1846.....	64.108	0.283	10.000	0.000	85.856	8.144
1847.....	63.897	0.118	10.000	0.000	80.376	5.656
1848.....	64.042	5.488	10.000	0.000	81.715	4.591
1849.....	63.601	0.375	10.000	0.000	87.775	8.766
1850.....	61.722	0.613	9.281	0.354	113.327	20.001
1851.....	62.977	0.536	9.537	4.515	106.783	24.780
1852.....	63.496	1.719	9.624	0.094	77.416	4.655
1853.....	64.999	2.926	9.766	0.166	91.987	8.573
1854.....	70.694	45.644	9.865	0.172	95.621	8.915
1855.....	68.791	1.089	10.112	0.978	74.721	3.477
1856.....	70.150	0.687	10.425	0.068	76.316	4.798
1857.....	71.040	0.918	10.620	0.122	91.506	7.599
1858.....	72.448	0.811	10.656	0.066	116.572	7.490
1859.....	73.068	1.647	10.692	0.351	114.939	5.036
1860.....	72.912	2.352	11.224	0.213	134.812	16.793
1861.....	72.551	0.654	11.496	0.398	163.034	27.482
1862.....	75.239	4.240	11.782	0.734	148.020	15.428
1863.....	83.692	2.702	12.982	0.416	156.947	18.878
1864.....	90.254	7.632	13.920	1.390	183.703	59.252
1865.....	103.083	44.103	15.106	0.611	137.103	111.753
1866.....	115.770	12.352	14.569	0.893	97.744	27.573
1867.....	129.373	11.431	14.532	0.928	95.016	28.324
1868.....	200.391	14.957	19.297	1.163	64.593	4.492

* The unit is *momme* per *ryō*.
† The unit is *momme* per *kan*.
‡ The unit is *momme* per adjusted *koku*.

TABLE A2

ANNUAL MEANS AND SDs OF THE DIFFERENCE BETWEEN
GOLD BILL PRICE AND GOLD PRICE* (1787–1868)

Year	Mean of Difference	SD	Year	Mean of Difference	SD
1787.......	−0.166	0.161	1837	−0.220	1.440
1788.......	0.154	0.741	1838	−2.117	0.996
1793.......	0.101	0.879	1840	−1.145	1.478
1794.......	0.039	1.087	1841	−0.366	1.010
1795.......	0.082	0.981	1842	−1.601	2.302
1798.......	0.116	0.341	1843	−1.086	1.506
1799.......	0.040	0.184	1844	−0.379	1.851
1800.......	−0.143	0.908	1845	−0.330	1.343
1801.......	−0.313	0.726	1846	−0.493	1.339
1804.......	−0.016	0.415	1847	−0.041	1.225
1805.......	0.228	0.850	1848	−0.105	1.420
1806.......	−0.027	1.470	1849	−0.250	1.442
1808.......	−0.600	1.016	1850	−0.114	1.513
1809.......	−0.602	1.021	1851	0.085	1.112
1810.......	−0.323	0.790	1852	−1.512	1.422
1811.......	−0.631	1.625	1853	−0.231	1.486
1812.......	−0.084	0.588	1854	−0.911	2.131
1813.......	0.126	1.436	1855	−1.267	2.077
1814.......	0.294	0.362	1856	−1.599	1.797
1816.......	−0.173	0.372	1857	−2.732	2.305
1817.......	−0.315	0.408	1858	−1.718	2.316
1820.......	−0.029	0.467	1859	−1.520	2.010
1822.......	−0.376	0.296	1860	−9.421	8.886
1823.......	−0.342	0.632	1861	−2.819	2.161
1824.......	−0.428	0.464	1862	−1.857	1.751
1825.......	−1.266	0.733	1863	−5.614	6.256
1827.......	−1.218	0.733	1864	−8.195	8.183
1828.......	0.089	0.454	1865	−5.522	4.603
1830.......	−0.241	0.406	1866	−3.725	10.730
1832.......	−0.215	1.169	1867	3.644	6.850
1836.......	0.448	1.303	1868	−1.828	6.276

* Unit is in *fun* per *ryō*.

TABLE A3
KYOTO PRICE INDEXES, 1751–1817
(1751 = 100)

Year	Polished Rice (Hakumai)	Soy Bean Paste (miso)	Soy Sauce (shōyu)	Wine (Sake)	Lamp Oil (tōyu)	Sauerbeck Index
1751..	100.00	100.00	100.00	100.00	100.00	100.00
1752..	87.38	87.50	98.98	96.69	94.29	92.97
1753..	72.11	81.25	92.23	79.61	88.57	82.75
1754..	62.28	81.25	94.27	78.50	74.29	78.12
1755..	78.22	106.25	93.66	80.12	80.00	87.65
1756..	119.65	112.50	95.19	106.97	94.29	105.72
1757..	104.65	118.75	94.99	116.06	91.43	105.18
1758..	96.28	118.75	97.44	105.01	94.29	102.35
1759..	97.61	106.25	94.79	106.03	105.71	102.08
1760..	86.06	87.50	94.58	100.08	94.29	92.70
1761..	79.02	93.75	92.94	99.83	82.86	89.68
1762..	73.44	87.50	92.43	100.08	94.29	84.09
1773..	74.37	...	102.25	114.70	85.71	94.26
1774..	70.39	...	102.25	107.05	82.86	90.64
1775..	74.37	...	102.25	107.05	102.86	96.63
1776..	82.34	...	102.25	99.41	97.14	95.29
1777..	95.75	...	102.25	99.41	82.86	95.07
1778..	87.65	...	102.25	99.41	68.57	89.47
1779..	84.46	...	102.25	99.41	68.57	88.67
1780..	71.85	...	81.80	99.41	...	84.35
1781..	78.09	...	81.80	99.41	71.43	82.68
1782..	102.66	...	81.80	99.41	...	94.62
1783..	130.54	...	81.80	102.72	80.00	98.77
1784..	147.68	...	81.80	129.99	105.71	116.30
1785..	107.17	...	81.80	103.65	94.29	96.73
1786..	92.96	...	81.80	103.65	105.71	96.03
1787..	222.97	...	81.80	137.64	...	147.47
1788..	118.86	...	81.80	133.22	...	111.29
1789..	109.30	...	133.95	132.54	...	125.26
1790..	90.70	...	...	111.30	...	101.00
1791..	80.48	106.25	76.69	96.86	77.14	87.48
1792..	121.91	125.00	76.69	117.25	94.29	107.03
1793..	131.87	131.25	78.73	131.44	85.71	111.80
1794..	97.34	112.50	117.59	103.40	94.29	105.02
1795..	99.87	112.50	78.43	101.10	94.29	97.24
1796..	118.06	118.75	77.91	110.88	97.14	104.55
1797..	109.69	118.75	77.51	108.75	97.14	102.36

TABLE A3 (continued)

Year	Polished Rice (Hakumai)	Soy Bean Paste (miso)	Soy Sauce (shōyu)	Wine (Sake)	Lamp Oil (tōyu)	Sauerbeck Index
1798..	113.01	118.75	79.24	106.29	85.71	100.60
1799..	106.24	106.25	70.55	118.95	88.57	98.11
1800..	119.39	112.50	69.53	110.11	94.29	101.16
1801..	110.76	125.00	69.53	114.70	91.43	102.28
1802..	99.60	106.25	68.61	100.34	77.14	90.39
1803..	98.94	112.50	68.40	108.75	91.43	96.00
1804..	80.21	106.25	63.80	93.03	85.71	85.80
1805..	80.74	118.75	62.68	97.03	80.00	87.84
1806..	85.66	112.50	66.05	93.71	80.00	87.58
1807..	84.20	106.25	76.89	94.14	74.29	87.15
1808..	108.10	118.75	73.42	110.62	77.14	97.61
1809..	113.28	118.75	70.45	102.72	80.00	97.04
1810..	87.65	106.25	70.25	100.93	77.14	88.44
1811..	87.65	100.00	70.04	101.95	85.71	89.07
1812..	90.04	100.00	69.43	101.95	80.00	88.28
1813..	82.87	100.00	70.86	96.01	74.29	84.81
1814..	105.58	112.50	71.68	103.65	77.14	94.11
1815..	105.44	112.50	71.06	105.01	71.43	93.09
1816..	98.14	112.50	71.37	99.41	65.71	89.43
1817..	111.69	118.75	72.60	103.23	62.86	93.83

NOTE.—The source of the data is *Kinsei kōki ni okeru shuyō bukka no dōtai* [Movements of major commodity prices during the late Tokugawa period], ed. Nakai Nobuhiko (Nihon Gakujutsu Shinkō-kai, 1952), pp. 69–72. The original data were compiled by the House of Mitsui which has had offices in Edo, Osaka, and Kyoto for their money-changing and retail (textile goods) business since the late seventeenth century. The data included, in addition to the five commodities used in this Appendix, the price of salt and four wage series. (The salt series was not included because it was missing nearly 50 percent of the time and the prices were for various types of salt whose quality differentials we were unable to ascertain. Neither were the wage data, as they are not directly relevant for our purpose at hand, are also incomplete, and, since they are fixed by guilds, are not sensitive to prices.) The prices were recorded only for spring and fall. We chose the spring prices which are normally closer to the annual average than the fall prices. The five commodities used accounted for a significant proportion of expenditure of consumers of the time, and therefore provide reasonably accurate reflections of the general trends of consumer prices. The last column, the Sauerbeck index, is an unweighted mean of the five price indexes, i.e.,

$$\sum_{i=1}^{n} \frac{P_{it}}{P_{io}}/n$$

where P_{io} is the base price of ith commodity and n is the number of commodity indexes available for that year. As the original source noted, "these prices might understate the actual prices somewhat since they were the prices which the Mitsui shops paid," i.e., "their bulk buying undoubtedly enabled them to buy at lower prices." This, however, should not affect the *trend* of prices.

28

TABLE A4
SAUERBECK PRICE INDEXES OF OSAKA WHOLESALE (EXPORT),
KAMIGATA (KYOTO), AND EDO CONSUMER GOODS, 1802–1868
(1818 = 100)

Year	Osaka Wholesale*	Kyoto Consumer†	Edo Consumer†
1802.........	112.25	...	...
1803.........	119.59	...	...
1804.........	114.68	...	...
1805.........	113.82	...	...
1806.........	116.80	...	...
1807.........	108.01	...	...
1808.........	115.55	...	...
1809.........	122.86	...	...
1810.........	119.18	...	...
1811.........	118.08	...	...
1812.........	116.02	...	...
1813.........	113.71	...	...
1814.........	112.77	...	...
1815.........	106.45	...	...
1816.........	103.98	...	...
1817.........	99.99	...	...
1818.........	100.00	100.00	100.00
1819.........	101.82	97.71	96.16
1820.........	102.19	91.95	95.74
1821.........	113.32	94.34	97.89
1822.........	106.40	95.55	101.50
1823.........	103.87	94.59	100.53
1824.........	111.03	96.47	100.76
1825.........	111.63	96.00	99.81
1826.........	125.81	105.14	112.91
1827.........	127.42	103.06	106.91
1828.........	117.34	103.49	108.31
1829.........	109.56	114.49	113.44
1830.........	109.22	109.68	111.36
1831.........	118.72	111.30	116.58
1832.........	124.72	103.87	113.75
1833.........	116.40	108.54	116.04
1834.........	114.84	130.93	148.63
1835.........	127.80	109.55	137.47
1836.........	131.57	116.58	143.20
1837.........	139.94	172.30	224.05
1838.........	136.76	143.23	189.65
1839.........	135.64	153.73	183.23

TABLE A4 (*continued*)

Year	Osaka Wholesale*	Kyoto Consumer†	Edo Consumer†
1840.........	169.05	118.43	156.93
1841.........	163.31	120.52	150.76
1842.........	159.51	116.13	146.82
1843.........	144.80	114.55	132.87
1844.........	133.66	107.45	139.30
1845.........	146.63	111.15	153.40
1846.........	156.48	115.36	168.29
1847.........	157.49	125.59	163.49
1848.........	151.05	127.95	163.60
1849.........	150.71	135.63	159.87
1850.........	138.29	133.52	172.63
1851.........	149.71	158.59	181.34
1852.........	173.81	122.29	162.76
1853.........	182.96	125.07	180.37
1854.........	168.91	135.28	175.63
1855.........	163.08	124.60	174.75
1856.........	184.07	121.31	169.84
1857.........	191.12	134.79	171.53
1858.........	184.45	147.24	186.56
1859.........	175.79	146.15	181.64
1860.........	199.49	163.81	207.11
1861.........	230.82	245.05	249.30
1862.........	210.07	203.61	236.20
1863.........	248.16	231.23	238.65
1864.........	424.08	270.51	269.08
1865.........	630.59	365.38	379.05
1866.........	804.69	719.82	502.19
1867.........	1077.74	1107.19‡	625.17
1868.........	1049.47	578.80	578.67

NOTE.—Source is same as table A3.

* This is the Sauerbeck price index for three commodities: rapeseed oil, charcoal, and cotton cloth. All three commodities were identified as of standard origin and quality. This index can be considered applicable to wholesale prices in *Kamigata* (Kyoto–Osaka region) and for exports to Edo and other parts of Japan. We used data for the fourth month of the Japanese calendar for the same seasonal reasons as stated in table A3.

† These series are the Sauerbeck price indexes calculated from the same five commodities as in table A3.

‡ This is due to an extremely bad harvest of 1867 which raised the rice price index from 907.09 in 1866 to 1534.22 in 1867.

THE VILLAGE AND AGRICULTURE
DURING THE EDO PERIOD

THE SENGOKU VILLAGE LEGACY

Near the end of the Tokugawa period, officials from the shogunate's Finance Office undertook a survey of villages in Musashi and Sagami provinces.[1] During the course of their investigations, the bakufu officials consulted documents preserved by prominent village families that traced their lineages back in time to samurai society of the sixteenth century. Some of the documents from the villages of Sagami had been issued by the Hōjō house of Odawara, and many of the Musashi documents carried the seal of the Uesugi daimyo. Among them were directives requiring the recipient to provide horses for military service, whereas others bestowed fiefs in reward for distinguished service in battle, an indication that some of the villagers' ancestors had served, nearly three centuries earlier, as warriors under the Sengoku daimyo. Other evidence corroborates this notion. In many cadastral survey registers from the early seventeenth century, it is not uncommon to find two persons listed as cultivators (*sakunin*). Usually the name of a samurai or priest appears first, below which is entered the name of the man who was presumably the actual cultivator, separated by the term *bun*. From this it is clear that many former samurai who had lived in the villages while serving the Sengoku daimyo as warriors remained on the land in the seventeenth century, thus establishing the lineages revealed in the survey at the end of the Edo period. Why these persons chose to remain on the land, abandoning samurai status for a life on the soil, remains an intriguing question that can be answered only by examining how the relationships among land tenure, taxation, agricultural technology, and the social composition of villages subtly yet irrevocably shifted over the course of time that separated the late Edo from the late Sengoku period.

Social stratification within the *shōen* estates of the medieval period

---

1 For a comprehensive explanation of these surveys, see Furushima Toshio, *Nihon nōgyōshi* (Tokyo: Iwanami shoten, 1956), pp. 177–9.

was very complex. Local landholders, known as *myōshu,* were the principal cultivators, and they paid an annual land rent to the estate's proprietors, most often temples or aristocratic families in Kyoto. These local landholders possessed legally protected entitlements to their lands, including the right to buy, sell, and bequeath their holdings. Landownership was transferable not only between fellow landholders but also to officials of the shogunate such as the military estate stewards (*jitō*), some of whom might reside within the boundaries of any given estate and ultimately become the vassals of that estate's proprietors. At this time in the Tōkai region, small-scale private landholders, who also constituted a portion of the lower stratum of the warrior class, were referred to as *kumon,* or native estate officers. Like the *myōshu* these men could buy and sell land, expand agricultural production, and open markets.

Many of the landholders of the medieval period had to fight when called upon by the daimyo with whom they had entered an alliance. To this end, members of this landowning warrior class were expected to supply their own provisions and military equipment and to lead their own retainers into battle. Moreover, this upper stratum of warrior-villagers also managed groups of "vassal peasants" (*hikan-byakushō*), who in peacetime worked land leased from the samurai but who in time of war accompanied their samurai masters into battle. More numerous were the villagers called *jige-byakushō,* men who engaged solely in agriculture under the direction of the *myōshu* and *kumon* but who were not required to fulfill any military service obligation. These numerous social differences indicate that the sharp division between the warrior and peasantry that distinguished the class structure of Tokugawa society had not yet come into existence even in the late Sengoku era.

Although the proprietary control wielded by the temples, shrines, and nobility over their *shōen* in the Kinai region gradually diminished, their vestigial authority over the land lingered on until Toyotomi Hideyoshi, as part of his drive to achieve national hegemony, began a comprehensive survey of Japanese agricultural land, the famous Taikō cadastral survey, which permanently altered the nature of rural land tenure in the final decades of the sixteenth century. Consequently, the offices of military estate steward (*jitō*) and estate officer (*shōkan*) also remained until Hideyoshi's time. Some of these officials had been able to accumulate considerable holdings within the villages that comprised the *shōen* and had built up sizable military followings. Some had even managed to acquire court rank by virtue of their political connections

33

with court-based proprietors, allowing them to become directly involved in the political machinations of the Kyoto court.

The cultivators-cum-samurai and the villagers who farmed but did not fight constituted different social classes in villages, living together and performing complementary functions. A community of such small-scale landowners usually constituted a *sō*, an autonomous body entrusted with resolving any problems that arose within its boundaries.[2] The right to convene assemblies to resolve *sō* matters was generally limited to samurai. Within the community, members with samurai status were called *otona-byakushō*, or senior farmers, and they had many special privileges. All festival activities of the village shrine dedicated to the local tutelary deity, for instance, were conducted by this group. The rise of the samurai marked an important stage in the transition from the increasingly ineffectual *shōen* system to the social institutions of Tokugawa society.

As Toyotomi Hideyoshi established his hegemony over the country, he and his fellow daimyo enacted policies that obliterated the old social composition of rural society.[3] Of all his policies, Hideyoshi's nationwide survey of all land under cultivation did more than anything else to redefine the composition of the peasant class and to establish the amount of land tax that the cultivators were capable of delivering to the overlord. Political motivations accompanied the social and economic aspects of the survey, for this was also Hideyoshi's means for safeguarding the authority he had acquired through conquest, as it enabled him to measure more accurately the worth of the fiefs he granted to his band of retainers.

The first land survey was carried out in Yamashiro Province in 1582, a month after Hideyoshi had hunted down Akechi Mitsuhide and extracted revenge for his having killed Oda Nobunaga. As the survey teams moved out across Japan, they discovered that not all villages were equally receptive to the inspection. In Kyushu, for instance, Hideyoshi was obliged to proceed more cautiously, because of the strength of the hostile local samurai. When one of Hideyoshi's commanders did begin a survey there, the indigenous samurai rose up in an ill-fated rebellion that was quashed by daimyo forces mobilized

2 The historical significance of *sō* is discussed in Keiji Nagahara, with Kozo Yamamura, "Village Communities and Daimyo Power," in John Whitney Hall and Takeshi Toyoda, eds., *Japan in the Muromachi Age* (Berkeley and Los Angeles: University of California Press, 1977), pp. 107–23.
3 Hideyoshi's career and policies are covered in Mary Elizabeth Berry, *Hideyoshi* (Cambridge, Mass.: Harvard University Press, 1982); and George Elison, "Hideyoshi, the Bountiful Minister," in George Elison and Bardwell L. Smith, eds. *Warlords, Artists, & Commoners: Japan in the Sixteenth Century* (Honolulu: University of Hawaii Press, 1981), pp. 223–44.

from throughout Kyushu. But soon after this, Hideyoshi was finally able to open up the entire island of Kyushu to survey teams. In 1590, after the Kantō and the Tōhoku regions were subjugated, Hideyoshi ordered a survey for the entire Tōhoku region. To encourage compliance, he promised to destroy the castles of any warrior who resisted and to slaughter all peasants who complained.

Survey teams measured the area of land cultivated by individual farmers, estimated the average productivity of the region, and on this basis calculated the potential yield of each plot of land. This calculation was referred to as the *kokudaka*, an assessment of the land's productive capacity in terms of *koku* (approximately five bushels) of rice. The name of the cultivator was entered into the cadastral register next to this figure. Before Hideyoshi's survey, landownership was usually verified through a process known as *sashidashi*, or a call for the submission of pertinent documents. The landowner would present documents describing his holdings, both fiefs and hereditary lands, together with documentary evidence to support his claims. Under Hideyoshi's procedures, however, verification of landownership by initiative from below was no longer considered adequate. Instead, the impetus now came from above. Typically, a proprietor dispatched his own officials to the countryside to measure all of the agricultural and residential land in a certain region, using the *chō* (approximately one hectare) as their standard. The "cultivator" listed in each entry of the register was then held responsible for paying the annual land rent, whether or not he actually tilled the land.

Regional differences were common, however. For instance, Yamashiro, the province surrounding the capital city of Kyoto, never came under the control of a strong, independent daimyo. Rather, it long remained an area of competition among small warrior families seeking influence in the Muromachi bakufu. The *myōshu* who served as estate officials or military estate stewards were rewarded with benefice land (*kyūbun*) for their service, and they were also allowed to buy up *myōshu* rights to additional landholdings. These privileges enabled many of the *myōshu* to accumulate extensive holdings, and a growing number became samurai. As a result, the gap widened between those with samurai status and those who remained mere peasants. Some of the landed samurai left their villages to become vassals of the nobility, but most chose to remain in their villages. When Hideyoshi's survey teams came to the lands in Yamashiro that belonged to the nobility and the religious organizations, the samurai and functionaries of the religious establishment who still resided in the villages were classified as "cultivators" (sakunin), even though they served simply as collectors of rent from the actual families who tilled the land. This meant that the actual cultivators, in this instance, were not accorded any status in the registers.

Consequently, historical debate has focused on questions of when and under what conditions the separation of status in rural society eventually took place.[4] In regions where the aims of Hideyoshi's survey were fully realized, the actual cultivator was usually recognized in the survey registers as the sakunin; in such areas most of the former warrior families, having relinquished their lands, did not appear on the register. Registration became more complex when Hideyoshi reassigned daimyo to different domains, however. In such circumstances, some of the rural vassals accompanied their lords to the new domains, but most remained behind in their villages. At this point they lost their official status as samurai and were carried on the village registers as sakunin, which meant that now the actual cultivator of the land might be listed below them in the register, separated by the character bun. This practice was known as bunzuke kisai, or joint registration, and was most common to Shinano and the provinces of the Kantō.

One objective that Hideyoshi hoped to achieve through the use of surveys was to establish a system of agriculture based on the small, independent farmer (shono). Discrete social units consisting of members of the immediate family were to become the principal source of the annual land revenues, and the act of cultivation was now deemed as the most important criterion for determining who possessed the land and who paid the annual rent. This basic intent can be further discerned from pertinent pronouncements issued during the late sixteenth century. A decree promulgated by Hideyoshi in 1594, for instance, forbade any peasant family from living with a collaterally related family if both families had independent incomes, and it further ordered such families to construct separate residences.[5] Similarly, Asano Nagamasa's decree of 1587 prohibited the upper stratum of

4 Among the major interpretative works are Araki Moriaki, Taikō kenchi to kokudakasei (Tokyo: Nihon hōsō shuppan kyōkai, 1959, 1982); Wakita Osamu, Shokuhō seiken no bunseki, 2 vols. (Tokyo: Tōkyō daigaku shuppankai, 1975–7); Osamu Wakita, "The Emergence of the State in Sixteenth Century Japan: From Oda to Tokugawa," Journal of Japanese Studies 8 (Summer 1982): 343–67; Kanzaki Akitoshi, Kenchi (Tokyo: Kyōikusha, 1983); and Miyakawa Mitsuru, Taikō kenchi ron, 3 vols. (Tokyo: Ochanomizu shobō, 1957–63).
5 Editor's note: Unless otherwise specified, the factual material for this article is contained in the very rich corpus of scholarship that Professor Furushima has published in Japanese. Those wishing further details should see his Nihon nōgyōshi and his Kinsei keizaishi no kiso katei – nengu shūdatsu to kyōdōtai (Tokyo: Iwanami shoten, 1978); Tochi ni kizamareta rekishi (Tokyo: Iwanami shoten, 1969); and Sangyōshi (Tokyo: Yamakawa shuppansha, 1966). These have been reprinted in Furushima Toshio chosakushū, 10 vols. (Tokyo: Tōkyō daikaku shuppankai, 1974).

peasantry from employing tenant farmers to work their lands, and it stipulated that the actual cultivator of the land had to forward the annual land rent directly to the proprietor in order to fulfill his obligations as a cultivator, thus preventing the village upper class and officialdom from employing peasants without remuneration.

The nature of Hideyoshi's prohibition against peasant ownership of weapons was revealed in another of his well-known policies, the "sword hunt," announced in a decree dated 1587/7. The previous year a rebellion in the province of Higo, led by local samurai and supported by elements of the cultivator-warrior stratum of rural society, had been suppressed only with great difficulty. In the wake of this incident, Hideyoshi punished many samurai, and in the following year he prohibited peasants from bearing weapons of any kind. Impounded were long swords as well as short swords, bows, spears, and firearms.

The total disarmament of the peasantry throughout the country moved in pace with the pacification of the daimyo. Previously, Nobunaga had depended on village warriors to fill out the ranks of his spear columns and infantry corps, and when the flintlock became the major weapon of warfare, they constituted the bulk of his musket corps and were officially designated as samurai. On the other hand, as Hideyoshi conducted land surveys and sword hunts, the former samurai who elected to remain in the village were no longer permitted to bear arms. They now had their lands confirmed by being listed in the survey registers as cultivators. Thus, these measures helped support the newly erected barrier between the farmer and warrior, and the two most important social groups of society were henceforth differentiated not only economically but also by social status, as symbolized by the bearing of swords. Of course, in rural areas farmers were permitted to keep guns for hunting and to fire blanks in order to prevent wildlife from destroying crops. They were, however, expected to register these guns with regional officials. The size of the ammunition they used was regulated, and the number of guns held by a village was checked annually.

Hideyoshi also sought to implement what can be called his small, independent farmer policy by prohibiting cultivators from migrating from their home villages or changing occupations. Consequently, although the samurai would accompany a daimyo who was transferred to a new domain, the peasants remained in place in their home villages. Daimyo sought to maintain or, if possible, to increase the number of households subject to payment of the annual land tax (*nengu*). This aim was repeatedly stressed in the ordinances banning the flight of cultivators, especially those who held official posts. When the number of farm families within a village decreased because of unavoidable mishaps, such as the death of a household head, the samurai officials demanded that village officials seek assistance from the farmer's widow and his surviving children to make certain that either their family or another would continue to cultivate the holding and pay taxes.

Still other policies, enacted later during the Tokugawa period, also promoted stability for the small-scale independent farmer. One matter of special concern was the effort to maintain the viability of agricultural households. A decree in 1649 dealt with a father's bequest to his children, and his wish to register each of his children who were engaged in agriculture. Not only did this decree acknowledge the farmer's right to divide the property, but it also recognized each of the inheritors as independent farmers. In the Kinai region in the seventeenth century, many personal servants (genin) began to acquire their own homes, and most gained official recognition as independent cultivators and full members of the village as well.

Two important decrees that significantly influenced affairs in the countryside were the prohibition against the permanent alienation of farmlands (dempata eitai baibai no kinshi) and the decree limiting the division of land (bunchi seigen rei).[6] Such prohibitions codified many measures announced earlier by individual daimyo before the appearance of Hideyoshi. According to the house laws issued by the Imagawa family of Tōtōmi in 1553, for instance, the sale (or mortgage) of private lands for a fixed time period after prior notification of the authorities was permitted, but the decree still prohibited the permanent alienation of land.[7] A placard from Kaga domain dated 1615 prohibited the sale of agricultural land, and a 1631 decree stipulated that when rice fields were sold, the purchaser was required to collect the annual land-tax payments from the original cultivator, serve as proxy for the seller, and promise not to sell the land later.[8] The prohibition against the permanent alienation of land was not incorporated into bakufu law until 1643. Up to that time, village deeds clearly recorded instances of the permanent sale of agricultural land. Thereafter, instances of mortgaging and foreclosure continued to occur, and al-

6 Furushima, Nihon nōgyōshi, chap. 7. See also Furushima Toshio chosakushū, vol. 3, pp. 49–59.
7 Katsumata Shizuo, "Imagawa Kana mokuroku," in Chūsei seiji shakai shisō, vol. 21 of Nihon shisō taikei (Tokyo: Iwanami shoten, 1972).
8 Nakamura Kichiji, Kinsei shoki nōseishi kenkyū (Tokyo: Iwanami shoten, 1938), p. 364.

though the prohibition was often repeated, the transfer of land became quite widespread by the beginning of the eighteenth century.[9]

Decrees that limited the subdivision of land also restricted the redistribution of land to children other than the eldest son in those cases in which the family head held less than a defined minimum amount of land. This minimum requirement varied from domain to domain and not infrequently changed over time, but a figure of ten *koku* was common. The first appearance of this sort of inheritance restriction came in the year 1673, when most people considered approximately one hectare of land as the minimum needed to support an ordinary small family for a year, and hence to ensure perpetual consanguineous possession.[10]

The cadastral surveys generally dealt only with cultivated land and residential plots. Individual possession and utilization of forestland and communal brushland, as well as the use of the lakes, seas, and coastlands, did not come under the jurisdiction of any clearly stated measure similar to the survey. In the sixteenth century, the rapid growth of waterborne commerce led to an increased demand for shipbuilding materials which, along with the growing demand for building materials for castles, warrior residences, and the houses and stores of the merchants, stipulated the demand for lumber. Consequently, many villages began communally to cut timber to sell commercially. Forestland also served as a crucial source of fuel necessary for the farmer's subsistence. Grass from pastures and forests provided fodder for both the samurai's riding horses and the farmers' own workhorses and oxen.

Even more importantly, woodlots became the single most important source of green fertilizer. Under the *shōen* system, the use of mountain woodlands, the collection of grasses for fertilizer, and fishing in the lakes and seas usually were regulated according to long-established customs that obviated the need for official guidelines. Local custom also prevailed with respect to the use of village communal forests and brushlands. Such lands might be owned by an estate proprietor or his officials who were empowered to grant access to the stewards, the *myōshu*, and the peasants who depended on such lands. Even after the Taikō survey clearly established the peasantry as a landed class, such long-standing local practices would not change until well into the Edo period.

---

9 *Furushima Toshio chosakushū*, vol. 3, pp. 57–8.   10 Ibid., pp. 59–61.

THE SOCIAL COMPOSITION OF THE EARLY MODERN
VILLAGE

Although the basic intent of the Taikō cadastral survey was to record the names of the heads of small peasant families that cultivated the land in order to bring social stability to the countryside and to make these families responsible for paying annual land taxes, this goal was not completely realized everywhere. Had it been, it would have resulted in a situation in which all peasants owned and worked parcels of land of approximately the same size. However, entries in registers dating from the late sixteenth and early seventeenth centuries reveal a considerable disparity in the assessed value of the lands held by individual farmers, even among inhabitants of the same village. A few large families might cultivate lands whose productive capacities amounted to as much as two hundred or three hundred *koku* of rice. On the other hand, some individual peasant families held less than five *koku*, and the putative yields of others did not amount to even one *koku*. This inequity arose because many village samurai in the regions of Kinai and the mountainous reaches of Kantō and Tōsan (the old provinces of Hida, Shinano, and Kai) were permitted to retain rights of possession and cultivation over their hereditary lands. These samurai-turned-peasants might hold lands assessed at upwards of three hundred *koku*, and they were able to manage such large possessions only by incorporating branch families into their own households and by employing hereditary servants, known as *hikan*, *nago*, or *kadoya*. These house servants were owned by the heads of households and could be sold or traded.

In contrast, a more common pattern could be seen among the farmers who worked lands estimated at ten to twenty *koku* and who cultivated these lands by relying on the labor of their immediate family and relatives. Those farm families who worked only tiny plots were forced to lease land from wealthier farmers and to pay rent in kind or in labor service. In some very remote villages, there were even some farmers who still used the primitive slash-and-burn and field rotation techniques, and these lands were usually not subject to the annual land tax.

Inequality in the distribution of individual family holdings was also reflected in social relationships within the villages. Those farmers who possessed large landholdings were able to monopolize the prized, honorary functions in ceremonies that evoked the village's protective deities. In villages near Kyoto such families in fact were considered to have the status of samurai. In Honden village in Kawachi, for example, only the upper-class villagers participated in the local religious ceremonies, and they claimed to be descended from the founders of the village.[11] Such farmers were referred to as "the rooted" (*neoi*) or as "the pioneers" (*kusawake*).

Quite common in the Kinki region and certain other areas in western Japan was the monopoly of religious and ceremonial duties by a *miyaza*, or shrine council, composed of the heads of landholding village families.[12] Moreover, in the early Togugawa period, village ceremonies were typically conducted by a select "privileged council," or *kabuza*. Still other customs that served to differentiate the older families who constituted the village's upper class from the rest of the villagers survived throughout Japan well into the Tokugawa period. Even in the early nineteenth century, elite villagers in Mino Province were still referred to as "elder" or "head" farmers (*otona-* or *kashira-byakushō*). In Kanō domain, official government edicts gave legal sanction to the traditional housing and clothing privileges that were reserved for this class. The smaller, more ordinary farmers were called "lower" or "adjunct" farmers (*jige-* or *waki-byakushō*), and they were upposed to live in more humble dwellings.[13] In some villages, the older and lower-class farmers even patronized separate shrines.

The gap between the upper-class farmers and the rest of the farming population was both a product of traditional social custom and a consequence of economic privileges and laws favorable to the elite rural families. For instance, in the Sengoku period it was common for only head farmers to have the right to own forestlands. Moreover, riparian works were often carried out by either a *sō* or a coalition of *myōshu*, and this often meant that the village's upper class was able to retain authority over the distribution of reservoir water. Such privileges and the concomitant economic advantages continued to be enjoyed by select groups well into the Edo period, and the accompanying social differences that had arisen among the inhabitants of pre-Tokugawa villages were often preserved for a considerable length of time.

Although the nationwide land surveys of the late sixteenth and early seventeenth centuries established a rough kind of horizontal equity among the cultivators, by requiring everyone listed in the survey registers to work the land and to pay the annual land taxes, in fact, condi-

11 See chap. 5 of Furushima Toshio and Nagahara Keiji, eds., *Shōhin seisan to kisei jinushisei* (Tokyo: Tōkyō daigaku shuppankai, 1954).
12 See the entry "miyaza" in Terao Hirotaka, comp., *Nihon keizaishi jiten*, vol 2 (Tokyo: Nihon hyōronsha, 1940).
13 See doc. 119 ("Motorogun Miederamura teishō") in *Gifu kenshi shiryō*, vol. 4.

tions in the early Tokugawa period allowed a privileged subclass to continue to dominate village politics. In some part this can be attributed to the concern of many daimyo governments with protecting small-scale farmers from falling victim to the insolvency that could be brought on by the combined onus of tax payments and the frequently heavy expenses associated with conducting official village duties. It should also be remembered that early Tokugawa village officials were often descended from a privileged class of local elites who had held official posts assigned by the earlier civilian proprietors or military lords. Thus they could claim that a prestigious lineage entitled them to positions of authority, especially as village headmen.

Beginning about the mid-seventeenth century, however, the practice of limiting formal membership in village organizations as well as positions of leadership to select members of the village's upper class gradually began to change, especially in response to transformations in the village economy and domain politics. Sometimes the initiative came from below. In many places where the "privileged councils," or *kabuza*, had dominated village affairs, for instance, protests by lower-class villagers, who not infrequently took their demands to daimyo or shogunal courts, brought about the establishment of "village councils," or *muraza*, which permitted all village families to be represented in such ceremonies. Another example, this time concerning access to forestlands, comes from Horado village in the mountainous region of northern Mino. In 1655 the long-standing claim by wealthy village landholders to the exclusive use of nearby forestlands was challenged by lower-class farmers who had been denied entry into the forest to collect materials for use as fertilizers. The dispute was eventually settled in favor of the lower-status farmers, and most of the forestland was opened for communal use.[14]

Another factor leading to change was the increasing tendency to apportion taxes and other dues in proportion to a family's holdings relative to the entire village *kokudaka*. This process can be traced in some detail for the villages of Tōdō domain, located in the ancient provinces of Iga and Ise.[15] In principle the annual land rent was based on the putative yields recorded in the cadastral survey, and it was paid by the cultivators as a percentage of these assessments. During the

14 Furushima, *Kinsei keizaishi no kiso katei*, pp. 189–92.
15 See the 1750 document "Sōkokushi," edited by Tōdō Kōbun, for specific ordinances. Particularly relevant are the details for 1692. This document was published in 1941 by the Kyōiku kai of Ueda-machi in Mie Prefecture.

early Tokugawa period, however, the Tōdō village officials, not the common cultivators, came to be held responsible for ensuring that their village as a unit delivered the specified amount of its total tax assessment to the appropriate domain official. Indeed, village leaders were sometimes even held hostage when defaults occurred.

At first, documents imposing the annual land tax tended merely to list a figure that represented the total *kokudaka* for all old and new paddies and dry fields within the village and then demanded a certain percentage of tax based on that total, thus treating the village as a single tax entity. Consequently, within any given village, taxes often were not apportioned according to an individual farmer's assessment as specified in the original cadastral survey records. Eventually the annual tax assessment documents began to include clauses providing that village meetings, in which all village households were represented, would decide how to apportion the village's tax burden. The earliest instances in Tōdō domain of villagewide participation in the apportionment process date back to 1610, but the practice did not appear in the tax documents of Tōdō domain until approximately 1650. Furthermore, the apportionments agreed upon within the Tōdō villages had to be written down and witnessed by everyone, and even other minor taxes, originally paid exclusively by upper-class households, were now divided into equal amounts and paid by all village households.

To continue with the Tōdō example, in 1649 the domain government conducted a survey of the rural households within its boundaries. A document summarizing the results of the survey noted that the number of village households had increased markedly, but it remarked on a decline in the number of so-called official farmers (*yakugi no hyakushō*), a term used in Tōdō to refer to households that had existed in the late Sengoku period and that were traditionally held responsible for paying an annual household levy known as the *yanami yaku*, a cash substitute for an older corvée levy. Based on this finding, domain officials recommended that the number of households subject to this levy be decreased in poor villages and increased in wealthier villages. This policy enabled the domain to restore the number of households obligated to pay this levy to a figure roughly equivalent to what it had been in previous years. Consequently, the term "official farmers" had now come to indicate one's degree of wealth, and not one's pedigree. Status within the village was now bestowed according to the farmer's actual holdings and his ability to pay the village assessment. Those who were able to pay the entire family allotment were considered "full" members. Less wealthy peasants who only paid seven or eight tenths of the tax were called "seventy percenters" or "eighty percenters."

Policies designed to alter the number and composition of officially recognized village members reflect a shift in the pattern of landholding that was taking place as a result of the sale of farmland. There was an increasing tendency among villagers to apportion all taxes, not just the land tax, in accordance with the *kokudaka* assessment for each family. For example, a 1690 decree in Tōdō ordered that village maintenance fees (*muranyūyō*) were to be borne by the entire village. Village officials were also prohibited from taking other farmers along on trips to the domain capital, nor were they to employ other farmers to cultivate their own lands. The decree also stipulated that servants and members of extended families, who had previously been denied standing as separate householders, now could become independent farmers if they received partitioned lands and established separate, detached domiciles. Two years later, in 1692, another decree stipulated that "from this date village maintenance fees are to be paid as a proportion of an individual family's *kokudaka* and are not to be divided among village households in a manner that fails to reflect differences in wealth." This decree also stated that "official farmers" had to pay the village maintenance fee as a proportion of their *kokudaka*. Significantly, the document justified this policy by noting that if equal fees were paid by all village households, the poorer farmers would be put at a disadvantage.

In short, the social structure commonly found in most villages in the latter half of the Tokugawa period emerged after tax assessments began to be levied in proportion to the size of an individual farmer's holdings and started to take account of disparities in wealth. New nomenclature also appeared that reflected these changes in village social stratification. For example, from the beginning of the eighteenth century, all cultivators with independent holdings were referred to as *hyakushō* or *hombyakushō*, and the poorer families who did not possess their own holdings, and hence did not have a *kokudaka* assignment, were known as *mizunomi* (literally, "those who drink water").

As the possession of holdings included in a village's official *kokudaka* became the sole criterion for determining *hyakushō* status, official administrative posts, such as village headmen, elder, group household head, and farmers' representative (*hyakushōdai*), gradually replaced the mixed bag of village-level positions that had been recognized in the early Tokugawa years.[16] Moreover, the method of selecting village officials became more open. In the early years of the Tokugawa period, village officials were usually appointed by the domain government, and almost all were drawn from the same traditional upper-class families, often referred to as the *otona-byakushō*, or elder farmers, who had dominated so many other aspects of village life. But as landholding patterns and taxation methods changed, new people felt that they had achieved a more equitable standing in the village, and so they began to press for administrative changes that would give them a larger voice in village political affairs.

In 1841, for example, a coalition of village officials and *otona-byakushō* of a village in Mino Province submitted a document to the local lord that set out guidelines for resolving a dispute that had erupted over nominating a man to serve as village headman.[17] These guidelines established new rules to govern the election of future village officials by providing that two members from a group of six former elders (*toshiyori*) would serve alternately as headman for three years while the other four continued to serve as elders. This measure essentially created a six-member council to govern the village. Routine village functions were to be carried out by the six elders in consultation. All "elder farmers" were allowed to participate in discussions of special matters such as the apportionment of the annual land tax, the official domain inspection of the rice crop, and the provision of lodging for visiting officials. Among the thirteen signatories of the document, social distinctions remained. Only one wrote *hyakushō* under his name. The remaining twelve listed themselves as *otona-byakushō*, one of whom was a farmer's representative, and six of whom were elders.

The sharp social barriers between farmers who had the status necessary to become village officials and the lower-class farmers began to crumble even more after the 1720s when disturbances and even violent demonstrations flared up concerning the election of ordinary peasants as village officials, usually in regions where viable markets had developed for agricultural goods.[18] For instance, in 1642 the shogunate

16 For a discussion of village offices in English, see Harumi Befu, "Duty, Reward, Sanction and Power: The Four Cornered Office of the Tokugawa Village Headman," in Bernard S. Silberman and Harry D. Harootunian, eds., *Modern Japanese Leadership* (Tucson: University of Arizona Press, 1966), pp. 25–50; and Harumi Befu, "Village Autonomy and Articulation with the State," in John Whitney Hall and Marius B. Jansen, eds., *Studies in the Institutional History of Early Modern Japan* (Princeton, N.J.: Princeton University Press, 1968), pp. 301–14.
17 *Gifu kenshi shiryō*, vol. 4, doc. 133, pp. 594–6.
18 A detailed discussion of this process in Kurashiki can be found in Thomas C. Smith, *The Agrarian Origins of Modern Japan* (Stanford, Calif.: Stanford University Press, 1959), pp. 180–200.

stationed an administrative representative (*daikan*) at Kurashiki in Bitchū, and the town prospered as a port from which the shogunate's rice tax was shipped. From this time, thirteen men, known as the *koroku* (ancient lineages), held positions of authority as village officials and landlords.

Beginning in 1700, new fields were developed near the sea, and cotton cultivation became increasingly widespread around Kurashiki. At the same time, wealthy men who engaged in the cotton trade began to appear. They became known as the *shinroku* (new lineages), and beginning in the late eighteenth century they opened a contest, at times edging on violence, with the old lineages for positions of authority in the village. By the 1818–30 period the so-called new lineages had emerged as the community's political elite. Under conditions such as these, elections in which ballots were formally cast for candidates began to be held in many areas throughout Japan. Peasant grievances over the unfair distribution of the land-tax burden and the unequal imposition of the village maintenance fees were the primary catalysts for these disturbances. Important also was dissatisfaction over the monopoly by an elite few of honorary positions in village festivals. More ordinary farmers now questioned the governing abilities of the once-wealthy farmers whose fortunes had declined but who nonetheless continued to hold sway over village politics.

LAND-TAX REVENUE AND GOVERNMENT FINANCES

Wealth came from many sources in the Tokugawa period. The mines and forests produced important primary resources, and Chapter 11 in this volume explains the dynamic growth in commerce during the seventeenth and eighteenth centuries. Yet for all the vitality and excitement associated with the expansion of cities and trade, it must be remembered that the rice taxes collected from rural villages constituted the basic wealth of the country throughout the entire early modern epoch. An appreciation of the important role of the peasantry in the economy can be gained from examining the income of the largest and most important of the military families, the Tokugawa house, for the last century of the regime.

The extensive Tokugawa domain was officially assessed at between 3.5 million to 4 million *koku*. By comparison, the domain of the next largest lord, the Maeda house of Kaga, was officially appraised at just over 1 million *koku*, although the annual rice crop was usually nearly a third more than that. The Tokugawa family enjoyed many other economic advantages beyond its landholdings. First, the Tokugawa house had the benefit of the services of an enormous bureaucracy that it entrusted with the task of administering its lands scattered throughout Japan. This bureaucracy was distinguished by its extensive organization, its systematic auditing of accounts, and other features that were later adopted by the Meiji civil service. Moreover, the Tokugawa house acquired control over the output of all mines throughout Japan, including the rich gold mines of Sado and the extensive silver mines of Ikuno and Ōmori. In addition the Tokugawa house managed the large tracts of forests situated in the Hida and Kiso mountains. And finally, the Tokugawa family was able to levy taxes on commerce and industry in Edo, Osaka, Kyoto, and other cities under its direct administration and to collect revenues from the Nagasaki trade.

Because only secondary sources survive, we do not have accurate figures on the shogunate's revenues for the entire Edo period. However, it is possible to make calculations derived from documents that are extant for certain years. In 1844, for instance, a year for which good documentation exists, gross bakufu revenues amounted to 4,011,766 *ryō* of gold, of which 1,827,879 *ryō* was categorized as "regular income" and 2,183,887 *ryō* as "extraordinary revenues."[19] The single most important source of revenue was the land tax, which amounted to the equivalent of some 1,660,000 *ryō* in 1844. The shogunate also netted about 583,000 *ryō* from loan repayments; 839,000 *ryō* as profits garnered from a recoinage that lowered the precious metal content of the coins it issued; and 23,629 *ryō* from forced loans and gifts extracted from wealthy merchants and peasants. Lesser but still significant amounts of income were derived from mining revenues (62,000 *ryō*) and transport fees (71,000 *ryō*).

Clearly, the land tax was the major source of revenues. Such tax payments made up 41 percent of the bakufu's total revenues in 1844, almost twice the 21 percent of total earnings represented by the second largest source of income: recoinage profits. Daimyo who could not avail themselves of the special sources of income restricted to the Tokugawa house were even more dependent on the land tax. In Kaga domain, to take but one example, the land tax during the early decades of the nineteenth century accounted for well over 80 percent of all domain revenues, or nearly 560,000 *koku* of rice annually. Although Kaga's landed income was exceptionally large in absolute terms, most

19 Furushima, *Kinsei keizaishi no kiso katei.*

domains derived approximately the same percentage of their total revenues from the rice tax.[20]

It is easy to imagine the burden that fulfilling the annual tax obligations presented to the average household farm. Many specific taxes were typically lumped together to make up the average family's annual tax obligation. The most important of these was the "basic tax" (honnengu), calculated as a proportion of the official, estimated yields on surveyed lands. Added to this were the various miscellaneous taxes (komononari) that were imposed on fixed assets: the boats that plied the rivers and seas, the soaking bins used for making paper, the large pots used for boiling seawater to make salt, and even the possession and use of forestland. These taxes were usually small sums paid as user or licensing fees rather than as a percentage of output or profit. In the early Edo period, there was also a labor corvée imposed on each registered farm household, and this was later converted into a cash payment calculated as a percentage of kokudaka holdings. Another levy – one that won little favor with local farmers – was imposed from the mid-Tokugawa period and required the villages located along the major highways maintained by the shogunate, the Tōkaidō, Nakasendō, Nikkō Kaidō, and Kōshū Kaidō, as well as those dotting the highways constructed by individual daimyo, to provide packhorses for official communications and transport.

The payment of these taxes resulted in severe hardships for most of the peasantry, and official policies often seemed to be designed to leave the peasants with only the minimal income necessary for their continued existence. The draconian spirit of the shogunate's officials is revealed in a few well-known sayings that have come down to us.[21] Honda Masanobu (1538–1616), a daimyo closely allied with Tokugawa Ieyasu, urged his officials to estimate a peasant's annual output and his consumption needs and then to calculate the basic tax so that it would soak up every surplus grain of rice. "The proper way to govern is to ensure that peasants don't accumulate wealth yet don't starve either." Ieyasu advised his rural intendants to govern the peasant by "making certain they can neither live nor die." Kan'o Haruhide, the finance magistrate in 1749 when the shogunate increased its tax levies, com-

---

20 For a general discussion of domain finances, see Aono Shunsui, Daimyō to ryōmin (Tokyo: Kyōikusha, 1983); pp. 70–91; and Kitajima Masamoto, Bakuhansei kokka kaitai katei no kenkyū (Tokyo: Yoshikawa kōbunkan, 1978), esp. pp. 1–28.
21 This quotation and others similar to those that follow can be found in many texts. See Furushima, Nihon nōgyōshi, pp. 173–6, as well as vol. 22 (Shiryō-hen, Nihon, kinsei-hen) of the Sekai rekishi jiten (Tokyo: Heibonsha, 1955).

pared the peasants to sesame seeds: "The harder you squeeze them, the more you can extract from them."

The harshness of the tax burden is also revealed in the expenditure records of village officials from several domains. During a normal harvest year, most peasant families could usually manage to make ends meet with the income left to them after paying the land tax. Successive poor harvests, however, could make it impossible for some households in hard-hit areas to survive. Rice production was frequently ruined by insect plagues, especially in the southwestern regions, by extended spells of cold weather during the summer growing season in the northeast, and by rain and wind damage during the autumn typhoon season across the entire country. Unseasonally cold weather brought special dread to farm villages throughout the Tokugawa period. During cool summers, outbreaks of rice blast could wipe out the year's entire rice harvest over large regions. Cold temperatures usually damaged other grain crops as well, leaving peasant families without any food at all to subsist on. During the Temmei famine, which lasted from 1782 to 1785, and the great Tempō famines that occurred in the 1830s, tens of thousands of peasants throughout Japan died from starvation and disease.

Adding to the crushing weight placed on the peasantry were the revised tax collection procedures authorized by the shogunate during the early eighteenth century in order to counter its own gradual decline in revenue collection. Many of these revisions were first ordered by the eighth shogun, Yoshimune, as part of his famous Kyōhō Reforms. Surviving documents permit a glimpse at the effect these new procedures had on tax rates and gross tax collections on shogunal lands over the subsequent century.

These changes can be divided into four distinct phases, the first covering the twenty years of the Kyōhō period itself, from 1716 to 1736. Among the reforms instituted during this period was the so-called *jōmen*, or fixed-rate system, first introduced to selected villages in 1724. Under this system, a village's tax rate would be set for a fixed period, usually three, five, or ten years. If more than 30 percent of the anticipated harvest was then destroyed by natural causes during one of the fixed periods, the tax rate would be temporarily lowered. Under the new procedures the taxation rate was reviewed after each period, and the government probably expected regular upward revisions. This reform had an immediate impact on the shogunate's income. Total annual revenues, which had previously hovered around 1.4 million *koku*, leapt immediately to 1.5 million *koku*. In 1727, the shogunate collected 1.62 million *koku*, and this caused rice prices to plunge. Five years later, in 1732, however, crop failures occurred in Kyushu and the Chūgoku region, and subsequent annual revenues returned to the 1.4 million-*koku* level.

During the second stage of reform, from 1737 to 1764, tax collections rose to new peak levels. Early in this phase, the shogunate initiated the use of the "actual inspection" method (*arige kemi*) in which the levy for each field was calculated as a fixed percentage of the putative yield, as determined by a visual inspection of the crop. This new practice permitted the shogunate's officials to monitor more closely the crop conditions, and it resulted in enhanced revenue collections. The well-known scholar and government adviser Honda Toshiaki (1744–1821), however, believed the actual inspection system to be a pernicious practice, and he attributed the frequent outbreaks of famine in the Kantō and Tōhoku regions to its widespread adoption. Be that as it may, in 1744, the revenues derived by the shogunate from land taxes reached a record high of 1.8 million *koku*. Five years later, in 1749, the system was officially extended over the entire country, and for the next sixteen years the shogunate's annual land-tax revenues ranged between 1.65 million and 1.7 million *koku*, with the exception of one year when they temporarily fell to 1.55 million *koku*.[22]

Such high levels of tax collection could not be maintained for long without inviting protest from the peasantry, who were wont to interpret any perceived hike in tax collections as unjust and unfair. Peasant attitudes had changed since 1710, the eve of the Kyōhō Reforms. Before the Kyōhō era, there were rarely more than ten incidents of violent protests by peasants in any given year. But fifteen violent protests erupted in the year following the record tax collections of 1744, and in 1749, thirty-one violent outbursts took place, with more than ten incidents recorded for each of nine of the thirteen years of the Hōreki era (1751–63).[23]

The third stage of tax reform witnessed even more agrarian unrest. In 1766, tax collections had receded to the 1.55 million-*koku* level, where they remained until 1780, only to decline rapidly again after the disastrous harvests of 1783 and 1786. These nationwide crop failures were caused by summer cold spells, which were due chiefly to the large

---

22 Furushima, *Kinsei keizaishi no kiso katei*, pp. 335–41.
23 Ibid., p. 271. A convenient introduction to recent interpretations concerning popular protest is Aoki Michio et al., eds., *Ikki*, 5 vols. (Tokyo: Tōkyō daigaku shuppankai, 1981–2). The most comprehensive listing of popular dissent is Aoki Kōji, *Hyakushō ikki no nenji-teki kenkyū* (Tokyo: Shinseisha, 1966).

amounts of volcanic ash thrown into the atmosphere by an eruption of Mt. Asama. The poor harvests brought on a significant number of peasant demonstrations, and the shogunate announced that penalties would be imposed on leaders of such protests and that government forces would be empowered to fire on rebellious peasants. Despite the threat of government suppression, continuing outrage against tax increases made it difficult for the shogunate to consider any further hikes.

The fourth stage spanned the period from 1787 to 1819, corresponding to the years that Matsudaira Sadanobu (1758–1829) served as senior councilor and to the first half of Shogun Ienari's administration. Although the shogunate's expenditures for the construction of temples, shrines, and coastal fortifications suddenly increased, the shogunate was able to keep its budget under control by compelling the daimyo to contribute significant portions of the expenses for these projects. Consequently, the shogunate was able to manage with less revenue, often with just 1.55 million *koku* a year, and tax rates fell accordingly. Indeed, the principal dissimilarity between the second and fourth stages was in the different rates of taxation. During the last sixteen years of the second stage (1748–64), the taxation rate hovered between 37 and 39 percent of the tax base, with the exception of one year. By contrast, during the fourth stage there were only three years in which the taxation rate approached 35 percent, and for three years the rate fell below 32 percent.

Despite the extreme hardship brought on by periodic famines and unpredictable yet sharp tax increases from time to time, living conditions for much of the peasantry improved during the course of the Edo period, thanks in part to advances in agricultural technology. A key factor in this process was that the rural upper classes accumulated large agricultural surpluses which they then used to develop and introduce the new technologies. These surpluses were a consequence of certain features of the tax collection system at the time it was first implemented. During the Taikō survey, all villages within a specified region were classified into three categories according to their total yields, and all farmland within a village was further graded as superior, average, poor, or even "especially poor" quality land. In mountainous regions, land was classified as either "mountain paddy" or "mountain field" land. In the Kinai region, the rank of "especially superior" was given to land of extremely high quality, and in other regions, similar distinctions were made among different grades of land to reflect expected variances in yields. Despite this multiplicity of grades, however, the documentary record for specific regions reveals that the gradations in the tax scale applied to lands of very different quality were actually quite small.

In the early Tokugawa period, moreover, land taxes were typically assessed as a percentage of the total village *kokudaka*, and this tended to translate into a low percentage tax rate for high-yield lands, and a relatively high tax rate for low-yield lands, if for no other reason than that the farmers who owned the better lands often had more influence in the village assemblies that apportioned the tax levy. Thus, the burden of meeting the annual tax payments fell inequitably on the small-scale farmers. Those who found themselves unable to pay their dues were forced to sell part or all of their land, falling into the status of indentured servant. While the small farmer eked out his living, the agrarian upper class, paying a lesser proportion of their yield as taxes, accumulated surpluses that provided the funds to develop and introduce new technology.

Changes in peasant life during the Edo period were also related to fluctuations in the amount of annual land-tax revenues collected over time. Thus the decline in the shogunate's tax revenues that began in the 1760s, as we noted, as well as the drop in percentage rates in the early nineteenth century, permitted some members of the agrarian class to gather funds to invest in technology. Moreover, it is clear that the amount of rice extracted through land taxes also began to level off in many individual daimyo domains during the eighteenth century.[24] This was the case in such widely separated domains as Satsuma, Kaga, and Aizu–Wakamatsu. As with shogunal lands, this left a surplus in the hands of the peasants, who could then plow them back into technological improvements or buy the new kinds of foods, clothing, and housing that did so much to change the quality of life in rural villages, as described in Chapter 13 in this volume.

IRRIGATION AND LAND RECLAMATION

Many of the rural upper classes who accumulated surpluses increasingly invested them in irrigation and land reclamation projects. They were joined in this effort by the daimyo, who anticipated that such projects would broaden their tax base by expanding rice production.[25]

24 Land taxes are discussed in Aono, *Daimyō to ryōmin*. In English, Thomas C. Smith examined the stabilization of rates, especially in Kaga domain, in his "The Land Tax in the Tokugawa Period," in Hall and Jansen, eds., *Studies*, pp. 283–99.
25 A thorough discussion of irrigation and land reclamation projects can be found in Kozo Yamamura, "Returns on Unification: Economic Growth in Japan, 1550–1560," in John Whitney Hall, Keiji Nagahara, and Kozo Yamamura, eds., *Japan Before Tokugawa: Political*

Indeed, in the late Sengoku and early Edo periods, the daimyo often took the initiative in sponsoring such projects, as they had the political authority needed to mobilize large labor forces and the capital necessary to finance these efforts.

One of the most noteworthy flood control and irrigation projects of the late sixteenth century was undertaken by the daimyo Takeda Shingen (1521–73) in the area between the Kamanashi and Fuefuki rivers to the south of Kōfu city, an area already blessed with one of Japan's highest per acre yields for wet-field rice. The Midai River, which fed into the Kamanashi, was redirected north to join the Kamanashi at a point where there are cliffs on the opposite shore. Over time, Shingen then constructed dikes that would direct water toward the Kamanashi in such a manner that whenever the rivers flooded, the spillover would flow gently onto the farmland behind the dikes. During the Edo period, these dikes were gradually moved closer to the river, and by the 1750s riparian technology had improved to a level that enabled the completion of a continuous dike encircling the entire southern section of Kōfu. During this period, the tributaries of the original Kamanashi River were then converted into irrigation canals.

Even more sophisticated projects later became possible as the Japanese improved the riparian technology available to them. For example, engineers learned how to construct sluices near the rapids that usually formed at the point where mountain rivers spilled out onto the plains, thus converting natural waterways into irrigation canals, so that a constant flow of water could be maintained through both dry and rainy seasons. Moreover, by the seventeenth century, domain construction offices were able to plan more complexly designed systems of reservoirs. In Sanuki Province on Shikoku, for example, construction teams blocked off ravines to provide reservoir storage during the autumn and winter, drawn from the upper reaches of rivers in that area.[26] These new reservoirs were linked to older, existing reservoirs in order to form an interlocking irrigation system that would ensure a steady supply of water throughout the growing season.

The new castle towns often benefited from these riparian projects. In Kanazawa, for instance, engineers designed a system of inter-

<hr>

Consolidation and Economic Growth, 1500–1650 (Princeton, N.J.: Princeton University Press, 1981), pp. 327–72. Also see William W. Kelly, "Water Control in Tokugawa Japan: Irrigation Organization in a Japanese River Basin, 1600–1870," in Cornell University East Asian Papers, no. 31 (Ithaca, N.Y.: Cornell University Press, 1982).

26 Furushima, *Nihon nōgyōshi*, pp. 231–2.

linking canals several dozens of miles in length that drew water from two rivers and delivered it to key points within the city. They even invented a unique siphon pump to move the water uphill at one point.[27] Initially, the city of Edo relied on Inogashira Pond, located some twenty kilometers to the west of the city, for its water supply. But from 1650, the city began to channel water in from the upper reaches of the Tama River, after an extensive canal system was laid out on the plateau west of Edo.[28]

Providing for a more constant supply of water was only one of many methods used to increase agricultural production during the Edo period. Land was also reclaimed from the bays and shallow tidal marshes facing the Pacific Ocean and the seas off western Kyushu, as well as from Seto Inland Sea. Most of this land was very fertile, as it was composed of rich silt deposited by rivers. Engineers constructed breakwaters, and the trapped saline water was pumped or allowed to flow out through the gates at low tide. The scale of reclamation projects grew considerably as technology improved. Often by the 1700s more than one hundred hectares of land were being reclaimed at a time.

At first, only the daimyo had the resources to carry out large-scale reclamation schemes, but during the seventeenth century, wealthy merchants and peasants also began to finance coastal projects. The funding provided by Yoshida Kambei (1611–86) for the reclamation of a portion of Edo Bay was one of the earliest examples of the merchants' participation in large-scale land development.[29] There, fields were reclaimed from the delta region of the Ōoka River, situated just behind what would later become the port of Yokohama. Drainage work for the project was initiated in 1656, although construction had to be halted the next year owing to tidal damage. Work was resumed in 1659, and the project was completed only after Edo merchants responded to a call for additional investment funds from Yoshida, whose name then became linked with the project. Another example comes from Osaka, where in 1685 merchants began to invest in the reclamation of the marshland located near the delta of the Yodo River.[30] Merchant-inspired land development projects continued for several decades in this region. The reclamation of an old riverbed of the

27 The siphon system is described in Nishi Setsuko, "Tatsumi yōsui repōto," *Rekishi techō* 2 (May 1974): 31–4.
28 Doboku gakkai, ed., *Meiji izen Nihon dobokushi*, vol. 7 (Tokyo: Iwanami shoten, 1936), pp. 1436–42.
29 Yokohama shiyakusho, ed., *Yokohama-shi shi*, vol. 3 (Yokohama: Yokohama shiyakusho, 1958), pp. 670–8.
30 Matsuyoshi Sadao, *Shinden no kenkyū* (Tokyo: Yūhikaku, 1936).

Yamato River, begun in 1707, as well as the drainage of additional marshes helped make the Osaka area the nation's most productive agricultural region, starting in the 1700s.

Many projects during the Edo period were made possible by the joint effort and investments of both political overlords and wealthy farmers and merchants. Governing officials, of course, saw such projects as a means of expanding the tax base, whereas farmers and merchants viewed them as a means of enhancing their own income. One famous example of such a joint effort occured in Echigo in the 1720s when the shogunate authorized Edo merchants to provide the financial backing that permitted local farmers to convert coastal swamps into paddy fields.

In some cases, however, land reclamation became a new source of friction that threatened village harmony or led to disagreements between farmers and government authorities. Kumazawa Banzan (1619–91), a seventeenth-century Confucian scholar, noted that the large amount of reclaimed paddy in Bizen Province would deprive the older fields of water and fertilizer.[31] To take another example, the increase in the amount of arable land forced some daimyo in Sanuki to measure the water level of the reservoirs during the spring and then to set limits on the acreage that the farmers could plant in rice during that year.[32]

Farmers everywhere were keen to secure sufficient supplies of water for the spring planting season and the months of rapid plant growth during the summer. This not infrequently set off a sharp competition among farmers from the same, or even different, villages whose irrigation systems shared the same water source. Consequently, care had to be taken to allocate water equitably over the entire irrigation system. Gates, locks, and other facilities were constructed to guarantee a fair distribution of water, and watering was often done on a daily or even hourly rotational basis. Decisions regarding the dispensation of water essentially defined the length of the rice-planting season and determined where the seedlings, later transplanted to rice paddies, were first set and the amount of land that could be planted with a winter grain crop. Because individual households were unable to secure water supplies on their own, they were forced into cooperating with other members of their or neighboring villages in order to carry out their

---

31 See Kumazawa's "Shugi gaisho," in Takimoto Seiichi, ed., *Nihon keizai sōsho*, vol. 33 (Tokyo: Nihon keizai sōsho kanōkai, 1917), p. 222. Chapter 3 in vol. 3 of my *Furushima Toshio chosakushū* has many examples in which people complain to the shogunate concerning the opening of new fields.
32 Furushima, *Nihon nōgyōshi*, pp. 234–5.

agricultural tasks. When quarrels erupted, officials often had to be called in to mediate a settlement.

The same was especially true in areas where double cropping was practiced. Typically, the second crop was barley, wheat, or rapeseed. In order to plant such grains, a farmer had to drain and till the fields after the fall harvest. Because the fields were kept dry during the winter, they required proportionately more water when reflooded in the spring, a time of peak demand. This contributed to water shortages and sparked additional disagreements among neighbors. To dissipate such frictions, officials in Tōdō domain in 1649 moved to discourage double cropping, ordering its peasants to reduce the size of the winter grain crop to two-thirds of normal yields. The same decree also stipulated that the land-tax rate would remain unchanged even when there were crop failures, and the officials warned that farmers who diverted their labor to tilling their newly reclaimed fields, to the detriment of their registered paddy fields, would not be granted tax relief.

AGRICULTURAL USE OF FORESTLAND

The availability of good land and an adequate supply of water were not, in themselves, sufficient to guarantee stable agricultural outputs during the early modern period. Farmers also had to maintain the fertility of their paddy fields by gathering shrubs, shoots, and grasses from marginal lands for use as green manure or for mixing with horse and cow manure. Nearby woodlands provided many of life's other necessities – wood for sheds, outbuildings, irrigation canals, and firewood; roof thatch; and such supplementary foods as greens, fruits, and mushrooms. Tree buds, grass shoots, and roots also served as emergency foods that helped the peasants survive, however miserably, through the worst stretches of famine. Because the woodlands played an indispensable role in the agricultural process and the daily lives of the agrarian population, the peasantry was intensely concerned about their supervision and use.

During the Sengoku period, the valuable woodlands and marginal wastelands usually belonged to the estate proprietor, and individual peasants could gain entry only on the basis of negotiations worked out between the proprietor and the village community, which over time tended to coalesce into an accepted definition of custom and precedent governing access to the bounty of the forests. In the Edo period, two forces worked to change these local traditions. The first came from the top down as daimyo moved to assert their authority over their realm.

From the late sixteenth century, daimyo needed building materials in order to construct their castle towns. Even later, demand remained high as the country's cities were ravaged periodically by fires. Consequently the daimyo regulated the felling of trees that could be used for construction materials. At first, they tended to declare the dense forests in remote mountains that contained the largest trees as being off limits to the farmers, though the lords still permitted villagers access to the smaller woodlands that surrounded the agricultural plots. Later, many daimyo barred the peasants from cutting zelkova, cedar, cypress, fir, hemlock, and other prime timber on these smaller woodlands. In time, the shogunate and most daimyo designated all timber stands as "the lord's forest" and strictly prohibited any unauthorized cutting of trees.[33]

The second force for change came from inside the village community itself. In the medieval period, the local conventions worked out with proprietors had typically provided only for a village's elite, landholding families to have access to the forests, whereas the commoner farmers usually could enter the forest only by virtue of their established relationships with the elites. In time, however, the commoner farmers became inclined to consider such privileges as rights, and they came to view nearby forestland as communal property from which they could gather firewood and materials for building and for aging into fertilizer. In many places by the mid-seventeenth century, villagers were demanding that the forests be opened to the whole community. Government officials were usually invited to mediate such disputes, and the typical solution was to reserve a small portion of the forestland for the person claiming ownership and to open most of the remaining land for communal use.

Although the documentation for this evolution of rights to forestland is sketchy, it appears that as elite control broke down, the use of communal forests came to be regulated by the village covenant, which guaranteed equal access to the forests.[34] Infractions of the village covenant could be punished by the withdrawal of such rights, and the eyes of the village youth association (*wakamonogumi*) enforced compliance. The covenant determined the opening day and length of the periods during which entry into the forests would be allowed. The first day of each gathering season was usually referred to as the day of "opening the gates to the mountains." After inspecting the growth of

33 Forestry policy is the subject of Conrad Totman, *The Origins of Japan's Modern Forests: The Case of Akita* (Honolulu: University of Hawaii Press, 1985).
34 Furushima, *Kinsei keizaishi no kiso katei*, pp. 186–94.

rice seedlings and meadow grasses, the village officials would designate a day during which grass used for mulch could be cut, usually two or three days before the seedlings were transplanted to the paddies. There were separate opening days and periods for collecting fodder that would be used for farm animals, for gathering the hay spread on barn floors during the winter, and for cutting firewood and roof thatch.

Daimyo and village alike enforced other restrictions so as to protect the forests' resources. Most daimyo permitted peasants to use only sickles and scythes when in the woodlands so that they would not damage large, valuable trees. Frequently, village covenants included a provision prohibiting the sale of harvested grasses, especially to peasants from other villages. Similarly, a farmer's consumption of forest products was limited to the amount of grass required to fertilize his paddy fields and the amount of hay that had to be mixed with the manure in his compost pits. Equal access did not mean equal division of forest and meadow products among all households. Instead, the yield from the meadows and forests was typically divided among farmers according to the size of a farmer's landholdings and the number of people in his family.

This system underwent additional changes during the latter half of the Tokugawa period. A farmer's yearly take from the woodlands came to be perceived as a right held by every farming household, and these allotments began to be bartered and sold. Some households were assigned plots in woodlands, initially for limited periods of time. Such assignments gradually became permanent, and individual households began to ignore village or communal claims to the forests and woodlands. Some farmers planted thickets in order to sell the yield as firewood, and others produced and marketed charcoal. Forestland was cleared and converted into paddy land, and meadowland was forested so that farmers could sell trees for use as lumber. This privatization and commercialization of communal lands became especially prevalent after 1800.

TECHNOLOGY AND COMMERCIAL AGRICULTURE

The previous sections have examined how several aspects of agricultural life changed over the seventeenth and eighteenth centuries. It is now possible to take a more comprehensive view of the evolving agricultural community and to elaborate on the relationship between the transformations in village life and the changes in the mode of agricultural production. During the Edo period, agriculture passed through three technological stages of varying degrees of complexity: the slash-and-burn technique, the self-contained village economy, and the commercialized cash crop economy – and the shift from one stage to another lay at the bottom of three different life-styles.[35]

Slash-and-burn farming

The most rudimentary type of farming relied on slash-and-burn techniques. The so-called agricultural servants such as *hikan* and *nago*, as well as other subordinate peasant families who provided labor services for the large farming households, often used this method on their marginal holdings in poor, upland areas. But in secluded mountains and on isolated islands, whole villages employed this primitive technology. The isolated regions of the Chichibu district in Musashi, the Shibayama district of Hyūga, and Tsushima Island are prominent examples. In these areas, farmers would typically raze sections of forestland. Trees, shrubs, and grasses within delineated areas were cut and burned on the site, and farmers could then grow crops in the ashes for two to five years. The farmers did not bother to apply fertilizers to preserve the soil's fertility, as the ashes usually provided sufficient nutrients to produce crops for several years. After yields fell to inefficient levels, the farmers would abandon the land. However, the land could be used again after a lapse of several years, once it had become overgrown with small trees and shrubs.

Another aspect of slash-and-burn farming was that fields did not need to be plowed. Plots were kept small enough to be leveled with rakes and bamboo brooms after removing any branches that had not been reduced to ashes in the fire. Hence, the only tools needed for cultivation were a sickle for cutting grass, hand axes for felling trees, and the rakes and bamboo brooms used to level the ashes. These plots were usually planted with such crops as buckwheat, soybeans, and foxtail millet, and farmers on Tsushima also grew wheat and barley. Productivity, however, was quite low; yields amounted to only three or four times the amount of seed sown, whereas ordinary rice paddies usually yielded between thirty to fifty times the amount of seed sown.

Because fields created with slash-and-burn techniques were often situated in hilly or mountainous areas, crops were vulnerable to dam-

---

35 Ibid., pp. 238–72, for additional details.

age from wildfowl, boar, and deer. When harvest time approached, the villagers put up temporary huts near the fields from which they kept watch in order to ward off predators. On Tsushima, for instance, farmers constructed wooden palisades to keep out wild boar. Hence, once fields had been burned over on this island, they had to be left idle until enough wood for making palisades could be cut from nearby trees. Good land thus had to be held out of production for fifteen years, poor land for up to twenty-five years.

Self-sufficient farming

The phrase "self-sufficient farming," used here in contrast with "commercialized farming," should not be taken to mean that individual farmers, or even entire villages, relied completely on the goods and crops they produced themselves. Rather, villagers who engaged in these self-sufficient practices had a traditional peasant mentality. That is, they did not engage in commercial agriculture in order to accumulate wealth that could then be used to create new and different modes of living. Rather, their aim was more modest and was bound by the concerns of their ancient village customs. Thus, they grew commercial crops and engaged in trade only to the extent necessary to acquire commodities that would permit them to sustain life at a traditional level. To this end, they tended to shun the market whenever possible and to produce items for sale only within the context of an assured production for subsistence. Typically, the proceeds from such sales would then be used to buy goods that could not be produced on the homestead.[36]

Examples of this kind of production are abundant for the early Tokugawa period. With the exception of those living near the sea, for instance, most farmers were forced to rely on outsiders for salt, because of the lack of rock salt deposits in Japan. Moreover, iron and other metals used for farm tools and household goods usually had to be acquired from a limited number of mining regions. After 1680, cotton replaced cruder fibers as the most common material for clothing, and peasants began to buy secondhand cotton clothes, ginned cotton, and cotton cloth from external sources. At first, the farmers simply bartered their crops for the goods they needed from outside, but then they started to pay for them more frequently with cash. People in the

36 Most readers will be aware of the similarity between this sort of peasant mentality in Japan and the general ideas about peasant attitudes toward commerce expressed by Eric Wolf in his *Peasant Wars of the Twentieth Century* (New York: Harper & Row, 1964), pp. xiv–v.

Tsuzuki district (*gun*) in Musashi, for example, acquired their salt in the early Tokugawa period from villages in the neighboring Kuraki district. The exchange was by barter, with the salt producers in Kuraki receiving firewood, which they used as a fuel to make the salt. Later, the Tsuzuki villagers began to sell their firewood to inns in Edo and along the Tōkaidō highway, where they got a better price, and they used that cash to buy salt.[37]

Villagers in many regions were able to remain self-sufficient during the early modern period because of their access to water and forestland. An abundant water supply was necessary for wet-rice cultivation, which provided the bulk of the land tax, and free use of forests provided the basis for self-sufficiency in everyday essentials. We have already noted that the ready availability of materials for constructing flood control and riparian works made cash expenditures unnecessary in most daily transactions. But even more important to agricultural self-sufficiency were the fertilizers gathered from the forests and the wild fodder collected from marginal lands. Farmers were thus able to continue self-sufficient farming on the same farmland despite intensive cultivation because they could maintain the fertility of the soil with these self-gathered fertilizers.

The three most important fertilizers were "gathered mulch" (*karishiki*), livestock manure, and human waste. Tall grasses, shoots that grew from the stumps of felled broad-leaved trees, and the leaves of shrubs were used for mulch and were laid directly on the paddies. Livestock manure was mixed with leftover fodder, dried autumn grasses, forage, and rice straw. Horses and cattle were used to till the fields and to transport goods, but their most important role was as a source of manure. This is revealed in the design of stables of this period. Stable floors were dug out to accommodate the addition of straw and grass, and the roofs were raised in order to allow the manure – hay mixture to pile up into large heaps. The stable manure was shoveled out monthly and piled in the yard. When it reached a sufficient age and height, the manure would be transferred to the fields. Farmers' almanacs recommended that hay and grasses be fed to animals from all four sides of the stable to ensure a proper blend of the manure and uneaten fodder.[38] Farmers who fertilized paddy fields with cut grasses used this fodder–manure mixture for dry fields. In villages without livestock, pits were dug in the yard and filled with cut

37 *Yokohama-shishi*, vol. 4, pp. 504–5. See also vol. 11, pp. 971–4.
38 Furushima, *Nihon nōgyōshi*, chap. 6, esp. pp. 250–3.

grass, straw, chaff, wastewater from the kitchen, and human waste. This mixture was allowed to decompose and then was then applied to the fields in place of the animal manure and fodder mixture.

Fertilization with night soil has often been viewed as a hallmark of Japanese agriculture. Naturally, the bodily waste from an average household was not sufficient to maintain the fertility of its farmlands. But farmers from villages located near cities and post towns were able to collect human waste from these communities in exchange for a few vegetables and some glutinous rice cakes during the New Year's season. Night soil was used to fertilize land planted with rice, grain, or, quite often, vegetables. A thriving night soil trade developed in cities like Edo and Osaka, as well as regional castle towns such as Kanazawa, and "ladler guilds" were formed in these cities to cater to outlying villages.[39]

Improved tools and their expanded availability were also responsible for helping Tokugawa villagers achieve self-sufficiency. Advances in agricultural efficiency came slowly in those isolated areas where most holdings were too small to utilize the new technology efficiently. Consequently, the farmer who held less than one hectare of farmland continued to rely on the hoe, which he used as an all-purpose tool for tilling, leveling the ground, preparing the soil, and even for cutting grass. In most regions, however, change came more quickly and was a product not only of the farmer's desire to grow more but also of his lord's will that he do so.

Studies of several domains reveal that blacksmiths residing in castle towns were frequently ordered by the daimyo to produce iron-bladed hoes for farmers who were unable to make them on their own. Initially, the blades were paid for in rice when the land tax was collected. By the 1680s, blacksmiths had begun to move permanently to villages so that they could expand their business of repairing and selling farm tools and blades. In some instances, the villages paid a small part of the village maintenance fee to the blacksmith for his services, and most repairs were probably paid for in kind. By the 1730s such smiths had invented several kinds of highly specialized hoes. The split-bladed "Bitchū hoe" was designed for improved tilling, and a hoe especially for cutting grass was also being manufactured. Wealthy farmers who employed servants and kept livestock would, of course, have used horse- or ox-drawn plows, but the ordinary peasants had to make do with a *nagatoko*. This was a plow with a long wooden base and a cast-

39 Kobayashi Shigeru, *Nihon shinyō mondai genryūkō* (Tokyo: Akashi shoten, 1984).

iron blade that had to be pushed by hand, and it could not cut even as deeply as a hoe could.[40]

The second most important farm tool was the sickle. It was usually used for weeding and cutting grass, as well as for chopping down shrubs, trimming branches, and even hacking down trunks of small trees. Sickles were even pressed into service as weapons by the disarmed peasantry. With the sickle and hoe, the peasants could carry out all of their farm duties. Moreover, they needed to buy only the blades for these tools, as the handles and all other farm implements could be made by using material gathered from the communal forestlands.[41]

Self-sufficient agriculture was also defined and limited by the variety of crops cultivated and by the tiny amount of land available to grow these different crops. Self-sufficient farmers paid their land taxes in kind and usually planted all of their arable paddies with rice. If they double-cropped their fields, they would most often grow wheat and barley (usually more of the former than the latter) as winter crops to feed their households. Wheat was usually ground into flour and eaten as noodles or dumplings. For home consumption, dry fields were planted with soybeans, millet, buckwheat, large white radishes, sweet potatoes (in western Japan), and taro, especially along the Pacific seacoast from Ise eastward into Suruga. Bits and pieces of spare land around residences were also turned into gardens and planted with a variety of vegetables.

An agricultural manual from a secluded mountain village in Shimotsuke with a preface dated 1808 describes a typical harvest.[42] The writer was a village headman (*nanushi*) who held nearly seven hectares of land, about half of which was cultivated by his household in 1814. However, the average peasant who appears in this manual farmed only 0.2 hectares of paddy and an equal amount of dry field. In one case mentioned in the document, a peasant who worked a tiny plot of land planted the paddy entirely with rice and cultivated other grains on the dry fields, typically millet, soybeans, cotton, adzuki beans, buckwheat, tobacco, and cowpeas. The borders of these fields and any remaining land were used for vegetables such as eggplant, autumn radishes, and taro. This peasant's fields gave only minimal yields.

40 Furushima, *Nihon nōgyōshi*, pp. 244–8.
41 Dai Nihon nōkai, ed., *Nihon no kama, kuwa, suki* (Tokyo: Nōsei chōsa iinkai, 1979). For a brief discussion in English of agrarian technology, see Kee Il Choi, "Technological Diffusion in Agriculture Under the Bakuhan System," *Journal of Asian Studies* 30 (August 1971): 749–59.
42 Furushima, *Nihon nōgyōshi*, pp. 344–6.

Cotton production for this secluded mountain village was perhaps no more than three to five *kan* per *tan* (1 *kan* = 8.267 lb.), which meant that in the average year this man grew only enough to meet the clothing needs of his own family. The tobacco yield was also not large enough to market. However, by 1808 even a small household such as this sold some of its produce, most often the surplus rice that remained after paying the land tax. This household ate almost none of its rice crop, instead relying chiefly on the grains from its dry fields. But this farmer owned a horse, and by using night soil, grass mulch, and the animal's manure, he was able to maintain the fertility of his fields without having to buy commercial fertilizers.

Commercialized agriculture

In some parts of Japan during the seventeenth century, and in most parts of the country after that, subsistence farming gave way to more commercialized forms of agriculture, and the traditional peasant mentality was increasingly displaced by more modern attitudes toward farm production. The key to this transformation was increased interaction with the marketplace. If the older peasant kept the market at arm's length, the new farmer embraced it more fully, opening his land and labor to competition and exploring alternatives to the factors of production so as to maximize returns. In this process the new cultivator came to favor those products with a potential of commercial profit over the more traditional, less risky crops cultivated for family subsistence. The changeover to cash crops was first seen among the upper-class farmers in the Osaka region around the middle of the seventeenth century. By 1770 commercial crops were grown by all peasant classes in the Kinai region. Within the next half-century, they were also being widely adopted in the Kantō region.

The first great cash crop of Tokugawa Japan was cotton. Even as early as the Muromachi period, cotton was imported, first as cloth and later as thread, which was woven into "Ise cotton cloth" and other designed cloths, and then sold to the nobility and clergy. During the Sengoku period, cotton was used to pay the fees charged at checkpoints along major transportation routes. Later, as farmers began to cultivate cotton for commercial purposes, cotton fields acquired sufficient importance to be listed separately in the land survey registers of Mikawa, Tōtōmi, and Shinano provinces, as well as those from the Kantō region. By the beginning of the nineteenth century, the area stretching west from Kyoto along the Inland Sea and east as far as Mikawa had become a major cotton-growing region.[43]

The agrarian upper class was most responsible for introducing cotton as a cash crop, for their lands generated the surpluses that permitted them to risk introducing such an innovation. From a village in the Ōtori district of Izumi in 1605 comes an example of a farm household that possessed lands assessed at ninety-five *koku* and given over entirely to growing rice as well as a small amount of other cereals. By contrast, seventy years later, in a neighboring village within the same Ōtori district, farmers grew rice and cotton on alternate years.

One household in this village that rotated between rice and cotton cultivation had its total landholdings assessed at 69 *koku* during the 1594 survey. By 1647, the family's holdings (including scattered possessions in neighboring villages) had swollen to 165 *koku*, 8 *to*, and by 1666 had increased to 190 *koku*. From harvest records, we discover that this family planted dry fields near the foot of the mountains with cotton, but they rotated cotton and indigo on the other dry fields and alternately grew cotton and rice in the paddy fields. The family leased the paddy fields to tenant farmers during the years when they were planted with rice. Because this region was subject to water shortages, portions of the paddy land were left unirrigated and used for cultivating cotton during drought years. This family could afford to purchase sardine-meal fertilizer by selling the surplus from their cotton crop. In 1665 the family fertilized between seven *tan* to one *chō* of its lands with sardine meal, and the cotton yield from these lands far surpassed the clothing needs of the family's four members and twelve servants.[44] Although there are no extant records that document the transition from a rice-based to multicrop agriculture, the introduction of cotton can safely be attributed to farmers from the agrarian upper class.

Clearly, we have evidence here of the influence of demand on supply. The emergence during the seventeenth century of massive urban populations, especially in Edo, Osaka, Kyoto, and Kanazawa, increased the demand for cotton and other commercial crops. Yanagita Kunio in his "Before Cotton Wear" (*Momen izen no koto*) concludes from the description of clothing colors and textures found in *haikai* poems that cotton clothing had become quite widely used by urban

43 The most detailed study in English examining the spread of cotton as a commercial crop is William B. Hauser, *Economic Institutional Change in Tokugawa Japan: Osaka and the Kinai Cotton Trade* (Cambridge, England: Cambridge University Press, 1974).
44 Furushima, *Nihon nōgyōshi*, chap. 6, esp. pp. 217–19.

residents before the Genroku era (1688–1704).[45] Indeed, sumptuary regulations promulgated in many domains in the 1650s and 1660s called for merchants and peasants to use cotton rather than silk.[46] Other kinds of documentary evidence from the early 1700s show that 40 to 50 percent of the land in some villages surrounding Osaka were given over to the cultivation of cotton.

In this region, farmers from all economic strata grew cotton. A detailed study of a village in the Kawachi district found that in 1705 nearly 41 percent of this village's paddy fields were planted with cotton; by 1747 this figure had climbed to 50 percent. By then the villagers had even blocked off the irrigation ditches leading to the paddies, in order to concentrate the village's water resources on the fields planted with rice. Sections for growing cotton were rotated annually. This meant that each farmer had to grow on his land the crop selected by the village for that portion of fields during that year.[47]

Other changes accompanied the increasingly widespread cultivation of cotton by large- and medium-scale farmers in the Osaka area. During the 1700s, for instance, live-in servants began to build their own homes, and many were able to establish themselves as full-fledged independent farming households on the basis of their increased output. In addition to household reorganization, several technological innovations also played an important role in increasing production. These were designed to improve yields for all crops, and the most remarkable were related to methods of fertilization, farm tools, and agricultural management.

Commercial fertilizers appeared during the seventeenth century. As early as 1673 sardine meal had been adopted by the wealthier members of the agrarian class to fertilize cotton fields. Initially, merchants sold dried sardines to urban dwellers for consumption as an ordinary foodstuff. Chapter 11 in this volume explains in some detail how dried sardines came to be used as a fertilizer and how merchant guilds that specialized in this product were formed in response to this new and growing demand. Sardine guilds cooperated in helping increase the size of sardine hauls, because the farms consumed sardines in much greater volume than did the urban consumers, and extremely large seines, which had to be hauled in by several fishermen, were intro-

45 Yanagita Kunio, *Momen izen no koto*, in *Teihon Yanagita Kunio shū*, vol. 14 (Tokyo: Chikuma shobō, 1962).
46 Furushima, *Nihon nōgyōshi*, pp. 209–10.
47 Furushima, *Nihon nōgyōshi*, pp. 347–50; and Hayama Teisaku, *Kinsei nōgyō hatten no seisanryoku bunseki* (Tokyo: Ochanomizu shobō, 1969).

duced. These nets required large sandy beaches and were used only during sardine runs. Sardine fishing required large amounts of capital, both to purchase the nets and to mobilize a large force of fishermen. Osaka's sardine merchants provided the necessary capital and opened up many new fishing grounds. At first, sardines were caught off the coasts of Bungo, Hyūga, and Iyo, and later off the coasts of Kujūkurigahama beach in modern-day Chiba Prefecture, from whence they were shipped to Osaka. During the nineteenth century, herring and whale by-products were shipped from ports in Hokkaido to Osaka.

In time, bricks or cakes of pressed rapeseed, sesame seed, and cottonseed were used as fertilizers. Merchants tested the fertilizing potential of numerous organic materials and began to market a variety of new products as well. The result of the opening of new fishing grounds and the ensuing leaps in the quantities and varieties of catches not only boosted the quantity of fertilizers produced but also led to the adoption of fertilizers for all crops, resulting in the greater productivity of food crops as well as cash crops. For example, some documents show that farmers who once had averaged one *koku,* six *to* of rice per *tan* on high-quality fields were, by the beginning of the nineteenth century, able to harvest between two *koku,* five *to,* and two *koku,* eight *to.*[48]

Throughout Japan new fertilizers naturally led to new methods of fertilization. At first, grass–manure mixtures had been applied once a year to fields before sowing or transplanting seedlings. When first introduced, dried whole sardines were also laid on the fields just once a year. But later, sardines were ground in mortars and applied several times a year in quantities that corresponded to the crops' rate of growth. These methods were later applied to traditionally self-supplied fertilizers. Urine, for instance, was separated from night soil and ladled around crops late in the growing season as a supplemental fertilizer.

Farmers in the Osaka region who grew commercial crops such as cotton and rapeseed led the move to new fertilizers as a way of improving yields. These same cultivators also sought to improve farm tool technology, although here their interest was directed as much at reducing labor costs as at increasing yields. For instance, on an average farm with a yield of nineteen *koku,* threshing done by hand required approximately 111 days of labor, more time than any other farm task took after fertilizers were improved. To reduce this cost, some farmers

---

48 Furushima Toshio, *Kinsei Nihon nōgyō no tenkai* (Tokyo: Tōkyō daigaku shuppankai, 1963), p. 345.

first employed a new tool known colloquially as the "threshing chop-sticks," two, thirty-centimeter-long bamboo sticks used to scissor ears and kernels of grain. By the 1680s, the "threshing chopsticks" had been replaced in the Osaka area by the one-thousand-tooth thresher, whose split bamboo teeth were fastened in rows to a wooden block. This one-thousand-tooth thresher was reputed to be ten times more efficient than the threshing chopsticks. These farm implements helped decrease labor requirements during the autumn harvest and threshing season and reduced the total labor input for cotton and rapeseed culti-vation. In 1720, iron teeth had replaced the bamboo in the one-thousand-tooth thresher, and this version was subsequently intro-duced to all regions of Japan.

These many improvements in agricultural technology, when applied systematically by farm households, led to intensive cultivation. The literature of the Edo period, especially that written by Confucian schol-ars, often gives the impression that farmland in general was tilled only once in several years and that seeds were sown in a haphazard fashion. Casual cultivation methods were, however, limited to the fields opened up by slash-and-burn techniques. Otherwise, seeds were sown on up-land dry fields in rows or clusters. Although rice seedlings were not transplanted to paddies in precise rows, they were planted in bunches adjusted so that a certain number covered a fixed area. Moreover, the more effective management of nursery beds and rice seed meant that fewer seeds had to be sown per *tan* of paddy, and upland fields were managed with more care as cash crops were introduced.

As rice came to be grown as a commercial crop, wealthy, elite farm-ers, especially village headmen, often kept farm journals in which they recorded the types of crops, amounts of fertilizer, strains of rice, and annual yield for each plot of village farmland.[49] Strains were selected after comparing the yields recorded in such documents. In this man-ner, farmers were able to discover rice plants with especially produc-tive ears, and eventually even to breed new varieties systematically. At the same time, farmers tried to reduce the amount of seed sown. In the Kantō region, where seeds were thickly sown, one *tan* of rice paddy usually was sown with somewhere from one *to*, two *shō*, to one *to*, five *shō* of unhulled rice. By 1720, farmers were only sowing three *sho* of rice per *tan*. This improvement resulted from the adoption of new sowing methods. Previously, unhulled rice was sown after being

49 A general discussion of this kind of manual can be found in Jennifer Robertson, "Japanese Farm Manuals: A Literature of Discovery," *Peasant Studies* 11 (Spring 1984).

soaked in water until sprouts began to appear. But by soaking the unhulled rice for only one day, draining the seeds, and sowing them immediately, farmers were able to save seeds. Additional savings were achieved by selecting seeds through testing for resistance to wind and water damage.

Innovative methods of intensive agricultural management were also devised by farmers who grew fruits and vegetables for sale to the urban market. In the Kyoto region, for instance, melons known as *makuwa uri* were highly prized. By 1680 several villages had become well-known for producing handsome melon specimens, the best of which were produced near Tōji (temple) and sold with an affixed seal testifying to their origin.[50] Farmers prepared and fertilized the plots for these melons during the preceding winter. When the plants first appeared in the spring, the farmers carefully observed each plant, keeping the most promising and thinning out the others. They even counted the leaves and cut the tops of branching vines to permit the main stem to grow larger and stronger. The top of the main vine was also pruned, and the next generation of vines was then allowed to bear fruit. Though time-consuming, such intensive horticultural techniques were already widely employed before the eighteenth century in regions where agriculture had been influenced by the growth of markets.

COOPERATIVE ASPECTS OF VILLAGE SOCIETY

Despite the great changes that surged through the villages during the Edo period, many cooperative aspects of village life provided elements of continuity that linked together the new and the old. The inhabitants of the early modern village may have possessed differing levels of political responsibility and observed distinctions based on lineage, but they also worked together, functioning as a coordinated unit to engage in agriculture. Village unity was fostered by a system of social relationships that encouraged cooperation and promoted a sense of community. Moreover, all village inhabitants were obliged to work together for mutual advantage in a variety of agricultural and social activities, of which irrigation provides a good example.

The construction and maintenance of an irrigation system was a complex undertaking. In addition to the initial investment of labor for

---

50 Furushima Toshio, *Nihon nōgyō gijutsushi*, vol. 6 of *Furushima Toshio chosakushū*, pp. 426–7, 543–8.

the construction of the irrigation canals that enabled the expansion of rice cultivation, constant maintenance was necessary to keep the irrigation system in operation. Locks, sluice gates, and other flood control devices that were erected to hold back rivers during the typhoon season required periodic maintenance and frequent repair. These facilities were made of wood, bamboo, stone, and sand, that is, from materials gathered by mutual consent and effort from the village's communal lands. Furthermore, irrigation ditches had to be dredged and repaired before the planting season, and the weeds that sprouted along ditches during the summer required constant attention. Villages that shared water supplies with neighboring villages or that were allowed to irrigate their fields only during certain times of the day shared the responsibility for opening and closing the water locks at the water sources, yet another task that required the full cooperation of all villagers.

In regions where double cropping was possible, rice seedling nurseries were begun before the winter grain was harvested. The young rice plants had to be irrigated as soon as they were put into the nursery plot, but diverting water to the seedbeds often lowered the level of the groundwater in adjacent fields that were planted in a winter grain crop. Consequently, where to locate a seedling nursery was a delicate question, requiring the consent of the entire village. As a general rule, farmers had to cooperate in order to be ensured of adequate water supplies. Moreover, they were forced to work their lands according to identical schedules, because adjoining fields in the same irrigation system were watered at the same time.

Cooperation was also the order of the day in villages that specialization in commercial crops. Cotton farming required dry fields, which were often constructed from paddy fields by cutting off the flow of irrigation water. Hence, cotton could be grown only with the cooperation of farmers whose lands shared the same irrigation ditch, as all land downstream within an irrigation system would be simultaneously converted into dry fields when the irrigation water was blocked off, unless the cultivators were willing to expend the time and funds to redirect the irrigation canals.

The rethatching of roofs was typically a community matter as well. Although it was possible for the average farmer to save enough straw from successive wheat harvests to cover his roof, the accumulated straw would not be of uniform age or dryness. Hence, special roof thatch was grown for covering roofs, and villagers set aside specific fields to grow enough thatch to reroof one or two villages homes every year, although the large houses of wealthy villagers usually required a double portion of thatch. All healthy male members of the village would help harvest the reeds and thatch the house selected for that year, and all families contributed to providing the bamboo supports and straw ropes needed for tying down the thatch. Because thatching the eaves of roofs required special skills, one person from every village (or sometimes every other village) was usually trained for this task, and the more elementary chores would be performed by ordinary villagers under his guidance.

Close cooperation among village members and the need for joint effort and consensus also had another side, making it difficult for innovations in life-styles, farm tools, and crops to penetrate village life. Traditions of cooperation tended to survive longest in those villages that were most self-sufficient and isolated from the outside world. On the other hand, the relative importance of village cooperation tended to diminish in areas where the market economy had made inroads and market-bound crops were widely cultivated.

CONCLUSION

When the farmers in Musashi and Sagami dug out their old family records to show the officials of the shogunate's Finance Office near the end of the Tokugawa period, what they found must have excited them. Verification of one's lineage, especially a tie to samurai origins nearly three centuries earlier, would have provided psychological satisfaction by placing one in the great flow of tradition and the village's history. Even more pleasing, one could now boast with confidence about one's elite heritage and claim a special niche in village lore.

But if one reads between the lines of those musty documents, what is even more startling is the change that time had wrought. The shift from subsistence to commercial farming; the appearance of new implements, seeds, and farming techniques; the expanded use of irrigation and fertilizers; the development of new means of village administration; and the steady improvement of diet, clothing, and housing – all of these had so far removed the farmer of the mid-nineteenth century from his samurai ancestors that he must have wondered whether his predecessors had ever existed at all.

The late Edo period farmers also stood, perhaps unknowingly, at the brink of another revolutionary transformation that would propel their own successors into the modern age. The shift from "peasant" to "farmer" that had occurred over the course of two centuries had not been simply a psychological reorientation. Rather, as depicted in the

71

other chapters in this volume, it had also involved a major shift in the institutional context within which the Japanese farmer lived. That institutional context was powerfully conditioned by the massive commercial developments in central Japan, developments that are beyond the purview of this chapter and that are treated in Chapter 11 of this volume and in volume 5 of *The Cambridge History of Japan*.

As a result of these changes, the expansion of national and international markets in the 1850s and 1860s would shake the foundations of Japan's institutional structure, inviting a group of leaders from western Japan to overthrow the shogunate and launch Japan on the course of modernization. Few farmers participated in the revolutionary struggles – perhaps because commercialization had proceeded so far as to dissolve the traditional cohesiveness of the peasant community – but all would be profoundly affected by its outcome.

POPULATION CHANGES*

BY AKIRA HAYAMI

A careful study of Japan's population on the eve of industrialization will help resolve the longstanding debate over which came first—population growth or modern economic development. It should shed light on the crucial problem of how the demographic indices of a premodern society, such as general population trends, birth and death rates, average age at marriage, and average life expectancy, can affect that society's subsequent industrialization. Finally, it should even allow us to determine which indices contributed to industrialization, and to what extent, so that we can posit population as an independent variable against economic development. One of the essential steps toward these goals is to decide whether population increase stems from a rising birth rate or a falling death rate, which indicates whether or not the demographic transition theory holds true for a given society. Yet even this basic question has not been answered for Japan. Despite an obvious need to clarify the nature of Japan's demography from *bakumatsu*[1] to mid-Meiji, on the eve of industrialization, we have surprisingly few such demographic studies. In this chapter I seek to show that by re-examining the data of the 1820-1850 and 1870-1910 periods, together with other evidence on the transition decades themselves, it is possible to clear up many uncertainties about population change in Japan.

Japan is blessed with an unusually rich store of source materials for the historical study of its population: *bakufu* and *han* population surveys based on village or town religious-investigation registers (*shumon ara-*

---

* The author gratefully acknowledges the contribution made by Bob Tadashi Wakabayashi, not only for his patient translation work, but also for many helpful comments and suggestions made during the preparation of this chapter.
[1] We shall here consider the *bakumatsu* era to be 1843-1868.

tame cho)[2] allow us to obtain precise figures for such demographic indices as long-range population trends and changing patterns of birth, death, and marriage. Furthermore, the establishment of the local administrative system in the 1890s and the appearance of fairly reliable demographic statistics for the first decade of the twentieth century mean that good data, on both the regional and the national level, are available for part of the Meiji period. But we lack national population data for the period from 1846, when *bakufu* population surveys ended, to 1872, when Meiji surveys began, and there is confusion about demographic rates over the following decades. We do have a national population figure for 1872 (33.1 million) based on data obtained from the domicile registration system (*koseki seido*) established by the Meiji government. The early Meiji population, however, has been the subject of much controversy. In 1930 the 1872 figure was revised upward to 34.8 million by the Cabinet Statistics Bureau (Naikaku Tōkeikyoku), which added the estimated number of persons missed in the registration process.[3] Yet, doubts persisted and re-estimates were made. The nation's population in 1875 was estimated variously as 35.3 million by the Cabinet Statistics Bureau, 34.8 million by Akasaka Keiko, and 37.2 million by Okazaki Yōichi.[4] The differences are not very great in absolute numbers, but as Umemura Mataji has shown, they assume critical significance when we attempt to determine the *rate* of population growth during that era.[5]

This problem is central to the mid-1960s Okazaki-Umemura debate over early Meiji population growth rates, a debate well known among Japanese economic historians. Okazaki's position was that since the early Meiji population was relatively large to begin with, its subsequent rate of increase should be interpreted as low. Umemura, on the other hand, while noting that his own view was still a "hypothesis," opposed Okazaki's assertion from the standpoint that population increase preceded modern economic growth. Because an understanding of this debate is crucial to the problem at hand, we must examine the positions adopted by these two scholars in some detail.

---

[2] The *bakufu* conducted twenty-two national population surveys from 1721 to 1846, at six-year intervals. Of these surveys, twelve break down aggregate national figures province by province.

[3] Naikaku tōkei kyoku, ed., *Meiji gonen ikō waga kuni no jinkō* (Tokyo: Tokyo tōkei kyōkai, 1930).

[4] See Umemura Mataji, "Meijiki no jinkō seichō," in Shakai keizai shi gakkai, ed., *Keizai shi ni okeru jinkō* (Tokyo: Keiō tsūshin, 1969), pp. 118-141.

[5] Ibid. See also Okazaki Yōichi, "Meiji jidai no jinkō: toku ni shusshōritsu to shiboritsu ni tsuite," *Keizai kenkyū*, vol. 16, no. 3 (1965), pp. 207-213; Umemura Mataji, "Meiji jidai no jinkō ni tsuite: kommento" and Okazaki Yōichi, "Umemura Mataji-shi no kommento ni taisuru kaitō," both in *Keizai kenkyū*, vol. 16, no. 4 (1965), pp. 356-359.

First, Okazaki dismissed the birth and death rates published in the early Meiji period as being incredibly low. Instead, he used the first modern census of 1920 to project life tables backward and estimate birth, death, and growth rates for each time frame within the Meiji period. Using these tables, he estimated that Japan's population was 36.3 million in 1870 and 37.2 million in 1875. His results indicated that the Meiji birth rate remained at the level of thirty-five to thirty-seven per thousand, that it did not decline until after the turn of the century, and that the death rate fell almost continuously from the figure of thirty-one per thousand recorded at the start of the period. In short, Okazaki found that Meiji population increases stemmed solely from a decline in the death rate.

Akasaka's estimates, used by Umemura, were also derived from the 1920 census. Akasaka had projected these figures backward to obtain vital statistics, and her results were similar to the figures obtained in 1930 by the Cabinet Statistics Bureau—34.8 million in 1875. This figure was 2.4 million, or about 7 percent, lower than Okazaki's. But a more important difference was that, according to Akasaka, the birth rate jumped greatly, from twenty-six per thousand to thirty-five per thousand. These figures argued that Meiji population increases should be attributed solely to a rise in the birth rate. Umemura noted that Okazaki's findings conformed to the demographic transition theory, and he suspected that this conformity was more than coincidental. According to the demographic transition theory, a nation's population changes during modernization by stages: high birth rates and high death rates, then high birth rates and low death rates, and finally low birth rates and low death rates. Umemura argued that this theory was untenable, citing the example of the Scandinavian countries as well as Akasaka's figures for Meiji Japan. The astounding increase in Meiji Japan's birth rate noted by Akasaka, he asserted, could not be left unaccounted for.

The more important and relevant of Umemura's findings are as follows. First, he held that the decline in the death rate in an industrializing society often reflects an income level that rises owing to endogenous factors—the increased scope and wider distribution of that society's aggregate production. Thus, rising income levels lead to increased personal expenditures and then to a declining death rate. Population growth, when it is achieved in this manner, conforms to the theory that economic growth produces population increase. But—and this is of immense importance—a declining death rate does not always stem from endogenous economic betterment. In much of the Third World today, the death rate has been lowered by importing advanced technology and hygiene already developed in the industrialized nations, and this exogenously induced decline in the death rate actually *obstructs* economic growth and improvement of living standards.

In regard to the birth rate, Umemura wrote that so long as the death rate remains high, a desire to ensure the survival of offspring will prevent people from taking steps to reduce the birth rate to a level below that of the death rate. But after the death rate has fallen and people no longer feel a compelling need to ensure the survival of offspring, they will lower the number of births out of a desire to raise their standard of living. Moreover, when income levels are on the rise and seem likely to continue to do so indefinitely, forces that once held down the birth rate become relaxed, and an increasing birth rate may accompany or even precede modern economic growth.

Of course, Umemura's views presuppose that the increase in modern Japan's birth rate began in the *bakumatsu* and Restoration era, prior to large-scale industrialization or economic growth. Some form of the theory that population increase produces economic growth, he hypothesized, may hold true for Japan, where factors during the Tokugawa period probably had worked to raise the birth rate.

Umemura's hypothesis has been neither confirmed nor refuted by later Japanese scholars studying the historical demography of Japan. For one thing, intensive research on the Tokugawa period can be conducted only at the village-survey level. Second, vital statistics for the early Meiji period are unreliable. And third, there is a dearth of economic statistics in contrast to the wealth of population statistics available.

Even so, we who specialize in Tokugawa economic and demographic history look with envy upon the national population data available for the early Meiji era, since the *bakufu* surveys upon which we must rely are less reliable as quantitative sources. For example: population figures for samurai households are omitted; statistics for certain domains or provinces do not contain child populations; and domain surveys were not conducted in a uniform, consistent manner. *Bakufu* surveys yield figures that are significantly lower than actual population levels, but we do not know how much lower;[6] nor do we have firm evidence to deter-

---

[6] Sekiyama Naotarō has gone over these materials with the utmost care, and probably for that reason they are known to foreign researchers as "the Sekiyama data." His estimates, though not precise, place the unreported population count at between 4.5 million and 5 million. See Sekiyama Naotarō, *Kinsei Nihon no jinkō kōzō* (Tokyo: Yoshikawa kōbunkan, 1969), p. 117. However, we should note that Sekiyama's estimate was made by "logically linking" a national population figure based on the 1846 *bakufu* survey with early Meiji government statistics. These early Meiji statistics are themselves by no means reliable. Moreover, given the fluid social and political conditions that did so much to reduce *bakufu* and daimyo authority in the late Tokugawa period, Sekiyama's estimate should not be accepted as an absolute of the highest accuracy. We must take into consideration regional

mine whether or not underreporting continued at the same rate and in the same numbers throughout the Tokugawa. Hence, these imperfect source materials pose many pitfalls.

Regardless of such pitfalls, we continue to use *bakufu* survey data to plot Tokugawa demographic trends.[7] Indeed, these surveys are the only quantitative source materials available that indicate national population levels and break them down province by province.[8] Without them, our understanding of Tokugawa society certainly would be much more limited than it is now. Thus, the early Meiji population data that have been virtually ignored (particularly by demographers) for being statistically flawed appear, to Tokugawa specialists, as a hitherto undiscovered Treasure Island awaiting exploitation. Their value in clarifying the nature of that momentous transition from Tokugawa to Meiji must be immense.

In the late Tokugawa and early Meiji, modernization had yet to be pursued in earnest; accordingly, population changes that accompanied it were still of minimal importance. This is not to ignore the rapid development of port cities, the appearance of export-oriented industrial areas centered on raw silk production, the opening of Japan to foreign trade and diplomatic intercourse, the changes in politics and military organization that accompanied the Meiji Restoration, and the modern means of transportation imported soon after that event. There have been many demographic changes produced by these developments, but prior to the Matsukata deflation policy of 1881 and the establishment of railroad networks and new political institutions in the early 1890s, Japan's population composition and distribution were not drastically altered. True, the early Meiji government did introduce vaccination and other public health measures but many of these policies had already been initiated in the *bakumatsu* era, and their effects on Japan's population were therefore gradual rather than sudden and disruptive. Thus, early Meiji population data, although they do not reflect late Tokugawa demographic conditions as accurately as modern statistics might, nonetheless present a picture that is remarkably clear—there was no radical disjunction between *bakumatsu* and early Meiji population structure and composition.

Many of the demographic statistics published in the early Meiji period

---

variations in the source materials that yielded his figures as well as periodic fluctuations in them.

[7] For example: Hayami Akira, "Tokugawa kōki jinkō hendō no chiikiteki tokusei," *Mita gakkai zasshi*, vol. 64, no. 3 (1971); Umemura Mataji, "Tokugawa jidai no jinkō to keizai," in Umemura et al., eds., *Suryō keizai shi ronshū: 1, Nihon no keizai hatten* (Tokyo: Nihon keizai shimbunsha, 1976), pp. 3-18; Susan B. Hanley and Kozo Yamamura, *Economic and Demographic Change in Preindustrial Japan, 1600-1868* (Princeton: Princeton University Press, 1977), pp. 38-68.

[8] Surveys by the *bakufu* and a few of the domains, often listing little more than population figures by sex, constitute the exception.

are given in units of the old Tokugawa-period "provinces" (*kuni*) as well as in the newly established "prefectures" (*fu* or *ken*).[9] A problem with the prefectures of this period is that their boundaries changed frequently. On the other hand, although the old Tokugawa provinces officially ceased to exist as administrative units, they were clearly defined geographic entities. Even if statistics using these provinces as units were not published, we can still produce figures for them by first finding data for the subadministrative units of *gun* (counties) and *ku* (large cities or their wards) that constituted the provinces, and then adding these subtotals together. This is possible because the *gun* units themselves did not change (except to be appended to, or detached from, one or another prefecture).

It would be wonderful if we could treat early Meiji "province" figures as simple extensions of Tokugawa province figures, but so uncritical a use of source materials is not permissible. Tokugawa province statistics were compiled from *han*-gathered data, and the gathering process differed from domain to domain. For example, the 1846 figure for Satsuma, which contained a high proportion of unenumerated samurai, stood at 242,000. But the total for Meiji-period Satsuma "province" came to 549,000—a jump of 227 percent, which is utterly implausible even in light of the 23 percent increase registered for the nation as a whole during that same period.[10] Yet, despite this shortcoming, a comparison of Tokugawa and Meiji general population *trends* is permitted: if the historian is not overly rigid in his attitude toward the limitations and imperfections found in early Meiji demographic data, they can be employed with great profit.[11]

[9] Published demographic statistics on the early Meiji are to be found in Naimushō, ed., *Nihon zenkoku kosekihyō* (1872-1876) and *Nihon zenkoku kokōhyō* (1877-1878). These two works are available in reprint editions: Nihon tōkei kyōkai, ed., *Tōkei kosho shiriizu*, vol. 4 (Tokyo: Nihon Tōkei Kyōkai, 1965); Naimushō kosekikyoku, ed., *Nihon zenkoku gun-ku bun jinkō hyō* (Tokyo: Naimushō kosekikyoku, 1879) and *Nihon zenkoku jinkō hyō* (Tokyo: Naimushō kosekikyoku, 1880-1885).

We are able to use these early Meiji statistics with confidence owing to the splendid annotated bibliography compiled by Hosoya Shinji, *Meiji zenki Nihon keizai tōkei kaidai shoshi* (Tokyo: Hitotsubashi daigaku keizai kenkyūjo, 1974-1980). Professor Hosoya, of the Nihon Keizai Tōkei Bunken Center at Hitotsubashi University, has listed the legal basis, statistical genealogies, and contents of individual records. In addition, the Sōrifu Tōkei-kyoku has published (Tokyo: 1976) *Sōrifu Tōkeikyoku hyakunen shi shiryō shūsei*; vol. 2, pt. 1, "Population," lists laws, regulations, and other legal documents that bear on population studies. Thanks to these two works, we can approach early Meiji statistics in an orderly fashion and can utilize a particular set of data with secure knowledge of its relationship to other kinds of data.

[10] See the "Kunibetsu jinkōhyō," in Sekiyama, *Kinsei Nihon no jinkō kōzō*, pp. 137-138. Between 1846 and 1872, there were extremely high jumps—150 percent or more—in the provinces of Kaga, Etchū, Hizen, Hyūga, Osumi, Satsuma, and Tsushima. In these areas, populations were systematically underreported in the Tokugawa period.

[11] One promising avenue of future research is to use the *gun* or *ku* units (of which there were over 700) as a framework to set up manageable or appropriate-size populations for

Before discussing the results of my research, I should explain my basic assumption about the nature of the "population" that emerges from Tokugawa and Meiji statistics. As discussed above, *bakufu* statistics suffer from a variety of imperfections—omission of samurai households, non-standardized methods of census taking by the various domains, occasional double counting of individuals or groups, and so on. Absolute figures obtained from Tokugawa population surveys, then, are not always reliable. To skirt the pitfalls involved, I adopted the following strategy. I have considered the population given for each province to be an index, and from the annual provincial or regional population, I sought to determine changes for every era under consideration. Assuming that there were no variations in survey methods within each domain throughout the Tokugawa period—and there is a good possibility that there were none—the figures derived should then be amenable to statistical treatment.

As far as Meiji populations are concerned, the registered population after the 1872 registration (*jinshin koseki*) became the basis of my calculations, and I added or deleted changes in the register from that year until 1885. The allowances made for births, deaths, and entries (by marriage and adoption) into and deletions from the register are known as "legally domiciled population" (*honseki jinkō*). Those who left their place of legally registered domicile, resided in one place for ninety days or more, and followed legal procedures to declare themselves to be living in a temporary domicile are known as "temporary-resident population" (*kiryū jinkō*). Finally, the "resident population" (*genjū jinkō*) is calculated from the "legally domiciled" population: registered temporary incoming residents are added, and temporary outgoing residents subtracted, to obtain the "resident populaton." This "resident population," then, is a purely theoretical calculation and is different from the resident population counted in Japan's truly modern censuses, which begin in 1920. In those censuses, the census takers actually met the people they counted.[12] Yet the Meiji population counts derived by this method are still much more accurate than those available for the Tokugawa period.

One noteworthy fact is that surveys conducted from domicile registers produce cumulative distortions in population statistics; in other words, population figures based on domicile registers become progressively more divorced from reality. In the early Meiji period, there may have been

---

investigation in conjunction with other statistics, say of prices or production (though these are even less reliable than demographic data). Detailed studies of early Meiji demographic and economic history can be undertaken in this manner.

[12] This is discussed by Osamu Saitō, "Migration and the Labour Market in Japan, 1872-1920: A Regional Study," *Keiō Economic Studies*, vol. 10, no. 2 (1973), p. 48.

omissions in the registers, but the inaccuracies they produce are not blatant. Instead, our chief problem is how to determine the true size of the migrating population. The number of out-migrants should theoretically equal that of in-migrants—at least in the domestic sphere. But in almost all cases, the recorded population of the latter group was greater than that of the former. Many migrants terminated their domiciled residence in one area and re-migrated to another without duly reporting the fact. Because of this, and given the natural increase in the proportion of in-migrants that accompanied urbanization and rising population-mobility rates, it eventually becomes impossible to determine the resident population. In 1908, the difference between in- and out-migrating populations reached 2,420,000—about 4 percent of Japan's total population. Earlier in the Meiji period the discrepancy was less serious: the first statistics available on a nationwide scale for migrating populations (in 1884) show that there were 230,000 more out-migrants than in-migrants, and this accounted for 0.7 percent of the national population.

I have noted conspicuous flaws that skew statistical data derived from early Meiji domicile registers. Nevertheless, we must recognize that these and other Meiji data *are* amenable to quantitative analysis, and we should make full use of them to clarify conditions in nineteenth-century Japan.

THE DEBATE AMONG AMERICAN SCHOLARS

National population statistics derived from *bakufu* population surveys, which are extant for the years 1721-1846, seem to provide quantitative evidence of population stagnation. Some have even described the situation as a Malthusian trap. In 1721, the population was 26.1 million; in 1846, 26.9 million. The highest figure recorded in these surveys is 27.2 million; the lowest, 24.9 million. We get a mean figure of 26.0 million for the period, plus or minus 1.2 million (or 4.6 percent).

Scholars who emphasize the dark side of Tokugawa society, particularly those who consider population to be a dependent variable of the economy, are quick to interpret such population "stagnation" as resulting from economic stagnation. Then again, those who attribute a lack of Tokugawa population growth to abortion and infanticide resorted to by commoners find in these figures just what they are looking for—proof of the poverty and despair that plagued Japanese society in that "feudalistic" era. But are such perceptions accurate?

Recently, certain American specialists on Tokugawa demographic and economic history have published important studies that shed light on these issues. In one such work, by Susan B. Hanley and Kozo Yamamura,

it is argued that 1) because of relatively low birth rates in Tokugawa
Japan, the concept of "demographic transition" is not applicable and 2)
in most cases, death rates approximately equaled birth rates, resulting in
a stable population. The authors found a slight increase in Japan's population after the Tempō mortality crisis of 1837-1838, an increase that
continued throughout the Meiji period but did not begin with it. In
addition, they saw "a remarkable similarity with pre- and early-industrial
population trends in Europe and no similarity at all between Tokugawa
Japan and the other nations of Asia today."[13]

In another study, Thomas Smith put forth the following conclusions
about one village located in central Japan:

> Both mortality and fertility . . . were low to moderate in Nakahara
> as compared to eighteenth-century European parishes. . . . [T]here
> can be little doubt that one of the reasons for low registered fertility
> was the practice of infanticide. . . . What is surprising is that the
> practice does not appear to have been primarily a response to pov-
> erty. . . . In short, it gives the impression of a kind of family
> planning.[14]

From the overall tone of Smith's book, we may infer his position: 1) at
least during the eighteenth century, steps taken by peasants to maintain
families at a certain size held down population increase; 2) this presents
a marked contrast to Ch'ing China, where the population is believed to
have doubled between 1749 and 1819; and 3) this contrast may have
much to do with Japan's earlier and more rapid economic development.
Smith notes:

> If population was held in check by deliberate controls over fertility,
> we should have in some respects a functional equivalent of the Eu-
> ropean marriage pattern [late marriage and high celibacy]. But if
> population was checked mainly by famine, as some historians be-
> lieve, we should have reason to doubt the economic expansion and
> consequent rise in per capita income after 1721.[15]

James Nakamura and Matao Miyamoto also believe that in contrast
to Ch'ing China, which experienced a tremendous population increase
during roughly the same period, Tokugawa Japan's basically "stagnant"
population created relatively higher per capita income, paving the way
for Japan to industrialize successfully and achieve high economic growth.

[13] Hanley and Yamamura, *Economic and Demographic Change*, p. 318.
[14] Thomas C. Smith, *Nakahara: Family Farming and Population in a Japanese Village,
1717-1830* (Stanford: Stanford University Press, 1977), p. 147.
[15] Ibid., p. 5.

Nakamura and Miyamoto stress differences in social and political institutions between Tokugawa Japan and Ch'ing China. For example, the Japanese *ie* (household) system "that tied the Japanese to a fixed vertical structure of mutual obligations and responsibilities and impartible inheritance" was in direct opposition to the family system of Ch'ing China. "In Japan," they write, "this took the form of population control and long-run investment, both of which tended to cause per capita output to rise."[16]

Of course these scholars do have differences of opinion. But they all agree that 1) the Tokugawa population did not increase; 2) this nonincrease resulted from the "rational" behavior of Japanese peasants who sought to maintain or improve their standard of living; and 3) these factors help explain Meiji Japan's rapid and "successful" modernization, in contrast to that of late Ch'ing China.

One American scholar, however, takes exception to these views. Carl Mosk, in a recent article, wrote:

> They [Hanley and Smith] argue that peasant families in Tokugawa Japan deliberately kept family size small through infanticide to maintain a relatively comfortable standard of living. To the contrary, I suggest that fecundity was low and the chances of infant survival poor, so parents were forced to adopt strategies about the sex of the births they would permit to survive in addition to eliminating many weak and sickly offspring soon after birth.[17]

Mosk estimated statistical data on food consumption and physical characteristics and discovered that, between 1874 and 1877, daily food consumption per individual was no more than 1,530 calories and 47.4 grams of protein, levels that subsequently rose along with per capita income. From these findings, he argued that "during the Tokugawa period *desired* fertility exceeded actual for the bulk of the population and this negative gap closed during the Meiji era."

Mosk's statement contradicts the findings of Hanley and Yamamura, Smith, and Nakamura and Miyamoto. "The concept of a demographic transition is applicable to Japan," Mosk suggested:

> If we think of demographic transition theory as explaining why *desired* fertility falls from relatively high levels prior to and in the

[16] James I. Nakamura and Matao Miyamoto, "Social Structure and Population Change: A Comparative Study of Tokugawa Japan and Ch'ing China," *Economic Development and Cultural Change*, vol. 30, no. 2 (1982), p. 262.

[17] Carl Mosk, "The Decline of Marital Fertility in Japan," *Population Studies*, vol. 33, no. 1 (1979), p. 37.

early period of modernization to low levels as modernization spreads, it is my contention that Japanese demographic history does not deviate from the main lines of demographic transition theory. ... [T]he Japanese demographic transition experience conforms in its essential features to the experiences of Europe, North America, Australia, and New Zealand.[18]

Mosk's challenge is clearly relevant to the Okazaki-Umemura debate on population trends in Japan. According to Mosk, the demographic transition theory once refuted by Umemura may hold true for the Tokugawa period after all—if we can certify that physical reasons made fertility lower than *desired* fertility and that this low fertility stemmed from inadequate food consumption and malnutrition. (Of course Mosk did not deny that abortion and infanticide were practiced.)

It now appears certain that new debates will emerge over why fertility was low in the Tokugawa period and what this fact means to the historian. Before those debates can be resolved, we must accumulate many regional studies—each based on reliable source materials that have been subjected to rigorous demographic and economic analysis, performed with the aim of determining the general standard of living and the actual steps taken to alter it, if any.[19] Mind-boggling amounts of time, money, and energy will doubtless be required to complete this task, but I believe it can be done.

THE LATTER HALF OF TOKUGAWA

Assuming that a useful purpose can be served now by viewing overall population trends before seeking out detailed demographic indices, I will look at provincial and regional data, derived mainly from *bakufu* and domain surveys in the Tokugawa period, and will attempt to link these figures to early Meiji population statistics for corresponding geographic areas.[20] *Bakufu* population surveys, which are extant from 1721 to 1846,

[18] Carl Mosk, "Fecundity, Infanticide, and Food Consumption in Japan," *Explorations in Economic History*, vol. 15, no. 1 (1978), pp. 269-289.

[19] I have published a book-length regional study of Tokugawa population in Suwa county, Shinano province: *Kinsei nōson no rekishi jinkō gakuteki kenkyū* (Tokyo: Tōyō keizai shuppansha, 1973). A similar study on Owari and Mino provinces is in preparation.

[20] Province-by-province Tokugawa population figures are available for 1721, 1750, 1786, 1792, 1798, 1804, 1822, 1828, 1834, 1840, and 1846. The figures for 1792 are published in Minami Kazuo, "Kansei yonen no shokoku jinkō ni tsuite," in *Nihon rekishi*, no. 432 (May 1984), pp. 42-47, and those for 1840 are published in Minami Kazuo, *Bakumatsu Edo shakai no kenkyū* (Tokyo: Yoshikawa kōbunkan, 1978), pp. 164-185. Figures for the other years can be found in Sekiyama, *Kinsei Nihon no jinkō kōzō*, pp. 137-139.

contain various noteworthy characteristics and problems. First, although absolute national population figures show stagnation, regional variation was pronounced: in some areas the population rose continuously, while in others it fell. These increases and decreases offset each other to give the overall appearance of "stagnation," or a lack of aggregate population growth. Generally speaking, in the Kantō and Tōhoku areas, population decline was the rule; in Kyūshū, Shikoku, and Chūgoku, increases predominated; and in central Japan, there was a slight population decrease in the Kinki region and an increase in Hokuriku. Map 11.1 shows that Tokugawa Japan's "demographic center of gravity" moved across Lake Biwa from east to west, as eastern areas decreased in population and western areas rose.

In 1721, the three northern Kantō provinces of Kōzuke, Shimotsuke, and Hitachi as well as the six Sanyō provinces of Bizen, Bitchū, Bingo, Aki, Suō, and Nagato both had populations of 1.8 million. But by 1846, the Kantō region had lost 0.5 million while the Sanyō area had gained the same number, so that the total difference in population was roughly 1 million. Thus, the aggregate population count for these two areas shows an undeniable, yet purely accidental, form of "stagnation" that disguises the sharply contrasting regional population changes which actually took place.

Tokugawa peasants were not tied to the land, notwithstanding what we are told in most high school textbooks: they were free to migrate as individuals, and they moved from village to city in surprisingly large numbers to look for work.[21] However, their geographical mobility was not limitless. Such movement was generally restricted to a hundred-mile radius of towns and cities within a specific region, such as Edo in the Kantō, or Kyoto and Osaka in the Kinki.[22] Population increase in western Japan and population decline in eastern Japan *just happened*: these contrasting trends did not result from economic rationality—the migration of peasants in search of work—as asserted by Yamamura in his two-region model of Tokugawa Japan.[23]

Instead, I propose the following explanation. In the eighteenth century,

---

[21] Akira Hayami, "Labor Migration in a Pre-Industrial Society: A Study Tracing the Life Histories of the Inhabitants of a Village," *Keiō Economic Studies*, vol. 10, no. 2 (1973), pp. 1-18. In the same issue, see also Susan B. Hanley, "Migration and Economic Change in Okayama during the Tokugawa Period," pp. 19-36, and W. Mark Fruin, "Farm Family Migration: The Case of Echizen in the Nineteenth Century," pp. 37-46.

[22] For Edo, see Minami, *Bakumatsu Edo shakai no kenkyū*; for Kyoto, Hayami Akira, "Kyōto machikata no shumon aratamechō," in *Kenkyū kiyō Shōwa 55–nendo* (Tokyo: Tokugawa rinsei shi kenkyūsho, 1981).

[23] Hanley and Yamamura, *Economic and Demographic Change*, pp. 28-37.

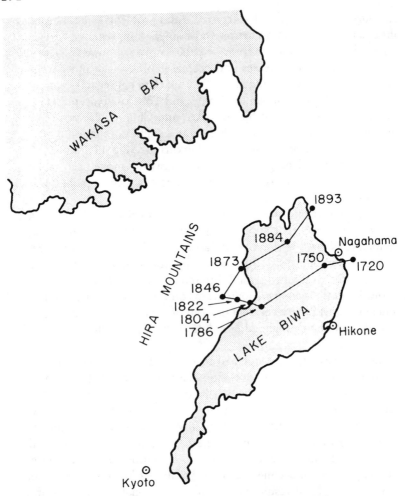

Map 11.1.   The Shifting Demographic Center of Gravity, 1720-1893
Redrawn from *Nihon rettō ni okeru jinkō bumpu no chōki jikeiritsu bunseki* (Tokyo:
Shakai kōgaku kenkyūsho, 1974), p. 125.

eastern Japan suffered from chronic bad weather which produced a long-term drop in agricultural production, but western Japan was largely unaffected.[24] Owing to the high death rate in cities, which teemed with workers who had migrated from the depressed countryside, the Kantō and Kinki regions (which included Edo, Kyoto, and Osaka) were subject to the negative-feedback function and their populations stagnated.

The long-term decline of northeastern Japan's population in the eighteenth century can be understood better by examining the annual domain-population surveys of Yonezawa and Aizu *han*. As shown in Figure 11.1, these two domains enjoyed population growth throughout the seventeenth century; but from the start of the eighteenth, decline set in, and owing to the calamitous Hōreki and Temmei famines of 1756 and the 1780s, their populations fell precipitously to a level two-thirds that of their seventeenth-century peak. In Yonezawa *han*, the population had not quite recovered to its earlier peak level even by *bakumatsu* times, which means that this *han* contained more people in the late seventeenth century than in the mid-nineteenth.

These facts suggest that the eighteenth-century decline in eastern Japan's population was not a result of short-term famines—however devastating—during the 1750s and 1780s. Instead, the decrease was a long-term trend that was probably caused by chronic bad weather, which lowered agricultural output throughout the century. Although the population increase in western Japan during this same era was but 0.2 to 0.3 percent annually, it could not have occurred apart from the development of peasant by-employments, particularly in handicraft industries.

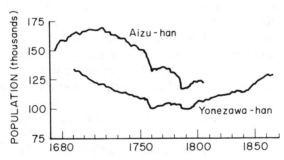

Figure 11.1.   Population Trends of Aizu *Han* and Yonezawa *Han*, 1680-1850
Data for Aizu *han* from Takahashi Bonsen, *Nihon jinkō shi no kenkyū* (Tokyo: Sanyūsha, 1941), pp. 208-217; for Yonezawa *han*, Yoshida Yoshinobu, *Oitama minshū seikatsu shi* (Tokyo: Kokusho kankōkai, 1973), pp. 113-118.

[24] From 1732 to 1733, however, western Japan did suffer from famines caused by pests, which bred in massive numbers and inflicted damage on rice plants.

One conspicuous example is Chōshū *han*, where about half of the peasant's income was earned from by-employments and nonagricultural activities, a fact that offers persuasive evidence of economic development having produced population growth in this period and area.[25]

In sum, by discussing Japan's population in the latter half of the Tokugawa period solely in terms of aggregate numbers, and then summarily labeling it "stagnant," we preclude an appreciation of its complexities and regional variations. Only through more detailed studies that account for geographic differences and changes over time can we attain a meaningful historical understanding of "Tokugawa Japan" as a whole.

A second problem has to do with the lack of *bakufu* survey statistics after 1846.[26] If the *bakufu* had continued conducting national surveys as usual up to the Restoration, population statistics for 1852, 1858, and 1864 would be available; but domestic and foreign crises left *bakufu* leaders with little time or inclination to conduct censuses. Since no further national population figures are available until 1872, when the new Meiji government instituted its registration system (*jinshin koseki*), we have a statistical blank space of twenty-six years—from 1846 to 1872. This mid-nineteenth-century era cannot be interpreted either as one of "stagnation" or as a simple continuation of eighteenth-century demographic trends.

To begin with, as shown in Map 11.1, the nation's "demographic center of gravity" during the period under consideration was furthest west in 1846, but by 1873 it had moved northeastward at considerable speed. Of course, Tokugawa and Meiji population statistics are not of uniform quality or accuracy, so the speed of this shift cannot be plotted with precision; but *general trends* can be determined. Clearly, Japan's "demographic center of gravity" had been moving westward at a rapid pace prior to 1846; this speed slackened considerably in *bakumatsu* times, and by the beginning of Meiji, the center of gravity was moving eastward swiftly. We may conclude, then, that the eastward shift in Japan's population distribution had already begun by the *bakumatsu* and Restoration era.

Next, as shown in Figure 11.1, the population of Yonezawa *han* (in present-day Yamagata prefecture) began to rise after the start of the nineteenth century, and by *bakumatsu* times it had just about recovered

---

[25] Thomas C. Smith, "Farm Family By-employments in Pre-Industrial Japan," *Journal of Economic History*, vol. 29, no. 4 (December 1969), pp. 397-423; Shunsaku Nishikawa, "Productivity, Subsistence, and By-employment in Mid-Nineteenth-Century Chōshū," in *Explorations in Economic History*, vol. 15, no. 1 (1978), pp. 69-83.

[26] Prior to the first *bakufu* survey of 1721, Japan's early Tokugawa population increase had already tapered off, but a discussion of that era lies beyond the scope of this study.

the population losses incurred during the eighteenth century. Hence we need to reconsider whether or not the general trends of rising population in the west and falling population in the east hold true for the nineteenth century. Fortunately, national population statistics, though flawed in some respects, do exist for every sixth year during the twenty-four-year period from 1822 to 1846; by using these data in a discriminating manner, we gain valuable information with which to solve this problem.

Finally, it should be noted that Japan suffered a disastrous mortality crisis triggered by nationwide epidemics in 1837 and 1838. Osaka, for example, lost 11 percent of its population during these two years. The disease in question remains unknown, but in the Owase area (of present-day Mie prefecture) it evidently was accompanied by high fever and diarrhea.[27] According to the death registers (kakochō) of a farm village near Hida-Takayama, seventy-three persons starved to death in 1837 alone; in addition, forty-nine children and twenty-three elderly persons died from the illness, and thirty-seven others died from acute infectious diseases. Infectious diseases took their greatest toll in lives during the sixth and seventh months of that year.[28]

The Tempō mortality crisis, then, stemmed not just from famine-induced starvation, but also from infectious diseases—probably ailments of the intestinal tract and/or measles. Here again, a cause-and-effect relationship in history is hard to determine. Were the deaths from infectious disease caused by weakened resistance, the result of poor harvests that reduced food consumption and brought on malnutrition? Or did the poor harvests stem from widespread disease that was produced by some new, virulent strain of virus that sapped peasants of the strength to farm? The resolution of this problem will have to await identification of the culprit disease.

In any case, the immensity of this Tempō mortality crisis is beyond doubt. According to bakufu statistics, a 4.2 percent decline in Japan's total population occurred between 1834 and 1840. This was the second largest rate of decline for any six-year interval on record from 1721 to 1846; it was exceeded only during the 1780s. Between 1834 and 1840, only eight of Tokugawa Japan's sixty-eight provinces registered a population increase, while twenty-seven showed a decrease of 5 percent or more.

The area of most precipitous decline stretched from Tōhoku to Hokuriku, and traces of the decimation can be found in Meiji records.

[27] Hayami Akira, "Kishū Owase-gumi no jinkō sūsei," in Kenkyū kiyō Shōwa 43–nendo (Tokyo: Tokugawa rinsei shi kenkyūsho, 1969).
[28] Suda Keizō, Hida "O" jiin kakochō no kenkyū (private printing, 1973), pp. 154-155.

Statistics compiled in 1884 are the first for which quinquennial age structure is known.[29] From these data we find that, in fifteen of the nation's
forty-three prefectures, the number of 45-to-49-year-olds[30] (born between
1836 and 1840, the five-year interval in which the Tempō mortality crisis
occurred) was lower than the number of 50-to-54-year-olds (born in the
preceding five-year interval, from 1831 to 1835). Furthermore, those
fifteen prefectures were all on the Japan Sea coast stretching from Tōhoku
to Hokuriku. More detailed analysis reveals the following. Statistics in
1886, the first year for which the national one-year age structure is
known,[31] show that the age-49 population (born in the crisis year 1837)
was 16 percent less than those age 50 (born in 1836). In theory, the
higher up in the age structure, the smaller the population should be, since
it normally is reduced to a greater degree through death by natural
causes—barring large-scale out-migration from a certain area, of course.
The above facts, then, mean either that there were few births in the crisis
year of 1837 or that the infant death rate was extremely high. These
Meiji data are many years removed from the crisis year; moreover, we
must take into account regional variations in the adult death rate. Even
so, regional statistics derived from *bakufu* surveys and Meiji source materials match beautifully.

One more short-term population change remains to be discussed—the
cholera epidemic that struck Japan right after the opening of the treaty
ports. During the nineteenth century, there were several worldwide cholera pandemics; the third just happened to coincide with *kaikoku* (the
opening of the country).[32] The disease raged throughout Japan, starting
at Nagasaki in 1858. Though there is no accurate record of how many
people died or suffered from it, its imprint, like that of the Tempō mortality crisis, was left indelibly on Meiji records. For example, there were
relatively few births in 1861, when the pestilence hit its peak. The 1884
records giving quinquennial age structure show that, in forty-one out of
forty-three prefectures, the number of 20-to-24-year-olds born in the five-
year interval including 1861 was lower than the number of 25-to-29-
year-olds born in the previous five-year interval (a national average of
93.2 percent). The one-year age-structure figures for 1886 reveal that the

---

[29] Naimushō kosekikyoku, ed., *Nihon zenkoku jinkōhyō* (surveyed January 1, 1884; date
of publication unknown).

[30] Throughout this chapter "year-old" will refer to *sai* in the Japanese method of reck-
oning ages.

[31] Naikaku tōkeikyoku, ed., *Nihon teikoku daishichi tōkei nenkan* (surveyed December
31, 1886; published in 1888).

[32] Tachikawa Shōzō, *Byōki no shakai shi* (Tokyo: Nihon hōsō shuppan kyōkai, 1971),
pp. 180-223.

national population born in 1861 was 12 percent less than that born in 1860. Statistics show that the epidemic raged most furiously in the Tōkai, Kinki, Chūgoku, and Shikoku areas, and that the greatest loss of life occurred in the five central prefectures of Aichi, Gifu, Mie, Nara, and Wakayama. In those prefectures, the number of persons born in 1861 fell to less than 80 percent of those born in 1860.

Thus, the mortality crises of the late 1830s and early 1860s were nationwide in scope and had brutal effects on Japan's population. Figure 11.2 shows one-year age structures for males and females at the end of 1886, plots their age backward, and shows changes in the population for each structure. This graph indicates that the Tokugawa population declined sharply on four separate occasions: the Tempō mortality crisis of 1837-1838; in 1846;[33] in 1851; and from 1859 to 1862. It is quite conceivable that either the birth rate was extremely low, or the infant death rate was extremely high for these years.

What we must keep in mind, however, is that such abnormal conditions were of short duration and were caused mainly by communicable diseases

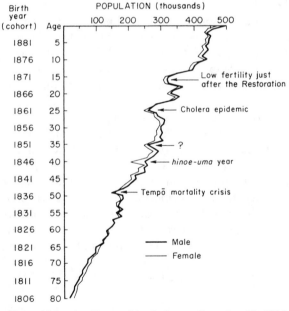

Figure 11.2.   Age Composition in Japan, December 31, 1886

[33] This was the year *hinoe-uma*, considered to be an inauspicious year for females to be born. Therefore, the "population decline" observed in statistics for that year actually stems from nonregistration of female births and, presumably, infanticide.

having little connection with national economic conditions. In sum, from the beginning of the nineteenth century down to the Restoration, exogenous short-term factors worked to hold down population increase on a few occasions; what is more, there took place pronounced regional variations in population change that cannot be ignored. The Tempō mortality crisis and *bakumatsu* cholera epidemics were most devastating in areas where population was on the rise (except for Tōhoku); the *bakumatsu* epidemics, in particular, wrought their greatest havoc in Japan's economically advanced regions.

Before we can sort out the cause-and-effect relationship between population growth and economic development in Tokugawa Japan, we must discount such short-term, exogenously induced negative effects on population change. The lack of population surveys broken down by province for the *bakumatsu* era prevents us from measuring the precise impact that the cholera epidemics had on Japan's population, but existing statistics do shed some light on the Tempō crisis. The twenty-four years from 1822 to 1846, for which surveys were taken every sixth year, can be divided up into four intervals of six years each. When we disregard the 1834-1840 interval (in which the Tempō mortality crisis occurred) we obtain a picture of long-term, overall national population trends on a province-by-province basis. During the other three six-year intervals, the population increased 5.2 percent, and of the sixty-seven provinces for which reliable data exist,[34] all but eleven showed an increase. Without a doubt, this means that Japan's early-nineteenth-century population was growing.

More detailed analysis of provincial figures for those three six-year intervals reveals that in thirty-five provinces the population showed some growth in all three intervals. Furthermore, among these thirty-five provinces, Echigo, Hōki, Izumo, Bingo, Aki, and Sanuki enjoyed a population increase of more than 2 percent in all three intervals. Thus, in the first half of the nineteenth century, most of Japan's provinces were enjoying steady population growth. Chūgoku, Shikoku, and northern Kyūshū, areas that enclose the Inland Sea, displayed continuous growth, as did certain provinces in the Tōhoku, Hokuriku, and Tōsan regions. By way of contrast, Kantō and Kinai—the core areas of Tokugawa Japan and the economically most advanced—failed to grow. (See Maps 11.2 and 11.3.)

We may summarize the significance of these observations on late Tokugawa population as follows. In the first half of the nineteenth century, western Japan (particularly areas surrounding the Inland Sea) enjoyed

[34] This excludes Shimōsa, where records are poor.

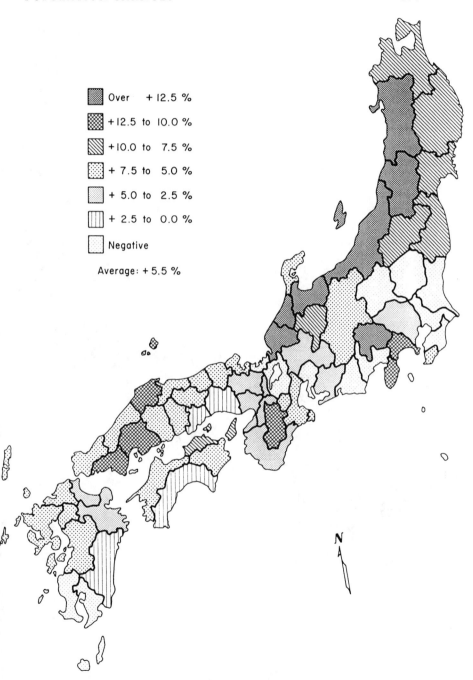

Over   + 12.5 %

+ 12.5 to 10.0 %

+ 10.0 to 7.5 %

+ 7.5 to 5.0 %

+ 5.0 to 2.5 %

+ 2.5 to 0.0 %

Negative

Average: + 5.5 %

N

Map 11.2.   Population Change in Japan, 1822-1846 (Except 1834-1840)

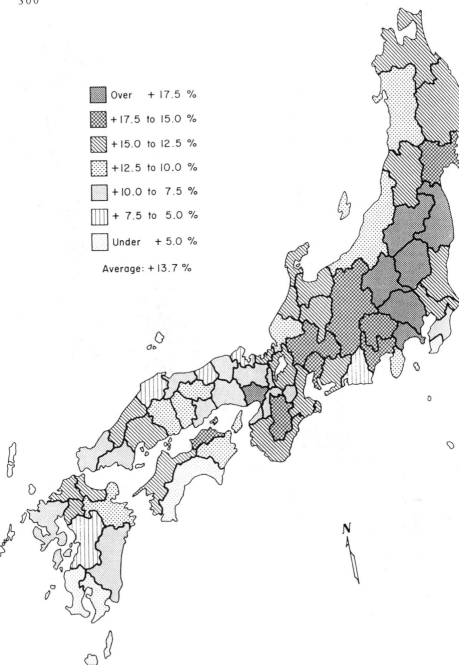

Map 11.3. Population Change in Japan, 1872-1885

steady population growth. Such growth, though to a lesser extent, also took place in other parts of the country—even in Tōhoku. Japan's population was on the upswing, and this increase continued throughout the *bakumatsu* era; although temporarily checked by the Tempō mortality crisis, late Tokugawa population growth soon resumed. Why was it that the areas around Edo, Kyoto, and Osaka—the nation's heartland—enjoyed no large population increases, while western Japan and Tōhoku, whose population had been decimated in the eighteenth century, did? One reason may lie in the high death rate found in all preindustrial cities; but the real answer, I think, should be sought outside of population structure, in economic development. In the Inland Sea area, village industries and peasant by-employments were developing during this period, and sericulture and the silk-reeling industry were beginning to emerge in Tōhoku. But the Kantō and Kinai, in contrast to these "developing" areas, were already "developed." The divergent forms of population change that occurred in these two types of regions conform precisely to phenomena that characterize periods of proto-industrialization. Yet until we obtain detailed regional and, if possible, village-level studies, the question of whether population growth engendered economic development or vice versa will remain unsolved.

THE EARLY MEIJI

The first national population statistics available for post-Restoration Japan date from 1872, and are derived from the new Meiji government's domicile registration system. From this time on, Japan's population continued to rise each and every year. The average annual growth rate was, it is true, less than 1.0 percent during the period under consideration, but it is nevertheless important to emphasize that national statistics show sustained growth in the Meiji population. Modern medicine and sanitation were implemented to prevent epidemics of typhoid fever and cholera, which had taken a great toll in lives during the Tokugawa period. Consequently, acute short-term fluctuations in Japan's population were eliminated. (See Figure 11.3.)

But when we examine regional population growth trends and the reasons for population change in early Meiji Japan, we find clear differences from the Tokugawa period. Map 11.3 indicates that southern Tōhoku, northern Kantō, Kai and Shinano, Tokyo, and Osaka enjoyed the greatest population growth in early Meiji; yet most of these areas were *not* growing in the first half of the nineteenth century or in the latter half of the Tokugawa period. (See Map 11.2 for Tokugawa trends.) Thus, the na-

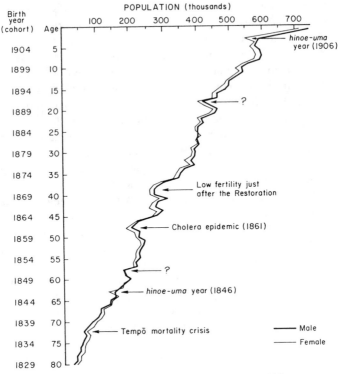

Figure 11.3. Age Composition in Japan, December 31, 1908
Data from Naikaku-tōkeikyoku, *Nihon zenkoku jinkō seitai tōkei* (1911).

tion's population was definitely increasing during the early Meiji era, and the regions that spurted ahead to take the lead in this increase were those that had been "also-rans" during the late Tokugawa.

Figure 11.4 shows the relationships between various types of population change from 1822 to 1846 and from 1872 to 1885 in fourteen regions. (Note, however, that I have omitted changes from 1834 to 1840 in order to minimize the effects of the Tempō mortality crisis.) In late Tokugawa, we see that the population was rising in all regions except northern Kantō. Hokuriku and the side of the Tōhoku region along the Japan Sea showed the highest growth; Tōkai, Kinai, and the areas surrounding Kinai had little growth. The figure for southern Kyūshū is surprisingly low, probably because of the dubious, misleading counting methods employed by Satsuma *han*: population growth in this region was most likely much greater. In early Meiji, eastern Japan (from Hokuriku and Tōkai eastward) recorded a higher growth rate than western Japan; and, surprisingly enough, the region of greatest increase was north-

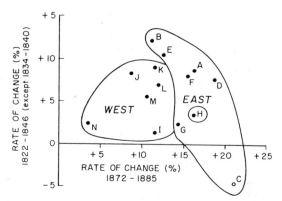

Figure 11.4. Comparison of Population Change, by Region, 1822-1846 and 1872-1885

KEY:

A. East Tōhoku: Mutsu (in 1868 divided into Mutsu, Rikuchū, Rikuzen, Iwaki, and Iwashiro)
B. West Tōhoku: Dewa (in 1868 divided into Uzen and Ugo)
C. North Kantō: Kōzuke, Shimotsuke, and Hitachi
D. South Kantō: Musashi, Sagami, Kazusa, Shimoosa, and Awa
E. Hokuriku: Sado, Echigo, Etchū, Noto, Kaga, Echizen, and Wakasa
F. Tōsan: Kai, Shinano, and Hida
G. Tōkai: Izu, Suruga, Tōtōmi, Mikawa, Owari, and Mino
H. Kinai: Yamashiro, Yamato, Kawachi, Izumi, and Settsu
I. Peripheral Kinai: Ōmi, Iga, Ise, Shin, Kii, Awaji, Harima, and Tanba
J. San'in: Tango, Tajima, Inaba, Hōki, Oki, Izumo, and Iwami
K. Sanyō: Mimasaka, Bizen, Bitchū, Bingo, Aki, Suwō, and Nagato
L. Shikoku: Awa, Sanuki, Iyo, and Tosa
M. North Kyūshū: Chikuzen, Chikugo, Hizen, Iki, Tsushima, Buzen, and Bungo
N. South Kyūshū: Higo, Hyūga, Osumi, and Satsuma

ern Kantō which had been declining at the most precipitous rate in the nation during the latter half of the Tokugawa period. Next came southern Kantō and the Pacific coast of Tōhoku. From 1872 to 1885, Japan's greatest population growth occurred precisely in those areas where it had failed to increase significantly from 1822 to 1846.

During the early Meiji era, the regions in eastern Japan that enjoyed the fastest growth in population were those in which sericulture, silk reeling, and textile industries were the most developed; the regions that showed the least growth were those in which rice was the most important single agricultural product. These two facts lead us to believe, as independent evidence confirms, that the terms of trade shifted in favor of silk and against rice. In fact, the eight provinces that displayed the greatest population increase between 1872 and 1885 (over 18 percent) were Shimotsuke, Kōzuke, Musashi, Iwaki, Sagami, Settsu, Iwashiro, and Mino, in that order. Except for Settsu, which includes the metropolis of Osaka, all were located in eastern Japan; moreover, all were centers of sericulture. Kai and Shinano, the nation's most important sericulture centers, both enjoyed more than a 15 percent increase. (See Map 11.3.) Hokuriku and the Japan Sea coast of Tōhoku became the areas of least population growth in eastern Japan.

As for western Japan, population increase did continue in early Meiji, but at a low rate. Map 11.3 shows that except for Settsu (Osaka), no western province is included in Cluster I, which denotes a 17.5 percent rate of increase or higher. Furthermore, Cluster II contains only the four western provinces of Yamato, Kawachi, and Izumi (which surround Osaka) and Sanuki (in Shikoku). The low figure for southern Kyūshū may be the result of casualties suffered in the Satsuma Rebellion of 1877. In western Japan as well, Kinai, which had a rather low rate of population increase from 1822 to 1846, enjoyed the highest growth rate in early Meiji. This turnabout probably can be explained by improved urban living conditions in Kinai, one of the nation's two highly urbanized areas. Improved hygiene no doubt lowered the high mortality rate that had afflicted this urban region in Tokugawa days.

All of this means that Japan's "demographic center of gravity" moved eastward during the Tokugawa-Meiji transition (see Map 11.1).

Figure 11.4 shows "eastern" Japan as everything eastward from Hokuriku and Tōkai and "western" Japan as everything from Kinki westward. After the beginning of Meiji, eastern Japan's rate of population increase outstripped that of western Japan. The relationship between rates of population change in the east for these two periods shows that regression is negative and that the correlation coefficient is quite high ($r = -.745$). By way of contrast, the dotting is scattered in the west, and the correlation coefficient is not at all significant. Our problem is to determine precisely when this "turnabout" in rates of increase between east and west took place and to discover what caused it.

Japan's national population began to rise after the start of the nineteenth century. As previously noted, if we disregard the short-term Tempō mortality crisis, we find that the population in about 80 percent of the Tokugawa provinces was growing during the first half of that century. Later, in the *bakumatsu* era, there is strong evidence to indicate that an onslaught of cholera lowered the population for a short time, especially in central Japan. But pestilence did not halt the general trend of national population increase. The emergence of export-oriented industries such as raw silk, textiles, and tea meant increased opportunities for employment in the regions where those industries flourished, and this new economic development did much to alter demographic conditions in Japan.

By emphasizing the trend of population growth in nineteenth-century Japan, we should not lose sight of the short-term negative factors which lessened that growth. We have already mentioned one of those negative factors—the cholera epidemics of the 1860s. But Figure 11.3 shows that another fairly sharp drop in the number of births occurred from 1869 to 1872. This latter decrease can be accounted for partly by undercounting, but a more important cause lies in the warfare and social disorder that occurred during and immediately after the Restoration. Combined with the cholera epidemics of the same decade, then, two significant decreases in the number of births took place during this ten-year *baku-matsu*-Restoration era, which may mean that the national population fell for a short time in this period. By 1872 or 1873, the causes of this short-term decrease clearly were eliminated, and Japan's sustained population growth began. Yet we must remember that the latent potential for this continued growth had existed from the 1820s.

The Satsuma Rebellion may have affected regional population change in southern Kyūshū, but the number of casualties was relatively small when viewed on the level of national population statistics. Of greater consequence were the cholera epidemics of 1879 and 1886, for on both occasions more than 100,000 people died. By the late 1870s, however, the Meiji government was moving to eliminate cholera, infectious diseases of the intestinal tract, typhoid fever, and venereal disease, all of which had hitherto taken a great toll in lives. This stepped-up government program to eliminate disease and improve hygiene is overshadowed by its larger goal—to achieve "national wealth and strength"—and, indeed, some scholars interpret modern medicine and hygiene as having been *sacrificed to that end*.[35] This is clearly untrue. Modern medicine and hygiene were essential means to attain that end, and the Meiji government actively sought to disseminate them throughout society. The police were mobilized to combat cholera, and vaccination against smallpox became obligatory, though not everywhere in Japan. Between 1874 and 1882, the construction of hospitals increased tenfold.[36] Medical schools were established at a fast clip. Of course, these measures did not prove effective overnight: it took time to lower the death rate for normal years, but infectious diseases and typhoid, which had decimated Tokugawa populations, virtually disappeared. Not counting the two cholera epidemics already mentioned, no plague resulted in 100,000 or more deaths. Such improvements in hygiene and medicine raised the reproductive capacities of urban populations, which had suffered from high death rates during

[35] Tachikawa, *Byōki no shakai shi*.
[36] Ibid.

the Tokugawa period: the negative feedback function between urbanization and population increase was definitely eliminated at some point in the early Meiji.

Thus far, we have outlined the factors behind post-Restoration national population growth. We should now discuss the problem of regional variation, particularly with respect to geographic areas in which Meiji population trends represented turnabouts in relation to Tokugawa trends.

In the first half of the Meiji period, the two areas that displayed the highest rate of population increase were 1) southern Tōhoku, northern Kantō, and Tōsan, where the sericulture and silk-reeling industries flourished; and 2) the cities of Tokyo, Yokohama, Osaka, and Kobe, where modern industry and the military establishment produced population growth. The former regions had the highest growth rate for rural areas in Japan, and the latter regions, the highest for urban areas. By province, Shimotsuke, Kōzuke, Musashi, Iwaki, and Sagami led the nation in that order; and all of these provinces lay in the east. Moreover, the major centers of Japan's export-oriented industries—sericulture, silk reeling, and tea—were also located in the east. Statistics for the twelve provinces of Iwaki, Iwashiro, Uzen, Kōzuke, Musashi, Sagami, Kaga, Kai, Shinano, Hida, Mino, and Tajima show that in 1882 the per-villager production of raw silk and silk thread accounted for 20 percent of the total value of agricultural output. Except for Tajima, all twelve lay in the east.[37]

By comparing these eleven eastern silk-producing provinces and the eleven provinces that lay in the Sanyō and Shikoku regions, we get markedly different pictures of population change. In nine of the eleven Sanyō and Shikoku provinces, the value of ordinary agricultural products (rice and other foodstuffs) per person accounted for more than 75 percent of total agricultural output. Table 11.1 shows the rates of population change for the two regions between 1872 and 1885 as well as their respective per capita values for silk-related production and ordinary agricultural production (cereals and foodstuffs). We should keep in mind that the statistics for agricultural production used here are by no means highly reliable and that they do not include the villagers' earnings from non-agricultural by-employments. Nevertheless, it is clear that in the silk-producing provinces, not only did the value of silk production account for a much greater percentage of total agricultural output than in Sanyō

---

[37] On the value of agricultural production, see Nōmushō nōmukyoku, ed., *Meiji jūgonen nōsanhyō* (Tokyo: Meiji bunken shiryō kankōkai, Meiji zenki sangyō hattatsu shi shiryō, 1965 reprint of 1882 ed.), *bessatsu 5*. For village population, I have used Sambō Hombu, ed., *Kyōbuseihyō Meiji jūninen*, 2 vols. (Kyoto: Yanagihara shoten, 1978 reprint of 1879 ed.). I considered every administrative unit of 5,000 persons or more to be an "urban area" or "city" (*toshi*) and subtracted these urban populations in my estimates for each province.

TABLE 11.1
Population Growth and Per Capita Agricultural Production, 1872-1185

Province	Growth Rate	Food Production		Silk Production	
		%	yen	%	yen
SILK-PRODUCING AREAS					
Iwaki	22.0	66.6	8.80	26.5	3.51
Iwashiro	18.3	54.7	9.63	41.0	7.22
Uzen	12.6	74.8	8.82	25.0	2.95
Kōzuke	24.8	31.7	6.83	65.4	14.08
Musashi	23.9	68.7	12.05	21.9	3.85
Sagami	19.3	70.5	8.04	23.0	2.63
Kaga	12.8	67.4	10.86	22.1	3.57
Kai	17.1	61.4	9.48	33.9	5.23
Shinano	15.0	53.4	9.30	42.6	7.43
Hida	14.6	66.3	19.44	32.6	9.56
Mino	18.0	67.0	6.67	23.0	2.29
AVERAGE	18.0	62.0		32.5	
(Average income per capita)	(16.47)		(9.99)		(5.67)
SANYŌ AND SHIKOKU					
Mimasaka	11.9	82.9	6.36	1.3	0.10
Bizen	7.5	78.5	10.95	0.3	0.05
Bitchū	12.8	83.9	6.83	0.9	0.08
Bingo	14.2	77.8	6.61	0.2	0.02
Aki	13.9	76.5	6.59	0.1	0.01
Suō	9.9	76.2	6.98	0.3	0.03
Nagato	8.5	93.0	8.52	0.2	0.02
Awa	11.9	65.1	7.49	3.0	0.35
Sanuki	15.3	74.3	9.12	—	—
Iyo	14.5	84.5	5.95	0.7	0.05
Tosa	4.8	81.0	7.57	1.2	0.12
AVERAGE	11.4	79.5		0.7	
(Average income per capita)	(9.57)		(7.54)		(0.07)

and Shikoku, but the per capita value of food production was also higher than in Sanyō and Shikoku.

To a certain extent this contrast stems from the spread in food prices between these two regions, since interregional differences in rice prices were great during the 1880s. In the silk-producing provinces as a whole,

the average price of rice per *koku* was 7.4 yen; in the six Kantō and
Tōsan provinces, it was as high as 8.4 yen. But in Sanyō and Shikoku,
the price averaged 6.4 yen. In the Japan Sea coastal provinces, the price
was roughly 4.2 yen per *koku*; in consuming areas of the Pacific coast,
it was 7 to 8 yen. Given these regional price variations, it seems that the
higher cost of food products in the silk-producing regions was related
not only to proximity to the Tokyo market, but also to increased demand
caused by rapid population growth and by growing purchasing power.

These investigations allow us to draw the following tentative conclusions. First, sometime between 1846 and 1872, the rate of population
increase for eastern Japan surpassed that for western Japan. Second, this
spurt in population growth rates was most pronounced in eastern silk-
producing provinces.

A REGIONAL COMPARISON

In this section we will compare the early Meiji demographic development of two selected areas that had displayed significantly different
patterns of population change during the Tokugawa period, particularly
in the eighteenth century. Of course, comparative analyses of this type
must be conducted for many other areas as well, but limitations of time
and space force us to focus on these two regions of marked contrast.

One area, Kōzuke and Shimotsuke provinces, lies in northern Kantō
and constitutes the modern prefectures of Gumma and Tochigi; the other
area, Bingo and Aki provinces, is located in the Sanyō region and forms
present-day Hiroshima prefecture.[38] I chose these two areas because 1)
both had roughly the same size population at the beginning of the nineteenth century—852,000 for Kōzuke-Shimotsuke and 889,000 for Bingo-
Aki—according to the *bakufu* survey of 1804; 2) these eastern and western areas displayed contrasting patterns of population change in the
Tokugawa and Meiji periods, as shown on Maps 11.2 and 11.3; and 3)
provincial and prefectural boundaries coincide in both areas, which allows
us to link their respective Tokugawa and Meiji statistics.

Between 1721 and 1846, the population of Kōzuke-Shimotsuke fell a
full 29 percent, from 1,130,000 to 807,000—an annual decrease of 0.2
percent. During the same period, in contrast, the population of Bingo-
Aki rose 34 percent, from 682,000 to 915,000—an annual increase of
more than 0.2 percent.[39] As noted earlier, the population loss in Kōzuke-

[38] These areas are abbreviated "KS Area" and "BA Area," respectively, in Figures 11.5-
11.8 and Table 11.2.
[39] On source materials for the Tokugawa period, see fn. 20, above.

Shimotsuke, the area of greatest population decline in the nation, was caused by bad weather in the eighteenth century and by heavy out-migration to Edo. Even within the limited interval of 1822-1846, Kōzuke-Shimotsuke suffered a 5.3 percent population loss, while Bingo-Aki enjoyed an 8.9 percent gain. As revealed in Figure 11.5, the population of the BA Area was definitely on the upswing and, if not for the Tempō mortality crisis of 1837-1838, would have grown 0.4 percent annually during this interval, which is a fairly high sustained growth rate for a preindustrial society.[40]

But from 1872 on, the wide spread in population figures for these two regions rapidly began to close.[41] Between 1872 and 1885, Bingo-Aki registered a population increase of 14 percent, or 0.9 percent annually—which is by no means low, even when early Meiji underregistration is taken into consideration. On the other hand, Kōzuke-Shimotsuke recorded an astounding 25.6 percent increase, or 1.7 percent annually, during the same period. According to *bakufu* surveys, the Bingo-Aki population had overtaken that of Kōzuke-Shimotsuke sometime between

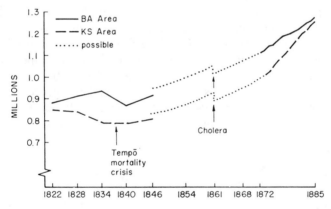

Figure 11.5. Population Trends in KS (Kōzuke-Shimotsuke) and BA (Bingo-Aki) Areas, 1822-1885

[40] Any direct linkage of the figures for 1846 with those for 1872 (see Figure 11.5) is purely speculative. To do this, I added the estimated unreported population to the 1846 figure, and arbitrarily set the death rate from the 1861 cholera epidemic at 5 percent. The estimates of unreported population for 1846 were derived from statistics compiled by status (*mibun*) in 1881; these amount to 4 and 5 percent, respectively, for the Kōzuke-Shimotsuke and Bingo-Aki areas. I also assumed that there was no change in their rates of population increase between 1846 and 1872 except for the year 1861. Of course, these presuppositions must be verified by future town- and village-level studies, but population age-structures (to be discussed below) lend credence to such assumptions.

[41] On source materials for the Meiji period, see fn. 9, above.

1804 and 1822; yet we now see that by 1885 the two areas had roughly the same number of inhabitants. And if figures for migrating populations (discussed below) are added, Kōzuke-Shimotsuke has clearly overtaken Bingo-Aki once again.

Precisely when did this unusual population growth in Kōzuke-Shimotsuke begin? Statistics for 1885, the first year for which province-by-province quinquennial age structures are known, provide a clue, for they permit us to compare population age-structures in the two areas. (See Figure 11.6.) The decrease in 46-to-50-year-olds and 21-to-25-year-olds in Bingo-Aki indicates the damage inflicted by mortality crises in 1837-1838 and 1861. Although there are no pronounced drops in the Kōzuke-Shimotsuke age structures, the KS Area has higher (by 1.3 percent) component ratios than Bingo-Aki for 6-to-10-year-olds and 1-to-5-year-olds. If we assume that there was no great difference in child mortality rates between the two areas, this last discrepancy points to the emergence of a high birth rate in Kōzuke-Shimotsuke, beginning from about 1875.

As mentioned earlier, provincial and prefectural vital statistics are available from 1877, but their reliability is by no means great. Figure 11.7 drawn up from those vital statistics, shows that although there clearly was a difference in crude birth rates between the two areas, their crude death rates were not far apart. But these figures are inconceivably low, to be sure. To obtain more precise statistics on births, I compiled ratios of the number of females of childbearing age to the number of births for the respective areas, which also permitted me to address general fertility. Unfortunately, age differentials for 1880-1883 are different from those for 1884-1885, so I could not obtain consecutive statistics. Therefore, I

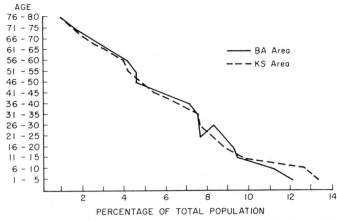

Figure 11.6. Age Components in KS (Kōzuke-Shimotsuke) and BA (Bingo-Aki) Areas, 1885

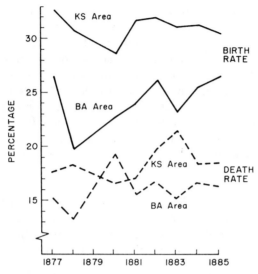

Figure 11.7.   Crude Birth and Death Rates in KS (Kōzuke-Shimotsuke) and BA (Bingo-Aki) Areas, 1877-1885

sought to determine ratios of the number of females aged 20-49 to the number of births for the period 1880-1883, and of the number of females aged 20-39 to the number of births for 1884-1885. The averages for 1880-1883 were 0.158 for Kōzuke-Shimotsuke, 0.124 for Bingo-Aki, and 0.125 for the nation as a whole. Averages for 1884-1885 were 0.216 for Kōzuke-Shimotsuke, 0.177 for Bingo-Aki, and 0.178 for the nation as a whole. Thus we see that Bingo-Aki averages were virtually the same as national averages, but that those for Kōzuke-Shimotsuke were 26 and 21 percent higher, which shows that fertility clearly was high in the KS Area.

One further factor behind population change—a social factor—should be discussed. This has to do with in-migrating and out-migrating populations as they appear in domicile registers. Needless to say, when one area has a greater number of register entries and in-migrants than it has register deletions and out-migrants, that area in theory should be taking people away from other areas. But in actuality, the number of out-migrants never equals that of in-migrants as they should when national totals are made from register counts. For example, on January 1, 1884, there were 520,000 in-migrants and 290,000 out-migrants. But there was little difference in the register entries and register deletions—both were about 110,000. We should not lose sight of this statistical shortcoming when assessing the social changes in population shown in Table 11.2.

Note that there were more register entries and legally recognized in-migrants coming into Kōzuke-Shimotsuke than there were persons leaving that area. For Bingo-Aki, on the other hand, out-migration was greater than in-migration. But we should note that the population turnover thus produced was not of significant size: it was less than the turnover produced by natural causes. Thus, there was not much difference between the "legally domiciled population" (*honseki jinkō*) and the "resident population" (*genjū jinkō*) in this period. Yet, as Table 11.2 shows, when we compare "resident population" figures for the two areas, we find that Kōzuke-Shimotsuke had already surpassed Bingo-Aki by the beginning of 1884.

The reader no doubt has already guessed the causes of this rapid population increase in the Kōzuke-Shimotsuke area. According to agricultural output statistics for both areas in 1882, the per capita value of agricultural output in Kōzuke was 21.5 yen; in Shimotsuke, 10.6 yen.[42] When we consider that the national average for this year was 11.9 yen

TABLE 11.2
Population Indices for Kōzuke-Shimotsuke (KS) and
Bingo-Aki (BA) Areas, 1884

	KS Area	BA Area
Legally domiciled population	1,246,151	1,262,561
Births	39,043	32,142
In-registered	5,338	2,325
Deaths	23,088	21,271
Out-registered	4,411	3,634
Total entries	45,417	36,227
Total deletions	27,830	25,326
SUBTOTAL	+ 17,587	+ 10,901
In-migration	27,338	2,745
Out-migration	9,966	6,159
SUBTOTAL	+ 17,372	− 3,774
Resident population	1,263,523	1,258,787

NOTE: All changes occurred in 1883. "Legally domiciled population" = *honseki jinkō*; "resident population" = *genjū jinkō*.

[42] See fn. 38, above.

(s.d. + 3.8 yen), we see that, in contrast, Kōzuke's figure is extremely high. Moreover, the figure for Kōzuke, when broken down, shows that the value of ordinary agricultural production (mainly cereals and other foodstuffs) was 6.8 yen, or 32 percent of the total, while that for specialized agricultural production (raw materials for industry) was 14.7 yen, or 68 percent of the total. Of these specialized products, the value of silk thread and raw silk output was 14.1 yen, accounting for 65 percent of total agricultural output. No similar example can be found elsewhere in Japan.

By way of contrast, in Bingo-Aki the average per capita value of agricultural output was 8.6 yen. Ordinary agricultural production accounted for 77 percent of total output, specialized agricultural production, 23 percent. Rice made up approximately 60 percent of the former production figure and comprised 49 percent of total agricultural production in the area. In Kōzuke, the price of rice was 8.6 yen per *koku*; in Aki, 6.1 yen. In Kōzuke, the amount of rice produced per farmer was 0.53 *koku*; in Aki, 0.69 *koku*; and on the national average, 0.99 *koku*. The value of rice production per farmer, however, was another matter, with Kōzuke showing 4.6 yen to Aki's 4.3 yen.

Figure 11.8 shows trends in sex ratios for the two areas.[43] In 1750, the first year for which figures are available, the sex ratio for Kōzuke-Shimotsuke was 123.5 (females = 100), but by 1846 it had dropped sharply, to 106.5. On the other hand, the sex ratio for Bingo-Aki increased slightly, from 104.8 to 106.5, during the same period. In Kōzuke-Shimotsuke, population decline was combined with a lowering of the sex ratio: the male population fell to approximately 67 percent of its original

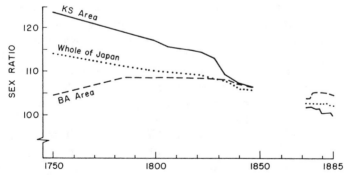

Figure 11.8. Sex Ratio Trends in KS (Kōzuke-Shimotsuke) and BA (Bingo-Aki) Areas, 1750-1885

[43] Statistics for sex ratios derive from source materials listed in fn. 20, above.

size during this period; the decline in the female population was limited to about 20 percent.

At present it is impossible to ascertain just what caused this decline. In general, the sex ratio for central Japan during the late Tokugawa period remained at a normal level, while in the Kantō and Tōhoku regions, and in Shikoku and Kyūshū, it fell from a high to a normal level.[44] No single factor can explain the changes that occurred in the Tokugawa sex ratio as well as the diverse population changes that took place simultaneously thoughout Japan. Rather, the answer lies in the changing position of women in society and in the family, in the rising value of women's labor, and in the declining mortality rate for females during pregnancy and childbirth. These changes, moreover, took place according to regional time lags during the Tokugawa period—beginning and taking hold earliest in central Japan, and extending to remoter areas by the early eighteenth century. These changes then spread to all parts of the nation more or less evenly after the period when population data became available.

Sex ratios in the early Meiji era for our two areas are as follows. In 1872, Kōzuke-Shimotsuke had a ratio of 101.9 and Bingo-Aki 104.1; the national average was 103.0. In 1885, the Kōzuke-Shimotsuke ratio was 100.0; Bingo-Aki's was 104.9; and the national average was 102.4. During the twenty-six year statistical gap from 1846 to 1872, then, there was a turnabout in the sex ratios for the two areas. Figure 11.8 shows that in 1750 the sex ratios for the two areas were far apart—one far above and the other far below the national average. But like the original difference in population size between these two areas, this wide divergence in sex ratios gradually narrowed. By 1830, both were about the same as the national average, and by the early Meiji era, both were slightly below it. All of this indicates a turnabout in the relative standings held by the two areas with respect to sex ratios. Perhaps most impressive is the rapid decline of the sex ratio in Kōzuke-Shimotsuke after 1828. Most likely the sex ratio of surviving babies had become balanced a few decades before that year; or there may have been a lowering of the death rate in women (which had been high until 1828). In any case, something important must have occurred to lower the sex ratio. At this point, I can offer only the following observations. The sex ratio in Kōzuke-Shimotsuke became moderate completely apart from any change in population size. If we are to interpret this fact as resulting from the "rational"

---

[44] See Hayami Akira, "Tokugawa kōki jinkō no chiikiteki tokusei," *Mita gakkai zasshi*, vol. 64, no. 8 (1971), pp. 67-80. Recently, Thomas C. Smith, Susan B. Hanley and Kozo Yamamura, and Carl C. Mosk have entered the debate on changes in the Tokugawa sex ratio.

behavior of peasants, who made up the vast majority of Japan's population, we must first come up with an explanation as to why the balancing of the sex ratio was a "rational" occurrence.

CONCLUSION

We have come to see that Japan's national population began increasing from the start of the nineteenth century and that, after the 1820s, this trend of stable growth held true for virtually all localities. The mortality crises of 1837-1838 and 1861 cannot be overlooked; yet, despite these temporary setbacks, the population grew at an annual rate of 0.3 to 0.4 percent.

Regional variations did exist; but on the whole Japan's population continued to rise during the statistical gap from 1846 to 1872. Toward the end of this quarter-century, those regions where the sericulture and silk-reeling industries had developed recorded an annual population growth on the order of 1 percent. This growth probably stemmed mainly from an increased birth rate; but a lowered sex ratio or, in other words, a higher percentage of females to males (beginning in the 1830s) may also have been a contributory factor.

What do these findings tell us about the relationship between population and the economy, a problem introduced at the beginning of this chapter? No firm conclusions can be arrived at until many, many more empirical studies have been conducted; at this time, I can submit the following very tentative answer.

During the Tokugawa period, there was moderate population growth in the nation's most economically advanced region—the west—particularly in areas surrounding the Inland Sea, where opportunities were plentiful for nonagricultural by-employments in cottage industries. The Hokuriku area, where rice was cultivated successfully as a cash crop, also enjoyed moderate growth. The apparent "stagnation" in aggregate national population figures was a purely chance occurrence caused by exogenously induced population decreases in Tōhoku and northern Kantō that offset gains in western Japan and Hokuriku. The nation's most highly urbanized areas—southern Kantō and the Kinai—failed to grow, or even declined slightly in population, owing to the negative feedback function. Considered together, these facts suggest that economic development and population increase in Tokugawa farming villages went hand in hand: population stagnancy was definitely *not* a precondition of economic development.

I wish to reserve judgment as to whether or not the demographic transition theory applies to the period under examination, since the early Meiji birth rate did in fact rise in those regions where export-oriented industries developed. Even so, no proper conclusion can be drawn until we take into consideration the period after 1890, when industrialization began in earnest—and such an inquiry lies beyond the scope of this study.

Japan's population increase, which began at the start of the nineteenth century and picked up speed after the 1850s, stemmed mainly from a rising birth rate. Yet this does not necessarily mean that the death rate did not fall. In many of the villages that I have surveyed, mortality did in fact decline after the 1840s.[45] However, empirical studies are too few to be able to draw any definite conclusion on this matter, and in any case, the short-term death rate jumped abnormally during the mortality crises of 1837-1838 and 1861. Japan was free from the horrors of pestilence only after the 1870s, when it imported modern science and hygiene from the West. Prior to that, Japan's population increase was interrupted by exogenously induced crises on a few occasions, but the latent potential for increase surfaced undeniably in the nineteenth century.

What phrase should we use to describe the pattern of population increase that took place in nineteenth-century Japan—an increase whose causes have yet to be identified fully? Western Japan's population had been growing at approximately 0.2 percent annually since 1822; it did not begin increasing suddenly in the nineteenth century. So it was for the nation as a whole. Japan's national population was on the upswing during the late Tokugawa period; this increase only accelerated in the nineteenth century. I believe that the emergence of the stem family as the unit of agricultural production in Tokugawa Japan provided Japan with the potential for population growth. Therefore, growth was *to be expected* in the Tokugawa population; indeed, the *absence* of population increase would have required explanation. When we consider the low ratio of urban population and the impressive rural economic expansion that took place in areas where population increased, we cannot but conclude that moderate population growth in farming villages went hand in hand with economic development in this preindustrial society. During

---

[45] In Yokouchi village, Shinano province, the crude death rate was 19.5 per thousand from 1826 to 1850, and 17.5 per thousand from 1851 to 1871. In Nishijo village, Mino province, the death rate fell from an average of 21 per thousand before 1830 to 16 per thousand after 1845-1850. See Akira Hayami, "Demographic Aspects of a Village in Tokugawa Japan," in Paul Deprez, ed., *Population and Economics* (Winnipeg: University of Manitoba Press, 1970), pp. 109-125, as well as Hayami Akira, "Nōshū Nishijō mura no jinkō shiryō," in *Kenkyū kiyō Shōwa 47–nendo* (Tokyo: Tokugawa rinsei shi kenkyūsho, 1973). From just two village surveys, of course, nothing can be said about Tokugawa Japan as a whole. Scores of similar studies must be accumulated.

the statistically desolate quarter-century from 1846 to 1872, this combination of moderate population increase accompanied by economic development spread throughout Japan, spurred on by irreversible domestic commercial advances plus the appearance of export-oriented industries after the opening of the treaty ports. After 1872, this trend became the sustained population growth that continues to our day.

Proto-Industrial Origins of
Japanese Capitalism

DAVID L. HOWELL

Proto-industrialization has been defined as a transitional phase on the way to modern, factory industrialization, characterized by "the development of rural regions in which a large part of the population lived entirely or to a considerable extent from industrial mass production for inter-regional and international markets" (Kriedte, Medick, and Schlumbohm [KMS] 1981:6). This article will use proto-industrialization as a lens through which to reexamine a number of issues in early modern Japanese history, including the relationship between commercial agriculture and rural industry, the role of the state in economic development, and the economic geography of the late Tokugawa period. Perhaps most importantly, I hope by looking at proto-industrialization to reach a better understanding of the transition from the feudalism of the Tokugawa era to the capitalist development of the Meiji period and beyond.

The past decades have been good to the Tokugawa period. Raised from the depths of feudal stagnation, it is now appreciated as a time of cultural awakening and intellectual vitality. Its economy is looking better all the time, too, thanks to the efforts of historians and demographers who have uncovered clear evidence of a rising standard of living during the latter part of the period. "Revisionists"—the term hardly seems appropriate anymore—have demonstrated that per capita incomes grew during the century leading up to the Meiji Restoration. This growth resulted when the population stopped rising while peasants' access to cash income increased through activities such as commercial agriculture, rural by-employments, and manufacturing. Indeed, so convincing is this new picture of the Tokugawa period that E. L. Jones (1988) counts it—along with early modern Western Europe and Song China—as one of only three readily demonstrable cases in world history of what he calls "intensive" economic growth before industrialization.

Saying that the late Tokugawa economy was growing is one thing; assessing the significance of that growth is another question entirely. In 1965, more than a decade before the Tokugawa period's historiographical rehabilitation, Kazushi Ohkawa

David L. Howell is Assistant Professor of History at the University of Texas at Austin.

Earlier versions of this article were presented at the 1990 Joint Meeting of the Western and Southwestern Conferences of the Association for Asian Studies and the 1991 Annual Meeting of the Association for Asian Studies. The author would like to thank Gary D. Allinson, Myron Gutmann, Edward J. R. Rhoads, Kären Wigen, and an anonymous reviewer for the *JAS* for their helpful comments and suggestions. Research for this article was supported in part by a grant from the University Research Institute of the University of Texas at Austin.

The Journal of Asian Studies 51, no. 2 (May 1992):269–286.
© 1992 by the Association for Asian Studies, Inc.

and Henry Rosovsky (1965:58) dismissed all evidence of economic development before the Meiji period as nothing more than "isolated islands of modernity" typical of "backward countries" like Japan. Since then, however, scholars' assessments have been decidedly more upbeat. Susan B. Hanley and Kozo Yamamura (1977; Yamamura 1973; Hanley 1983) see cultivators as rational actors in control of their economic lives; for them the very fact of growth says much about Japan's successes after 1868. For others, such as Thomas C. Smith (1986), Tokugawa economic development fostered attitudes toward work and time management that prepared the Japanese peasantry for the discipline of the factory. Hayami Akira (1989) takes a similar approach when he argues that an "industrious revolution," predicated upon heavy investments of labor (rather than capital) in production, occurred in late Tokugawa Japan. In Hayami's view, the commercialization of the agricultural economy gave peasants greater independence, but at the same time forced them to work longer and harder to raise the productivity of their landholdings.

Each of these approaches is instructive, but questions persist concerning *structural* changes linking the Tokugawa peasant economy to Meiji industrialization. One way to find such structural changes is to look at rural industry and its role in the economic development of nineteenth-century Japan. The concept of proto-industrialization, originally articulated by European historians, provides a useful framework to address this problem.

Historians of proto-industrialization in Europe have yet to reach a consensus on the exact relationship between proto-industry and capitalism,[1] but it is clear that "proto-industrialization preceded factory industrialization where it occurred, and paved the way for it" (Mendels 1972:246). Proto-industrial development did not, however, lead inevitably to full factory industrialization, as a proto-industrial region could stagnate or even "de-industrialize" (KMS 1981:147–48).

The proto-industrialization model includes an important demographic element (Gutmann 1988). Proto-industrial regions in Europe typically saw an increase in population as people married earlier and had more children once the value of household labor was not constrained by the size of a family's landholdings. That is, people could support larger families on less land because of the opportunities for non-agricultural employment. Ironically, the economic growth engendered by proto-industrialization was often accompanied by a *decline* in living standards because incomes, while much higher than in an agricultural economy, did not keep pace with the growth in household size (Mendels 1972:252). For this reason, we cannot sanguinely assume, as many analyses of Japan seem to, that economic growth necessarily translated into better lives for people in the countryside.

The remainder of this article will present a brief overview of one example of proto-industrial development in nineteenth-century Japan, the herring fishery of

---

[1]See the discussion in KMS 1981:1–11. For the sake of clarity and consistency, let us use both "feudalism" and "capitalism" in a Marxian sense here. The feudal mode of production is characterized, according to Rodney Hilton 1978:30, by an "exploitative relationship between landowners and subordinated peasants, in which the surplus beyond subsistence of the latter, whether in direct labour or in rent in kind or in money, is transferred under coercive sanction to the former." Conversely, capitalism, according to Maurice Dobb 1947:7, is a mode of production characterized by "the concentration of ownership of the means of production in the hands of a class, consisting of only a minor section of society, and the consequential emergence of a propertyless class for whom the sale of their labour-power was their only source of livelihood." It is important to add that the presence of isolated instances of capitalist production does not mean that society has undergone a fundamental transformation to capitalism; only when capitalist relations of production predominate can society as a whole be characterized as capitalist.

Hokkaido. The fishery produced commercial fertilizer for sale in Honshu on a large scale throughout the nineteenth and early twentieth centuries. It will then turn to a discussion of some of the critical issues raised by the application of the proto-industrialization model to Hokkaido specifically and to Japan in general, particularly those concerning the links between Tokugawa proto-industrialization and Meiji capitalism.

Proto-Industry and Capitalism in Hokkaido

The Hokkaido fishery is an attractive case study of proto-industrialization for a number of reasons. First, Hokkaido, better than any other region in Japan, fits the proto-industrialization paradigm of rural industry for distant trade. No domestic trade was more distant than that between Hokkaido and central Honshu, and no people more dependent on industrial production than those of Hokkaido, who lived under climatic conditions too harsh to support much agriculture before the mid-Meiji period.

Second, unlike silk and cotton textile manufacturing or other important early industries, fertilizer production in Hokkaido was not affected by Japan's opening to trade with the West after 1854.[2] Technology and labor were native and demand and supply remained domestic until the fishery's collapse after World War II. The fishery therefore provides an opportunity to trace indigenous Japanese developments, and thus strengthens the case for proto-industrialization as a model of economic development not bound to the European experience. This speaks to Frank Perlin's (1985:386–87) call for a conceptualization of proto-industrialization as a tool to analyze historical change rather than simply as a euphemism to describe the phenomenon of rural manufacturing for long-distance trade.

Finally, it was those peculiarly "proto-industrial" features of the fishery in the early nineteenth century that contributed to the emergence of capitalism in Hokkaido. That is, fertilizer production for distant markets gave rise to an economy only partially subordinated to the institutions of the local political authority, the Matsumae domain. Capitalism emerged through a dialectical process of change in the organization of production within the fishery and domain-level institutional response.

Hokkaido's commercial herring fishery originated in the early eighteenth century as merchants, based mostly in central Honshu, responded to a growing demand for herring-meal fertilizer (*nishin shimekasu*) among cultivators in the Kinai and elsewhere.[3] During the Tokugawa period, production took two basic forms: the family fishery, in which a multitude of independent petty fishers worked with household members and perhaps a few hired hands; and the contract fishery (*basho ukeoisei*), in which merchants specially licensed by the Matsumae domain (or the bakufu) enjoyed a variety of economic and administrative powers, particularly the right to supervise large-scale fishing operations using mostly Ainu labor. The family fishery was Matsumae's answer to a peasantry of smallholders, while the contract fishery was an integral part of the domain institutional structure insofar as it evolved out of

---

[2]Saitō Osamu's (1985) discussion of Japanese proto-industrialization, which is summarized below, is framed largely in terms of the different courses taken by silk-reeling areas of northern Kantō and Shinano and cotton-spinning regions in the Kinai after foreign trade was reopened.

[3]The following discussion of the evolution of the Hokkaido fishery is based on Howell 1989a: chaps. 2–5, although the attempt to frame the material in terms of proto-industrialization is new.

272 DAVID L. HOWELL

the official trade between the daimyo and his leading retainers and the native people.

After the Meiji Restoration, the contract-fishery operators (*basho ukeoinin*) lost their privileges and the entire fishery was opened to exploitation by anyone who cared to participate, although production remained divided between family and entrepreneurial fisheries. The period from about 1870 to 1900 saw a rapid expansion of the fishery, fed in no small part by strong demand for herring by-products in Honshu. Indeed, by the latter part of the nineteenth century, Hokkaido was by far Japan's most important source of commercial fertilizer. However, overfishing—the result of intensive production with increasingly efficient technology—depleted the stocks so that catches declined steadily throughout the first half of the twentieth century. The last herring run took place in 1958, although boats operating in deep water offshore continue to haul small catches to this day.

The Hokkaido fishery was a large but hardly heavy industry: at its peak up to a quarter-million people processed several hundred thousand tons of fish into fertilizer each year, yet the technology remained fairly simple and the capital requirements, while well beyond the means of ordinary fishers, were small compared to highly mechanized enterprises. Even as the fishery expanded and the organization of production changed, moreover, the mechanics of transforming large shoals of fish into large bales of fertilizer remained remarkably constant. Regardless of the size of the individual fishing operation, labor was divided between skilled fishers, who piloted the boats and worked the nets, and semiskilled or unskilled workers, who hauled the fish onshore and processed it into fertilizer. Processing the fish was a simple if malodorous procedure: herring was boiled, pressed, and dried into a mealy state, then packed into straw bales for shipment.

The only significant change in the way fish were caught and processed came with the introduction of a large and efficient but expensive net known as the pound trap (*tateami*) in the 1850s. The salient feature of the pound trap for our purposes was that it required at least fifteen to twenty (mostly unskilled) workers to operate, and was thus ideally suited to capitalist production. Conversely, household fishers used small, easily manipulable gill nets (*sashiami*), a set of which could be worked by just two or three skilled men. It is important to stress that, differences in scale notwithstanding, the final product in either case was the same, and was marketed as such.

The fishery underwent a period of rapid development in the middle decades of the nineteenth century. Capital began to move from the realm of circulation—that is, the buying and selling of herring-meal fertilizer—into the realm of production. By the end of the century, structural change within the fishery, bolstered by the active sponsorship of the Meiji state, had resulted in a fully developed capitalism in which small, independent proprietors found themselves increasingly vulnerable to the economic and political power of entrepreneurs.

Entrepreneurs were able to establish capitalist production in the fishery thanks to a confluence of developments in labor, technology, and capital allocation, all fed by vibrant demand for fertilizer. Demand for herring meal in markets throughout Japan grew steadily during the first half of the nineteenth century, partly because the growth of the agricultural economy had led more farmers to use commercial fertilizers, and partly because herring meal's main competitor, dried sardines, had become prohibitively expensive.

With steadily expanding demand for herring, fishers had a strong incentive to raise production, but many found it difficult to do so because of a paucity of labor. Contract fishers had traditionally relied on Ainu labor, but its availability declined as the native population was ravaged by diseases such as smallpox and measles.

Independent fishers, prohibited by the Matsumae domain from employing Ainu workers, drew upon a small pool of non-Ainu wage workers in southern Hokkaido. Formally free, wage labor entered the fishery in large numbers for the first time after the Tenpō famine hit northeastern Honshu between 1832 and 1838. Hunger drove peasants to Hokkaido, where, thanks to the herring trade, food from western Japan was available. While Tōhoku workers had always been employed in the fishery, the influx during the Tenpō famine established a pattern of seasonal and permanent migration that was to last well into the twentieth century. Contract fishery operators hired some of the newcomers, but many others found employment with independent fishers based in southern Hokkaido, where they became the core of a seasonal proletariat of fishery workers.

Once wage labor became readily available, fishers were motivated to develop fishing gear that could make efficient use of that labor. Contractors had experimented with various types of large-scale gear intermittently since the late eighteenth century, but attempts to use large nets had inevitably met with the opposition of small fishers, who feared for the resource and hence for their livelihood. Lacking a supply of labor to work the nets, the early experiments were doomed to failure. Once the Tenpō famine made labor available, however, contractors—and, for the first time, the larger independent fishers—had an incentive to push for the use of pound traps over the opposition of small fishers. The Matsumae domain supported the small fishers, but the bakufu, which assumed administration over most of Hokkaido in 1854, permitted pound-trap use, thus clearing the way for the emergence of a capitalist fishery under independent operators employing wage labor from Honshu.

The introduction of new technology alone was not enough to establish the capitalist mode of production in the fishery. Capitalists, after all, need capital. The two dozen or so contractors with fisheries on the west coast of Hokkaido had the capital to make good use of the new technology and labor, but very few of them were interested in investing in expanded production. Most were satisfied to use the privileges accorded to them by the Matsumae domain to profit from low-risk, high-yield ventures such as dealing in the wholesale fertilizer market, usury and supply lending, and—lowest risk and highest yield of all—collecting taxes and access fees from small fishers operating in areas under their control.

Given the conservatism of the contractors, capitalists in the fishery came instead from the ranks of independent fishers and even complete outsiders. All the burgeoning entrepreneurs needed was capital. In fact, it was already there, thanks to the demand for herring meal, but it had to be reallocated before capitalists could dominate the fishery. This occurred through a transformation of credit relations, in which capital, formerly parceled out to small fishers in the form of credit, was instead concentrated in the hands of a few entrepreneurs.

Small fishers in Hokkaido had long depended on supply merchants (*shikomi oyakata*) to provide them with advances of cash, food, and gear before each herring season. In return, the merchants claimed substantial interest and fees as well as first lien on the catch, which they bought below the prevailing market price. It was a lucrative livelihood for the merchants and, while exploitative (insofar as it undermined fishers' independence), met a real need within the fishing population.[4]

Supply lending did not disappear with the advent of the pound-trap fishery, but it did become a harsher institution. That is, whereas merchants in the past had

[4]Given the erratic and often seasonal nature of fishing, credit arrangements of this sort were quite common. See Kalland 1981 and 1984 for discussions of credit systems financed by merchants and the Fukuoka domain, respectively, and Sider 1986 for a description of credit institutions in the Newfoundland cod fishery that resembled those of Hokkaido.

often carried defaulting fishers for a long time—years or even decades—without foreclosing, after the mid-1850s they became stricter in their enforcement of loan contracts. The reasons for this hardened attitude are simple. Before the introduction of wage labor on a large scale, it was usually to the supply lender's advantage to continue to provide credit to defaulting clients, first, to ensure a steady supply of fertilizer from those clients (which the merchant would then market for a profit) and, second, to allow for the possibility that the clients would be able to repay the principal of their loans over time. With the advent of the pound trap, however, the supply merchant had a new option: to foreclose on defaulting fishers and reduce them to wage labor in a capitalist fishery—run either by the merchant himself or by another client with an operation large enough to convert to pound traps. Capital that had once been directed into the household fishery was redirected to more efficient capitalist enterprises, and formerly independent small fishers were hired for skilled positions in those enterprises. By no means did every merchant exercise this option at every opportunity; supply lending persisted in various forms into the twentieth century and, for even the largest fishers, credit was always a fact of life. Nonetheless, the emergence of a market for the labor of skilled fishers imperiled many marginal operators in southern Hokkaido.

The situation for small fishers worsened after 1868, for the Meiji state implemented a series of institutional changes that made it even more tempting for creditors to enforce contracts to the letter. The right to fish, which had previously been free to all comers, was gradually made into a commodity as exclusive access, first, to land to process fish and, later, to the sea itself, was granted to individual fishers. This made it extremely difficult for small operators to move about in search of good catches, as they had often done in the past; it left them even less able to pay their debts and hence more liable to suffer proletarianization, with the rest of their lives spent working for wages. Thus, ironically, the condition of small producers steadily declined even as the fishing economy grew rapidly in the late nineteenth century. Nevertheless, beleaguered though they were, family fishers did not completely disappear even after a century of steady decline.

The basic changes in labor, technology, and capital were effected before the Meiji Restoration, but the establishment of a Westward-looking state, eager for rapid economic growth, helped bring about the final transformation of the fishery. Aside from institutional changes, mentioned above, that made the right to fish a commodity, the new regime stripped the contract-fishery operators of their economic and administrative privileges, which diverted even more financial and human resources toward capitalist development, much of it directed by entrepreneurs with a background in commerce but not fishing. Moreover, the Meiji government's policies consistently put economic growth ahead of other considerations, so that any support dispossessed fishers got from the state in their efforts to avoid proletarianization came grudgingly at best.

Given the nature of the Hokkaido herring fishery, with production dispersed among hundreds of fishing grounds of unequal and unstable value, it is not surprising to learn that factory industrialization never took place. In the 1920s and 1930s, however, a surrogate for full industrialization did emerge in the factory ships that canned crab and salmon in the Sea of Okhotsk.[5] Unlike the comparatively small capitalist enterprises of Hokkaido, the factory ships were owned and operated by large, modern corporations based in Hakodate or Tokyo.

[5] For a discussion of the factory ships, see Howell 1989a:210–12. See also Kobayashi Takiji's (1973 [1929]) fictional account, Kani kōsen. The events in Kobayashi's account are mostly true, although they did not occur during a single voyage.

The factory ships' ties to the herring fishery were twofold. First, many of the entrepreneurs who made fortunes in the crab fishery had begun their careers in the herring fisheries of Hokkaido and Karafuto (southern Sakhalin). Thus, there was a certain continuity of both purpose and capital. Second, and more important, the work force was drawn from the same pool of poor, unskilled peasants from northeastern Honshu, and poor, skilled fishers from southern Hokkaido. These were men (and a few women) for whom the declining Hokkaido fishery no longer had any use, so they had little choice but to endure the long hours and arduous routine of the six-month voyages into Soviet waters. The pay was good, at least compared to what was available at home, but it was scant compensation for the danger and indignity the workers suffered. But the capitalist transformation of the fishing economy was complete and, as one veteran of the factory ships later recalled, "the time would come and there'd be no other way to make any money, so we all had to endure the hardship and go back" (Kuwabara 1987:26).

Proto-Industrialization, Capitalism and the Tokugawa Economy

The Hokkaido fishery stands out in the history of the Japanese economy because the fundamental transformation to capitalism was complete *before* the establishment of a regime dedicated to Western-style economic development. But the fishery, for all its precocity, was not an isolated "capitalist sprout." Rather, the development of the fishery during the late Tokugawa period was part of a broader process of proto-industrial development that affected social and economic relations throughout Japan. In the remainder of this article I will examine how the proto-industrialization model can help us better understand the development of the late Tokugawa economy in general and the Hokkaido fishery in particular. And since it is better to give than to receive, I will suggest ways that the Japanese experience can contribute to the refinement of the proto-industrialization model as it applies across societal boundaries.

The Hokkaido fishery was by no means the only, or even the best known, example of proto-industrial development in nineteenth-century Japan. The textile industry stands out in particular, but others included papermaking, sake and soy-sauce brewing, iron and other metalworking, and the processing of agricultural and marine products, such as tea, indigo, sugar, wax, vegetable oil, whale by-products, and a variety of fertilizers.[6] The historical significance of these industries is obscured by the course of Japanese development after the opening to the West in the 1850s. Factory industrialization did not occur as the result of natural evolution so much as through a deliberate policy of modernization implemented by a state anxious to emulate the more advanced West. Given the dramatic transformation of the Meiji years, it is natural enough to ascribe the origins of Japanese industrialization to the policies of the Meiji state. But overlooking the existing base of proto-industrial development restricts our understanding of Japan's rapid and successful transformation.

Application of the proto-industrial model to late Tokugawa Japan is not, however, without its pitfalls. Saitō Osamu, who has made the most extensive study of the problem to date (1985:168–69; see also Saitō 1983), concludes that the differences

[6]See Leupp 1989:500–45, for an overview of rural industries in Tokugawa Japan. See also a number of case studies: Hauser 1974; Howell 1989b; Kalland 1986; Nishikawa 1986; Saitō 1986; Smith 1969; Wigen 1990.

between Europe and Japan were such as to make the model basically inapplicable in the Japanese case, the widespread incidence of rural industry notwithstanding. Saitō (1985:197–205) sees three critical differences between the two cases. First, in Japan there was never a clear-cut distinction between agricultural and industrial regions. While some regions did rely heavily on rural industry, and others on grain production, it was not enough, in his view, to spark a fundamental transformation of the peasant economy. This was because the inseparability of agriculture and industry in the peasant household, as reflected in the sexual division of labor, inhibited regional specialization. Second, even in those regions with rural industry, Japan did not conform to the demographic model of European proto-industrialization, which predicts a drop in age at first marriage, leading to higher fertility and a decline in living standards. If anything, people in proto-industrial regions in Japan tended to marry later than those in agricultural ones, with the result that they benefited from the economic growth engendered by manufacturing. Saitō (1985:173) sees this as a function of the fact that proto-industrial development generally followed agricultural expansion, so that population densities were already high before the onset of proto-industrialization. This meant, third, that Japanese proto-industrial regions did not develop higher population densities than agricultural ones, and thus did not generate a large pool of dispossessed peasants vulnerable to proletarianization.

While Saitō's misgivings about the applicability of a European model of proto-industrialization to Japan are certainly compelling, they should not obscure the fact that rural industry was an important and widespread phenomenon in nineteenth-century Japan; Saitō himself says as much (1985:168). In fact, many of his objections can be accommodated by examining the political constraints placed upon the late Tokugawa economy, for the role of the state was critical in determining the degree and significance of rural industrialization in any given area. Before turning to a discussion of this problem, however, we must first locate proto-industrialization relative to commercialization and capitalism.

Proto-industrialization was distinct from the expansion of commercial agriculture. Whereas the growth of commercial agriculture changed the way things were bought and sold, but not the way they were produced, proto-industrialization facilitated the penetration of capital into the realm of production, thus—potentially, at least— leading to the emergence of capitalism. To be sure, commercialization affected the peasant economy in important ways: Thomas C. Smith (1959) has shown how the expansion of the money economy after the middle of the Tokugawa period weakened hereditary bonds of dependency and led to a restratification of society on the basis of wealth as village elites came to function as landlords, merchants, and moneylenders. Nevertheless, insofar as household rather than wage labor remained primary, the growth of commercial agriculture did not immediately affect the social relations of agricultural production. While rural industry could and sometimes did emerge in regions with highly commercialized agriculture—and often involved the processing of agricultural products—there was no necessary connection between the two; indeed, industrialization frequently proceeded more rapidly in regions without much commercial agriculture.[7]

---

[7]According to Mendels 1972:245, "Those [in continental Europe] who had remained isolated from market forces and those who had become fully specialized in commercial agriculture did not feel the necessity of turning to modern industry as much as those who had been depending on handicrafts." On the other hand, Gay L. Gullickson (1986:65), while conceding that "proto-industrialization may have occurred more often in subsistence farming or pastoral regions," argues that "seasonal unemployment and landlessness, not poor land, were the distinguishing features of proto-industrial regions."

But if proto-industry was qualitatively different from commercial agriculture, so, too, was it distinct from modern industry. Proto-industrialization, instead, occupied a sort of middle ground between the two. Peasants working in or near their homes provided the labor for rural industry, and most no doubt maintained a strong identity as tillers of the soil. Although such peasants were assuredly not an industrial proletariat, their participation in proto-industrial production did affect the household economy in profound ways.

Ultimately more important than the identity of the producers or the location of production, however, is the organization and purpose of production. As Jürgen Schlumbohm (KMS 1981:108) writes, "There exists . . . a basic distinction between the two forms of commodity production: either its goals are in principle limited to satisfying the needs of the producers, or its goals consist in the essentially unlimited maximization of profit." Peasant production is geared to the producer's subsistence, in the broadest sense of the word. That is, the market does no more for the peasant than to facilitate the exchange of commodities he cannot produce for himself. While the use of cash in exchange is certainly significant, it does not affect the fundamental nature of the transaction. In other words, the peasant uses money to obtain goods, and is thus distinct from the capitalist entrepreneur who uses money to make more money. With proto-industrialization, the economy goes beyond "mere" commercialization, as capital moves from the realm of circulation (the buying and selling of goods) into the realm of production (investment in tools, raw materials, and labor) for the first time, thereby opening the door to the possibility of capitalism and sustained economic growth.

The critical difference between commercialization and capitalism lies in the impact capitalism has on social relations. While commercialization refers to the widespread commodification of agricultural produce and other goods, under capitalism the last great commodity—people's labor-power—is bought and sold on a large scale and, for the first time, the organization of production becomes characterized by that buying and selling.

Proto-industrialization represents the nexus between commercialization and capitalism. To illustrate this point, let us return for a moment to Hokkaido. The division of the Tokugawa fishery into a mass of petty, independent producers, on the one hand, and a small group of fishing contractors who received administrative and economic privileges from the Matsumae domain, on the other hand, parallels an internal division within proto-industry between putting-out and manufactures, recently described by Gary Leupp (1989:500–8). Putting-out, in which a merchant provided raw materials, credit, and sometimes tools to a peasant who then engaged in handicraft production at home, was the most common form of proto-industrial production in both Europe and Japan. Its functional equivalent in Hokkaido was the supply-lending institution described above, in which merchants provided advances of cash, daily necessities, and gear to small fishers in return for exclusive marketing rights to the fishers' herring, in addition to interest and commissions. Insofar as the individual fisher had control over his productive activities and usually owned his means of production, the arrangement was not capitalist: the fisher sold fertilizer—not labor-power—to the merchant. The same could be said of other putting-out arrangements, making them akin to commercial agriculture (which often entailed credit relationships between cultivators and merchants).

Production at the contract fisheries, on the other hand, corresponded to manufactures, in which an entrepreneur brought peasant workers together at a single location, provided them with tools and raw materials, and oversaw their labor. Thus at contract fisheries, merchants supervised the fishing operations of Ainu and other laborers, to whom they provided boats, nets, and other equipment. Non-Ainu workers received a seasonal wage in cash; Ainu generally received commodities like rice, sake, tobacco, and ironware in lieu of a cash payment.

Manufactures differed from factory industrialization in two respects. First, there was relatively little division of labor within the manufactories (workers performed tasks similar to those performed by peasants engaged in putting-out arrangements at home) and, second, there was little or no mechanization. These differences aside, the manufactories were at least *superficially* capitalist enterprises in the sense that the workers sold their labor-power rather than some other commodity to their employer.[8]

I say *superficially* capitalist because the manufactories often emerged out of a close relationship between privileged merchants and feudal authorities. At the contract fisheries, for example, the merchants' control of land to process fish (tantamount under the circumstances to the right to fish) and their access to Ainu workers (who were not formally free to enter into a wage-contract) were both derived from their privileged position vis-à-vis the Matsumae domain.[9] Look beneath the veneer of apparently capitalist production and one finds merchants whose control over both the means of production and their workers' labor were linked so closely to the protection of the domain that once that protection was removed—as indeed it was after 1868—their operations ceased to be viable. In other words, the contract-fishery operators were "capitalists" who needed feudalism to survive.

But even if production at the contract fisheries was not "really" capitalist, there is no question that they established the model for capitalist production later emulated by entrepreneurs independent of the feudal regime. In that sense, the contractors played a critical role in the process of transformation—one typical of merchant capitalists in a declining feudal economy—by acting as a solvent of the old forms of production (see Fox-Genovese and Genovese 1983:6–7).

Proto-Industrialization and the Economic Geography of Nineteenth-Century Japan

The failure to distinguish between commercial agriculture and rural industry has resulted in an unfortunate rendering of the economic geography of late Tokugawa Japan. Economic historians commonly classify regions as "advanced" or "backward" based on the extent of commercial agriculture and the development of local markets. According to this view, central Honshu—particularly Osaka and the surrounding Kinai plain—is the archetypical advanced region, and the northeastern and southwestern peripheries of the country the most backward.[10] While this dichotomy

[8]It is worthwhile to note, however, that the merchant overseeing a putting-out operation was just as interested as the proto-factory operator in getting the surplus-value of peasant labor—rather than the use-value of the commodities being produced—and thus equally fulfilled a key criterion of capitalist production. In other words, Leupp's distinction between putting-out and manufactures is more valuable when looking at labor than when considering the purposes of production. See the discussion of the so-called manufactures debate among pre-World War II Japanese Marxist historians, and particularly the analysis of the work of Hattori Shisō in Hoston 1986:95–126.

[9]For an elaboration of these points, see Howell 1989a:41–65.

[10]Hanley and Yamamura 1977 organize their book in terms of this dichotomy, but in doing so follow common practice. For a discussion of the innovative aspects of their treatment of regional differences, see Wigen 1990:31–34.

works well when talking about markets, it unfortunately diverts attention from those "backward" areas where critical changes in the organization of production— the key to the development of capitalism—were occurring.

Rural districts in the Kinai, where commercial agriculture developed early and effectively, did see some proto-industrialization, but the impetus for industrial development was weak because villagers could easily participate in commercial agriculture to meet urban demand for foodstuffs (Saitō 1985:176). Conversely, proto-industry thrived in many ostensibly backward regions. For example, the northern Kantō plain and Shinano were centers of silk thread production, Tosa was a leading producer of paper, Nanbu had a large iron-working industry, and Hokkaido, of course, was a center of commercial fertilizer production. These regions lagged in agricultural development and lacked extensive internal demand for industrial commodities, but were well-suited to proto-industry. Indeed, since in some cases even subsistence agriculture was impractical because of poor soil or climate, people had little choice but to turn to proto-industrial endeavors and long-distance trade with the Kinai and similar areas. The influx of industrial products from peripheral areas in turn spurred growth in commercial agricultural regions and thus furthered the development of the economy as a whole.

Rather than looking at Tokugawa economic history in terms of a dichotomy between "advanced" and "backward" areas, it is better to see the regions as complementing one another. Given the importance of long-distance trade—both in industrial products and tax rice—"backward" areas were hardly isolated from market forces, even if commercial agriculture was slow to develop (Hayami 1989:22). Indeed, "backward" regions turned to proto-industrial production for distant markets in more developed areas—instead of developing commercial agriculture and local markets for industrial commodities of their own—in response to developments that had already occurred elsewhere.[11]

Moreover, dividing Japan into just two or three regions does not do justice to the complexity of development at a lower level of geographical abstraction (Wigen 1990:41). This point is especially important if considered in conjunction with Thomas C. Smith's (1973) observations about the movement of industry from urban to rural areas during the latter part of the Tokugawa period. Shinbo Hiroshi and Hasegawa Akira (1988) discuss urban deindustrialization in the Kinai soy-sauce brewing and cotton textile industries, and I have elsewhere (1989b) looked at intraregional specialization in the southern Kantō plain. By looking at economic differentiation as a phenomenon that occurred within broad regions more than between them, we can, at least, circumvent the questions raised by Saitō's observation that Japan lacked regional specialization on a scale comparable to Europe. Perhaps there need not be much specialization—whether within regions or among households—to get the proto-industrial engine of economic growth and institutional tension started.

A telling example of regional differences within a single political unit was the Nanbu (Morioka) domain in northeastern Honshu—the classic "backward" region (Hanley and Yamamura 1977). Nanbu can be seen as a microcosm of the entire country, with the central Kitakami river valley representing the "advanced" agricultural regions and the mountains and coast the "backward" centers of proto-industrial development. Agricultural, but not industrial, production in the domain was centered on the Kitakami valley, which included the castle town of Morioka. Proto-industry— most notably large-scale commercial fishing and fish processing (not herring, alas!)

---

[11]In Europe, too, "proto-industrialization was most likely to occur where urban and rural needs complemented each other" (Gullickson 1986:67).

and iron working—was found along the Pacific coast and in the mountains separating the coast from the Kitakami valley.

Interestingly, the most highly industrialized parts of the domain saw the most serious occurrences of unrest among Nanbu's notoriously contentious peasants; the best-known instances of conflict (the Sanhei rebellions of 1847 and 1853) involved disputes over domain commercial and industrial policies, and were directed in large part against merchants who had purchased samurai status from the domain. The disorder in Nanbu may be attributed to the fact that the impetus for economic growth came from the proto-industrial hinterland, and the feudal institutional structure—located as it was both physically and ideologically in the agricultural core—could not adapt.[12]

As important as geographical factors in proto-industrialization were political and institutional ones. After all, proto-industrialization in Japan, as elsewhere, occurred only within the framework of the political structure. The structure of the Japanese polity helps to explain why it did not conform to the European pattern of proto-industrialization and, in particular, was slower to make the transition to industrial capitalism. The Japanese case was complicated by the critical importance of agriculture—especially rice—in the political economy. The emphasis on rice cultivation, as manifested in the *kokudaka* system, may have inhibited the sort of broad regional specialization found in Europe and thus prevented the demographic transformation necessary to fuel full factory industrialization.

Under the *kokudaka* system a daimyo's place in the institutional hierarchy of the Tokugawa state was measured in terms of the putative agricultural productivity of his domain.[13] Although it very quickly ceased to reflect actual economic conditions, the *kokudaka* system retained its institutional importance throughout the Tokugawa period. Even as many domains came to tolerate and even actively foster a wide variety of economic activities, peasants were expected to grow grain—preferably rice—unless there was some compelling reason for them not to do so. When officials pressed peasants to produce as much rice as possible—even where climatic or technological conditions made rice cultivation impractical—they were responding to the position of rice as a measure not only of wealth but also of status in the feudal polity.

The *kokudaka* system thus represented an institutional hurdle to economic development, although not an insurmountable one. For daimyo and their officials the critical distinction was not between subsistence and commercial agriculture, or even between agriculture and industry, but rather between rice and non-rice production.[14] Whether proto-industrialization occurred or not became largely a question of a domain's attitude toward non-rice production—or, more precisely, whether other commodities could supplement or even replace rice in the domain economy.[15]

In Hokkaido, to take an extreme example, rice cultivation was impossible, so the herring fishery became a proxy for agriculture. In a sense, herring was "rice"

---

[12]For treatments of economic development and peasant rebellion in Nanbu see, in addition to Hanley and Yamamura 1977: Iwamoto 1977; Mori 1974:345–570; Moriya 1975; and Yokoyama 1977:173–96.

[13]See Wakita 1975 for an overview of the origins of the *kokudaka* system.

[14]As Mintz 1985 demonstrates so well, the preoccupation of the Japanese with rice as a staple food is consistent with practice in most world cultures. See also Braudel 1979 for a discussion of staple grains throughout the world.

[15]Much of the economic thought of the Tokugawa period can be seen as an attempt to rationalize commerce and industry as legitimate alternatives to a rice-based economy. See, for example, Najita 1987 and Roberts 1991.

in Matsumae:[16] its economy revolved around the fishery in a way that satisfied the requirements of the feudal polity while opening the door for considerable proto-industrial and eventually even capitalist development. In other domains, where rice cultivation was more feasible, the authorities could adopt a narrower definition of "rice," with the result that support for industry—and even commercial agriculture—was not readily forthcoming. For instance, the southern Kantō was the locus of a number of industries, most notably soy-sauce brewing and sardine fertilizer processing, that drew labor from the peasant population. However, local authorities were either unwilling or unable to appreciate the value of these industries. Instead of seeing their potential benefits, all they saw was the decline of agriculture. Rather than profiting from industrial growth, they vainly tried to get villagers to go back to the fields (Howell 1989b:357–64).

Interestingly, in this case it does not really matter whether the failure of officials to capitalize on industrial endeavors was the result of a Confucian reverence for grain cultivation or a structural inability to tap the wealth created by industry; one reinforced the other. The centrality of rice in the Tokugawa political economy, as reflected in the *kokudaka* system, was ultimately responsible for an atomized administrative structure in places like the Kantō, where it was not unusual for a half-dozen or more bakufu retainers to share tax revenues from a single village. Ironically, this may actually have contributed to proto-industrialization in some cases because, as Kären Wigen (1991:1) has noted, "commercial ventures followed their own spatial logic, which was not that of the Tokugawa feudal settlement; economic regions coexisted with political regions, but did not conform to them." In other words, parcelized sovereignty made it difficult for feudal authorities to tax the commercial sphere. This explains the apparent anomaly seen in the Kantō of rapidly rising material standards of living in the face of what in the authorities' eyes was widespread rural decline.

The inability of the Tokugawa state to take full advantage of proto-industrial development reflects the rigidity of a feudal polity. Economic institutions may come under pressure and begin to change, but they cannot complete the process of transformation so long as political impediments remain (KMS 1981:95–96). In Japan proto-industrialization had its ultimate origins in the political integration of the early Tokugawa period and the subsequent development of transportation routes and markets to handle tax grain.[17] Later, however, the sort of structural change prompted—indeed, required—by proto-industrialization was impeded by the inflexible institutional structure of the Tokugawa polity. Once the feudal polity was eliminated by the reforms following the Meiji Restoration, economic change proceeded at a rapid pace, so that Japan was a genuinely capitalist economy by the beginning of the twentieth century. One casualty of this transformation was rice, which lost its ideological and institutional place of honor in the Japanese political economy with the enactment of the land-tax reform of 1873.

Conclusion

The proto-industrialization model has run into criticism from various quarters, some of it prompted by the confusion concerning the precise role rural industry is

[16]The Chinese character used for "herring" in Matsumae was a compound of the characters for "fish" and "not" [鯡], signifying (at least in the folk etymology) that herring was more than just a fish in that riceless domain. The usual character is 鰊 .
[17]See Miyamoto and Uemura 1988. Also useful are Furuta 1988, for his discussion of early sea transportation, and Kawana 1982, for his discussion of transportation in the Kantō region.

supposed to have played in the process of structural transformation.[18] Part of the problem is that the "model" is not a single model at all, but rather a number of distinct constructs organized loosely around the notion that early industry belongs in some broader context; what sort of context, though, depends on one's perspective. Thus we have demographically oriented studies of proto-industrialization like those of Saitō, as well as those that are more concerned with the structural transformation from feudalism to capitalism, such as the work of Kriedte, Medick, and Schlumbohm. This study, of course, falls very much into the latter category, in part because reliable demographic data are simply unavailable for Hokkaido before the Meiji period. That is not the problem it might appear to be, however, since it at least shifts the focus from demography to the proto-industrialization model's ultimate goal of accounting for the rise of modern industry.

This brings us back to the role of rural industry in Japan's structural transformation. The mere existence of rural manufacturing did not of itself cause capitalism; it did, however, open a window of opportunity for the emergence of capitalism. Whether capitalist production actually arose or not hinged on the place of merchant capital in the feudal structure of a given location. In Hokkaido, merchant capital, as represented by the contract-fishery operators, laid the groundwork for large-scale production, but resisted taking the final step to capitalism. Once the series of changes set into motion by the influx of labor and adoption of new technology began, the contractors lost the initiative and independent capitalist entrepreneurs appeared and eventually came to dominate the fishery.

In other domains, the situation was similarly linked to local circumstances. In a large domain like Nanbu, the regional diversity of economic activity encouraged the development of proto-industry, but manufacturing remained under the domination of merchant capital, backed by the sanction of domain monopolies and monopsonies. Incidents like the Sanhei rebellions, in which peasants reacted against tight domain (and hence merchant capital) control over the economy, may have represented failed attempts to open the door to future capitalist development. Conversely, in areas without centralized control, such as the Kantō plain and southern Shinano, the course of proto-industrialization was not tied so closely to the feudal structure; there is evidence (Wigen 1991) to suggest the evolution of capitalist production in at least some sectors.

If proto-industrialization was not the direct cause of capitalism in Japan, it was a symptom of stress in the structure of the feudal polity. This is perhaps about as much as we can ask of the concept of proto-industrialization as an explanatory tool. After all, the push for structural transformation was not a foregone conclusion; the rent-seeking tendency of feudalism was much more the "natural" state of affairs.[19]

This view of the role of proto-industrialization in the emergence of capitalism contributes not only to our understanding of Japanese economic history, but it refines the proto-industrialization model as a theoretical construct as well. The emergence of capitalism from a proto-industrial base within the Hokkaido fishery, before the transformation of the Japanese economy as a whole, supports Jürgen

[18]For a critique of the proto-industrialization model in general, and particularly its claims for universal applicability, see Coleman 1983. See also the debate surrounding the value of Kriedte, Medick, and Schlumbohm 1981, particularly Geoff Eley's (1984) defense of that work, the response by Frank Perlin (1985), and the numerous works cited in those articles, especially Berg, Hudson, and Sonenscher 1983. For a response to their German critics, see Kriedte, Medick, and Schlumbohm 1986. See also the discussions in Wigen 1990:35–41 and Wray 1989:365–71.

[19]Although he eschews terms like feudalism and capitalism, Jones (1988) organizes his argument around this point.

Schlumbohm's characterization (KMS 1981:10) of proto-industrialization as a process in which the structural transformation from feudalism to capitalism is played out in microcosm within a region. In contrast, Schlumbohm's collaborators, Peter Kriedte and Hans Medick (as well as Franklin Mendels), see proto-industrialization as an intermediate stage between feudalism and capitalism,[20] but the Hokkaido evidence, when seen in the full context of Japanese history, does not support the teleology suggested by their model. That is, although (1) the preconditions for Hokkaido's development as a proto-industrial region lay in the structure of Japanese feudalism, and (2) capitalism could not have emerged in the fishery had it not undergone a proto-industrial stage first, there was nothing inevitable about the course of development in the industry.

Proto-industrialization in the Hokkaido fishery did not represent a distinct stage of historical development, but rather consisted of a series of interrelated developments—in demand, labor, technology, capital, and state institutions—the net effect of which was to undermine feudalism and replace it with something new—capitalism. Until that theoretical magic moment when capitalism was born in Japan, the fishery was still very much part of the Tokugawa feudal economy, even as it served to undermine the social and economic foundations of that economy.

List of References

BERG, MAXINE, PAT HUDSON, and MICHAEL SONENSCHER, eds. 1983. *Manufacture in Town and Country Before the Factory.* Cambridge: Cambridge University Press.

BRAUDEL, FERNAND. 1979. *The Structure of Everyday Life: The Limits of the Possible (Civilization and Capitalism, 15th–18th Century,* vol. 1). New York: Harper and Row.

COLEMAN, D. C. 1983. "Proto-Industrialization: A Concept Too Many." *Economic History Review,* 2nd series, 36:435–48.

DOBB, MAURICE. 1947. *Studies in the Development of Capitalism.* New York: International Publishers.

ELEY, GEOFF. 1984. "The Social History of Industrialization: 'Proto-Industry' and the Origins of Capitalism." *Economy and Society* 13:519–39.

FOX-GENOVESE, ELIZABETH, and EUGENE D. GENOVESE. 1983. *Fruits of Merchant Capital: Slavery and Bourgeois Property in the Rise and Expansion of Capitalism.* New York: Oxford University Press.

FURUTA RYŌICHI. 1988. *Kawamura Zuiken.* Tokyo: Yoshikawa kōbunkan.

GULLICKSON, GAY L. 1986. *Spinners and Weavers of Auffay: Rural Industry and the Sexual Division of Labor in a French Village, 1750–1850.* Cambridge: Cambridge University Press.

GUTMANN, MYRON. 1988. *Toward the Modern Economy: Early Industry in Europe.* Philadelphia: Temple University Press.

HANLEY, SUSAN B. 1983. "A High Standard of Living in Nineteenth-Century Japan: Fact or Fantasy?" *Journal of Economic History* 43:183–92.

HANLEY, SUSAN B., and KOZO YAMAMURA. 1977. *Economic and Demographic Change in Preindustrial Japan.* Princeton: Princeton University Press.

[20]See KMS 1981:9–10 and Eley 1984:523–26 on the differences among the authors' conceptions of proto-industrialization. Mendels 1972 subtitled the article in which he coined the term "proto-industrialization" "the first phase of the industrialization process," which certainly suggests a teleology.

HAUSER, WILLIAM B. 1974. *Economic Institutional Change in Tokugawa Japan: Ōsaka and the Kinai Cotton Trade.* Cambridge: Cambridge University Press.

HAYAMI AKIRA. 1989. "Kinsei Nihon no keizai hatten to 'Industrious Revolution' " [Economic development in early modern Japan and the "industrious revolution"]. In Hayami Akira, Saitō Osamu, and Sugiyama Shin'ya, eds., *Tokugawa shakai kara no tenbō: Hatten, kōzō, kokusai kankei* [A view from Tokugawa society: Development, structure, international relations], 19–32. Tokyo: Dōbunkan.

HILTON, RODNEY. 1978. "Introduction." In Rodney Hilton, ed., *The Transition from Feudalism to Capitalism,* 9–30. London: Verso Editions.

HOSTON, GERMAINE A. 1986. *Marxism and the Crisis of Development in Prewar Japan.* Princeton: Princeton University Press.

HOWELL, DAVID L. 1989a. "The Capitalist Transformation of the Hokkaidō Fishery, 1672–1935." Ph.D. diss., Princeton University.

———. 1989b. "Hard Times in the Kantō: Economic Change and Village Life in Late Tokugawa Japan." *Modern Asian Studies* 23:349–71.

IWAMOTO YOSHITERU. 1977. *Kinsei gyoson kyōdōtai no hensen katei* [The process of change in early modern fishing communities]. Tokyo: Ochanomizu shobō.

JONES, ERIC L. 1988. *Growth Recurring: Economic Change in World History.* Oxford: Clarendon Press.

KALLAND, ARNE. 1981. *Shingū: A Study of a Japanese Fishing Community.* (Scandinavian Institute of Asian Studies Monograph Series, No. 44.) London and Malmö: Curzon Press.

———. 1984. "A Credit Institution in Tokugawa Japan: The *Ura-tamegin* Fund of Chikuzen Province." In Gordon Daniels, ed., *Europe Interprets Japan,* 3–12. Tenterden, Kent: Paul Norbury Publications.

———. 1986. "Pre-modern Whaling in Northern Kyūshū." In Erich Pauer, ed., *Silkworms, Oil, and Chips . . .* (Proceedings of the Economics and Economic History Section of the Fourth International Conference on Japanese Studies, Paris, September 1985), 29–50. Bonn: Josef Kreiner.

KAWANA NOBORU. 1982. *Kashi ni ikiru hitobito: Tonegawa suiun no shakaishi* [The people of the river ports: A social history of transportation on the Tone River]. Tokyo: Heibonsha.

KOBAYASHI TAKIJI. 1973 [1929]. *"The Factory Ship" and "The Absentee Landlord,"* trans. Frank Motofuji. Tokyo: University of Tokyo Press and Seattle: University of Washington Press.

KRIEDTE, PETER, HANS MEDICK, and JÜRGEN SCHLUMBOHM [KMS]. 1981. *Industrialization before Industrialization.* Cambridge: Cambridge University Press and Paris: Editions de la Maison des Sciences de l'Homme.

———. 1986. "Proto-industrialization on Test with the Guild of Historians: Response to Some Critics," trans. Leena Turner. *Economy and Society* 15:254–72.

KUWABARA MASATO, ed. 1987. "Kyōdo ni ikiru" [Life at home in the country] (oral history project). *Matsumae han to Matsumae* [The Matsumae domain and Matsumae] 27: entire issue.

LEUPP, GARY. 1989. " 'One Drink from a Gourd': Servants, Shophands, and Laborers in the Cities of Tokugawa Japan." Ph.D. diss., University of Michigan.

MENDELS, FRANKLIN. 1972. "Proto-industrialization: The First Phase of the Industrialization Process." *Journal of Economic History* 32:241–61.

MINTZ, SIDNEY W. 1985. *Sweetness and Power: The Place of Sugar in Modern History.* New York: Viking Press.

MIYAMOTO MATAO and UEMURA MASAHIRO. 1988. "Tokugawa keizai no junkan kōzō" [The structure of circulation in the Tokugawa economy]. In Hayami

Akira and Miyamoto Matao, eds., *Keizai shakai no seiritsu* [The formation of an economic society] (*Nihon keizai shi* [An economic history of Japan], vol. 1), 271–324. Tokyo: Iwanami shoten.

MORI KAHEI. 1974 [1935]. *Nanbu han hyakushō ikki no kenkyū* [A study of peasant uprisings in the Nanbu domain] (*Mori Kahei chosakushū* [The selected works of Mori Kahei], vol. 7). Tokyo: Hōsei daigaku shuppan kyoku.

MORIYA YOSHIMI. 1975. "Bakuhan kōshin han no keizai jōkyō: Morioka han bakumatsu hyakushō ikki no yobiteki kōsatsu no tame ni" [Economic conditions in an underdeveloped domain during the Tokugawa era: Toward a preliminary study of peasant uprisings in the Morioka domain in the Bakumatsu period]. *Nihonshi kenkyū* [Japanese history], 150–51; 184–202.

NAJITA, TETSUO. 1987. *Visions of Virtue: The Kaitokudō Merchant Academy in Tokugawa Japan.* Chicago: University of Chicago Press.

NISHIKAWA, SHUNSAKU. 1986. "Grain Consumption: The Case of Chōshū." In Marius B. Jansen and Gilbert Rozman, eds., *Japan in Transition: From Tokugawa to Meiji,* 447–70. Princeton: Princeton University Press.

OHKAWA, KAZUSHI, and HENRY ROSOVSKY. 1965. "A Century of Economic Growth." In William W. Lockwood, ed., *The State and Economic Enterprise in Japan: Essays in the Political Economy of Growth,* 47–92. Princeton: Princeton University Press.

PERLIN, FRANK. 1985. "Scrutinizing Which Moment?" *Economy and Society* 14: 374–98.

ROBERTS, LUKE S. 1991. "The Merchant Origins of National Prosperity Thought in Eighteenth Century Tosa." Ph.D. diss., Princeton University.

SAITŌ OSAMU. 1983. "Population and the Peasant Family Economy in Proto-Industrial Japan." *Journal of Family History* 8:30–54.

———. 1985. *Puroto-kōgyōka no jidai* [The age of proto-industrialization]. Tokyo: Hyōronsha.

———. 1986. "The Rural Economy: Commercial Agriculture, By-employment, and Wage Work." In Marius B. Jansen and Gilbert Rozman, eds., *Japan in Transition: From Tokugawa to Meiji,* 400–20. Princeton: Princeton University Press.

SHINBO HIROSHI and HASEGAWA AKIRA. 1988. "Shōhin seisan, ryūtsū no dainamikkusu" [The dynamics of commodity production and circulation]. In Hayami Akira and Miyamoto Matao, eds., *Keizai shakai no seiritsu* [The formation of an economic society] (*Nihon keizai shi* [An economic history of Japan], vol. 1), 217–70. Tokyo: Iwanami shoten.

SIDER, GERALD M. 1986. *Culture and Class in Anthropology and History: A Newfoundland Illustration.* Cambridge: Cambridge University Press and Paris: Editions de la Maison des Sciences de l'Homme.

SMITH, THOMAS C. 1959. *The Agrarian Origins of Modern Japan.* Stanford: Stanford University Press.

———. 1969. "Farm Family By-Employments in Preindustrial Japan." *Journal of Economic History* 29:687–715.

———. 1973. "Pre-Modern Economic Growth: Japan and the West." *Past and Present* 60:127–60.

———. 1986. "Peasant Time and Factory Time in Japan." *Past and Present* 111:165–97.

WAKITA OSAMU. 1975. "The *Kokudaka* System: A Device for Unification." *Journal of Japanese Studies* 1:297–320.

WIGEN, KÄREN. 1990. "Regional Inversions: The Spatial Contours of Economic Change in the Southern Japanese Alps, 1750–1920." Ph.D. diss., University of California, Berkeley.

————. 1991. "Social and Spatial Divisions of Labor in Nineteenth Century Shinano: Mapping the Contested Terrain of Paper Craft Production." Paper delivered at the 43rd Meeting of the Association for Asian Studies, New Orleans, La.

WRAY, WILLIAM D. 1989. "Afterword." In William D. Wray, ed., *Managing Industrial Enterprise: Cases from Japan's Prewar Experience*. 317–74. Cambridge: Council on East Asian Studies, Harvard University.

YAMAMURA, KOZO. 1973. "Toward a Reexamination of the Economic History of Tokugawa Japan, 1600–1867." *Journal of Economic History* 33:509–41.

YOKOYAMA TOSHIO. 1977. *Hyakushō ikki to gimin denshō* [Peasant uprisings and martyrdom traditions]. Tokyo: Kyōikusha.

COMMERCIAL CHANGE AND URBAN GROWTH IN EARLY MODERN JAPAN

AN ERA OF URBAN GROWTH

During the first century and a half of the early modern period, between 1550 and 1700, Japan became one of the most urbanized societies in the world. At the beginning of this era, the ancient imperial capital of Kyoto was the only city with more than 100,000 residents, and a mere handful of other settlements held as many as 10,000 persons. But by the year 1700, four new Japanese communities had exceeded the 100,000 mark, and approximately 5 to 7 percent of all Japanese lived in such large cities. This compared with a figure of 2 percent in Europe, where only fourteen cities had reached the 100,000 level, and only the Netherlands and England–Wales could boast of urban concentrations greater than Japan's. Edo had become the world's largest city by the end of the seventeenth century, and the populations of Osaka and Kyoto approached those of London and Paris, the two largest cities in the West.

The meteoric urban growth that occurred in Japan at the beginning of the early modern period had profound and diverse consequences for Japanese history. First, the cities acted as large magnets, creating energy fields that set in motion large-scale population movements and propelled hundreds of thousands of persons into the cities to fill burgeoning job opportunities. The growing urban centers served as enormous consumption centers as well, and across Japan farmers changed their cropping patterns to meet new demands for vegetables, fruits, and plant materials for clothes. Consequently, regional specialization increasingly became a feature of early modern commerce, and new transportation networks and post towns sprang up everywhere to cater to mobile traders. In time, a fresh, spirited set of urban entertainments came into being as well, thus enriching the texture of Japanese cultural history. Finally, the unprecedented concentrations of people – vigorous, creative, and at times unruly – compelled the authorities to devise new kinds of political and administrative institutions.

The Sengoku period background

The quest to understand how and why this urban growth took place, and to appreciate as well the historical significance of the cities, takes us back in time to the middle of the sixteenth century – to the Sengoku period and the genesis of Japan's extraordinary epoch of urban development.[1] There were three principal types of urban settlement at that time. The most common, and the seed of what ultimately would become the dominant urban force in the early modern period in Japan, was the castle town, or *jōkamachi*, literally a community that grew up around a castle. During the first half of the sixteenth century, the bushi tended to live in agricultural villages, where they managed their fiefs and the affairs of the villagers. Gradually, during the decades of continual warfare that marked this era, these bushi emerged as an elite, arms-bearing class. As this happened, their leaders began to move out of the villages and to establish fortified residences at more easily defended locations. As revealed in names such as Negoya (literally, the huts at the base of the mountain) and Yamashita (at the foot of the mountain), these strongholds were usually situated where plains meet mountains, and they provided assembly points where, in times of crisis, the lord could gather his military band of retainers, relatives, and vassal samurai.[2]

These military centers quickly came to be the home for civilians as well. As combat spread into even remote parts of the country during the later decades of the sixteenth century, the castellans (now more familiarly known as daimyo), found it advantageous to gather into their castle headquarters larger and larger numbers of artisans who could manufacture weapons such as swords, lances, and even firearms; merchants who could transport these goods; and finally, groups of laborers to work on construction projects. It was also useful for the daimyo to establish within the precincts of the new castle towns officially authorized marketplaces where commodity transactions could

---

1 For a convenient overview of the issues that have occupied the attention of historians concerning Sengoku period cities, see Nakabe Yoshiko, "Sengoku jidai daimyō kyojū toshi ni kansuru shomondai," in Chihōshi kenkyū kyōgikai, ed., *Toshi no chihōshi* (Tokyo: Yūsankaku, 1980), pp. 56–79. In English, see Haruko Wakita, with Susan B. Hanley, "Dimensions of Development: Cities in Fifteenth-Century Japan," in John Whitney Hall, Keiji Nagahara, and Kozo Yamamura, eds., *Japan Before Tokugawa: Political Consolidation and Economic Growth, 1500–1650* (Princeton, N.J.: Princeton University Press, 1981), pp. 295–326.
2 Nishikawa Kōji, *Nihon toshishi no kenkyū* (Tokyo: Nihon hōsō shuppan kyōkai, 1972), pp. 167–202.

take place peacefully, and this too encouraged permanent residence in the towns.[3]

As the daimyo's policies gave rise to larger and more prosperous communities, the towns also became centers of local religious and cultural activities. Moreover, as life in the imperial capital of Kyoto became less secure after the Ōnin War (1467–77), men of artistic and literary accomplishment, such as the landscape artist and garden designer Sesshū, left the capital and took refuge in the provinces. And like Sesshu, who was employed by the Ōuchi daimyo of western Japan, such persons often were taken into service by the daimyo, thus ultimately bringing a measure of cultural refinement to the lives of the bushi and cementing the tie between artist and military figures that would endure into the early modern period.

Some notion of the vitality of these communities can be found in the epistles of the Jesuit missionaries, who openly admired the castle towns of the Sengoku period.[4] When visiting Gifu in 1575, for instance, Luis Frois wrote: "At this point I wish I were a skilled architect or had the gift of describing places well, because I sincerely assure you that of all the palaces and houses I have seen in Portugal, India, and Japan, there has been nothing to compare with this as regards luxury, wealth, and cleanliness." And after visiting Azuchi in 1584, Lourenço Mexia remarked that Japanese houses were as neat and clean as sacristies and that at Nobunaga's palace "the gardens and corridors were such that one could not spit in them." Such praise, however, should not obscure the fact that these castle towns were still relatively small; even in the 1580s most had populations of only a few thousand persons. Still, more than a hundred such settlements dotted the countryside of Japan, and these would provide one of the seedbeds for the rapid urbanization of the seventeenth century, growth that would propel Japan into the leading ranks of the urbanized countries.

Although these rustic castle towns represented the principal urban creation of the late Sengoku period, they were not without competitors. The warfare of that age was fought at two different levels. The first and most visible was the struggle among daimyo to expand their domains by military means; the other was the contest for supremacy within domains between individual daimyo and armed elements of the peasantry. In some instances, groups of such peasants were members

3 Nakabe Yoshiko, *Jōkamachi* (Kyoto: Yanagihara shoten, 1978), pp. 9–64.
4 Michael Cooper, ed., *They Came to Japan: An Anthology of European Reports on Japan, 1543–1640* (Berkeley and Los Angeles: University of California Press, 1965), pp. 131, 145.

of secularly powerful Buddhist sects, such as the Ikkō, or True Pure Land sect (*Jōdo Shinshū*), which permitted the peasants, together with merchants and artisans who were also sect members, to take up residence in and around a sect temple. These settlements then became known as "temple towns" (*jinaimachi*), and their residents often claimed autonomy from daimyo control.[5]

These temple towns were distinct from the so-called *monzenmachi* (literally, towns in front of the gates), which were concentrations of inns and souvenir shops clustered together around the entrances to those famous shrines and temples that attracted large numbers of worshipers and pilgrims.[6] The essential difference between the two urban types is that the temple towns formed under the auspices of major temples had a distinctive religious character and asserted their independence from the daimyo's authority. That is, these communities as corporate groups exercised judicial and police powers, apportioned and at times even levied their own tax dues, and undertook self-defense projects such as the construction of moats. The possession of these special immunities permitted the temple towns to carry out certain functions outside the direct purview of daimyo authority, and it is this latitude for independent action that has prompted historians to see them as autonomous, self-governing communities.[7]

Historians have identified seventeen temple towns, all founded in the middle decades of the sixteenth century.[8] These settlements, however, tended to have very short life spans. As daimyo put together greater and greater concentrations of military and political might during the latter half of the sixteenth century, they attacked the major religious sects and cut away the independent power basis of the temple towns. In some cases, the daimyo actually converted the temple towns into their own castle headquarters. For instance, Osaka was known at that time as Ishiyama and was built up as an armed community of Honganji believers. In 1580, Oda Nobunaga destroyed this fortified town after a decade of fighting, and subsequently Toyotomi Hideyoshi erected his own

5 The term is also read as *jinaichō*. A good introduction to this type of settlement can be found in Wakita Osamu, "Jinaimachi no kōzō to tenkai," *Shirin* 41 (January 1958): 1–24.
6 Harada Tomohiko, "Kinsei no monzenmachi," in Toyoda Takeshi, Harada Tomohiko, and Yamori Kazuhiko, eds., *Kōza: Nihon no hōken toshi*, 3 vols. (Tokyo: Bun'ichi sōgō shuppan, 1981–2), vol. 3, pp. 201–23.
7 In certain *jinaimachi* the temple priests retained ultimate political authority and managed the affairs of the community. See Osamu Wakita, with James L. McClain, "The Commercial and Urban Policies of Oda Nobunaga and Toyotomi Hideyoshi," in Hall, Nagahara, and Yamamura, eds., *Japan Before Tokugawa*, pp. 231–7.
8 For a careful discussion of the origins of temple towns and their historical significance, see Wakita Osamu, "Jinaimachi no rekishi-teki tokushitsu," in Toyoda, Harada, and Yamori, eds., *Kōza: Nihon no hōken toshi*, vol. 1, pp. 143–64.

castle headquarters on its ashes. Similarly, the castle town of Kanazawa, which by 1700 would become the fourth largest city in Japan under the rule of the Maeda family of daimyo, was built on the site of an earlier temple town named Kanazawa Gobō, which had existed under the protection of the Ikkō sect. In other instances, conquering daimyo left the towns in place as local merchant settlements. But in these cases as well, the military lords stripped the communities of their self-governing responsibilities and fully incorporated them into the tightening web of daimyo authority. The town of Imai, associated with Yanenji temple in Nara Prefecture, is a typical example of a temple town that lost its immunities and became purely a commercial settlement populated by small-scale merchants.

If the temple towns represented impediments to daimyo power, there was another type of sixteenth-century community that served an essential purpose for the daimyo. These were centers of trade and transshipment, or what might be called entrepôt towns. Some of these were inland post towns, but most were ports, such as Sakai on Osaka Bay, Kuwana on Ise Bay, and Hakata on the bay of the same name in Kyushu. In some instances, these settlements exercised self-governing powers similar to those claimed by the temple towns. In Sakai, for example, influential merchants managed urban administration and maintained armed forces.[9] But whether fortified or not, these merchant communities received different treatment from the daimyo than did the temple towns. Their strategic locations made them useful to daimyo, almost all of whom had to engage in some trade in order to acquire goods that were produced beyond their own borders. Indeed, most daimyo believed these entrepôt towns to be so central to their own ultimate economic success that they adhered to a tacit agreement to maintain a policy of nonaggression toward the settlements.

Interestingly enough, certain features of urban life and the cityscape in sixteenth-century Japanese cities reminded the first Westerner visitors of European urban settlements. One missionary noted the similarity between Japanese temple towns and Venice, which was also governed through administrative offices staffed by merchants. When visiting Nara, Gaspar Vilela wrote, "I spent some days there and saw three outstanding things of note. One of them is a great

9 For a detailed study of Sakai, see Izumi Chōichi, *Sakai: chūsei jiyū toshi* (Tokyo: Kyōikusha, 1981). In English, see V. Dixon Morris, "Sakai: From Shōen to Port City," in John W. Hall and Takeshi Toyoda, eds., *Japan in the Muromachi Age* (Berkeley and Los Angeles: University of California Press, 1977), pp. 145–58; and V. Dixon Morris, "The City of Sakai and Urban Autonomy," in George Elison and Bardwell L. Smith, eds., *Warlords, Artists, & Commoners: Japan in the Sixteenth Century* (Honolulu: University of Hawaii Press, 1981), pp. 23–54.

metal idol as big as the tower of the gate of Evora."[10] However impressed those European visitors might have been, no medieval city would survive unscathed the wars of reunification at the end of the sixteenth century, and the powerfully centralized state that resulted from that unification would call into being new cities, larger and more grand than anything those first European visitors saw.

National unification and early modern castle towns

It has become a historical truism to say that Oda Nobunaga initiated the political and economic programs that resulted in the early modern state; that Toyotomi Hideyoshi amplified them; and that Tokugawa Ieyasu supplied the final institutional refinements. As familiar as that paradigm might be, however, it is still relevant to a discussion of those social policies that had the most significant impact on urban growth – the separation of the peasants from the warriors (*heinō-bunri*) and of the peasants from the merchants (*nōshō-bunri*).

Oda Nobunaga's first step in imposing a new social order came after a bitter and bloody campaign against the forces of the Honganji sect gathered at their stronghold at Ishiyama. It took Nobunaga the full decade of the 1570s, and the sacrifice of tens of thousands of lives, before he could defeat the Honganji army, a mix of peasants, local samurai, and even merchants and artisans from the local temple town. As a consequence of this victory, Nobunaga acquired the strength and reputation to begin a policy of disarming peasants on some portions of his holdings. He also initiated steps to separate the warriors from agricultural management by conducting a cadastral survey (*kenchi*) in his home provinces of Yamato and Harima.

What lay behind Nobunaga's actions was the fear of an aroused peasantry and of an alliance between his retainers and villagers.[11] As long as the vassal warriors resided in the countryside and oversaw village affairs, they held the potential to threaten the lord. Indeed, in the middle decades of the sixteenth century, so many retainers turned their village holdings into independent power bases from which they defied daimyo orders, or even rose in revolt against their masters, that these years became popularly known as the era of *gekokujō*, of the inferiors overthrowing their superiors. The ultimate motive of Nobunaga, and of the daimyo who followed his example, was to drive a

---

10 Cooper, eds., *They Came to Japan*, pp. 282.
11 On the importance of peasant actions, see Keiji Nagahara, with Kozo Yamamura, "Village Communities and Daimyo Power," in Hall and Toyoda, eds., *Japan in the Muromachi Age*, pp. 107–23.

wedge between the retainers and vassals in order to bring each under more direct control.

Hideyoshi extended these policies of status separation.[12] As detailed in Chapters 2 and 4 of this volume, from the mid-1580s Hideyoshi began to expand the survey of rice-producing lands first started by Nobunaga, a policy that eventually produced a new village and administrative system, as well as a much more closely regulated peasantry. In 1588 he ordered a nationwide "sword hunt" to confiscate arms from villagers and to etch more clearly the status lines between peasant and warrior. Three years later, in 1591, Hideyoshi instructed the daimyo to conduct a village-by-village census (hitobarai) of their domains, a recording of the population and the numbers of households in rural areas that was designed to prevent the peasants from absconding and to bind them more tightly to the land. In that same year Hideyoshi also issued his famous edict that prohibited changes of status from samurai to merchant or from farmer to merchant. Although none of these policies could ever be fully enforced, they did provide a clear conceptual and legal differentiation of warrior, peasant, and merchant.

Tokugawa Ieyasu and his successors brought these policies to their completion. During the seventeenth century, the Tokugawa line of shoguns completely disarmed the peasantry and summoned the bushi class into the areas around its castles, moves that were repeated in nearly every daimyo domain. To be sure, in places where agriculture developed more slowly – generally in Shikoku, Kyushu, and in the north of Honshu – some lower-ranking bushi continued to live in villages. But with these exceptions, the imposition of status distinctions and the severing of the samurai from the management of agricultural affairs gave the shogun and daimyo the opening they needed to compel the warriors to move out of the villages and to take up residence around the lord's castle. At the same time, the overlords held out more positive incentives, by granting their vassal warriors residential sites and guaranteeing them annual stipends.

One consequence of these social policies was the large-scale growth of castle towns.[13] If the populations of the rudimentary castle towns of the Sengoku era tended to number in the low thousands, now cities of

12 Cities and the policies of the first two unifiers are discussed in Takamaki Minoru, "Shokuhō seiken to toshi," in Toyoda, Harada, and Yamori, eds., Kōza: Nihon no hōken toshi, vol. 3, pp. 189–211.

13 A discussion of the historiographical issues can be found in Matsumoto Shirō, "Kinsei toshiron," in Fukaya Katsumi and Matsumoto Shirō, eds., Bakuhansei shakai no kōzō (Tokyo: Yūhikaku, 1980), pp. 109–21.

thirty, forty, and even a hundred thousand persons became common-place. The core population for these cities were those samurai who had been forcefully uprooted from the countryside by the social policies of the unifiers. Between the 1580s and the 1650s, for example, some 50,000 samurai, including their families and attendants, moved into the shadow of the Maeda daimyo's castle at Kanazawa. By the end of the seventeenth century, more than half that number had taken up residence at Sendai, the headquarters of the Date family of daimyo, while nearly 25,000 samurai and their dependents lived at Tottori and 18,000 at Okayama. In all, the bushi class comprised approximately 5 to 8 percent of Japan's total population. As they settled into the areas around some 250 or so daimyo castles that dotted the Japanese country-side, they became the stable nucleus around which the urban popula-tion formed.[14]

A second migration, this one among rural villagers who hoped to become the merchants, artisans, and laborers of the new cities, accom-panied the movement of the samurai into the communities around the castles. The construction of the castle and samurai residences entailed a tremendous outlay of capital expenditures, and thousands of rural men poured into the city to take up jobs in the booming construction trades. As the samurai set up urban households, they hired servants – even a humble warrior family would usually employ an attendant, a valet, and a couple of women servants – thus creating additional em-ployment opportunities for rural immigrants.

Urban bushi households also generated enormous consumption de-mands. Restricted by daimyo fiat to military and bureaucratic careers, the samurai relied on the commoners to provide them with both mili-tary equipment and a variety of everyday goods and services, a situation that naturally attracted would-be merchants and artisans to the city. A fraction of them came because they were invited to sell specialty goods such as swords and armor to the daimyo and his warrior followers, but most of the prospective merchants arrived on their own, hoping to take advantage of the new commercial opportunities by setting up shops to sell more ordinary goods: umbrellas, footwear, wooden buckets, and pots and pans. It was this civilian migration that pushed the population of Tottori to 35,000 persons, Okayama to 40,000, Sendai to 50,000, and Kanazawa to nearly 120,000 persons by the year 1700.

14 The three classic works on premodern Japanese cities are Ono Hitoshi, *Kinsei jōkamachi no kenkyū* (Tokyo: Shibundō, 1928); Toyoda Takeshi, *Nihon no hōken toshi* (Tokyo: Iwanami shoten, 1952); and Harada Tomohiko, *Nihon hōken toshi kenkyū* (Tokyo: Tōkyō daigaku shuppankai, 1973).

Although the castles and surrounding environs were originally planned as defensive enclaves, the mass migration of merchants and artisans into the new communities quickly gave them well-defined economic functions, as nodes of both consumption and production, so that their commercial significance far exceeded the capacities of the Sengoku period towns. The economic needs of the daimyo lords during the seventeenth century also contributed to the burgeoning importance of these castle town communities. Probably no daimyo domain was ever totally self-sufficient in goods or currency. Some had to import crockery or clothing materials such as cotton or silk; others had to acquire foodstuffs such as tea, salt, or fish from outside sources. Moreover, whenever the Tokugawa shogunate made demands on the daimyo for contributions to construction projects, some lords had to go outside the local economy for cash or building materials. Consequently, no daimyo could escape the need to participate, at least to some extent, in the broader, national network of economic exchange that was taking shape around these cities.

The policies of the shogunate toward currency and the minting of coins also encouraged an expansion in the volume of commercial transactions and contributed to the emergence of castle towns as nodes of economic exchange. Most major daimyo minted their own coins in the early decades of the seventeenth century. The shogunate, however, began to produce gold and silver coins in 1601 and copper coins five years later, and it soon claimed a monopoly on the right to issue currency that circulated throughout the entire nation. This meant that coins minted by the daimyo could be spent legitimately only inside the domain of origin and that the lords were compelled to spend the shogunate's currency to pay for imported goods, as well as to meet the extraordinary construction levies imposed by the shogunate and the expenses associated with the alternate residence system (*sankin-kōtai*) that was institutionalized during the decade of the 1630s. To acquire these coins meant that each daimyo had to sell a portion of his tax rice in the national, shogunate-controlled markets of Edo and Osaka, thus contributing to their growth and importance.

In addition, most daimyo also marketed some exportable local specialty products that could be collected from the peasantry in place of rice. These specialty goods were determined by the topographical conditions within each domain but many, at least in the early seventeenth century, consisted of raw materials such as lumber or hemp harvested from mountainous regions, copper and iron dug from the earth, and dried fish and salt hauled from the sea. During the opening decades of the seventeenth century, castle towns soon became the focal points not only of commercial activity but also of the collection and transshipment of these items.

The geographic location of the new castle towns within the daimyo domains reflected their twin importance as military and economic centers.[15] Toward the end of the sixteenth century, as the daimyo began to consolidate their grasp over increasingly large territorial units, they moved out of the narrow confines of the mountains and built new, more massive moat-and-tower fortresses on the wide plains that constituted the strategic and economic heart of their holdings. Here, the daimyo could assemble and hold in readiness their growing warrior bands, protected by walls and moats constructed at sufficient distance from the castle nerve center to safeguard it from musket and cannon, the new implements of siege and destruction. But the new locations conferred economic advantages as well, for these citadels towered over the villages of the domains and permitted the daimyo easier access to the agricultural surpluses that they could tax and use for trade and to support their regimes. Most of the new castle towns were also situated directly on or close to major transportation routes, an important consideration for the merchants and artisans whom the daimyo lords hoped to attract to their communities.

Because most bulk commodities were transported by ship, the daimyo took into consideration the proximity of bays and harbors when choosing locations for their castle towns. If a castle could not be located directly on the coast, a daimyo would often construct port facilities as close to the castle town as possible and then dig a connecting canal so that barges and small boats could transport goods into the castle town. The castle town of Kanazawa, for instance, was located several kilometers inland from the Sea of Japan, and so the Maeda daimyo encouraged the development of Miyanokoshi as a port and in the early seventeenth century went to considerable expense to dredge out two rivers connecting the port to Kanazawa so that the castle town merchants could profit from easier access to oceangoing transportation. Between the 1580s and 1630s, several dozen new port towns

15 The bulk of research in Japan concerning the relationship between economic growth and the geographic distribution of castle towns has been conducted not by historians but, rather, by specialists known as historical geographers, who have tended to use one variety or another of central place theory. Two of the more influential works in this genre are Yamori Kazuhiko, *Toshizu no rekishi: Nihon hen* (Tokyo: Kōdansha, 1974); and Matsumoto Toyotoshi, *Jōkamachi no rekishi chirigaku-teki kenkyū* (Tokyo: Yoshikawa kōbunkan, 1967). In English the fullest discussion of economic linkages among Tokugawa period cities can be found in Gilbert Rozman, *Urban Networks in Ch'ing China and Tokugawa Japan* (Princeton, N.J.: Princeton University Press, 1974).

sprang up along the harbors of Japan, one example of the secondary urban construction stimulated by the growth of the early modern castle towns.

One disadvantage of the new locations was that the castles and their adjoining communities were usually located at some distance from the materials necessary to construct them. The mammoth stones used for the walls of Edo Castle, for example, had to be quarried in the higher mountains along the rugged western coast of the Izu peninsula. They then had to be lowered by ropes down the steep, treacherous mountain-sides and loaded onto the nearly three thousand barges that had been assembled to ship the stone blocks to Edo.[16] In Kanazawa, the stones were carved out of Mt. Tomuro, nearly eighty miles to the east of the city. Labor gangs rolled them overland on logs to a staging area near the castle where they were cut to shape by stone masons before being lifted and fitted into place. Such undertakings were hazardous. Countless numbers of men died while lowering the stones down the Izu mountains, and in Kanazawa portions of the walls collapsed twice during construction, killing dozens and injuring hundreds of laborers.[17]

Indeed, the epic nature attributed to these endeavors became part of the country's folklore as the peasant families who were compelled to supply the labor for these construction project left their feelings in a tradition of sorrowful folk songs and legends about those who toiled, and sometimes died, to erect the castles. For others, however, the sacrifices of the laborers were quickly overshadowed by the magnificence of the new castles, which were praised both as works of beauty as well as strength. In Kanazawa, one samurai wrote with pride that the long sweep of the walls gave the castle a sense of permanence, while the white stucco watchtowers gracefully, yet dramatically, set off the massive turrets and gates. Awed, he boasted that Kanazawa Castle was equal to the Toyotomi fortress in Osaka.[18]

To a large degree, the military and economic requirements of the age influenced the internal spatial arrangement of the castle towns.[19] Cer-

16 For a wonderfully illustrated history of the building of Edo, see Naitō Akira, *Edo no machi*, 2 vols. (Tokyo: Sōshisha, 1982).
17 James L. McClain, *Kanazawa: A Seventeenth-Century Japanese Castle Town* (New Haven, Conn.: Yale University Press, 1982), p. 33.
18 McClain, *Kanazawa,* p. 33. The construction of Osaka Castle is discussed in William B. Hauser, "Osaka Castle and Tokugawa Authority in Western Japan," in Jeffrey P. Mass and William B. Hauser, eds., *The Bakufu in Japanese History* (Stanford, Calif.: Stanford University Press, 1985).
19 The most detailed mapping of the castle towns has been completed by historical geographers. Especially influential has been Yamori's *Toshizu no rekishi.* Yamori divided castle town layouts into five general types, a classification that has been generally accepted as a working model by most researchers.

tainly, the physical layout of the communities embodied the status assumptions imposed by the lord on his domain. In the most common pattern, the residence of the daimyo lord and his family, as well as the most important administrative offices, were located in an area known as the *naikaku*, or central keep, an enclosure securely protected by stone walls and a network of moats, canals, and rivers. Around this inner redoubt lay the residences assigned to the band of vassal retainers, generally in two zones. The more important and unquestionably loyal samurai received rather large residences with perhaps as many as a dozen or more rooms and graced with landscape gardens. These were generally clustered together near the castle walls, protected by the ramparts and close to the administrative offices where these high-ranking retainers spent their working hours. Quarters for lower-ranking retainers were located in a second belt, usually far removed from the castle and often unprotected except perhaps for a single outer moat or sometimes a simple earthen barricade. The accommodations here accorded with the more humble status of these warriors, who, divided by occupational rank (riflers, foot soldiers, and the like), were crowded together with their families into tiny apartments inside long, narrow, barracks-style tenement houses known as *nagaya*.

Most of the merchants and artisans lived between the two groups of warriors. This residential area for the urban commoners was divided into wards (*machi*). Most commonly, these were oblong quarters, strung out along the roads which were planned to cross at right angles, with the houses facing each other across a street constituting a single ward. To some extent, the composition of these wards reflected the status and economic gradations that subdivided the merchant and artisan classes. Within any castle town, some wards were made up almost entirely of a small group of elite merchants who supplied certain crucial military or prized luxury goods to the daimyo, items such as munitions or arms, rice in bulk shipments, silks and other quality clothing materials, or cakes and saké. The daimyo would grant charters to these men, vouching that he would buy their products and thus coining the generic term, *goyō shōnin*, purveyors to the lord, that defined this distinctive group. In addition to the charters, the lord often bestowed on these merchants tax exemptions and residential housing plots within the better wards, generally known as the *hommachi*, that were close to the castle and among the first laid out, locations that had the additional advantage of being near the wealthier samurai customers.

Also given preferential treatment were the forwarding agents, the men who procured packhorses, arranged coolie labor, and otherwise managed the details of the daimyo's export trade.[20] Typically they received residential plots in the center of the commercial section, an area that then became known as Temmamachi, literally the post horse ward. Similarly, each daimyo required the services of certain kinds of artisans – swordsmiths, armorers, carpenters, stone cutters, plasterers, and tatami makers – and to entice them to his domain he would offer guarantees of employment, tax exemptions, and housing that was conveniently situated close to the castle.[21] Often those with the same occupation were clustered together in a specific ward, and even today ancient names such as carpenters' ward, swordsmiths' ward, and so forth can be found in the modern cities that evolved from former castle towns.[22]

Beyond the quarters dominated by the commoner elites were the more numerous wards populated by the merchants who dealt in ordinary goods such as vegetables, tea, oil, charcoal, and paper, and by artisans such as umbrella makers, coopers, dyers, and barbers.[23] Although separated from the elite areas, these wards usually still enjoyed a favorable location within the belt between the two main zones of samurai residences. Beyond the outer ring of lower-ranking samurai, on the outskirts of the town, were the slumlike areas of the urban poor, outcast groups, and day laborers who toiled in the lowest-paid and least-skilled construction jobs.[24]

The rapid growth of the castle towns during the late sixteenth century and early seventeenth centuries forced the Japanese daimyo to devise new systems of urban administration. Such a task defied easy solution, however, and it was not until the middle of the seventeenth century that most daimyo could set in place the administrative structures that served as the basis of urban government for the balance of the Tokugawa period. Unfortunately, the specific steps that the daimyo took to build these urban political structures cannot be easily traced, for natural disasters have destroyed much of the documentary base in most cities, and so the events in the first half of the seventeenth

20 Tsuchida Ryōichi, "Kinsei jōkamachi no temmayaku," in Chihōshi kenkyū kyōgikai, ed., *Nihon no toshi to machi* (Tokyo: Yūzankaku, 1982), pp. 146–75.
21 The residential clustering of persons according to occupation is the topic of Fujimoto Toshiharu, "Toshi no dōgyōsha-machi to sangyō," in Toyoda, Harada, and Yamori, eds., *Kōza: Nihon no hōken toshi*, vol. 2, pp. 35–7.
22 For a recent study of artisan groups, see Yokota Fuyuhiko, "Shokunin to shokunin dantai," in Rekishigaku kenkyūkai, ed., *Kōza Nihon rekishi*, vol. 5 (Tokyo: Tōkyō daigaku shuppankai, 1985), pp. 189–226.
23 Fukai Jinzō, "Kinsei toshi no hattatsu," in Matsumoto Shirō and Yamada Tadao, eds., *Genroku, Kyōhō-ki no seiji to shakai* (Tokyo: Yūhikaku, 1980), pp. 148–59.
24 For a discussion of outcast groups, see Harada Tomohiko, "Kinsei toshi no hisabetsu buraku," in Toyoda, Harada, and Yamori, eds., *Kōza: Nihon no hōken toshi*, vol. 2, pp. 389–412.

century often must be conjectured from the later records of the eighteenth and early nineteenth centuries.

One exception to this rule is the castle town of Kanazawa, where a variety of early-seventeenth-century documents have been preserved. Although there was perhaps no such creature as a perfectly typical castle town, the general evolution of Kanazawa paralleled that of other such cities. Consequently, the details observed there can provide a useful example of how urban government commonly developed. Moreover, because urban governance has received little attention from historians to date, a close examination of Kanazawa can help illuminate how the castle towns served as important units of local government and how the daimyo's efforts to govern the cities fit into the pattern of domain and village governance, as explained in Chapters 4, 5, and 10 of this volume.[25]

The administrative arm of the city government in Kanazawa, as in other castle towns, could be functionally divided into two principal components: one designed to rule the merchants and artisans and the other to govern the samurai. The samurai's administrative apparatus was the direct heir of the battlefield chain of command established in the late sixteenth century as the Maeda daimyo fought their way to power in the hills and plains of the Hokuriku region. During their rise to power, the Maeda had put into place a military organization in which authority passed from daimyo to individual retainers through a hierarchy of command that permitted the daimyo to mobilize and deploy military personnel easily during the years of constant warfare. As the Maeda summoned the samurai into the castle town between 1580 and 1620, they began to add civil administrative functions to this system of command. The highest level of the Maeda band of retainers, known collectively as the Eight Houses (hakka), served as the lord's leading military tacticians and commanders during times of warfare, but after the move into Kanazawa they were named as chief advisers and made responsible for formulating the political and administrative policies for the entire domain. Consequently, after the 1620s every important political decision that affected life in Kanazawa was made by either the daimyo or this body of chief advisers. In addition, these men were responsible for overseeing the activities of the next lower status group, the commanders (hitomochi).[26]

25 The most complete general coverage of castle town governments can be found in Nakabe, *Jōkamachi*, pp. 239–300; Tanaka Yoshio, *Jōkamachi Kanazawa* (Tokyo: Nihon shoin, 1966); and McClain, *Kanazawa*, pp. 85–101.

26 This pattern was similar to that observed in other domains; see, for example, John Whitney Hall, "The Ikeda House and Its Retainers in Bizen," in John W. Hall and Marius B. Jansen, eds., *Studies in the Institutional History of Early Modern Japan* (Princeton, N.J.: Princeton

The commanders were relatively high-ranking samurai (they had stipends ranging between one thousand and fourteen thousand *koku*), who had led troops on the field of battle. After being withdrawn to the city, they were assigned to significant posts in the civilian government. Four of the most influential domain offices, for example, were the offices of comptroller, rural magistrates, city magistrates, and magistrates for shrine and temple affairs, and all were staffed by men from this status group. Strictly speaking, these posts were not usually endowed with specific policymaking powers. However, the incumbents had frequent contact with the daimyo and the chief advisers, who often solicited their opinions, and this gave the commanders an informal mechanism for influencing policy decisions. Thus, for example, when the daimyo and the chief advisers were deadlocked over whether or not to license a kabuki and prostitution district in Kanazawa in the 1820s, the decision turned on the recommendations submitted by the city magistrates.

In addition to their posts within the formal administrative structure, the commanders were also held accountable for the civil conduct of the samurai under their jurisdiction. Any one commander might oversee as many as 150 warriors, who were then divided into several units, each captained by a unit leader (*kumigashira*). The commander was responsible for ensuring that all members of these units, as well as their families and attendants, obeyed the laws and edicts issued by the daimyo. If a rear vassal committed a crime involving violence, for instance, he had to be turned over to the appropriate domain police officials for punishment. In other cases, however, the unit leaders would meet with the parties involved in a dispute and attempt to arrange a mutually agreeable settlement. If that proved impossible, the commander would enter the case and could even mete out punishments, subject to the approval of his own superiors.

A much more elaborate administrative apparatus specifically designed to handle the affairs of the merchant and artisan status groups was created during the opening decades of the seventeenth century. In its final form, the city government became highly bureaucratic. Perhaps the most crucial officials were the city magistrates (*machi bugyō*). The first appointments to this office were made irregularly from the 1590s and permanently from 1641. These officials were entrusted with

University Press, 1968), pp. 79–88; and Madoka Kanai, "Fukui, Domain of a Tokugawa Collateral Daimyo: Its Traditions and Transition," in Ardath W. Burks, ed., *The Modernizers* (Boulder, Colo.: Westview Press, 1985), pp. 33–68.

implementing policies established by the daimyo and the chief advisers, and to this end, they supervised the City Office (Machi kaisho) that by the end of the seventeenth century had come to include more than three hundred employees.

A great number of merchants and artisans also served as lesser officials in urban administration. The post of city elder (*machidoshiyori*) was the most important of these. This term appears in documents as early as 1594, but appointments were not made on a regular basis until the late 1640s and early 1650s, when the number of elders was fixed at twenty.[27] The daimyo appointed as city elders merchants who had made their marks in business, men who possessed administrative skills and enjoyed a high reputation, as defined in terms of commercial success. Not unexpectedly, many came from the ranks of the chartered merchants, the merchant elite who enjoyed commercial privileges and an especially close relationship with the lord and high retainers.

The elders performed a variety of duties. They received written requests and complaints from the townspeople, attached their own opinions, and then submitted the paperwork to the samurai officials at the City Office. They also checked tax receipts and submitted statements that the proper amount had been collected. The elders accompanied the police officials who investigated the crimes of merchants and artisans and then attended hearings. Finally, they helped supervise the activities of other commoners who worked at the City Office. In a more general way, they were expected to promote good behavior and filial piety among the townspeople, to mediate civil disagreements between commoners, and to encourage diligence by merchants and artisans.

Several dozen other offices that functioned under the jurisdiction of the city elders in Kanazawa also became institutionalized during the middle decades of the seventeenth century. It became common practice, for example, to appoint inspectors (*yokome kimoiri*) and ward representatives (*machi kimoiri*) to assist the city elders. The inspectors helped with tax collection and investigated charges of questionable administration by city officials. Each representative served several wards (in the 1690s there were approximately forty representatives and slightly more than one hundred commoner wards), and they were specifically instructed to help compile census reports, examine commoner com-

---

27 The number was reduced to ten in 1669. *Machidoshiyori rekimei narabi ni tsutomekatachō*, ms. copy, Kanazawa City Library.

plaints about allegedly exorbitant and unfair prices, hold conciliation talks in commercial disputes, and investigate suspicious deaths. For this, the representatives were paid a salary of a little less than five *koku* of rice each, about one-half of what the city elders received.

The groups of ten households (*jūningumi*) constituted the final link in the administrative chain. The groups had a long history in Kanazawa, and the term can be found in early-seventeenth-century documents. Apparently not all urban commoners formed themselves into such groups, however, until domain proclamations issued in the 1640s instructed them to do so. These groups of ten households (in reality, the number of households in any one group often exceeded that number) were the functional equivalent of the household groups established in the rural villages in most domains.

In one sense, the groups preserved the interests of the merchant and artisan neighborhoods, since they functioned as units of mutual aid and self-help. In Kanazawa, for instance, members were supposed to assist neighbors who fell on hard times financially, and from the mid-seventeenth century each group maintained firefighting equipment such as ladders, rakes, and rain barrels. Looked at from another perspective, the groups reflected an effort by the daimyo to extend his authority and laws over the commoner populace, as the group members were held jointly responsible for obeying the law and, in theory, could be collectively punished for the actions of any single member. Beyond this, the groups also carried out a variety of administrative functions. They assembled periodically to hear a reading of legal codes, enforced the provisions of wills and decided the disposition of property when a member died without leaving such a document, and verified that any member who moved to a new ward left no debts behind. Moreover, they conducted conciliation talks whenever quarrels, commercial disagreements, or land disputes among group members interrupted neighborhood tranquility. If no satisfactory solution could be found, then the ward representative, and ultimately the city elder if necessary, would be called in for further rounds of negotiation. Only if the mediation at all these levels failed did the dispute move up the ladder for settlement by samurai officialdom.

In pace with the amplification of the urban administrative apparatus during the first half of the seventeenth century, Kaga's officials acted to establish a written, legal basis for their political authority by issuing codifications of laws and ordinances. These were promulgated according to status group, with different codes for the samurai and for the urban commoners. During the early years of the castle town's growth, the Maeda daimyo issued three separate codes regulating the samurai life: in 1601, 1605, and 1612 (with a set of supplements in 1613). Here, daimyo law was very limited in scope and intent. For instance, the 1605 code, issued under the personal seal of Maeda Toshinaga (1562–1614), prohibited the following:

1. Walking on the streets at night.
2. Loitering on the streets.
3. Singing on the streets.
4. Playing the flute (*shakuhachi*).
5. Holding sumo matches on the street.
6. Dancing in the streets.
7. Masking one's face with a scarf.

Clearly, the government's chief concern was to preserve law and order and to establish procedures for the adjudication of disputes. The other samurai codes played on the same themes: They forbade cliques, declared that retainers should not harbor thieves or suspected criminals among their rear vassals, specified that all parties involved in violent quarrels were to be judged equally guilty, irrespective of who was at fault, and prohibited gambling, with specific rewards for anyone who supplied information about violators.

The laws directed at the merchants and artisans were much more numerous, and major codifications were issued in 1642 and 1660. A concern with peace on the city streets could also be detected in these documents. The 1642 code, for instance, carried prohibitions against gambling, gossiping, and keeping dogs as pets; whereas the 1660 edition repeated earlier injunctions against prostitution, wearing swords, and urinating from the second floor of houses.

But these merchant codes could intrude more into the lives of the urban commoners than did the samurai codes. Particularly noticeable was the expansion of government involvement in the economic life of the townspeople. The 1660 code stipulated that maximum interest rates be fixed at 1.7 percent per month and prohibited any joint samurai–merchant business ventures. Yet another article announced that a representative from the City Office would visit any person who fell behind in his debt repayments or credit obligations, an especially important clause for the merchants and artisans of Kanazawa, as it promised government assistance in collecting all debts. Another feature of merchant codes was a concern with public services. The 1660 code contained clauses concerning garbage disposal, the firefighting responsibilities of the household groups, and the duties of the ward patrols (*teishūban*), whose chief responsibility, which rotated among the residents of each ward, was to patrol nightly the ward's streets, watching for fire and criminal activity.

In addition to the major legal codifications, the domain government issued a mass of ordinances during the middle of seventeenth century that attempted both to regulate behavior and to further refine status distinctions. An important ordinance in 1661, for example, attempted to synchronize clothing with status. Regulations that took effect on New Year's Day of that year established the types of clothing fabrics permitted to peasants, townspeople, and each major subdivision of the samurai status group. Accordingly, high-level retainers such as members of the Eight Houses and the commanders could wear thirteen kinds of high-quality silk; retainers from the middle ranks were permitted four kinds of lesser silk; and those such as the more minor archers and riflers were restricted to pongee, cotton, and the rougher fibers of flax, hemp, and vines, known collectively under the rubric of *nuno*. The regulations provided that townspeople could wear plain silk (*kinu*) and pongee, whereas the peasants were held to pongee and the rougher fibers.

The domain complemented these clothing regulations with other status decrees. Some laws set limits on the amounts and kinds of foods that could be served on holidays and ceremonial days, with the samurai permitted more opulent indulgences than merchants were. According to other laws, townspeople were not supposed to have carved wooden beams or doors made from cedar in their homes, because these were perquisites of the samurai class. Nor could townspeople, unless they were seriously ill or over sixty years of age, ride in palanquins, whose use was normally restricted to high-ranking samurai and certain city officials.

The establishment of patterns of urban governance in early modern Japan paralleled the transformations in the exercise of political authority in rural areas and on the domain level, as explained in Chapters 5 and 9 of this volume. The daimyo of the late sixteenth century had been personal autocrats who led armies, enfeoffed retainers, issued decrees, and set policy. By the second half of the seventeenth century, most of their successors had withdrawn from the direct, day-to-day management of the affairs of government and, instead, had become more nominal rulers whose chief function was to serve as the legitimizing agent of the administrative structure.

The retreat of the daimyo as personal leaders, however, did not portend a decline in state powers, for the new bureaucracies of the seventeenth century had more ability to tax, legislate, and punish than did the daimyo of the previous age. Yet, in a profound historical twist, the exercise of this power was also newly tempered; first, by the government's need to harmonize its policies with the aspirations and wishes of the merchants and artisans in the cities and, second, by the obligation of government to subordinate its impulses to the requirements imposed by the new bureaucratic practices, legal codes, and standardized procedures that grew up during Japan's transition from the medieval to the early modern polity. The history of cities such as Kanazawa demonstrate how castle towns brought together the concentrations of wealth and power that made possible this shift away from personal forms of authority toward a new style of bureaucratic statism.

CITIES AND COMMERCE IN THE SEVENTEENTH CENTURY

Castle towns and the agricultural revolution

The commercial economy grew significantly during the period of Japan's political unification, from the middle sixteenth down to the end of the seventeenth century. The point of departure for this expansion was a revolution in agricultural production. Although the statistical data are not without shortcomings, some scholars have estimated that the amount of cultivated paddy more than doubled in the century from 1550 to 1650 alone.[28] Productivity and yields also increased as better fertilizers, improved farm tools, and new strains of seeds made their appearance. Important as well were reclamation and large-scale irrigation projects, many underwritten by daimyo who hoped to expand the taxable revenue base of their domains. Another factor was the role played by the individual peasant household. As rural residents acquired more secure rights to their holdings, a process discussed in Chapters 3 and 10 in this volume, the farmers came to believe that significant portions of any increase in yield would accrue to them, and thus they were more willing to make the investments necessary to boost productivity and to bring formerly marginal fields into cultivation.[29] Indeed, signs of a growing rural prosperity – new and larger houses, improved diet, better clothing – were evident in most areas of Japan by the middle of the seventeenth century.

These improvements in the nation's productive capacity touched off

---

28 Kozo Yamamura, "Returns on Unification: Economic Growth in Japan, 1550–1650," in Hall, Nagahara, and Yamamura, eds., *Japan Before Tokugawa*, p. 334.
29 Ibid., pp. 339–57.

a dynamic spurt in population growth. Although accurate statistics were not kept at that time, some demographers and historians place the growth rate in the range of 0.78 to 1.34 percent annually between 1550 and 1700. Others posit an accelerating rate during the seventeenth century, rising from 0.5 percent in the early decades of the century to nearly 1.4 percent between 1650 and 1670.[30] Despite these differences of opinion, most scholars agree that the greatest population increases took place in the last half of the seventeenth century and that, in aggregate, the country's total population grew from roughly 12 million persons to approximately 26 million to 30 million at the time of the shogun's census in 1721.

The rapid increase in both productive capacity and population also brought about changes in household composition. The number of individual farm households increased at a faster rate than did overall production growth, and this statistic indicates a rearrangement of household configuration away from a complex, extended family toward smaller nuclear families, many of which were created as branches and given land by the stem family. The disappearance of the extended farm family meant that the small independent cultivator (*jisakushonō*) who farmed his holding with the labor of his own family became the most common type of peasant household. As the process of subdivision continued, however, there eventually came into being a growing number of families who possessed land that was barely sufficient for their needs. Indeed, by the 1670s the shogunate had become so concerned about the destabilizing aspects of the further subdivision of farmland that it issued a "law restricting the division of farmland" (*bunchi seigen-rei*).[31]

The evolution of the farm family also brought about conditions that favored urban migration. As families shed surplus members during the first half of the seventeenth century, there were always some who did not have enough land to establish branch families. These disfranchised men and women often moved into the growing castle towns, where they could hope to find work as day laborers or unskilled artisans, although the poorest of the women were sometimes forced into prostitution. Similarly, those new branches who had received only marginal amounts of land were in a position of continuous economic

30 Hayami Akira, *Kinsei nōson no rekishi jinkōgaku-teki kenkyū* (Tokyo: Tōyō keizai shimpōsha, 1973), p. 23; and Shakai kōgaku kenkyūjo, ed., *Nihon rettō ni okeru jinkō bumpu no chōki jikeiretsu bunseki* (Tokyo: Shakai kōgaku kenkyūjo, 1974), pp. 42–57.
31 The fullest discussion of the relationship between the commercialization of agriculture and household composition remains Thomas C. Smith, *The Agrarian Origins of Modern Japan* (Stanford, Calif.: Stanford University Press, 1959).

jeopardy, and in years of even slight drought or cold weather they might have to abandon their homes to search for work, or even to beg, in the castle towns.

There is no way of knowing the exact magnitude of migration in the seventeenth century, but given the rapid growth of the castle towns, surely several hundreds of thousands of persons were on the move in the middle decades of the century. In Kanazawa alone, to take one example, between 1660 to 1663, arriving would-be merchants and artisans leased well over 300,000 square meters of farmland on the fringes of the city.[32] Regardless of the exact scale of migration, however, local officials were clearly worried, and many castle towns enacted special ordinances in the middle of the seventeenth century that discouraged further movement into their cities and that attempted to bring beggars under closer supervision.[33]

The ongoing migration from village to city also prompted the shogunate to introduce the system of family census registers (koseki) as one way of gaining some measure of control over this migrant population. Before this, the shogunate had compelled each temple to conduct a religious investigation (shūshi aratame) as a means of suppressing Christianity. It had also ordered a census and household count in each village for the purpose of making corvée levies, and at the same time, it instructed peasants to report the number of cattle and horses they were raising. In 1670, however, these two records were combined in the religious and census investigation (shūmon aratame). This new reporting system began the practice of requiring all the households of each domain, without exception, to register the names of their members with ward or village officials and to identify their temple of affiliation. Once a person was registered, if he wanted to migrate, he had to prove that he had obtained the permission of his temple and his ward or village.

In addition to provoking the imposition of stricter political controls, the large influx of population into the cities in the middle decades of the seventeenth century affected the physical layout of the castle towns. First, the castle towns started to expand into areas beyond the geographic limits that the daimyo founders had envisioned. The migrants, mostly poor, tended to live where rents were lowest, on the rural fringes of the castle towns. Increasingly, the boundaries between urban wards and agricultural villages became blurred as men and

32 Tanaka Yoshio, "Kinsei jōkamachi hatten no ichi kōsatsu – 'Aitaiukechi' kara mita jōkamachi, Kanazawa no baai," *Hokuriku shigaku* 8 (1959): 19–37.
33 For a specific example, see McClain, *Kanazawa*, pp. 124–32.

women who worked as laborers, craftsmen, or bushi household servants rented lodgings in settlements that were under the administrative jurisdiction of the rural magistrates (*kōri bugyō*). Moreover, theaters and houses of prostitution often sprouted up in these fringe areas. This growth caused, in turn, a whole new set of problems, as farmers complained about the newcomers trampling over fields, breaking down dikes, or otherwise disrupting the rhythm of agricultural life. Many urban governments responded by transferring these areas to the jurisdiction of the city magistrates, thus making the merchant–farmer wards part of the cityscape.

The physical expansion of the cities played havoc with older notions of urban planning. Originally, for instance, most daimyo had preferred, for defensive purposes, to situate their foot soldiers and the large Buddhist temples in a concentric circle around the outer limits of the city. Now many had to abandon that design or else undertake considerable expense and trouble to relocate the warrior residences and religious institutions. Predictably, this kind of urban reorganization most frequently occurred in cities that had the misfortune of suffering a major fire. Such conflagrations provided a convenient pretext for the daimyo to relocate people who otherwise would have been reluctant to move to strange neighborhoods, away from old friends and familiar shops and places of worship. Following such fires, many daimyo also widened the streets and established open areas as firebreaks at strategic points.

Concurrently, the principle that persons of the same occupation ought to live together in the same wards suffered serious erosion, and except for some special occupations such as that of gunsmith or swordsmith, artisans as well as merchants began to reside in scattered locations throughout the expanding cities. One reason contributing to this process was that some established merchants and artisans voluntarily moved into the newly created fringe wards, in search of new customers or lower shop rents. A second reason was that the forced relocation of some bushi turned the fringe areas into real residential hodgepodges, adding samurai to the merchant, artisan, and day laborer populations. In Kanazawa, for instance, seven of the households in one ward on the outskirts of the city belonged to artisans, twenty-eight to merchants, six to day laborers, and thirteen to samurai.[34]

The complexion of the inner city changed as well. As some of the

---

34 For this and other examples, see Tanaka, *Jōkamachi Kanazawa*, pp. 103–106; and Tanaka Yoshio, *Kaga han ni okeru toshi no kenkyū* (Tokyo: Bun'ichi sōgō shuppan, 1978), pp. 140–5.

newcomers prospered, they moved into the older, more prestigious sections of the city, usually choosing sites that suited their fancy and commercial needs, rather than adhering to the artificial occupation divisions of an earlier age. Finally, many were tempted by the empty land within the new firebreaks. Not uncommonly, poorer merchants and artisans squatted on this land, much to the chagrin of those domain authorities who were still wedded to the notion of a planned city. But the perseverance of the homesteaders to stay was usually greater than the resolve of the city authorities to evict them.

The expansion of cities in the middle and later decades of the seventeenth century was only one factor working to change the character and function of cities. By the end of the century, the commoners of the castle towns had also achieved new levels of economic prosperity and brought into being a distinctive urban-based culture. The interaction of the population migration with the commercial and cultural developoment inside the city created a new kind of castle town, as we shall see, one that was very different from the expectations of the daimyo during the period of urban creation at the beginning of the century.

Commercial development and castle town merchants

Paralleling the agricultural revolution was a spectacular expansion in the volume of commercial exchange that began during the middle decades of the sixteenth century and continued until the end of the seventeenth century. Historians have identified several causes that contributed to this process, including the policies implemented by the daimyo during the late Sengoku period in order to strengthen the economic basis of their rule, such as the abolition of toll gate barriers and the promotion of periodic markets that would be open to all traders.[35]

Daimyo of the seventeenth century continued these policies and also vigorously promoted the expansion of permanent markets within the new castle towns, such as when the Maeda daimyo set aside two plots of land in the commercial heart of Kanazawa to be used by fish and vegetable dealers.[36] Other significant stimulants included the standard-

35 The classic work on this topic is Sasaki Gin'ya, *Chūsei shōhin ryūtsū no kenkyū* (Tokyo: Hōsei daigaku shuppankyoku, 1972). In English, see Gin'ya Sasaki, with William B. Hauser, "Sengoku Daimyo Rule and Commerce," in Hall, Nagahara, and Yamamura, eds., *Japan Before Tokugawa*, pp. 125–48; and Kozo Yamamura, "Returns on Unification," on pp. 327–72 of the same volume.

36 Kanazawa-shi Ōmichō ichiba-shi hensan iinkai, ed., *Kanazawa-shi Ōmichō ichiba-shi* (Kanazawa: Hokkoku shuppansha, 1979), pp. 10–25.

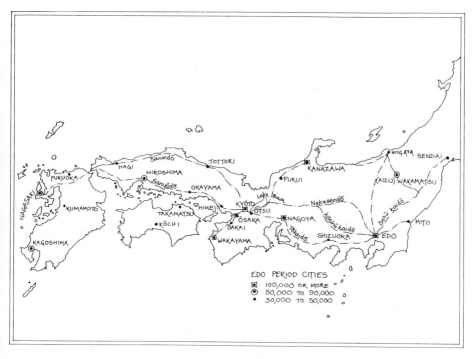

Map 11.1 Major cities and transportation routes, eighteenth century.

ization of weights and measures and the minting of coins by the Tokugawa shogunate that were accepted nationwide as units of exchange.
Important, too, was the growth of transportation facilities.[37] Beyond
constructing port facilities and dredging rivers and canals to link castle
towns to ports, the Tokugawa shogunate and individual daimyo also
laid out large sums of money to develop overland transportation facilities. The keystone of these projects was the linking of Edo with distant
localities by the construction of several major roadways, including the
great Tōkaidō highway between Edo and Kyoto, whose more than
fifty post towns provided the supplies, horses, and resting places that
made possible transportation between the emperor's and the shogun's
home cities. Within the domains, too, the daimyo built roads and
bridges to ease the transport of foodstuffs and raw materials from the
rural villages into the castle towns.[38] (See Map 11.1)

37 Maruyama Yasunari, "Toshi to rikujō kōtsū," in Toyoda, Harada, and Yamori, eds., Kōza:
Nihon no hōken toshi, vol. 2, pp. 119–44.
38 For a very useful study of the post towns, see Haga Noboru, Shukuba-machi (Kyoto:
Yanagihara shoten, 1977).

Another factor was the institutionalization of the system of alternate residence. Although the custom of personal attendance on one's superior and the submission of hostages as an expression of loyalty had become fairly common during the sixteenth century, these practices were made a permanent obligation for the daimyo only after 1633. From that date, daimyo were compelled to alternate their residences between Edo and their home domains, to build elaborate mansions in Edo, and to leave appropriate retinues, including their wives and children, permanently in the shogun's city. This system was designed to permit the shogunate to maintain a close surveillance over the daimyo, but it also had the consequence of stimulating the nation's volume of commercial exchange as the daimyo processions moved back and forth along the new highways that crossed Japan.[39]

The growing wave of commercial transactions had several important consequences. Agricultural patterns changed enormously, for now farmers were able to concentrate more profitably their energies on growing commercial crops, such as cotton, tea, hemp, mulberry, indigo, vegetables, and tobacco, for sale to the urban markets.[40] Regional specialization also became a feature of economic life, as great numbers of villagers around Osaka, for instance, started to switch over to cotton cultivation while farmers in northern Japan began to raise horses and cattle for sale as draft animals.[41] Individual rural households began to develop by-employments or simple rural industries, so that even within a single domain certain villages became known for their production of goods such as paper, charcoal, ink, pottery, lacquer ware, or spun cloth.

Concurrent with the commercial growth of Tokugawa Japan was the daimyo's increasing need for cash revenues, which could come only through participation in interregional trade. One part of the story is simply that the daimyo needed money to buy the growing number of specialized goods that were produced outside their own domains. But the system of alternate residence also put a strain on the daimyo's finances. The experience of the Maedo daimyo of Kaga was fairly typical. By the end of the seventeenth century, their journeys to Edo

---

39 The most complete treatment of the alternate residence system in English is Toshio George Tsukahira, *Feudal Control in Tokugawa Japan: The Sankin Kōtai System*, Harvard East Asian Monographs, no. 20 (Cambridge, Mass.: Harvard University Press, 1966).

40 This shift in cropping patterns is discussed in Watanabe Zenjirō, *Toshi to nōson no aida* (Tokyo: Ronsōsha, 1983), esp. pp. 121–49, 241–76.

41 For examples of this sort of regional specialization in the Kinai, Morioka, and Okayama, see Susan B. Hanley and Kozo Yamamura, *Economic and Demographic Change in Preindustrial Japan, 1600–1868* (Princeton, N.J.: Princeton University Press, 1977), pp. 91–198.

and the expenses associated with maintaining the nearly three thousand persons from Kaga who lived year-round in the Edo mansion often consumed at least one-third and sometimes as much as one-half of all annual domain expenditures.[42] The occasional extraordinary levies made by the shogunate were also burdensome. The Tokugawa rulers demanded economic assistance when they rebuilt Osaka Castle after the siege of 1614–15, constructed a castle residence for the retired Ieyasu at Sumpu, and repaired Edo Castle after fires in 1636, 1657, and 1658. The shogunate also made fairly regular exactions for the construction of roads, bridges, and waterways. The cash requirements dictated by the shogun's levies, when added to burdens associated with the system of alternate residence, contributed greatly to the domains' growing indebtedness. By the end of the seventeenth century, nearly all domains were spending in some years more than they could collect in agricultural levies, and many daimyo had turned to borrowing funds from wealthy merchants in Edo and Osaka. To return to the Kaga example, annual domain expenses amounted to nearly 15 percent more than its revenues in the 1690s, and within another two generations the total of its outstanding loans to wealthy merchants probably amounted to more than twice the sum of all annual domain revenues.[43]

Commercial growth and the expanding needs of most domains for new sources of revenues prompted many daimyo to revise their policies toward the merchants in their castle towns. In particular, many daimyo began to cast aside their ties with the older class of privileged merchants, the *goyō* purveyors to the lord, and, instead, began to nurture relationships with other groups of businessmen who could best meet the changing requirements for increasing the flow of goods into castle towns and promoting interdomain trade.

In most castle towns, the daimyo and their governments now forged ties with *ton'ya*, or groups of wholesalers and forwarding agents, to whom the lords granted monopoly rights over specific commodities and commercial crops. Some of these associations participated in interregional trade. In Kaga domain, for instance, an association of tea wholesalers had been formed by the 1650s and had been granted sole rights to import tea from other domains. The wholesalers' own profits came from a commission, which was authorized by the domain and added to the basic price before the wholesalers sold the tea to peddlers

42 For the figures for Kaga and several other domains, see Tsukahira, *Feudal Control*, pp. 81–102.
43 Kuranami Seiji, *Kaga: Hyakumangoku* (Tokyo: Hachiyo shuppan, 1974), pp. 101–28.

who then retailed it throughout the domain.[44] Other wholesale groups specialized in moving goods from the closer rural hinterlands to castle town customers. Thus by the 1680s several different wholesale groups were authorized to buy charcoal, paper, ink, cloth, cooking oil, and firewood from villagers throughout Kaga domain, who produced these items at slack times in the agriculture season, and to sell them, after adding a commission, to retailers in the castle town of Kanazawa.[45]

In other cases, wholesalers were responsible for directing the complex flow of raw materials that were used to produce local specialities for sale outside the domain. An example of how many layers of wholesalers might be involved in such a process comes from the castle town of Hikone, headquarters of the famous Ii family of *fudai* daimyo. There, the most marketable local product was clothing made from jute (*asa*), which was prized for its coolness and breathability in the warmer, more humid regions of Japan. Farmers in mountainous areas around Hikone collected the jute and sold it to designated groups of wholesalers, who in turn resold it to artisans, who then spun it into thread. A different group of wholesalers known as *asaya*, or jute dealers, then purchased this thread, added an authorized markup, and sold it to craftsmen who wove it into cloth. Finally, yet another authorized group of wholesalers purchased the cloth and marketed it outside the domain.

In other circumstances, a domain might pursue policies that favored particular artisan groups. In the castle town of Wakamatsu in Aizu domain (the present-day city of Aizu–Wakamatsu), about 10 percent of all the artisans in the city produced lacquer ware, a local product that won fame nationwide and was in great demand in central markets such as Edo and Osaka. The domain designated the trees and bushes from which lacquer base was extracted as *yakuboku*, or "tax trees," and the domain ordered the peasants to collect the liquid extracted from the trees and to pay it as a tax. The government later sold the extract to castle town artisans and then purchased the output, mostly wooden soup bowls, for sale outside the domain. Although no figures for the seventeenth century are available, by the middle of the eighteenth century, exports of such lacquer ware accounted for 84 percent of all domain exports. Indeed, the fact that the domain imported beech and magnolia trees, which provided sap that could be turned into the lacquer base, indicates that demand for Aizu lacquer ware far outstripped the amount of raw material available in the domain.

44 Heki Ken, eds., *Kaga han shiryō*, 18 vols. (Tokyo: Ishiguro bunkichi, 1928–58), vol. 4 (Kambun 3 [1663]/3/6), pp. 10–12.
45 McClain, *Kanazawa*, pp. 131–4.

Government policy in almost every castle town gave preferential treatment to rice dealers. The reason for this had to do with the tax and stipendiary systems. When the diamyo across Japan pulled the samurai into the castle towns and abolished their prerogative to extract dues from the peasants directly, the lords began to compensate their retainers by providing stipends, denominated in units of rice. By the middle of the seventeenth century, it had become standard practice in most parts of Japan to pay samurai with certificates, good for the amount of their stipends and collectible from the daimyo's granary. Very soon, rice dealers who bought the certificates from the samurai, and even from the daimyo himself, and then sold the rice on the open market became a prominent part of the merchant class in nearly every castle town.

Because it was in the daimyo's interest to have rice sell at as high a price as possible, most daimyo governments enacted laws that, in effect, gave special protection to the rice dealers. For example, almost every daimyo strictly prohibited the importation of rice from outside his home domain, except during times of famine. Moreover, most daimyo formally recognized groups of rice dealers, who could then form a protective association, or *kabunakama*, with monopoly rights to purchase rice certificates from the samurai.

Finally, many daimyo enacted policies that favored saké brewing as a way of encouraging rice consumption. One way that they did this was to specify the amounts of rice to be set aside for saké production. Beyond this, many daimyo also protected the brewers by authorizing the formation of protective associations, prohibiting the importation of saké from outside the domain, and granting special payment terms to brewers for the rice they used in their business.[46] By the end of the seventeenth century, saké brewers in the castle towns had become as important as their rural counterparts and were among the more prosperous elements of the urban merchant class.

Local towns

Closely related to the increasing volume of commercial exchange was the appearance of what were called local towns, or *zaigōmachi*. As

---

46 Numerous restrictive regulations concerning saké brewing can be found in compilations of laws in the Tokugawa period, and so it has been argued that saké brewing was generally carried out under very severe production restrictions. However, these regulations were typically issued on a temporary basis during the periods of poor harvest or crop failures. In normal times, saké brewers were valued as large-scale consumers of rice.

farmers engaged more and more in by-employments, merchants began to move into rural areas in order to help the farmers assemble raw materials, process those into finished products, and then transport the goods into the urban retail markets. In time, the percentage of the rural population engaged in trade grew, and many of the villages lost their agricultural identity. The evolution of villages into local towns is often considered to be a nineteenth-century phenomenon, but the process certainly began earlier. For instance, in Kaga domain alone, by the close of the seventeenth century the government had recognized the commercial growth of fifteen villages by redesignating them as towns (*machi*) and placing them under the jurisdiction of their own town magistrates.[47]

The village of Jōhana, located not far from Kanazawa in Kaga domain, can serve as a useful example of the trend toward small-scale rural urbanization.[48] Jōhana sits on a large alluvial delta at the point where the famous Mt. Gokayama faces Tonami Plain. Farmers who lived in the foothills around the mountains grew cocoons that were used to manufacture silk thread. These farmers, however, had only a few plots of rice paddy, and after they paid their taxes and fed their families, few had enough capital to cover the cost of producing the cocoons. Consequently, certain urban-based rice merchants and financiers came to Jōhana and began to lend rice and money to farmers so that they could raise cocoons, with the understanding that these merchant financiers would be permitted to buy the crop. The merchants then turned over the cocoons to artisans in Jōhana who would spin them into thread, which in turn was sold to another group for weaving into silk cloth. Finally, wholesalers, also based in Jōhana, would sell the silk cloth outside the domain, especially to merchants in Kyoto. This kind of commercial opportunity transformed Jōhana from an agricultural village at mid-century into a community in which the majority of households in 1693 were engaged in some aspect of the silk business. Indeed, about 30 percent of Jōhana's residents had migrated there between 1683 and 1693 in order to take advantage of these commercial opportunities.

Raw cotton was another commercial crop whose increased popular-

---

47 *Kaga han shiryō*, vol. 5 (Genroku 13 [1700]), p. 515. For more on Japan in general, see Thomas C. Smith, "Pre-modern Economic Growth: Japan and the West," *Past and Present* 43 (1973): 127–60.

48 Jōhana is the topic of several articles in Mizushima Shigeru, *Kaga han, Toyama han no shakai keizaishi no kenkyū* (Tokyo: Bunken shuppan, 1982), pp. 41–64.

ity had significant repercussions on urbanization and the emergence of local towns.[49] Cotton was first grown extensively as a cash crop in the Yamato region (present-day Nara Prefecture), and the provinces of Settsu, Kawachi, and Izumi quickly became centers of cotton cultivation. Later, production moved further into western Japan. The rapid expansion of cotton production at the end of the seventeenth century touched off a clothing revolution, for farmers and lower-class urban dwellers quickly began to replace their rough hemp and jute clothing with cotton products.

At first cotton was grown on dry fields in the Yamato region, but farmers soon changed to wet-field production. In many villages, more than 50 percent of the wet-field area was given over to cotton production. At the beginning of the eighteenth century, the shogunate sponsored a construction project on the Yodo River, which flowed into the sea at Osaka, and completed a channel that emptied into the ocean at Sakai. At that time, old residences, ponds, and swamps along the river were converted into wet fields, most of which were used to grow cotton. Indeed, there were even some villages where all the land was turned over to cotton cultivation.

Farmers typically held back a portion of the cotton crop that they harvested and processed it themselves by stripping the seeds and spinning the cotton into thread for weaving into cloth on home looms. Normally, they did this as a form of by-employment in the slack season and sold the output to cotton cloth dealers. The farmers sold any remaining portion of the crop in its unprocessed state to wholesale agents, who turned it over to local artisans who ginned the cotton, some using an instrument called a *wataguri*, a tool imported from China through the port of Nagasaki. Next, other local artisans spun the cotton into thread and wove it into cloth for sale by retailers. Any remaining portion was bought up by traveling wholesalers who peddled it in various individual domains across Japan.

In the Yamato region, the collection of raw cotton from farmers and the processing into thread and cotton cloth took place chiefly in the castle town of Kōriyama.[50] But in the Osaka area, where cotton growing developed on a wide scale, several local towns sprang up to house

49 For a study of the causes leading to the growth of local towns in one region, see Omura Hajime, "Echigo no zaigō-machi," in Toyoda, Harada, and Yamori, eds., *Kōza: Nihon no hōken toshi*, vol. 3, pp. 354–91.
50 Kobayashi Shigeru, "Kinai no zaigō-machi," in Toyoda, Harada, and Yamori, eds., *Kōza: Nihon no hōken toshi*, vol. 3, pp. 392–422.

the merchants and artisans engaged in the trade.[51] Examples include Hiranogō, Kashiwabara, Furuichi, Tondabayashi, Daigazuka, Izumisano, and Kaizuka, many of which once had been temple towns. The largest of these old temple towns that emerged as a commercial center was Hiranogō, which, according to a 1704 census, had 2,543 households and 9,272 persons. Among these households, 1,331 were listed as agriculturalists, and thus Hiranogō might be labeled an "agricultural town" (nōson-toshi), that is, one in which approximately half the population engaged in agriculture and half in commerce. Among the 1,212 households engaged in commerce in Hiranogō, 254 were involved in some aspect of the cotton business, from the wholesaling through the winnowing stages. In addition, 60 households purchased cottonseeds and manufactured oil. If the dyers of cotton cloth, dealers in used cotton clothing, fertilizer manufacturers, and shipping agents are also included, then 44 percent of all the merchants in the city managed businesses that were related in some way to the cotton trade. Day laborers accounted for 313 households, and many were undoubtedly employed in some aspect of the cotton business. Thus it is clear that Hiranogō was supported by the cotton production of surrounding agricultural areas and that the cotton trade within the city was characterized by a highly developed functional specialization.

There were some ten other, similar "agriculture towns" in the region, including Kaizuka, which also had previously been a temple town. Kaizuka was the home port for eleven oceangoing ships and forty-one coastal boats used to export cotton and cloth and to import rice from Shikoku and Hokuriku and fish fertilizer from Edo and Uraga. This indicated that the production of cotton was not dominated solely by capital financiers from Osaka but, rather, flourished in the various "agricultural towns" and in large part involved small-scale, independent traders and producers. Moreover, the Kaizuka example shows how the development of the cotton business brought about a new marketing structure that stimulated the commercial rice business in Shikoku and Hokuriku as well as the fish business in the Kantō region.

The commercialization of agriculture and the emergence of new patterns of marketing during the seventeenth century also created fresh opportunities for new groups of men to compete with the older,

51 For a full discussion of the spread of the cotton trade into local towns, especially those such as Hiranogō and Kaizuka in the Osaka region, see Nakai Nobuhiko, Tenkan-ki bakuhansei no kenkyū (Tokyo: Hanawa shobō, 1971), pp. 237–321. In English, see William B. Hauser, Economic Institutional Change in Tokugawa Japan: Osaka and the Kinai Cotton Trade (Cambridge, England: Cambridge University Press, 1974), pp. 143–60.

established shipping agents who were based in castle towns and who monopolized the transportation of goods under charters authorized by their daimyo. That is, during the first half of the century, goods were typically transported along a limited number of prescribed roadways by officially designated transportation agents or shippers, who handled cargo at prescribed places called *toiyaba* within the cities. In exchange for this monopoly right, the shippers had to handle freight for the daimyo and his retainers either free of charge or at reduced rates. However, some commodities, especially those that had to be carted into a castle town from its hinterland villages, were transported outside of the official system. In these cases, farmers simply packed goods that they had made themselves onto horses or other draft animals, which they otherwise used for agricultural purposes, and took these products into the cities.

During the seventeenth century, some of these farmers started to transport goods to more distant places, shipping agricultural products and rural handicrafts, and even finished goods from the castle towns, to central markets outside of their own domains. For many merchants the new services offered by the farmers turned part-time shippers were cheaper and more convenient than the official system, which by law required that loads be placed on fresh horses at the *toiyaba* of each post town, which were located about ten kilometers apart along the major roadways. Consequently, many customers began to use the services of these farmer-agents. As they accumulated capital, some of these new shippers also became wholesalers, buying up goods in rural areas and selling them to urban merchants. In this way there emerged a new group of former agriculturalists who moved into the cities during the final decades of the seventeenth century and who came to specialize in the purchase, handling, storage, and sales of various commodities.

Because the public transportation system had been set up by the shogunate and the individual daimyo domains, the older, officially recognized forwarding agents and wholesalers in the post towns now protested to the shogunate and requested that prohibitions be directed against the newly emerging shippers and wholesalers in both cities and rural areas. Often, however, daimyo supported the newer shippers. The reason was that the daimyo were hoping that the greater volume of commerce generated by the new shippers would help enhance the prosperity of their domains, especially the castle towns.[52]

52 For a study of the transportation system and of some of the contentions that could arise, see Constantine N. Vaporis, "Post Station and Assisting Village," *Monumenta Nipponica* 41 (Winter 1986): 377–414.

It was also during the latter half of the seventeenth century that ocean transport developed rapidly, especially between Edo and Osaka. The enormous consumption demands generated by the residents of Edo, the de facto political capital of the country, were satisfied in large part by supplies from advanced economic areas in western Japan. Consequently, great importance was attached to the development of an ocean link with Osaka, which had emerged as a collection and distribution center. The Inland Sea, used for shipping from the earliest times, formed the principal route between Osaka and Kyushu, Shikoku, and western Honshu. Usually goods sent to Edo from the Pacific coast region of northern Japan were shipped by oceangoing transport to Naha Bay (near Mito in present-day Ibaraki Prefecture) where they were off-loaded and forwarded to Edo via land, river, and lake routes. A second ocean link involved shipping the goods to Chōshi Bay (present-day Chiba Prefecture) and then sending them up the Tone River on barges to Edo. Ships avoided going around Bōsō peninsula and directly into Edo Bay because of the danger of shipwreck off the southern tip of the peninsula. Goods from the Japan Sea side of Tōhoku and from Hokuriku were first shipped to Tsuruga (Fukui Prefecture) or Obama on Wakasa Bay. They were off-loaded at these ports and sent overland to the northern shore of Lake Biwa where they were put on boats and transshipped to Ōtsu before being forwarded overland to Kyoto and Osaka.

Shipping was still divided into these circuits at the middle of the seventeenth century, although all had the disadvantage of requiring that the goods be hauled overland for a portion of the journey. That state of affairs was remedied and the Japan Sea coast transformed into one complete circuit when the shogunate instructed the entrepreneur Kawamura Zuiken to develop the sea routes known as the eastern sea circuit (*higashi mawari*) and the western sea circuit (*nishi mawari*). Kawamura accomplished this by charting coastal waters, erecting beacons and lighthouses at dangerous points where the shipping lanes came close to rocks, and providing disaster relief facilities. With the backing of the shogunate, he was also able to convince many daimyo to abolish port taxes and to issue regulations that permitted freedom of cargo handling so that ships from every domain could enter all ports. Ultimately, the eastern sea circuit connected the most distant parts of Tōhoku directly with Edo, and the western sea circuit went from the Japan Sea coast side of Tōhoku through Hokuriku, then around the Straits of Shimonoseki and into the Inland Sea, before continuing directly to Osaka. The Edo–Osaka route connected the two circuits.[53]

The establishment of the two coastal shipping circuits in 1671 and 1672 was a direct response to the growth of Edo's population. In other words, Edo's demands for foodstuffs, which had increased markedly just before this period, far outstripped supplies from the city's nearby hinterland, which were unusually scarce because of several poor harvests, and this threatened social unrest in the city. Consequently, the shogunate was anxious to find a way to ship tax rice from its holdings in the Tōhoku area quickly and safely to Edo.

The consolidation of the shipping circuits, however, also encouraged private traders and stimulated the development of a nationwide commercial economy by fostering the manufacture of goods for export outside the area of production. One example of this is commercial fertilizers which became necessary for the cultivation of raw cotton as the acreage dedicated to that crop expanded explosively in the Nara and Osaka areas. The most common kind of fertilizer was made from dried sardines, and at first fish taken from the Inland Sea were used for this purpose. In response to the rapid increase in demand for this kind of commercial fertilizer, new businesses were established on Bōsō peninsula, especially at Kujūkuri beach. At first, the fishing grounds around Bōsō were worked by fishermen who came up from Wakayama during the fishing season and toiled for a daily wage on boats owned and managed by men who lived in the Kujūkuri area. They dried the sardines on the sands of the beach and then sent them to ports in Uraga. Fertilizer merchants from Kansai opened branch stores in the port towns around Uraga Bay to buy up fertilizer for shipment to cotton-growing areas in western Japan.[54]

Until this time, the broad sands of Kujūkuri beach had been used to produce modest amounts of salt, which the local farmers made by boiling off salt water in large cauldrons. Now, however, the farmers learned from the men of Wakayama new methods of netting fish. In time, some of the villagers even abandoned their agricultural homes in

---

53 For a thorough study in English, see E. Sydney Crawcour, "Kawamura Zuiken: A Seventeenth Century Entrepreneur," *Transactions of the Asiatic Society of Japan* 9, 3rd series (1966): 1–23. A detailed analysis of the impact of the new routes on local commerce is contained in Takase Tamotsu, *Kaga han kaiunshi no kenkyū* (Tokyo: Yūhikaku, 1979).

54 For an account of how the development of shipping routes influenced commercial production on the opposite side of Japan, see Makino Ryūshin, *Kitamaebune no jidai* (Tokyo: Kyōikusha, 1979). In English, see Robert G. Flershem, "Some Aspects of Japan Sea Trade in the Tokugawa Period," *Journal of Asian Studies* 23 (May 1964): 405–16.

order to establish fishing villages on the seashore. An improved, larger net that could be stretched between two boats came into general use, and this made the Kujūkuri area Japan's richest sardine-fishing grounds. The farmers-turned-fishermen capitalized on this by opening up a wholesale office on the banks of the Fuka River in Edo, and even the fertilizer dealers from the Kansai region had to purchase supplies through this office. Gradually, the Edo wholesale office also took over the collection of cargoes, which had previously been handled by merchants in Uraga.

In this way, the fishing villages located along the Bōsō coastline increased their catches of fish that were processed into fertilizer for use in cotton cultivation in the Kansai region, and the residents of Kujūkuri beach, who had given up making salt to concentrate on producing fish fertilizer, began instead to purchase salt that was produced in villages along the Inland Sea, an area where salt production grew rapidly at the end of the seventeenth century. The abandonment of salt production at Kujūkuri beach was not an isolated event. The demands of the great urban markets at Edo and Osaka stimulated the production of salt in the villages along the Inland Sea, and this salt, cheaper because of large-scale production techniques, came to be sold commercially along the western circuit and almost completely displaced local, small-scale salt manufacturers, such as those at Kujūkuri. The only exception to this trend were those special cases in which daimyo supported salt production through the grant of special privileges.

In short, the expansion of urban markets was closely linked to the emergence of local towns, such as Jōhana, where businessmen could produce competitively priced goods, and to the more intensified regional specialization in the production of commercial items such as fertilizers and salt. In turn, the new production locales and marketing networks triggered further transformations in the three major metropolises of Edo, Kyoto, and Osaka, as we shall see next.

The three metropolises

Kyoto. Nestled at the top of the urban hierarchy in early modern Japan were the three large metropolises of Edo, Osaka, and Kyoto. Of these, Kyoto was the most ancient and the most highly regarded as a cultural center. Kyoto's artistic and literary achievements had sparkled most brightly during the classical golden age of the early eleventh century, when court mimes, pageants, and processions were held regularly at palatial residences around the city, when artists unrolled their stories on narrative scrolls (*emakimono*), and when court ladies such as Murasaki Shikibu and Sei Shōnagon penned novels and literary diaries of unsurpassed elegance and style.

During a large portion of the medieval period, Kyoto functioned as the nation's undisputed administrative center.[55] From its founding in 794 Kyoto had been home to the emperor and his court, but from 1338 until 1573 Kyoto became as well the headquarters for the shogunate. From the thirteenth century, the city also served as Japan's primary religious center when the new, popularly oriented Jōdo and Nichiren sects, as well as the more rigorous Rinzai branch of the Zen sect, established their chief temples in Kyoto or else in the city's immediate environs. Concurrently, as the priesthood and warrior class joined the nobility in the city as a consuming elite, Kyoto became a center of trade, manufacturing, and exchange. Artisans who produced handicrafts of exceptional quality for the courtiers had long been a permanent feature of Kyoto life, but now they worked alongside merchants, known as *toiya* or *ton'ya*, who served the military elite by forwarding to the city tax revenues and other goods from the warriors' home provinces. Within Kyoto, the Ashikaga shogunate also encouraged the development of guilds (*za*) to control the production and distribution of certain crucial commercial products such as lamp oil and salted fish.[56]

Kyoto reached another crossroads in 1573 when Oda Nobunaga forced the last Ashikaga shogun to flee and then burned and pillaged Kamigyō, the aristocratic northern half of the city. Hideyoshi began to refashion the city into a military strongpoint by girdling the city with an earthen rampart and compelling religious establishments to congregate in Teramachi and Tera-no-uchi, areas set aside for that specific purpose. Tokugawa Ieyasu then capped this process by placing Nijō Castle and a military garrison in the midst of the city.[57]

The rich history of the city during the early modern period is reflected in an occupation register compiled in 1685.[58] According to this

55 The leading scholar on premodern Kyoto is Hayashiya Tatsusaburō. See especially his *Machishū: Kyōto ni okeru "shimin" keisei shi* (Tokyo: Chūō Kōronsha, 1964). In English, see Tatsusaburō Hayashiya, with George Elison, "Kyoto in the Muromachi Age," in Hall and Toyoda, eds., *Japan in the Muromachi Age*, pp. 15–36.
56 These issues are covered in Takeshi Toyoda and Sugiyama Hiroshi, with V. Dixon Morris, "The Growth of Commerce and Trades," in Hall and Toyoda, eds., *Japan in the Muromachi Age*, pp. 129–44.
57 Ashikaga Kenryō, "Kyōto jōkamachi no keisei," in Toyoda, Harada, and Yamori, eds., *Kōza: Nihon no hōken toshi*, vol. 3, pp. 68–97.
58 Nakai Nobuhiko, "Kinsei toshi no hatten," in *Iwanami kōza Nihon no rekishi*, vol. 11 (*kinsei* 3) (Tokyo: Iwanami shoten, 1963), pp. 37–100. The population composition of the city is also discussed in Moriya Takeshi, *Kyō no chōnin* (Tokyo: Kyōikusha, 1980), pp. 55–70.

document, Kyoto was home to 51 doctors, categorized as physicians, surgeons, pediatricians, obstetricians, ophthalmologists, and dentists. In addition, two other registers list 41 "men of letters" (*bungakusha*), including poets and specialists of Chinese classics; 16 "experts" (*kanteinin*) on painting and calligraphy; and 125 "masters" (*shishō*) of the tea ceremony, flower arrangement, the noh theater, and the board games *go* and *shōgi*.

Skilled artisans also made Kyoto the nation's center of traditional fine arts and handicrafts. The population registers of 1685 also list famous shops by specialty, and among these we can find dealers with national reputations for their musical instruments, writing brushes, and implements for the tea ceremony. A separate register contains the names of craftsmen who produced such high-quality artistic goods as crowns, folding fans, porcelain, *tabi* footwear, special clothing for use in the tea ceremony, fixtures for Buddhist household altars, and high-quality paper used by the emperor, courtiers, and the warrior elite.

Beyond this, the weaving of silk goods and textile dyeing added a distinctive touch to craft production in Kyoto. The number of weavers in the seventeenth century is not known for certain, but some documents state that a fire in 1730 destroyed nearly three thousand looms, out of a total of more than seven thousand in the city.[59] If this is so, then it would seem likely that more than ten thousand persons were engaged in textile production at that time, if the dyers are included. During the late medieval period, weaving spread to Kaga and then other parts of the country, but in general regional production concentrated on more ordinary, plain silk, whereas the techniques for expert dyeing and for making complicated patterns and crests remained an exclusive monopoly of the Kyoto craftsmen.

The great economic transformation of the seventeenth century changed the nature of the silk trade in Kyoto. The growth in wealth nationwide generated new demands for Kyoto silk, and over the century the ancient imperial capital became as well known for its commercial production as it had been for its aristocratic traditions. Some of the new demand came from daimyo and upper-level samurai, who had become the country's new social nobility. Keenly aware of the need to develop symbols of their new status, they began to consider the expensive, high-quality silk of Kyoto as indispensable for use in their own clothing. They also gave presents of this silk to the shogun and his

59 Hayashiya Tatsusaburō and Katō Hidetoshi, *Chōnin kara shimin e* (Tokyo: Kōdansha, 1979), pp. 65–83.

officials. Many daimyo even sent retainers to Kyoto to purchase silk so that they could make certain that they were acquiring genuine, Kyoto-produced textiles.

Other specific policies implemented by the Edo shogunate also had an impact on the high-quality silk-weaving trade that was concentrated in the Nishijin section of Kyoto. The restriction of foreign trade to Nagasaki, a city under direct shogunal administration; the beginning of the tally trade in silk thread with China; and the granting to designated merchants of exclusive rights to deal in imported raw silk thread (referred to as *shiraito*) all affected business conditions in Kyoto. The raw silk thread imported through Nagasaki was shipped to Kyoto, along with high-quality silk cloth and other textiles produced in China. These goods passed from the tally-trade merchants, who were the importers, to the thread-shipping agents (*nakagai*), who were concentrated in Nishijin, and then to the weavers. The 1685 occupation register lists seventy-six tally-trade merchants, thirty-eight shipping agents for imported silk thread, and thirteen wholesalers who handled imported goods other than raw silk thread.

This same register also lists forty-six silk wholesalers who dealt in unfinished silk cloth that was produced outside Kyoto. Silk cloth usually was not shipped directly from local production areas to large consumption centers such as Edo and Osaka. Rather, because the Kyoto craftsmen had exclusive knowledge of certain dyeing and processing techniques, silk cloth from other regions was sent to Kyoto where it was glossed, dyed, embroidered, and rolled into finished bolts. The Kyoto-based wholesalers not only handled unglossed silk cloth, but they also acted as purchasing agents and wholesalers for raw silk thread that was produced in various regions in Japan. These same purchasing agent–wholesaler houses also helped establish silkworm cultivation in various regions at the end of the seventeenth century, and Nishijin weavers quickly began to use this locally produced raw silk thread instead of imported thread. As a consequence, Nagasaki's importance as an entry point for foreign trade rapidly declined.

The 1689 occupation register lists fifty-four money changers in the city of Kyoto.[60] These coinage specialists not only assayed and exchanged coins minted in various domains, but they also provided several forms of rudimentary banking services, by advancing loans and issuing letters of credit. The cash holdings of wealthy persons such as importers of raw silk thread were concentrated in Kyoto by the

---

60 Nakai, "Kinsei toshi no hatten," pp. 37–100.

middle of the seventeenth century. The daimyo, who had no means of obtaining cash other than from the sale of tax rice and who needed large amounts of cash for obligations to the shogunate, often borrowed money from wealthy merchants, using future tax proceeds as collateral. Moreover, merchants found it necessary to exchange among themselves coins minted in various parts of Japan in order to purchase semiprocessed goods and raw materials such as silk thread and cloth and also to complete the sales of processed goods to outlets in Edo and Osaka. These kinds of monetary conditions gave rise to the business of money exchanging, the buying and selling of cash, and the issuing of letters of credit – all of which served to transform Kyoto into one of Japan's leading financial, as well as production, centers.

Osaka. Like Kyoto, Osaka could trace its history back into antiquity. A settlement had come into existence in prehistoric times, and this later served as a point of embarkation for embassies to Korea. The community then became the temporary site of an imperial capital before more permanent ones were established, first at Nara and then at Heian early in the eighth century. Several centuries later, in 1496, the monk Rennyō (1415–99) chose this site on Osaka Bay as the location for his Ishiyama Honganji temple complex. Over the next century, the population expanded rapidly, at first because of a sudden influx of migrants when the main Ishiyama temple in Kyoto was overrun by rivals in 1532, and then thanks to more modest but steady growth as merchants and artisans arrived to serve the needs of the temple personnel and their followers.[61]

In 1580 Oda Nobunaga, during his quest to unify Japan, overwhelmed this fortress after several unsuccessful attacks. Two years later Nobunaga's successor, Toyotomi Hideyoshi, took over what remained of the fortress and erected a large, formidable castle on the site. The city expanded under Toyotomi control, as several daimyo built residences near the castle to signify their loyalty to Japan's new military hegemon. Still more merchants and artisans arrived to cater to the daimyo's needs, and the city also expanded physically as the government filled in portions of the adjoining bay. By the battle of Osaka Castle in 1614–15, when Tokugawa Ieyasu obliterated the Toyotomi house and subsequently placed the city under the administrative super-

---

61 For a classic survey of Osaka's history, see Miyamoto Mataji, *Ōsaka* (Tokyo: Shibundō, 1957). More current is Wakita Osamu, *Kinsei Ōsaka no machi to hito* (Kyoto: Jimbun shoin, 1986). In English, see William B. Hauser, "Osaka: A Commercial City in Tokugawa Japan," *Urbanism Past and Present* 5 (Winter 1977–8).

vision of the shogunate, Osaka rivaled, and perhaps even surpassed, Kyoto in population.[62]

In the decades after the battle of Osaka Castle, the city was reconstructed, and by the middle of the seventeenth century Osaka had become one of the two greatest commercial and manufacturing centers in the country.[63] At the heart of this dramatic growth was Osaka's emergence as the central rice market for western Japan. Hideyoshi had shipped some of his tax rice from Shikoku to Osaka before his death in 1598, but the city's transformation into the nation's most important rice market followed the establishment of the Tokugawa hegemony and the imposition of the shogunate's authority over the city. As Osaka continued to grow in the early decades of the seventeenth century, daimyo from western Honshu, Kyushu, and Shikoku began to ship tax rice into the city. Concurrently, daimyo along the coast of the Japan Sea sent rice to Tsuruga or Obama, where it was transshipped overland and across Lake Biwa. In all, some estimates for the first quarter of the seventeenth century place the quantity of rice shipped into Osaka in the range of one million koku annually, and a century later, by the 1720s, this figure had increased more than fourfold.[64]

But Osaka did not prosper simply because of rice sales. According to 1714 statistics, the following categories of goods were shipped into Osaka: farm products, 40.9 percent of total imports; forest products, 24.4 percent; marine products, 14.1 percent; and mining products, 8.9 percent. The fertilizer made from sardines was 7.8 percent. The kinds of goods shipped out from Osaka in the same year were as diverse: farm products and processed agricultural goods, 72.8 percent; mining products, 12.6 percent; and processed forestry products, 12.6 percent.[65]

These statistics reveal a number of interesting points. Aside from rice, for example, forestry products constituted the chief imports. Most of the lumber was consumed in construction projects within the city, and the remainder were manufactured into household utensils and furniture, and then exported to other urban markets. After forest prod-

---

62 Osamu Wakita, with James L. McClain, "The Commercial and Urban Policies of Oda Nobunaga and Toyotomi Hideyoshi," in Hall, Nagahara, and Yamamura, eds., *Japan Before Tokugawa*, pp. 243–4.
63 The layout of the city is discussed in Yanai Akira, "Kinsei Ōsaka keikan fukugen e no kokoromi," in Toyoda, Harada, and Yamori, eds., *Kōza: Nihon no hōken toshi*, vol. 3, pp. 122–42.
64 Hauser, *Economic Institutional Change*, p. 13.
65 Nakai, "Kinsei toshi no hatten," p. 46. Occupation statistics are also a concern of Yasuoka Shigeaki, "Edo chūki no Ōsaka ni okeru torihiri soshiki," *Dōshisha shōgaku* 16 (November 1964): 290–307; and 16 (February 1965): 589–625.

ucts, the next largest import into Osaka was oil (15.8 percent), which was processed for use in lamps and cosmetics. Surplus oil not consumed in the city was exported. Similarly, mining products and imported raw materials were processed into iron or copper goods, or into refined copper, and also shipped out to other consumption centers.

Other statistics corroborate Osaka's emergence as a manufacturing and commercial center during the seventeenth and eighteenth centuries. Records dating from the 1710s, for instance, indicate that some two thousand ship's carpenters resided in the city, a clear indication that shipbuilding had become a major industry in Osaka. These statistics also record that fifty rapeseed oil producers and twenty-seven cottonseed oil producers lived in the city, and they turned out approximately seventy thousand kiloliters of oil annually. This should be regarded as a very large amount as no producers used waterwheels at that time but, rather, relied on the labor of humans and animals. Special wholesalers who shipped processed oil to Kyoto and Edo had made their appearance as early as the decade of the 1610s, and within a century a total of 360 wholesale houses handled raw, unprocessed seeds. Nine others shipped processed oil to Edo and Kyoto, and 250 agents shipped it to cities and villages in Hokuriku, Tōhoku, and western Japan. An additional 25 wholesalers dealt in oil cakes (*shimakasu*), a by-product of the oil-manufacturing process that was used for fertilizer.[66]

Perhaps the largest production facility in Osaka at this time was a copper-refining plant.[67] Virtually all mined copper in the entire country, about 3,257 tons annually, was brought to Osaka. There it was refined and nearly all, about 3,000 tons yearly, was reshipped to Nagasaki for export overseas. There were seventeen refiners in Osaka, and a total of approximately ten thousand men worked in the smelting plants. At that time, the Sumitomo family operated copper mines in Kyushu and was the largest refiner in Osaka. They later became, along with the Mitsui family, one of Japan's largest zaibatsu.

Osaka profited greatly from the nation's expanded agricultural production during the second half of the seventeenth century, as well as from the new opportunities afforded by the establishment of the Western Sea Circuit. Osaka quickly surpassed Kyoto in economic importance as it drew on products from many sections of Japan. Kyushu, Shikoku, and regions in northern Honshu supplied raw materials from

66 Exports are discussed in Nakai, "Kinsei toshi no hatten," p. 80.
67 Nakai, "Kinsei toshi no hatten"; and Yasuoka, "Edo chūki no Ōsaka ni okeru torihiki soshiki."

the primary sector, such as rice, soy beans, lumber, minerals, and fish, as well as a limited number of finished goods from the secondary sector such as paper, wax, and tatami-mat facing. The Kinki region emerged as the leading source of certain commercial agricultural goods such as cotton and rapeseed, processed goods made from these farm products, and such manufactured items as saké, soy sauce, and cotton cloth which were made from raw materials supplied from as far away as Kyushu and Shikoku. The coastal areas of the Inland Sea region, on the other hand, developed primary industries such as commercial agriculture and fishing.

All of these different goods were shipped to Osaka, where they were either consumed or reexported to other consumption centers such as Edo, Kyoto, and the cities and villages of the Kinki and Horuriku regions. Processed goods brought into Osaka were redistributed in that form, and the raw materials were manufactured into various products by artisans in the city. As Osaka became a hub of manufacturing and distribution, its population grew, and the city became the leading commercial center in western Japan, pushing Kyoto into the economic background.

As Osaka developed its commercial potential, new types of financial and credit institutions were established. These played an especially important role in promoting the flow of goods and raw materials into Osaka from surrounding rural areas. Essentially, there were two kinds of wholesalers: "provincial wholesalers" (kunidoiya) and "specialized wholesalers" (semmondoiya). As can be seen from such names as "the Satsuma wholesalers" and "the Awaji wholesalers," the provincial wholesalers derived their names from the old provincial units of the ancient imperial system established as part of the Taika Reforms in the seventh century, and they handled a complete line of commercial products and raw materials from that particular area. These provincial wholesalers were especially common in those regions that were linked to Osaka by shipping routes, and they sometimes included descendants of the wealthy merchants who helped make the Yodo River more suitable for shipping in the early Tokugawa period, as well as influential merchants who from the beginning had been engaged in ocean transport, cargo-handling, and warehousing services.

In the latter half of the seventeenth century there was a tendency for specialized wholesalers to split off from the provincial wholesalers.[68]

---

68 Nakabe Yoshiko, "Kinsei toshi Ōsaka no kakuritsu," in Toyoda, Harada, and Yamori, eds., Kōza: Nihon no hōken toshi, vol. 3, pp. 106–15.

For example, the Bingo tatami mat-cover wholesalers separated from the Bingo provincial wholesalers, and the Bizen pottery wholesalers amicably divorced themselves from a larger set of Bizen provincial wholesalers. In all, the number of provincial wholesalers tended to decline, and the specialized wholesalers started handling key commercial goods such as cotton and oil. Then, during the final decades of the seventeenth century, the number of specialized wholesalers increased sharply and subspecializations began to appear. For example, fish wholesalers broke away from the provincial groups, exerted their dominance over the market, and then subdivided into more narrowly specialized groups that dealt exclusively in fresh fish, dried and salted fish, dried bonito (*katsuobushi*), and river fish. In pace with these developments, the kinds and numbers of brokers and shipping agents multiplied, and nearly ten thousand were recorded in an Osaka census report from the 1710s.

New instruments of finance and credit were necessary in order to support this increased volume of trade. Among the first to invent these were the financiers associated with the marketing of daimyo rice. These financiers were known as *kakeya*, and they replaced the daimyo's own retainers as managers of the daimyo's warehouses (*kuramoto*). Serving on a contract basis, these *kakeya* disbursed warehouse rice, held cash on deposit, and supplied additional capital to the daimyo by making loans to them. So great was the lords' need for capital, however, that a daimyo often would approach a set of merchants in the same line of business, who would then pool their funds to make a joint loan and thus to share the risk of default. There were also financiers who solicited money from a number of merchants involved in different lines of business in order to acquire sufficient funds to make loans to daimyo.

The latter half of the seventeenth century also witnessed the growth of transactions among rice merchants who handled the sales of large volumes of daimyo tax rice after it reached the Osaka warehouses. In the 1710s, there were already some thirteen hundred rice brokers (*komenakagai*) in the city. These brokers bought and sold tax rice shipped through the daimyo warehouses at the new rice market established in a section of the city known as Dōjima. Soon they also started to deal in futures by buying and selling rice certificates as negotiable instruments that entitled the bearer to withdraw a specified amount of rice from the warehouses. By the 1710s some seventy money changers attached themselves to the rice market and offered guarantees for transactions made in the market.

As the Dōjima market flourished, the price of rice sold there tended to become the standard rice price for the entire nation, and this lent a certain stability to the finances of the daimyo who pledged their future tax levies as collateral for loans. Previously, the daimyo had frequently defaulted on the loans advanced by merchants, who understandably then became wary of making such loans. The establishment of the market at Dōjima, however, gave renewed confidence to Osaka merchants concerning the collectibility of daimyo loans. As a consequence, many money changers began to specialize in daimyo loans. One obvious example is the Kōnoike family, which became one of the wealthiest merchant houses of the Tokugawa period.[69]

In addition to the money changers associated with the rice market and those who specialized in daimyo loans, there were also many moneylenders who performed more generalized commercial services in Osaka. Like the money changers in Kyoto, these men issued letters of credit, bought and sold coins, changed coins, and advanced loans to wholesalers. As Osaka became the nation's largest commercial city, economic activity outpaced that of Kyoto and stimulated the development of a credit system whose most outstanding feature was the circulation of promissory notes, or *tegata*, which were secured by real estate or by current accounts.[70]

The moneylenders of Osaka devised other credit instruments as well. Merchants in Edo and Osaka, for instance, had often exchanged letters of credit, but the continuance of too many unbalanced accounts hindered the expansion of business activities. The solution to this problem came when the shogunate and daimyo accepted a new means of transmitting to Edo the proceeds from the sale of their tax rice through Osaka warehouses. Until the final decade of the seventeenth century, the shogunate and daimyo had sent cash overland to Edo. But from 1694 the warehouse managers began to take the receipts from the sale of tax rice to Osaka money exchangers, who would then purchase what was termed a "collectible credit draft" (*gyakugawase*) from a merchant who had an accounts receivable due from an Edo merchant. The Osaka money exchanger would then send this collectible credit draft to his own branch shop in Edo (or to a merchant in the same line of business), who would then collect the amount due from the Edo

69 Sakudō Yōtarō, "Kinsei Ōsaka ryōgae shō keiei no keisei katei – jūnin ryōgae no sōsetsu to Kōnoike ryōgaeten," *Bankingu* 175 (October 1962): 32–54.
70 For an informed discussion of new credit devices, see Sakudō Yōtarō, "Tokugawa chūki ni okeru shin'yō seido no tenkai – toku ni kin'yū to zaisei no kanren o chūshin to shite," *Rekishigaku kenkyū* 264 (April–May 1962): 66–70.

merchant. This money would then be turned over to the shogunate or to the Edo mansion of the daimyo within a fixed time limit, generally set at sixty days after the issuance of the draft in the case of the shogunate.

The Osaka money changers profited greatly from the commissions charged for such services. But even more significant was the impact that the use of these drafts had on the national economy. Because the person who held a collectible credit draft could in effect use it as collateral for sixty days, this system permitted a dramatic expansion in the volume of available commercial credit. As the system evolved in the early eighteenth century, promissory notes and credit drafts in circulation frequently amounted to several times the amount of actual currency in circulation, and this stimulated the growth of manufacturing and production throughout the entire country. The new credit system also drew more business to Osaka, making it a hub of finance as well as manufacturing and distribution. This contributed to the further centralization of economic activity in this city rather than Kyoto, so that by 1700 Osaka and Edo had emerged as Japan's leading commercial cities.

Edo. Of early modern Japan's three great cities, Edo was the youngest, and it grew the fastest.[71] The settlement was a small agricultural village until 1457, when Ōta Dōkan (1432–86), a retainer of the Uesugi family, built a small fortress on the site.[72] In 1590 Tokugawa Ieyasu, newly settled in the Kantō region, took over the castle, and after Ieyasu was appointed shogun in 1603, the surrounding community began to develop rapidly, both as the castle town headquarters of the Tokugawa family and also as the effective political and administrative capital of the country.[73]

Edo's population exploded in the seventeenth century. The nucleus for this growth was provided by the direct retainers of the shogun, the army of bannermen (*hatamoto*) and housemen (*gokenin*) who, together with their families and attached service personnel, were compelled to take up residence near the castle, just as the vassals of the daimyo were moved into the castle towns of their lords across all of Japan.[74] Once

71 A summary of the early growth of the city can be found in Haga Noboru, *Ō Edo no seiritsu* (Tokyo: Yoshikawa kōbunkan, 1980), pp. 1–64.
72 A fascinating introduction to the early history of the settlement can be found in Naitō Akira, *Edo to Edojō* (Tokyo: Kashima kinkyūjo shuppankai, 1966), pp. 14–40.
73 A fluent overview of the history of Edo can be found in Nishiyama Matsunosuke and Haga Noboru, eds., *Edo no sambyakunen*, 3 vols. (Tokyo: Kōdansha, 1975).
74 Nomura Kentarō, *Edo* (Tokyo: Shibundō, 1966), pp. 49–70.

the system of alternate residence was institutionalized in the 1630s, the daimyo, some members of their immediate families, and their extensive entourages established residences within the city, adding perhaps another third of a million persons to the city's growing population.[75] Merchants, artisans, and construction workers flowed into the city in response to the burgeoning occupational opportunities, and by the time this phase of rapid growth had exhausted itself in the 1720s, Edo's commoner population of merchants and artisans surely stood above the half-million mark, and the city's total population easily surpassed one million persons.

Some of these merchants and artisans accumulated considerable wealth and fame. The principal merchant wards of the city were referred to as *hommachi*, and many of these streets were lined with the shops of clothing and lumber merchants, who have come to represent the popular stereotype of the great Edo merchants.[76] In part, the popular image grew out of the special favors that the shogunate bestowed on some of these families. For instance, the headman (*tōryō*) of the chartered artisans (*goyō shokunin*) who were entrusted with minting coins on behalf of the shogunate, together with the headman of the chartered merchants (*goyō shōnin*) who specialized in silk goods, lived on large estates that were given to them by the shogunate. These were situated near the entrance to the castle, a location of very high status (today the Bank of Japan is located on the grounds of the former residence of the headman of the minters). In other cases, the stereotype derives from the lavish way in which these merchant princes displayed their wealth. In particular, the extravagant lifestyles of the lumber merchants, who took on construction projects during the great building booms of the second half of the seventeenth century and who made enormous fortunes, became central characters in folktales that still remain well known today. These men allegedly often reserved several large rooms in the pleasure quarters, summoned prostitutes beyond number, and threw gold coins around with reckless abandon.

Despite some similarities in growth patterns between Edo and the

75 Edo's population structure is discussed in Gilbert Rozman, "Edo's Importance in the Changing Tokugawa Society," *Journal of Japanese Studies* 1 (Autumn 1974): 93–4.
76 Some of the most imaginative research on the layout of Edo has been undertaken by Naitō Akira. See, for instance, his *Edo no machi* (cited in note 16); *Edo no toshi no kenchiku* (Tokyo: Mainichi shimbunsha, 1972); and "Edo no machi kōzō," in Nishiyama Matsunosuke and Yoshiwara Ken'ichirō, eds., *Edo jidai zushi*, vol. 4 (Tokyo: Chikuma shobō, 1975). A useful account of the spatial relationships between old Edo and modern Tokyo can be found in Jinnai Hidenobu, "Tōkyō no machi o yomu," *Bunka kaigi* (November 1985): 20–33.

other major metropolises, the city in eastern Japan retained a distinctive identity. Not only did more warriors live in Edo, but the city's merchant and artisan cultures also provided a contrast with those of Osaka and Kyoto. An Edo occupation register published in 1694 lists a total of 161 employment classifications and includes the names of important merchants and artisans. Among these are 68 doctors and 280 persons are identified as scholars, poets, painters, and noh actors, thus giving the impression that Edo was emerging as a city of culture and learning. But set against this is the fact that almost all the artisans were employed in the rougher construction trades or in the production of weapons. Moreover, there were in Edo no distinctive industries that were innovative technically or aesthetically, such as the copper refiners and shipbuilders of Osaka or the weavers and dyers of Kyoto.

In many ways the most visible merchants in Edo were those who dealt in fresh foods such as vegetables and fish. Edo's residents dined on a great variety of regional specialties shipped in from the city's hinterland: *daikon* radishes from Nerima, burdock from Iwafu (in modern-day Saitama), native Japanese melons from Kawagoe and Fuchū, and watermelons from Hachiōji.[77] Vegetables grown in villages within a forty-kilometer radius of Edo were sold daily by retailers at six markets in the city. Fish from nearby Tokyo, Sagami, and Suruga bays, as well as the coastal areas of Chiba and Ibaraki, were sent by ship from the fishing villages to riverside fish markets, and they were then sold at four markets in Edo. Because the volume of fresh foods consumed by all urban residents, including both warriors and commoners, was enormous, both the forwarding agents and retailers who handled goods needed in daily life, such as oil and wood and charcoal, together with the rice merchants, occupied an important niche in Edo's commercial activity.

Craft production developed slowly in the Edo region, and for a long time the city had to depend on the more economically advanced Kansai region, and on Osaka in particular, for supplies of those consumer goods that required sophisticated processing.[78] Other cities of the Kantō and Tōhoku regions faced similar circumstances, and wholesalers in Edo in the early seventeenth century functioned chiefly to

77 An early and still influential study concerning the spread of commercialized agriculture is Furushima Toshio, *Edo jidai no shōnin ryūtsū to kōtsū* (Tokyo: Ochanomizu shobō, 1951).
78 For a discussion in English of the relationship between Edo and its hinterland and Edo's dependence on Osaka, see William B. Hauser, *Economic Institutional Change*, pp. 14, 30; and Rozman, "Edo's Importance," pp. 105–6. For a classic study of Edo's commercial development, see Hayashi Reiko, *Edo ton'ya nakama no kenkyū* (Tokyo: Ochanomizu shobō, 1967).

distribute goods to outlets in these regions on behalf of shippers head-quartered in the Kansai region. However, by the end of the seventeenth century, wealthy merchants from Ise, Ōmi, and Kyoto who had extensive experience and reserves of capital expanded their operations into the Kantō area and Edo's extended hinterland. At that time they no longer functioned as simple forwarding agents on behalf of others, but, rather, they themselves directly purchased goods in Kansai and Osaka for sale in Edo. In this fashion, real economic power slipped from the hands of the old forwarding agents who handled sea shipping and warehousing services and passed into the hands of these more aggressive merchants.

Not unexpectedly, the more intense competition from these outside merchants set off a reaction among the merchants in Edo, first visible in their efforts to organize trade associations to meet the new challenges. In 1694, to take the most notable example of this, wholesalers in Edo who dealt in eighteen different kinds of goods shipped by sea from Kansai formed what was referred to as the *tokumidon'ya*, or ten groups of wholesale guilds.[79] As was the case with the formation of protective associations in the castle towns, the Edo wholesalers, through this agency, hoped to be able to better protect markets and restrict the operation of outsiders.

The Edo wholesalers also discovered ways to use their organization to provide more regular business practices and some degree of protection against the unexpected. Thus, they forbade group members from engaging in shipping practices that might give one house an unfair competitive advantage. To promote stability for the entire group, they also started to indemnify members whose goods were lost or damaged in transit. It was not uncommon at this time for the crews of hired ships to fake a shipwreck and then secretly sell the cargoes. Also, it was standard practice for a ship's captain to jettison deck cargoes in order to improve his ship's stability and seaworthiness whenever storms stirred up rough seas. Among the more valuable of these cargoes were casks of refined saké brewed in the Nada sections of Osaka. Because Nada saké enjoyed an especially proud reputation in Edo, wholesalers there quickly sold whatever stock they had, and the loss of a cargo of Nada saké represented an immediate and substantial financial loss. Indeed, the system of joint indemnification initiated by the Edo wholesalers was originally designed to cover losses of saké car-

79 For a recent study of the development of merchant associations, see Kagawa Takayuki, "Toshi shōten no hatten," in Rekishigaku kenkyūkai, ed., *Kōza Nihon rekishi*, vol. 6 (Tokyo: Tōkyō daigaku shuppankai, 1985), pp. 195–228.

goes, although indemnities were soon extended to cover the loss of any cargo that was tossed overboard or went down with a ship.

As the curtain fell on the seventeenth century, it was obvious that Japan's commercial economy had become urban centered. On the regional level, the castle town of each domain had become a nodal point of trade, drawing in raw materials, agricultural surpluses, and processed goods from the village and towns in its hinterland. Much of this was consumed by the residents of the castle towns, but an increasing fraction – either in its original state or after further processing – entered the new transportation conduits that served as the arteries of the emerging national economy. The great centers of Edo, Osaka, and Kyoto were the poles that defined the national economy's magnetic field. Their enormous populations needed to be fed, and this generated the currents that set in motion the transfers of materials, finished products, and the development as well of financial instruments that had come to define Japan's early modern economy.

CITIES AND COMMERCE IN THE EARLY EIGHTEENTH
CENTURY

The expanding commercial activity of the seventeenth century produced new and unprecedented levels of well-being and prosperity in Japan, especially for those segments of society that were most directly involved in economic production. Yet at the same time, the economic changes that surged through Tokugawa society also caused dislocations, created fresh problems for government, and stirred up waves of concern among the nation's political leaders. Ultimately, in the 1710s and 1720s the shogunate would address these challenges through a set of policies known as the Kyōhō Reforms. Chapter 9 in this volume details the political significance of this political program, but as we shall see, the reforms also held important implications concerning the economic life and well-being of Japan's urban residents.

The impact of the Kyōhō Reforms on the urban economy can best be understood by recalling some of the events and concerns that led up to them. Among these were the apprehensions of the nation's political leaders, who feared at the end of the seventeenth century that continued and unrestrained economic growth might have adverse consequences for the system of rule by status that they had worked so hard to implement earlier. Merchants were supposed to occupy the lowest rung of the Neo-Confucian hierarchy, but in some cases their business success had given them wealth and a reputation inconsistent with their theoretical position in society. As one city magistrate in Kanazawa noted in his office diary:

Merchants deal in goods. They buy and sell things which people need in their daily lives – food, shelter, and clothing. Merchants transport goods from one area to another. . . . They accumulate money. They lend out money and make a profit. Merchants who have a plan of operations and a good sense for profits do a large volume of business and make a great deal of money. When they have a favorable destiny, they can become rich in a single generation. Among the newly rich are some whose descendants are lazy and lack a profit sense, and they squander all of the accumulated wealth. In these troubled times, samurai households are suffering vicissitudes and changes of fortune. Persons who excel in business have become society's heroes. . . . A samurai can inherit [his father's] fief, but he cannot inherit his father's standing as a great man.[80]

The uneasiness of the political elite sprang from other, practical fiscal considerations as well. Despite the growth in the commercial economy, tax rice still remained the foundation of wealth for the shogun and daimyo. Too much commercial development, officials feared, might prompt farmers to take land out of rice production, thus jeopardizing their tax collection. Moreover, as ever more wealth flowed into the countryside to pay for commercial crops or the products of rural handicraft industries, the political leadership became increasingly concerned that farmers might become lazy and spendthrift, and thus less diligent in their efforts to produce rice and less able to pay taxes.

Finally, the shoguns Ietsuna (1651–80) and Tsunayoshi (1680–1709) pursued currency debasements in order to offset their well-known extravagant expenditures and to finance the resultant budget deficits. Specifically, for a fifteen-year period beginning in 1668, the shogunate minted large volumes of copper coins and then authorized the issuance of great amounts of gold and silver coins as well. This expansion of the money supply was designed to cover the increasing budgetary shortfalls of the period and to counterbalance the loss of coins that flowed out of Nagasaki to finance the export trade with Chinese, Dutch, and Korean merchants.

The shogunate's other chief concern at this time was to compensate for dislocations caused by the expansion of the commercial economy and its penetration into peasant villages. This is evident from the fact that the increase in minting activity emphasized those kinds of silver coins that were used in the Kansai regions and points farther west, where economic development and the commercialization of agricul-

80 Quoted in McClain, *Kanazawa*, p. 121.

ture had been most rapid.[81] Whatever the specific causes, however, the increase in the minting of silver coins took place at a time when the production of silver at Japan's mines was declining rapidly. As a result, the shogunate was forced to reduce the proportion of silver used in the coins to less than one-third of the coins' par value. In all, these various debasements sparked an inflationary fire, and, in the minds of policy-makers during the opening decade of the eighteenth century, fear of inflation combined with the apprehensions concerning the nature of economic growth to bring on a sense that an economic crisis was sweeping the country and undermining political authority.

The Kyōhō Reforms, merchant associations, and urban violence

The Kyōhō Reform program bundled together several specific policies that were aimed at dampening inflationary pressures, including calls for austerity in government; the issuance of detailed sumptuary regulations designed to encourage frugality in private life; the promulgation of moral injunctions exhorting the samurai to revive their martial spirit; a tightening up of rice-tax collections through the implementation of a fixed, annual payment system; a return to hard currency; and the wide-scale licensing of merchant protective associations (*kabuna-kama*) in the cities under the shogunate's jurisdiction. This set of policies, especially the authorization of merchant associations, would redefine the relationship between the urban and rural sectors of the economy, and the deflationary trends set in motion by the reforms would also have an impact on urban living standards, contributing, as we shall see, to the appearance of the first examples of organized violence by commoners in the urban centers of early modern Japan.

Merchant protective associations endowed with monopoly rights were not entirely new, of course.[82] We noted earlier how many individual daimyo during the seventeenth century had come to rely on certain wholesalers and transportation agents for the conduct of interregional trade and had consequently accorded exclusive prerogatives to these merchants houses. Similarly, those craftsmen who could produce certain goods – lacquer ware in Aizu–Wakamatsu, jute cloth in Hikone, and paper, ink, and charcoal in Kanazawa, to note but a few already familiar examples – not infrequently received special privileges as

---

81 Classic studies on currency problems include Kobata Atsushi, *Nihon no kahei* (Tokyo: Shibundō, 1958); and Sakudō Yōtarō, *Kinsei Nihon kaheishi* (Tokyo: Kōbundō, 1958).
82 An early and still frequently cited study of such associations is Miyamoto Mataji, *Nihon kinsei ton'yasei no kenkyū* (Tokyo: Tōkō shoin, 1951).

well. In all cases, the government and merchants could hope to derive certain obvious benefits. The merchants received monopoly rights and were able to reduce intragroup competition, while the government could offer protection to business enterprises that were important to the city's overall economy and well-being.

The authors of the Kyōhō Reforms also saw in these examples of protective associations, however, a way in which government might gain greater leverage over economic activity and the structure of prices. So excited were they by these possibilities that between 1721 and 1726 the reformers organized nearly all merchants in Edo into protective trade associations, a pattern followed by many daimyo in their own domains. Out of this burst of licensing came the form of protective association that is most familiar to historians. That is, the government authorized specific monopolies in exchange for the payment of annual licensing fees (myōgakin) and annual taxes (unjōkin), monies that could help the shogunate and the domains address their financial difficulties. In addition to a guaranteed monopoly, each merchant group acquired the rights to define its exact business activities, fix the number of licenses to be issued, decide who would be eligible to buy or inherit a license, determine their own internal regulations, and confiscate the licenses of those who violated the bylaws. They also jointly decided prices to be charged and apportioned the percentage of the licensing fees and annual taxes to be paid by each member. Moreover, the government typically required each association to include in its bylaws a promise to observe the laws of the shogunate or daimyo domain and to submit periodic reports to the appropriate officials concerning prices, fees, and recent business activities.

The shogunate, and the daimyo in their castle towns, had certain specific intentions in mind when they licensed protective associations, and they found ways to impose their policy considerations on association merchants. First, they used the submission of the periodic reports as opportunities to jawbone merchants into holding the line on prices. In addition, political leaders hoped to prohibit the production and sale of certain expensive luxury goods, such as some types of clothing, and of all kinds of new products, in order to be able to restrain consumption and, by extension, inflation. Moreover, government officials sought to regulate the volume of goods being shipped, in order to prevent unscrupulous merchants from buying up and hoarding commodities, and they acquired yet another means of influencing prices when they began to insist on making public their approval (or disapproval) of the handling fees and commissions that middlemen proposed charging. Finally, the shogunate and most daimyo wanted to prevent urban wholesalers from making purchases in producing areas and local towns, so as to isolate the producers, especially farmers, from what were seen as the debilitating effects of trade and commerce. One means they used to accomplish this was to enforce the descriptions of business activities included in association bylaws, although many daimyo governments also chose to issue new ordinances on the subject as well.

The impact of the Kyōhō Reforms on Japan's residents cut many ways. Some prospered. It is clear, for instance, that the leading houses within the merchant associations were sometimes able to amass considerable wealth in regional castle towns, such as Kanazawa, and that they came to constitute a new elite that could compete for the social and political prerogatives accorded the older, established merchant families.[83] In the major metropolises of Edo and Osaka as well, it was not difficult in the early eighteenth century to discover evidence of better housing and food in the wealthier merchant wards and, despite the disappearance of some of the vigor of Genroku culture, to find a proliferation of entertainment establishments that catered to the more well-to-do merchants, such as the leaders of the protective associations. Indeed, by mid-century some merchant houses had grown so rich that they were well known throughout the country, houses such as the Echigoya (the Mitsui family of the modern era) and the Shirokiya (founders of today's chain of Tōkyū department stores).

Yet, whatever prosperity the Kyōhō Reforms brought to merchant elites, on another social level the new policies caused distress that found its outlet in acts of collective violence. These were most common in the countryside, where the reforms squeezed the peasantry under a more severe tax system. Indeed, before the Kyōhō period, there had seldom been more than one or two examples a year of organized, violent rural protest, but by 1750 such incidents averaged more than six a year. The Kyōhō Reforms led to economic hardship for some segments of urban society as well. In urban centers, the policies of reducing consumption, controlling prices, and, from the 1710s, issuing gold and silver coins at previous standards of purity while prohibiting the circulation of older, debased coins all combined to produce a sharp, if short, depression toward the end of the 1720s.

In the midst of these economic difficulties, a widespread infestation of locusts in 1732 caused severe damage to the rice crop in western

---

83 Tanaka, *Kaga han ni okeru toshi no kenkyū*, pp. 129–98.

Japan, especially on the island of Kyushu. In order to stave off a famine in that region, the shogunate quickly purchased large amounts of rice in Osaka and Edo for shipment to western Japan. As a consequence, prices rose dramatically in these major cities. In Edo, some two thousand poor persons, believing that the price increases were due to a sinister plot by the rice merchants, rioted and broke into the shops of the largest chartered rice merchants (*kome goyō shōnin*). This disturbance occurred in 1733 and constituted the first riot by urban commoners in the city of Edo, the shogun's castle town.[84]

In that same year, riots also broke out in Nagasaki on Kyushu, and in Hida–Takayama (present-day Gifu Prefecture) where the city's residents smashed rice shops.[85] As was the case in the countryside, such urban food riots became increasingly common over the last century of Tokugawa rule. With increased numbers came, ultimately, new demands as well. Whereas the 1733 rioters had engaged in a typical struggle for control over the food supply and had simply demanded that government function as it ought to in accordance with Neo-Confucian concepts of benevolence and order, by the beginning of the nineteenth century the rioters were denouncing the entire political and social order. Even this was only a prelude to the call for a radical reordering of the polity that would resound throughout Japan at the middle of that century.

The Kyōhō Reforms, urban financiers, and marketing networks

As stressful as were the economic dislocations and human suffering associated with the deflationary period of the 1720s and 1730s, it is also important to note that in the long run of economic development, the Kyōhō Reforms accelerated already existing trends concerning Japan's protoindustrialization and the development of an integrated national marketing network.[86] This can be seen in the subsequent history of the merchant houses and associations: By the middle of the eighteenth century, for instance, there were more than five thousand wholesalers in over four hundred different kinds of businesses in Osaka alone, and

---

84 For a discussion of this event within the broader context of Edo period urban violence, see Sasaki Junnosuke, *Hyakushō ikki to uchikowashi* (Tokyo: Sanseidō, 1974), pp. 47–61, and Takeuchi Makoto, *Edo to Ōsaka* (Tokyo: Shōgakkan, 1989), pp. 112–38.
85 The most comprehensive listing of popular dissent can be found in Aoki Kōji, ed., *Hyakushō ikki no nenji-teki kenkyū* (Tokyo: Shinseisha, 1966). A convenient introduction to popular protest is Aoki Michio et al., eds., *Ikki*, 5 vols. (Tokyo: Tōkyō daigaku shuppankai, 1981–2).
86 Two influential studies concerning the development of national markets and regional commerce are Toyoda Takeshi and Kodama Kōta, eds., *Ryūtsūshi*, vol. 1 (Tokyo: Yamakawa shuppansha, 1969); and Hayashi, *Edo ton'ya nakama no kenkyū*.

despite what the Kyōhō Reforms had said about urban–rural separation, the Echigoya and the other urban retailers maintained large purchasing establishments that sometimes contracted for the textile output of an entire region.

The extensive commercial activity generated by the wholesalers injected fresh bursts of energy into the arteries of interregional trade, stimulating new growth and creating a need for larger sums of capital.[87] As the wholesalers fanned out across Japan, it became standard practice for them to make partial payments in advance of receiving orders and to lend capital for production purposes as well as for purchasing raw materials. In time, some merchants made as much or more from the interest earned on these loans as they did from the commissions they received for their shipping and marketing services.

The elaboration of the marketing activities of these wholesalers held other implications for capital formation. That is, although some merchants had functioned solely as wholesalers in the seventeenth century, more typically, men in local areas who themselves engaged in production also arranged to ship their goods and those of their neighbors and fellow villagers to customers of their own choosing. The appearance of the new wholesaler associations, however, meant that the local producer-cum-shipper was relegated to functioning as an agent who filled orders from the urban-based wholesalers, by using the wholesalers' capital to buy and transport goods. Now the incomes of the rural merchants no longer derived from profits they made on sales but, rather, came from commissions on the volume of goods they handled. In effect, the local men now functioned as buyers' representatives. In this capacity, they would host members of the wholesaler's shop who were dispatched to the producing areas, help them select and purchase goods, and arrange for shipping. For these services, the local merchants received their expenses and a commission. These local merchants were typically referred as *kaiyado*, or purchasing houses, and in many cases they had an exclusive contract with a particular wholesale association. Moreover, as local shippers came to function as the purchasing agents for urban-based wholesalers, they were increasingly isolated from the local commercial distribution system. In turn, this often meant that still new kinds of financing arrangements were necessary. In time, the producers themselves began to borrow money from the urban-based wholesalers, which they repaid in the form of manufactured goods.

87 Matsumoto Shirō, "Genroku, Kyōhō-ki no seiji to keizai," in Matsumoto and Yamada, eds., *Genroku, Kyōhō-ki no seiji to shakai*, pp. 1–35.

This process of commercially inspired changes came full circle when the new methods of finance and distribution began to influence the business practices of the great financiers. For example, large wholesale houses now had to create complex accounting systems, and some even developed a form of double-entry bookkeeping that permitted them to compare credits against debits and to register both capital accounts and profit accounts. Moreover, in accordance with an expansion in the scale of operations, shops began to separate business finances from household finances.

Increasingly as well, in a practice known as "dividing the shop curtain," some wholesale houses began to provide training for their most skilled employees and to help them establish their own branch shops.[88] Men were often first employed by a shop at the age of twelve or thirteen and were given training in mathematics at the shop while carrying out their job obligations. Future shop managers were chosen from this group. Even though an employee might not ultimately become a manager, if he worked diligently for a fixed number of years, he might be given a lump sum of money, the hereditary family shop name, and other assistance in order to help him start his own shop. The day-to-day management of the main shop was often entrusted to managers who were employed for life, were granted use of the hereditary family name, and were treated much like a family member. This style of operation became widespread after the 1820s, and a century later Japanese modern industrialists were able to refer back to this system and to use it to rationalize the new schemes of permanent employment and promotion by seniority that they were attempting to fashion.

The Kyōhō Reforms, fires, and local government

Although the economic consequences of the Kyōhō Reforms were complex and subtle, it should be remembered that the guiding motive behind them was simple and direct: The shogunate was seeking to regulate the economy more closely. The same desire for greater control can be seen in the shogunate's attempt to reorganize the Edo city government during the decade of the 1720s. As was the case with the economic side of reform, the administrative changes constituted a response to a century of growth and to many unexpected problems that had arisen during the era of unparalleled urbanization.

---

88 One standard account of this process can be found in Miyamoto Mataji, "Kinsei no shōka hōkōnin to shōten soshiki," in his *Kinsei shōgyō keiei no kenkyū* (Kyoto: Ōyashima shuppan, 1948), pp. 111–47.

One of these unanticipated problems was fires, often poetically referred to as "the flowers of Edo." Pestilence would be more like it, especially for the city's commoners. The merchants and artisan wards of Edo were densely populated, houses were constructed of wood and paper; and firefighting equipment was rudimentary. The hand-operated pump first came into use in Osaka only during the latter half of the eighteenth century; but even in the nineteenth century, this pump was used in just a few places and the most common means of stopping fires was simply to demolish wide rows of homes in order to create firebreaks.

Under these conditions, any fire could quickly become a major disaster, and the documentary record reveals that the central wards of Edo were destroyed by fire on the average of once every six years in the 178-year period between the middle of the seventeenth century and the 1830s.[89] In particular, exceptionally large numbers of fires occurred in the decades of the 1650s, 1710s, 1770s,and 1830s, and all of them contributed to the social unrest of those decades.[90]

Among these four periods, the largest number of fires broke out during the decade of the 1710s. Then in the 1720s, the shogunate changed its urban policy by forming a firefighting association and offering rewards to those who could identify arsonists. The transformation in urban policy also involved a reorganization of the city.[91] In order to prevent the spread of fires, the shogunate increased the number of public squares (*hiroba*) and issued an ordinance instructing people to use adobe or mud plaster in home construction and to tile their roofs, which previously had been made of wood or thatch. Although this decree was not uniformly observed in every ward, especially those whose residents had sunk into serious economic straits, the government did try to enforce it more strictly in certain designated wards, mainly those that had been rebuilt following a fire. In time, the practice of using the new building materials spread, and by the nineteenth century, streets with rows of houses constructed of adobe or plaster and roofed with tiles gradually started to appear in cities in all parts of Japan.

The government also began to organize firefighting brigades in almost all sections of Edo. Officials actually used red ink to divide a map

89 A useful introductory study to fires and fire fighting is Minami Kazuo, "Shōbō," in Toyoda, Harada, and Yamori, eds., *Kōza: Nihon no hōken toshi*, vol. 2, pp. 457–71.
90 Harada Tomohiko, *Kinsei toshi sōjōshi* (Kyoto: Shibunkaku shuppan, 1982), pp. 92–123.
91 Yoshioka Yuriko, "Kyōhō-ki Edo machikata ni okeru sogan undō no jittai," in Chihōshi kenkyūkai kyōgikai, ed., *Toshi no chihōshi*, pp. 108–58.

of the city into forty-seven firefighting precincts. Each administrative subdivision within a precinct had to supply a brigade of thirty men, and all of the brigades would be mustered whenever a fire broke out anywhere within the precinct. The individual brigades were captained by the ward elders, and the new post of precinct fire chief was rotated among them, each serving for a period of one month. All of the city's firefighting precincts were placed under the authority of six newly appointed fire superintendents (nine in winter), who reported to the city magistrates. Since the forty-seven precincts that served as the basis of the new system were named after the forty-seven characters of the syllabary, this was known as the *i-ro-ha* system.

Firefighting officials often enlisted special artisans known as "scaffolding men" (*tobi*), who normally worked in high places on construction projects, to help demolish houses in order to create firebreaks. In time, these scaffolding men were placed on fixed retainers, with the aim of ensuring a supply of reliable reinforcements for the firemen in each ward. However, scaffolding men were also infamous as *abaremono*, or rowdy, undisciplined members of the day laborer class of that era, and fights among the scaffolding men broke out at each fire, sometimes actually adding to the problems of the average urban dweller.

This attempt to fold the responsibility for firefighting into the general administrative duties assigned to the City Office should be seen as part of a broader attempt to restructure urban government and to redefine the tax responsibilities of the merchant class in Edo at the beginning of the eighteenth century.[92] The main thrust of this administrative reorganization was to restrict the number of ward elders while expanding the scope of their jurisdiction and strengthening their powers. As a consequence, their duties came to resemble closely those noted earlier for the ward representatives in the castle town of Kanazawa.

At the same time, the entire city of Edo was divided into seventeen "townships," each consisting of several of the original wards. An organization of ward elders (*machikuchō kumiai*) was established, and a ward elder head (*kumiaichō*) was appointed from among the ward elders for a one-year term for the purpose of maintaining a proper liaison with higher units of government. Specifically, there were 254 designated wards in the city and a total of 263 ward elders, with some

92 Yoshiwara Ken'ichirō, *Edo no machi yakunin* (Tokyo: Yoshikawa kōbunkan, 1980), pp. 92–128.

wards having joint appointments. In addition, some peripheral areas were not included among these designated wards. These were not eligible to have their own elder and so were placed under the supervision of an elder from a neighboring ward.

Below the elders, the urban residents in each ward were organized into neighborhood associations, or groups of households, just as in the castle towns and rural villages. Originally, the official, recognized members of a ward were those who could claim proprietary rights of possession to land within the ward. The individual members of the neighborhood associations would alternately serve one month each as household group head and assist the ward elders in the performance of their duties. For instance, all reports, petitions, and lawsuits had to bear the seal of the household group head and the ward elder before they could be submitted to higher officials.

In general, the wards' fiscal obligations to the shogunate, as well as other expenses such as the salaries of the ward elders, originally were apportioned among those who possessed land and who were thus formal members of the ward, in accordance with the physical size of each individual's landholdings. Many merchants, however, claimed that the value of any particular plot of land depended on location as well as size. To do away with the alleged irregularities, then, the reformers of the early eighteenth century created three new categories of land value, assigned each merchant plot to one of these categories, and made uniform levies based on territorial size on all plots in each category.

For the wards where the artisans lived, the shogunate imposed corvée obligations that were different from the property taxes levied in the merchant wards. For example, the members of the carpenters' ward owed a fixed number of days of service when they had to work on shogunal construction projects. However, after the artisans moved out of their original wards and began to live in scattered locations around the city, the service obligations that had been levied on artisan wards as a whole were redistributed and levied on the individual members of an occupational group, regardless of their place of residence. Thus, another reason that the shogunate, as part of the Kyōhō Reforms, decided to authorize and encourage the formation of protective associations of artisans throughout the city was to make it easier to identify those individuals subject to service levies.

These kinds of changes that the shogunate effected in the urban administrative machinery of Edo in the 1720s were also replicated to a large degree in Kyoto and Osaka, which the shogunate governed directly and which generally had been subject to the same social and economic transformations that had swept through Edo.[93] Then from the 1750s the daimyo throughout Japan instituted similar reforms in their castle towns, and although other, lesser reforms were introduced afterwards in response to the changing circumstances of the nineteenth century, the framework constructed in the early seventeenth century tended to endure until the collapse of the Tokugawa shogunate in the 1860s.

CITIES AND COMMERCE IN THE LATE EIGHTEENTH CENTURY

The regional spread of commercial production

As discussed in detail in Chapter 9 in this volume, the Kyōhō Reforms did not provide permanent solutions to the ongoing problems of economic growth that were satisfactory to the shogunate. In particular, the shogunate was not able to halt further commercialization of agriculture, and that, together with the explosive growth of processing industries in local areas, eventually led the shogunate, and many individual daimyo as well, to yet another round of economic reforms in the 1770s and 1780s.

Signs that the Japanese economy was moving into a new stage of development during the middle decades of the eighteenth century were first visible in the textile industry. Cotton cultivation, which had been concentrated at first in the Kinki region, spread throughout almost the entire nation during the middle and late eighteenth century, except for the Tōhoku area, where climatic conditions made such farming nearly impossible. As cotton cultivation spread out from the Osaka region, it soon became a particularly important crop on the Ise peninsula and in areas along the coast of the Inland Sea. As the farmers in these locales started to cultivate cotton, farm families also began to engage in spinning and weaving as forms of by-employment. Later, the bleaching of cotton and the processing of bleached cloth became concentrated along the southern and eastern shores of Lake Biwa, before spreading into the Ise area in the latter half of the eighteenth century.

In the 1760s the silk textile industry became established in the Kiryū region (modern-day Gumma Prefecture) when local weavers

---

93 See, for instance, Nakabe Yoshiko, "Kinsei toshi Ōsaka no kakuritsu," in Toyoda, Harada, and Yamori, eds., *Kōza: Nihon no hōken toshi*, vol. 3, pp. 98–121.

mastered some of the dyeing techniques for silk that previously had been an exclusive possession of craftsmen in the Nishijin section of Kyoto. As Kiryū silk became known for its fine quality and as sales increased, other farmers and merchants in the area started to engage in silkworm cultivation, silk thread manufacture, and the production of a variety of silk textiles. About the same time, farmers in the mountainous areas of the southern Kantō region started to produce raw silk thread and cotton cloth for use by the great mass of urban commoners. As this happened, towns like Hachiōji and Ōme became important collection and transshipment points. A similar story could be told for Hokuriku, when the area around the city of Toyama became a thriving center for the production of silk and cotton textiles.[94] This localization of production and the development of new networks of exchange during the last half of the eighteenth century meant that Kyoto's importance as the center of the silk trade diminished greatly.

There were similar changes in the production of lamp oil, another important product. Originally, a variety of fish and vegetables were refined into oil in Kobe and Nishinomiya, where waterpower was abundant. Later, refining spread into a great number of local areas that grew rapeseed, which producers, until that time, had exported in its raw state although they also processed small amounts for individual use. Not surprisingly, the emergence of competitive marketing systems for cotton, silk, and rapeseed generated some sharp tensions between the established merchants of Osaka and the local upstarts. Some sense of this can be felt in the organization of a new protective association of lamp-oil traders in Osaka in 1759, whose members then pressured the shogunate to decree that all oil seeds, including rape and cotton seed, be sent to Osaka for processing.[95]

It is also important to note that the regional growth of processing industries often stimulated the production of raw materials in local areas. For example, in the early seventeenth century, people in Edo relied on imports of soy sauce from areas in the Kinki region such as Yuasa (present-day Wakayama Prefecture) and Tatsuno (Hyōgo Prefecture). Then, by mid-century, the sardine fishermen discussed earlier took with them from Yuasa to Chōshi the manufacturing techniques employed by the soy sauce brewers of western Japan. From there, the brewing process became generally known among producers in such localities as Sawara and Noda (Chiba Prefecture) and Tsuchiura

94 See Mizushima Shigeru, "Etchū orimono no hattatsu," *Toyama shidan* 34 (1966): 35–51.
95 For further details, see Nakai, *Tenkan-ki bakuhansei no kenkyū*, pp. 118–23.

(Ibaraki Prefecture), and merchants in those areas started to brew soy sauce to suit the tastes of the residents of Edo, fond of a saltier, more intensely flavored seasoning than was marketed in Osaka. Soon, soy sauce manufactured in the urban centers of the Kansai region was driven from the markets of Edo. Thus in a variety of products ranging from soy sauce and cooking oil to silk and cotton cloth, rural producers were challenging the previously predominant position of the older, more established shops of Kyoto and Osaka, many of whom had enjoyed some form of favored government protection.

Commercial growth and new economic policies

Tanuma Okitsugu. The 1760s and 1770s witnessed the initiation of new economic policies by the leaders of the shogunate and individual domains. Often historians have focused less on this set of events than on the subsequent Kansei Reforms; yet the policies of the 1760s and 1770s had a significant impact on the structure of economic activity in Japan, and they deserve our close attention. To some extent, the new policies constituted a response to the problems brought on by the regional spread of commercial activity and the growth of local marketing systems. As we shall see, the aggressive behavior of rural-based merchants and the decline of the central role of Osaka merchants caused dislocations and difficulties that would force their attention on government officials when the established but threatened merchants appealed for protection.

The new policies also addressed some older, and frustratingly persistent, fiscal problems that had plagued the shogunate and daimyo governments. The central concern here was to find some way to eliminate what had by now become chronic budgetary shortfalls and to reduce reliance on loans from merchant houses. Moreover, government officials hoped to acquire some control over prices, in order to overcome the inflation that had reappeared after the economic recession of the late Kyōhō period and that was seen as being responsible for both driving up government expenditures and causing serious financial problems for the samurai status group.[96]

The contemporaries who struggled with these problems and the historians who have reviewed their policy decisions have not had an easy time understanding the causal relationships between persistent budgetary

---

96 An early and still useful study of domain indebtedness is Sekiyama Naotarō, *Nihon kahei kin'yūshi kenkyū* (Tokyo: Shinkeizaishi, 1943).

shortfalls and the resurgence of inflation. Research has shown that currency debasements and other policies concerning coinage were clearly a factor. On more than sixty occasions, for instance, the shogunate issued new varieties of gold or silver coins, typically in order to debase the currency and thus augment official revenues.[97] These debasements, some historians contend, acted to drive up commodity prices. Others, however, have suggested that despite the infusion of new coinage into the economy, the shogunate never did mint enough coins to meet demand, so that the gap between supply and demand for currency became the chief source of inflationary pressures.[98]

Yet other historians place the blame for inflation on the unwise policies of domain governments. The lords of many domains, for instance, began to issue paper notes (hansatsu) during the eighteenth century. But frequently these were inconvertible, and even when convertibility to coins was promised, domain officials tended to pay little or no attention to the relative quantities of paper currency issued or to the amount of metallic money that they were supposedly holding on reserve to back the issuance.[99] That was precisely what happened in Kanazawa in 1775 when the domain first printed an excessive amount of paper currency and concurrently banned the use of silver coins. The popular action was immediate: People shunned the notes; the currency rapidly depreciated in value; and prices rose sharply.[100]

As frustrating as it has been for historians to obtain a full understanding of the relationship between currency policies and inflation, they have had even more difficulty with other related questions, which constitute an agenda for future research. We still, for instance, do not know the exact extent to which the shogunate and daimyo bureaucracies taxed the growing merchant wealth; nor do we fully understand why they did not put into place more systematic methods for moving that wealth into official coffers, especially after the Kyōhō Reforms had secured the unquestioned right of governments to levy annual dues and licensing fees on protective associations. Moreover, we have not yet fully analyzed the relationship between the spread of commercial production and rising commodity prices. On the one hand, we might well expect

97 John Whitney Hall, Tanuma Okitsugu: Forerunner of Modern Japan (Cambridge, Mass.: Harvard University Press, 1955), p. 69.
98 Shimbō Hiroshi, "Kinsei kōki ni okeru bukka, kin sōba, kawase uchigin sōba, 1787–1867," in Umemura Mataji et al., eds., Nihon keizai no hatten (Tokyo: Nihon keizai shimbunsha, 1976), pp. 261–79; and Sakudō, "Tokugawa chūki ni okeru shin'yō seido no tenkai," pp. 66–70.
99 Sekiyama, Nihon kahei, presents several case studies; and a detailed analysis of Okayama can be found in Kokushō Iwao, Hōken shakai no tōsei to tōsō (Tokyo: Kaizōsha, 1928), pp. 53–102.
100 Tsuchiya Takao, Hōken shakai hōkai katei no kenkyū – Edo jidai ni okeru shokō no zaisei, pt. 2 (Kyoto: Kōbundō, 1927), pp. 239–309.

that the diffusion of commercial enterprises and technology would enhance competition, cut production costs, and reduce the prices of commercial goods; yet, officials in domains across Japan constantly complained of higher prices as people within their jurisdictions became
more actively involved in the commercialized sector of the economy.[101]
Further, we need to know more about the linkage between prices and
the formation of official merchant groups.[102] Useful, too, would be
more amply documented analyses of the impact on prices of other
daimyo policies, such as the frequent bans on the import into any one
domain of goods that competed with local products. Finally, it is necessary to uncover more precise and detailed information about the relationship between rice prices and commodity prices in general. It has
become somewhat of a truism that the eighteenth century witnessed a
rise in commodity prices in general, but a decline in rice prices.[103]
Indeed, one can find documentation that would support this conclusion.[104] Yet, most studies assume this inverse correlation between the
two price indices without offering a convincing explanation of why the
growth of the commercial economy should depress the rice price and
thus reduce the relative value of tax revenues and samurai incomes.[105]

Although shogunal and daimyo officials frequently had an even less
precise understanding than do modern-day historians about how their
economy worked, many in the 1760s realized that a new fiscal crisis
was at hand, and so they put together a set of fresh economic policies
to address the problems confronting them. On the national level,
Tanuma Okitsugu (1719–88) became the chief architect of the sho-

---

101 Dohi Noritaka, "Kinsei bukka-shi no ichi kōsatsu," in Nishiyama Matsunosuke sensei koki
kinenkai, ed., *Edo no minshū to shakai* (Tokyo: Yoshikawa kōbunkan, 1985), pp. 415–37.
102 The Edo city magistrates, for instance, in 1723 thought that creating licensed groups of
wholesalers would give them a way to reduce prices. "Prices have risen," they claimed,
"because of competition between traders, shippers, and producers. If producers were authorized to sell only to ton'ya, monopoly profits could be controlled." Quoted in Hauser,
Economic Institutional Change, p. 36. Yet, other officials would later condemn protective
associations on the grounds that their monopolistic practices acted to increase prices. See
James L. McClain, "Failed Expectations: Kaga Domain on the Eve of the Meiji Restoration," *Journal of Japanese Studies* 14 (Summer 1988).
103 See, for instance, Hauser, *Economic Institutional Change*, pp. 34–5; and Kitajima Masamoto,
Edo jidai (Tokyo: Iwanami shoten, 1958), pp. 125–40.
104 See, for example, Ono Takeo, *Edo bukka jiten* (Tokyo: Tembōsha, 1982). For information on
a local area, see Takase Tamotsu, "Kaga han no beika hyō," in Toyoda Takeshi, ed.,
Nihonkai chiikishi kenkyū, vol. 1 (Tokyo: Bunken shuppan, 1980), pp. 319–60.
105 See, for instance, Sasaki Junnosuke, *Daimyō to hyakushō*, vol. 15 of *Nihon no rekishi* (Tokyo:
Chūō kōronsha, 1966), p. 160; and Kitajima Masamoto, *Nihonshi gaisetsu*, vol. 2 (Tokyo:
Iwanami shoten, 1968), pp. 201–8. As might be expected, given the nature of the data
available, scholars do not even agree that all members of the samurai class suffered a relative
loss of income. See, for instance, Kozo Yamamura, *A Study of Samurai Income and Entrepreneurship* (Cambridge, Mass.: Harvard University Press, 1974), pp. 26–69.

gunate's economic initiatives. In the 1760s and 1770s he reversed the
old, Kyōhō-inspired policies of restraint and, instead, began to encourage the growth of the economy's commercial sector, in the hopes that
this would increase supplies, bring down prices, and create new
sources of revenues.[106]

Perhaps the most conspicuous aspect of Tanuma's program was to
add to the existing number of protective associations and to broaden
the official patronage of the great merchant families, in the hope that
this would stimulate production. Thus the 1760s witnessed the appearance of many new retail groups in Edo and Osaka with exclusive
privileges in the retail marketing of iron, brass, lime, and other staple
commodities. Concurrently, selected wholesale houses were granted
newly authorized monopsony rights over such products as oil, cottonseed, and sulfur. Similarly, the shogunate authorized associations
to organize all shipping on the Tone and Kinu rivers as well as along
the Kasumigaura coastal region, sô as to reduce transportation fees.

Individual merchant houses also prospered from the acquisition of
new privileges. The Sumitomo family, for instance, had been involved
in the pharmaceutical and iron-goods business in Kyoto from the early
years of the Tokugawa period. Later, it started to trade in copper,
opened a refinery in Osaka, and, as we saw, rose to a position of
economic and social prominence. Thus, when Tanuma decided to
establish a copper monopoly in 1783, the Sumitomo were given exclusive rights to the copper trade in the Kansai region and later were
permitted to develop the rich Besshi mines.[107]

The desire to promote development and growth was evident in other
initiatives as well. Tanuma, for instance, provided funds to bring new
lands under cultivation, and after the eruption of Mt. Asano in 1783
had raised the bed of the Tone River, the shogunate arranged for flood
prevention and other riparian works to be undertaken. In a more
grandiose and controversial move, Tanuma encouraged foreign trade
through Nagasaki to China. Particularly attractive as export items
were the so-called *tawaramono*, or bales of dried sea products such as
tangle (*kombu*), sea slugs (*iriko*), and abalone. Then he turned his

---

106 For a full study in English of this policymaker, see Hall, *Tanuma Okitsugu*.
107 The expanded licensing of protective associations in the 1760s and 1770s is often interpreted
    as an attempt by the shogunate to sell special privileges in order to increase its revenues, as
    each association had to pay an annual licensing fee to the shogunate. Licensing had this
    advantage, of course, but because the annual fees were rather small and contributed little to
    the shogunate's financial well-being, historians in recent years have come to see licensing
    only as one part of a broader set of economic objectives designed to stimulate production and
    promote lower commodity prices. For a discussion of the importance of these revenues for
    the shogunate, see Hauser, *Economic Institutional Change*, pp. 41–46.

attention to developing fishing around Hokkaido, an island also re-puted to be rich in gold and other minerals, and he converted the existing baled-goods business into a shogunal monopoly. In 1786 Tanuma ordered all merchants who had formerly engaged in the trade to become government agents, and he then established a Baled Goods Office (*tawaramono yakusho*) at Nagasaki to supply capital to fisher-men, set prices, and establish strict domestic consumption limits for exportable marine products. So successful were these efforts that some members of the shogunate even contemplated extending such activi-ties into Sakhalin and the southern part of the Bering Sea, a move that would have reversed Japan's traditional seclusion policy.

Finally, Tanuma tried to reform the currency. Notable here was the introduction of a new silver coin known as the *nanryō nishu*, minted at 98 percent pure silver. In an innovative move, the shogunate tried to fix the coin's exchange rate by stamping onto its face the legend "Eight *nanryō* will exchange for one gold *ryō*," and officials further announced that the shogunate would accept only the *nanryō* for the obligations owed to it. In a related policy development, Tanuma tried to overcome the shogunate's chronic scarcity of copper for minting purposes, not only by relying on important merchant families such as the Sumitomo, but also by actually taking over the direct operation of some mines. In Akita, for instance, the shogunate confiscated from the local Satake daimyo the lands surrounding the family's famous Ami mine so that the shogunate could take over its production. Finally, the shogunate augmented the supply of coins by opening a mint for *zeni* at Nagasaki in 1768 and also by issuing a new four-*mon* copper piece known as the *shimon sen* in that same year.

Historians have not generally credited much success to these cur-rency reforms, chiefly because the new policies aroused so much oppo-sition that Tanuma was rather quickly driven from office, when stories of unprecedented shogunal extravagance and corruption also came to light. Some of the strongest opposition to specific Tanuma policies came from merchants.[108] Many of them, for instance, refused to have anything to do with the new *nanryō nishu* silver coin, and so it was used only for the intrinsic value of the silver it contained, not the artificial rate stamped on its face.[109] Moreover, the government seems to have

---

108 Kitajima Masamoto, *Kinsei no minshū to toshi* (Tokyo: Meicho shuppan, 1984), pp. 292–313.
109 The popular rejection of the *nanryō nishu* was first reported by Getaya Jimbei in a 1787 memorial. Shortly thereafter, popular attitudes changed when people realized that the coin had a high degree of purity, and it continued to circulate until 1824. See Hall, *Tanuma Okitsugu*, pp. 71–3.

been somewhat too enthusiastic in minting *zeni* and copper coins, and it issued more than markets would accept. *Zeni*, for example, circulated at approximately 2,800 to one gold *ryō* in the late 1730s but fell to 5,780 to one *ryō* in 1773. The consequence was an immediate and disastrous rise in commodity prices that produced loud complaints from people all across Japan.

Even more troublesome for Tanuma was the manner in which the licensing of new protective associations created tensions between those merchants and the older, established families, leading the shogunate to exhaust considerable credibility in trying to resolve such conflicts. One example of this concerns oil dealers in and around Osaka. Before Tanuma's tenure as grand chamberlain, merchants in Osaka had monopolized the oil business. In order to encourage expanded production, Tanuma divided the area between Osaka and modern-day Kōbe into five geographic districts and granted special rights to purchase all raw materials in these districts to five newly created associations of oil dealers. When the established Osaka merchants complained, Tanuma shifted gears and gave them the right to buy specified amounts of raw materials for processing into oil in all five of the districts, although the Osaka merchants were instructed to pay a fee to each of the new rural associations for this privilege. This solution satisfied no one, and both sides bombarded the local daimyo and the shogunate's officials with objections, petitions, and protests. The bitterness ran deep, and ultimately a frustrated shogunate tried to demonstrate its authority by announcing a shocking final solution: It confiscated from the local daimyo most of the territory where the oil was being produced, placed towns such Nishinomiya under the direct jurisdiction of the Osaka city magistrates, and gave its own rural attendants (*daikan*) stationed in Osaka administrative authority in the rural areas.[110]

If merchants protested some policies, the daimyo were even more apprehensive about other ways in which Tanuma flexed the shogunate's muscles. The confiscation of land in the Kansai brought no joy to the daimyo there, of course, and those in the north were equally frightened by Tanuma's confiscation of territory surrounding the copper mines in Akita, although there a strong protest by the Satake family ultimately succeeded in getting the family lands returned.

Even more daimyo felt threatened by Tanuma's new policies concerning the way in which they financed their own debts. Throughout the

110 Nakai, *Tenkan-ki bakuhansei*, pp. 118–23.

Tanuma years, the shogunate held to the belief that its fiscal problems, as well as those of the daimyo, were caused essentially by a combination of falling rice prices and rising commodity prices. Tanuma and his associates further argued that one of the primary reasons for the decline in rice prices came from false market surpluses created when daimyo – who sold rice certificates in Osaka in order to finance their own domain governments – began to issue certificates for more rice than their domains could actually produce.

Consequently, the shogunate began to require each daimyo to report officially the total amount of rice certificates issued as well as the actual amount of tax rice that he shipped into the city. The shogunate also permitted the merchants at the rice market in Dōjima to buy and sell only those certificates that bore the seal of the rice certificate inspector, an official newly appointed by the shogunate. The shogunate added still more restrictions on the diamyo's financing when it began to impose extraordinary levies on moneylenders and then to lend these funds back to the moneylenders with instructions to make these monies available to daimyo. As complicated as these fiscal arrangements seem on the surface, the new system meant that loans to the daimyo in theory were now originating with the shogunate, and as a condition for receiving such loans, the shogunate could require that daimyo pledge as collateral a portion of the domain tax rice equal in value to the loan. Thus, whenever a particular daimyo defaulted on the repayment of a loan, the rights to that portion of the domain's tax rice could be transferred in theory to the shogunate until the loan was fully repaid. In hopes of making this a more general method for all daimyo financing, the shogunate even went so far as to announce that it was considering extracting forced loans from peasants and urban dwellers throughout the country. Had such a scheme materialized, it would have marked the first time in the shogunate's history that it had bypassed the daimyo and directly taxed the residents of individual domains.

Many daimyo were severely handicapped by the new financing system, and all were shaken by the shogunate's threat to usurp their taxing prerogatives. Soon the dissatisfactions of these daimyo boiled to the surface, and when Tanuma's protector, the shogun Ieharu, died in 1786, Tanuma's enemies conspired to force his resignation and to appoint Matsudaira Sadanobu (1758–1829) as senior adviser to the shogun. Together with his own supporters, Sadanobu then launched the so-called Kansei Reforms of the late 1780s and early 1790s, whose self-declared purpose was to "return to Yoshimune" by recreating the alleged golden age of Sadanobu's grandfather and the author of the Kyōhō Reforms.

As we have learned from Chapter 9 in this volume, the core of the Kansei Reforms consisted of the abolition of many of the protective associations, a reissuing of sumptuary regulations, retrenchment programs, decrees ordering reductions in commodity prices, and exhortations against corruption, prostitution, and bribery. The Kansei Reforms came to an abrupt halt when Sadanobu himself was removed from office in 1793, and they were not particularly successful. The reforms treated symptoms, not causes. They did not adequately address such fundamental problems as the growing gap between commercial reality, on the one hand, and the frequent misconceptions of the daimyo and shogun about how the economy worked, on the other. Nor did the reforms eliminate the destructive aspects of the rivalry between urban merchants and the producers and wholesalers based in local towns and commercial villages. With economic policy in near chaos, commercial and urban problems would continue to mount in the early decades of the nineteenth century, forming part of the process that ultimately led to the Meiji Restoration.

Daimyo commercial policies. As many daimyo confronted increasingly severe problems with deficit financing during the latter half of the eighteenth century, they began to encourage commercial development within their domains and attempted to develop new mechanisms for tapping that wealth.[111] The centerpieces of these efforts were usually the creation of domain monopolies over certain products that could profitably be produced locally and sold in the great urban metropolises. Some domains had established such monopolies as early as the seventeenth century, but the techniques employed at that time were not nearly as sophisticated as those deployed in the late eighteenth century, when domain governments introduced new products and encouraged production by importing technology and supplying raw materials and capital to producers. Another important difference was that whereas the domains established the earlier monopolies in order to increase official revenues by collecting annually taxes and licensing fees, in the late eighteenth century many domains hoped to accomplish the same ends by capturing a portion of the profits of the trade,

---

111 For a recent discussion of the spread of commerce into local areas, see Yamaguchi Tetsu, "Bakuhansei ichiba no saihen to shōhin seikatsu," in Rekishigaku kenkyūkai, Nihonshi kenkyūkai, eds., *Kōza Nihon rekishi,* vol. 6 (Tokyo: Tōkyō daigaku shuppankai, 1985), pp. 229–65.

typically by marketing themselves the final product or by taking a percentage of the price of the goods as they moved from producer to wholesaler or from wholesaler to retailers outside the domain. Kumamoto provides a good example of a domain that actively moved into new commercial endeavors. In the latter half of the eighteenth century, domain officials established a local silkwork culture industry by importing techniques originally developed at Nishijin in Kyoto. Those same officials promoted wax tree cultivation by advancing to farmers in producing areas interest-free loans for fertilizer, tools, and household expenses.[112] Similarly, officials in Yonezawa domain imported silkworms and technical advisers from the nearby Date and Fukushima domains, distributed pamphlets with advice on mulberry cultivation throughout the domain, and advanced loans to producers. In Kaga, the government coupled similar incentives with tax exemptions in order to promote the lacquer and gold leaf industries.[113]

In most instances, the domain governments also attempted to control distribution and thereby to reserve the bulk of the profits for themselves. That is, the monopolies' actual day-to-day operations were entrusted to wholesale merchants within the local castle town, who were placed under the jurisdiction of newly created offices that typically bore names such as the Office of Domain Products (Kokusankata) or Office for Domain Prosperity (Kokuekikata). These offices usually carried out a full range of services, such as researching production problems, introducing technology, advancing capital and loans, and setting up distribution systems for the sale of the final products. Thus, the Kaga Office of Domain Products, established in 1813, oversaw the production – and took a percentage on the sale of – a variety of products, including textiles, lacquer, gold leaf, pottery, gold and silver inlay, ink, and paper.[114] In Mito, the domain established an office to handle the sale of locally produced *konnyaku* (devil's tongue) and then applied the profits to discharge loans contracted earlier between the domain and merchants in Edo and Osaka.

The system of domain monopolies had a mixed record. Some suc-

112 Several examples of specific domain monopolies can be found in Fujino Tamotsu, *Daimyō: sono ryōkoku keiei* (Tokyo: Jimbutsu ōraisha, 1964), pp. 229–37.
113 For additional details, see Shimode Sekiyo, *Kaga Kanazawa no kimpaku* (Kanazawa: Hokkoku shuppansha, 1972); Mori Yoshinori, "Kanazawa no haku," *Gakuhō* 26 (1982): 79–85; Miyamoto Masahisa, *Ishikawa ken* (Tokyo: Shōheisha, 1982), pp. 43–5; and Wajima shishi hensan semmon iinkai, ed., *Wajima shishi*, vol. 1 (Wajima: Wajima shiyakusho, 1976), pp. 286–314.
114 See Tabata Tsutomu, "Bunsei, Tempō-ki no Kaga han sanbutsukata seisaku no igi ni tsuite," in Tanaka Yoshio, ed., *Nihonkai chiikishi no kenkyū*, vol. 4 (Tokyo: Bunken shuppan, 1982), pp. 67–9.

ceeded and provided revenues that the daimyo could use to decrease their indebtedness. But many more failed, leaving domain finances in worse shape than ever.[115] In other instances, the monopolies drew the ire of established merchants and commercial farmers, who saw them as new threats to their own enterprises, and there were several incidents when peasants and merchants banded together to protest violently the new monopolies, thus adding to the challenges to daimyo authority that began to mount as the eighteenth century gave way to the nineteenth. The monopolies also presented new problems to the shogunate, for the monopolies once again challenged the role of Osaka and Edo merchants and disrupted the established marketing systems that centered on these urban centers. In all, their intention ran counter to the policies of Matsudaira Sadanobu, and their legacy was a new set of problems with which the shogunate ultimately would have to contend.

CONCLUSIONS

Viewed from the long run of Japanese history, the emergence of a more urbanized society and the growth of a commercialized economy during the Tokugawa period contained significant implications for Japan's development after 1868. Others have explained in some detail, for instance, how such Tokugawa period innovations as insurance systems and improved facilities for banking and credit contributed to Japan's relatively rapid economic transformation in the second half of the nineteenth century.[116] As we have seen, the merchants of Osaka and Edo created a system of marine insurance, and the moneylenders in those two urban centers put in place a sophisticated set of practices concerning deposits, advances, bill discounting, exchange transactions, and financing programs for rural industry that anticipated many of the functions of a modern banking system.

Equally important were the economic developments that took place outside the major cities. The protoindustrialization that occurred in the local towns and commercialized villages of the Tokugawa period stimulated the growth of light industry in such diverse endeavors as

---

115 Yoshinaga Akira, "Sembai seido to shōhin ryūtsū," in *Rekishigaku kenkyū* 229 (March 1959): 48–54.
116 See, for instance, E. Sydney Crawcour, "The Tokugawa Period and Japan's Preparation for Modern Economic Growth," *Journal of Japanese Studies* I (Autumn 1974): 113–25, as well as his "The Tokugawa Heritage," in William W. Lockwood, ed., *The State and Economic Enterprise in Japan* (Princeton, N.J.: Princeton University Press, 1965), pp. 17–44. A particularly influential article concerning banking is Kozo Yamamura's "The Role of the Samurai in the Development of Modern Banking in Japan," *Journal of Economic History* 27 (June 1967): 198–220.

the production of textiles, pottery, saké brewing, lacquer ware, tatami matting, roofing tiles, and farm equipment. Historians have found it difficult to quantify precisely the exact level to which such production had risen by the 1860s, but most agree that from this base, these industries grew quite rapidly during the final decades of the nineteenth century. Again, the precise rates of growth in the modern period are disputed by historians, and in any case they seem to have varied regionally, but it is clear that after 1868 the broader diffusion of traditional technology, the importation of new materials and technology from the West, the availability of new markets, and an increase in personal incomes in Japan all combined to stimulate considerable growth in the rural-based industries. Over time, this confluence of factors created greater sources of capital accumulation, increased the level of output of the economy, and provided useful experience with early forms of mechanized manufacturing that made possible the growth of modern, heavy industry in Japan at the turn into the twentieth century.[117]

However salutary the long-term consequences of commercialization and urbanization, in the shorter run they generated dislocations, contention, and competition, all of which contributed to the growing domestic crisis that formed a prelude to the Meiji Restoration. One example of this was the change in the internal composition of urban populations seen in Japanese cities during the opening decades of the nineteenth century. An especially prominent trend was a growing gap between the wealthier and the poorer members of the population, as well as an apparent increase in the absolute number of very poor.

Although the documentation is not complete, it seems likely that the percentage of urban residents who rented lodgings in major cities such as Edo and Osaka increased rapidly, often by as much as one-third.[118] These renters worked as peddlers, day laborers, or artisans who, to use the shogunate's own contemporary parlance, "eke out their living one day at a time."

It is difficult to explain why the proportion of urban poor should have been growing at a time when the total urban population had

---

117 The classic study that initiated research concerning the role of traditional industries in Japan's transition to modern economic growth is Furushima Toshio, *Sangyōshi*, vol. 3 of *Taikei Nihonshi sōsho* (Tokyo: Yamakura shuppansha, 1966). One of the more optimistic estimates of the growth of traditional industries in the Meiji period, and still widely cited, is Yamada Yuzō, *Nihon kokumin shotoku suikei shiryō* (Tokyo: Tōyō keizai shimpōsha, 1957); and lower growth rates for western Japan are documented in Nishikawa Shunsaku, *Nihon keizai no seichōshi* (Tokyo: Tōyō keizai, 1985).

118 An insightful study about the urban poor is Minami Kazuo's *Edo no shakai kōzō* (Tokyo: Hanawa shobō, 1977).

leveled off and when there is compelling evidence, as demonstrated in Chapter 13 of this volume, that standards of living were improving for many segments of urban society. Some demographers argue that the marriage age in cities was relatively high, compared with that of the agricultural villages, and that consequently in-migration from rural areas was necessary in order to maintain urban populations at a steady level. Such migrations did in fact take place in many regions, and most likely it was the poorer elements of peasantry who moved into the cities in the late eighteenth century. Most were formerly independent farmers who had lost their lands when the commercial economy reached agricultural villages.

Moreover, poor harvests hit Japan several times in the late eighteenth century, resulting in widespread starvation. At that time, the poor in several cities, including Edo and Osaka, took part in food riots, inspiring the shogunate to fashion new social welfare schemes for urban centers. The system implemented in Edo came to serve as a model for many other cities. There, each person who owned land contributed annually to his ward an amount of money that was determined by the value of his land. The collected monies constituted a reserve fund that ward representatives used to buy and store rice for emergencies, to make grants to elderly persons who lived alone, and to finance low-interest loans for the construction and maintenance of homes and shops. These funds were referred to as the City Office reserve fund (*machi kaisho tsumikin*) and still existed at the time of the Meiji Restoration, when Edo passed to the control of the new Meiji oligarchy, and the office that controlled the funds became the focal point of the new movement to establish a City Assembly (*shikai*) in Tokyo after 1868.[119]

The economic and social problems of the early nineteenth century, especially the rapid increase in budget deficits on both the shogunal and domain levels, contributed to the well-known, relative decline of the economic lot of many samurai retainers in the decades immediately before the Meiji Restoration.[120] Equally obvious, both to the samurai who lived through the times and to modern historians, was the fact

119 For more on the life of the urban poor at this time, see Matsumoto Shirō, "Kinsei kōki no toshi to minshū," in *Iwanami kōza Nihon no rekishi*, vol. 12 (*kinsei* 4) (Tokyo: Iwanami shoten, 1976), pp. 89–146.

120 Discussions of domain deficits and the impact on the samurai can be found in Aono Shunsui, *Daimyō to ryōmin* (Tokyo: Kyōikusha, 1983); Kitajima Masamoto, "Tempō-ki no rekishiteki ichi," in Kitajima Masamoto, ed., *Bakuhansei kokka kaitai no kenkyū* (Tokyo: Yoshikawa kōbunkan, 1978), pp. 1–22; and Hanley and Yamamura, *Economic and Demographic Change*, pp. 131–60.

that the shogunate and the country's daimyo had been generally unable to implement policies that would provide long-term solutions to the economic problems experienced by the samurai. Tokugawa Ieyasu and his fellow daimyo had built a society based on the concept of rule by status, but two centuries of urbanization and commercial growth had created a new world in which such a political ideal no longer corresponded to economic and social reality. Agriculture had become commercialized and oriented toward the urban markets, and even domain governments had become involved in the production and sale of commercial products. While inflation ate away at the samurai's incomes, some merchants, and even peasants, grew wealthy and enjoyed life-styles that drew the envy of even the highest-ranking elements of the samurai status group. Yet during times of drought and famine, the rural poor would crush into the castle towns, and the sounds of the food riots and of shops being smashed could be heard even within samurai mansions. Increasingly, society seemed out of kilter.

Confusion and anger led many to question the legitimacy of the shogunate and daimyo governments, and the samurai seemed to grow less loyal. This was manifested in subtle ways: some warriors took handsomely dowered wives from the merchant class; others sold their birthrights and drifted off into mercantile occupations; and a few simply gave up in despair and committed suicide. From the 1830s, other samurai, no longer willing to bear the hardships forced on their class, began to pay more attention to domain affairs. For some, this meant listening more closely to critics of government policy, whereas others tried to gain bureaucratic positions that would enable them to redirect domain policy. Thus, when the nation's crisis worsened in the 1850s and 1860s, a great many samurai were prepared to enter the political arena, eager to defend Japan from without and to reform its political structure from within.

During the early nineteenth century, the bonds that had shaped the nation's status groups into a coherent whole began to fray along other seams as well. In the seventeenth century, society was symbiotically organized, held together by mutual obligations and the trust that each of society's status groups would perform the duties assigned to it. The daimyo relied on merchants and artisans to supply goods and services, and the lords reciprocated by providing an environment within the castle towns and domains that responded to the merchants' needs and desires. Samurai and merchants were also organically linked. The samurai handled military responsibilities and staffed the most important, decision-making offices in the domain government. The merchants catered to the samurai's daily needs for commercial goods and also fleshed out the lower, enforcement ranks of urban administration.

During the late eighteenth and early nineteenth centuries, however, the pressures of commercial growth and the problems associated with urbanization eroded the old organic bonds of interdependence. Derision replaced trust. Daimyo no longer voiced confidence in merchants but, rather, condemned them. The bitterness in the new attitudes is clearly revealed in the speeches and behavior of the lord's officials in Kaga domain. In 1835 the leading adviser to the Maeda daimyo called the city magistrates to his office. "Among the households of urban commoners," he complained, "are many, both high and low, rich and poor, who are audacious and who do not preserve their status." The more humble merchants, he lamented, purchased splendid clothing when attending ceremonial functions, or even worse, he cried out, borrowed large sums with which to rent such clothing. Criticisms rolled from his tongue. Some merchants "coveted the houses of those of higher status," whereas others served "expensive banquets at weddings, beyond their status and financial means. . . . Yearly the excesses have become greater as people strive to impress their neighbors." Sadly, he concluded, "There are many who no longer observe the status regulations, who spend too much money, who have a poor sense of social responsibility." In response to this outburst, the city magistrates reissued sumptuary regulations and instructed lower officials to make certain that they were read aloud to all of Kanazawa's residents.[121]

It was a short step from scorn for the merchants' social behavior to condemnation of their business ethics. In 1842 several of the lord's advisers in Kaga jointly set forth their complaints about higher commodity prices:

In recent years, there has been adequate production of rapeseed. However, merchants have spread rumors that shortages exist, and they charge higher prices. Merchants have claimed shortages of paper, firewood, and charcoal and then raised their prices. All merchants and artisans have been forgetting the dictates of status and moral behavior. The attitude that one can neglect to work hard and yet still make a large profit has become widespread. . . . Originally, in the past, people worked at their jobs with passion and sincerity, and they made a reasonable profit. Now, however, people concoct elaborate

121 *Kaga han shiryō*, vol. 14 (Tempō 6 [1835]/intercalary 7), pp. 597–602.

schemes that allow them to neglect the proper conduct of their profession but still make enormous profits.[122]

The new abusive rhetoric displaced the more expected discourse of respect and deference and thus put into place paving stones that others would tread when they moved toward a new formulation of the political norm at mid-century. Even in the face of such frustration and complicated economic change, the shogunate and daimyo stubbornly continued to cling to the tenets of class separation, agrarianism, and rule by status, and their dogmatism was increasingly interpreted as an arrogant attempt to preserve artificially their dominant position in politics and society. The failure of the Tempō Reforms in the 1830s and 1840s opened the door for even more doubts and questioning, and the edifice of shogunal and daimyo authority collapsed quickly when a foreign policy crisis became intertwined with domestic upheavals during the 1850s and 1860s. It was only in the process of building a new system to respond to the changing modern environment after 1868 that the Meiji leadership finally adopted policies that reached an accommodation with the forces set in motion by the waves of urban and commercial growth that Japan experienced during the seventeenth and eighteenth centuries.

---

122 *Kanshi zuihitsu* (The public service records of Okumura Hidezane), ms copy, Kanazawa City Library, Tempō 13 (1842)/5/29.

The Economic Studies Quarterly
Vol. 38, No. 4, December 1987

THE ECONOMY OF CHŌSHŪ
ON THE EVE OF INDUSTRIALIZATION*

By SHUNSAKU NISHIKAWA

1. Introduction

The domain, or *han*, of Chōshū was located at the southwestern extremity of the island of Honshū and was comprised of the two provinces of Suō and Nagato. The total area amounted to over 6,000 square kilometers, and in the 1840s had a population of roughly 520,000.[1] Considered one of the wealthier han, Chōshū was a major force which overthrew the Tokugawa shogunate and carried out the Meiji Restoration (see Craig, 1961).

It has been generally thought that in the period after the 18th century, the domains' economies stagnated or decayed. As data on manufacturing and commercial activities are either non-existent or woefully incomplete, this view has been derived merely from the surveys of agricultural output and arable land.

However, from the *Bōchō Fudo Chūshin-an*, (hereafter BFC) which is a collection of reports from village headman, we can obtain a wealth of data on commercial profit as well as industrial input and output. In Chōshū, according to the BFC, the agricultural output in an average year in the early 1840s was 800,000 koku, while non-agricultural output amounted to 450,000 koku, thus a total material product amounted to 1,250,000 koku.[2] Comparing this with the assessed rice yield in the land survey of 1763 of 710,000 koku,[3] the growth rate for the 80 years was .7%. With a population growth rate of .3% per year, the per capita growth rate was .4% per year, and thus the economy grew by nearly 40%. Apparently this growth was achieved mainly by gradual development of protoindustry, transportation, and commerce.

Depending upon the BFC data on input, output, profits, income and wages, and labor force, as

* I appreciate the assistance and endeavors given by Shōko Ishibe, Wilma Maki, and James White in preparing and translating this paper, however none of them is responsible for possible errors.

Table 1 was estimated in the collaboration with Hiroya Akimoto of Tōyō University (Nishikawa and Akimoto, 1977). I have subsequently made some changes in the format and stand responsible for both the revised estimates and present version.

1) One third of this territory was ceded to four collateral domains, so that the territory of Chōshū Han itself was reduced to roughly 4,000 square kilometers (see Figure 1).

2) The former figure is the agricultural output (64,000 kan) shown in Table 1; the latter total is Total 1 (36,092 kan) in Table 2, both divided by the price of rice (1 koku = 80 silver momme = .08 kan). One koku = c.5 bushels; one koku of rice weighs 150 kilograms. See note 5 for kan and momme.

3) This figure is the *kusadaka* or *uchidaka*—actually assessed yield of the domain, which was almost twofold of the official yield or *omotedaka* authorized by the shogunate. Earlier *kusadaka* were 475,000 in 1626 and 635,000 in 1688 (Ishikawa, 1968, p. 46, 94, & 151). The annual growth rate of *kusadaka* was .7% in 1626–1688 and .15% in 1688–1763. Agricultural growth such as this seems to have been common in western Japan.

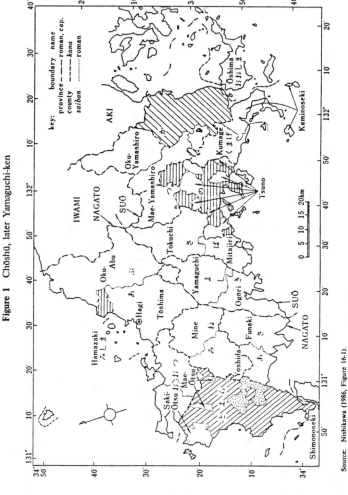

Figure 1 Chōshū, later Yamaguchi-ken

key:
boundary	name
province ——	roman, cap.
county ——	*kana*
saiban ·········	roman

AKI

IWAMI

NAGATO

SUO

Oku-Yamashiro

Mae-Yamashiro

Tokuchi

Mitajiri

Tsuno

Kumage くまげ

Oshima おほしま

Kaminoseki

Oku-Abu

Hamazaki はまざき

Hagi

Toshima

Yamaguchi

Mine

Okori

Funaki

Yoshida

Saki-Otsu さき

Mae-Otsu おつ

SUO

NAGATO

Shimonoseki

0 5 10 15 20km

Source: Nishikawa (1986, Figure 16-1).

Notes: a) Shaded areas were ceded to four collateral domains.
b) *Saiban* was a local administrative district in Chōshū Han. The lord appointed a magistrate and his clerks to each *saiban* among his vassals. The lord appointed a magistrate and his clerks to each *saiban* among his vassals.
Village headmen in the *saiban* assisted those samurai officials.

210

well as capital stock such as draft animals, ships and boats, we can estimate a *tableau économique à la* input-output table for Chōshū at that time. The table can provide us with a more real socio-economic picture of Japan on the eve of industrialization.[4]

2. The "Tableau Économique" of Chōshū

Table 1, to borrow the words of Barna (1975), presents a "tableau économique in modern guise" for Chōshū. Students of modern economics would refer to it as an "input-output table," in which the production sector is divided into agricultural (A) and non-agricultural (M) sectors, with commodities flowing from the left column to the top row of the table, and money flowing in the reverse direction.

Table 1 Tableau Économique of Chōshū for a Normal Year in the 1840s

(Unit: 1000s of paper kan)

From: \ To:	Intermediate demand		Final demand			Exports	Unallocated	Total
			Consumption C					
	Agri. A	Non-agri. M	Hsehold Ch	Han Cd	Samurai Cw	E	U	T
Intermed. input:								
Agri. A	2	5	42	2	5	8	0	64
Non-agri. M	4	10	18	3	5	13	5	58
Value added:								
Hsehold. income Vh	28	36						64
Taxes Vp	30	1						31
Imports F		6	13					19
Surplus R			4	2	1			7
Total T	64	58	64	20	11	21	5	

Source: Nishikawa (1985, Table 3-3, revised).

The upper lefthand block of Table 1 (the top 2 rows and 2 leftmost columns) contains four elements, the intermediate transactions between the two sectors of the economy. Final demand is comprised of consumption (C) and exports (E). Consumption is subdivided into household consumption (Ch), domain (including the lord) consumption (Cd), and samurai consumption (Cw). The total income of these three groups (95,000 *kan*) appears as income in the "Value

---

4) It is difficult to estimate the extent to which the economy of Chōshū was typical of the domainial economy. My impression is that Chōshū's protoindustry placed it among the most advanced. Thus other domains, although similar in overall structure, were probably not so strikingly protoindustrialized as Chōshū.

Added" rows of the table.[5] Row Vh represents household income after taxes: 28,000 kan from agriculture and 36,000 from non-agricultural sources. Domain and samurai incomes (row Vp) consisted of 30,000 kan from the land tax—paid primarily in rice—and the strikingly meager amount of 1,000 kan from non-agricultural taxes. This unbalanced taxation system was characteristic of the Tokugawa system. In this regard the ruling class was quite "physiocratic."

The two entries in row F represent 6,000 kan worth of imports of non-agricultural raw materials (dyestuffs, coal, iron, etc.) into the domain, and 13,000 kan worth of domain expenses incurred outside the domain. The latter figure involved the cost of the lord's household and the expense of upkeep of the lord's residences and offices in the three major cities of Edo, Osaka, and Kyoto. It also includes interest payments on loans from Osaka merchants, which sometimes amounted to substantial sums. Thus some 40% of the han's total income flowed out of the domain, a considerable loss for the domestic economy. However, the economies of the three major cities depended on exports from and expenditures by the domains, not only of Chōshū but also of many other ones, and the populations of these cities used the money thus earned to buy rice and other products from local domains.

The han extracted 31,000 kan in tax revenues from the people. Besides the 13,000 kan discussed above, vassal stipends took another 11,000 kan, and household expenses of the lord plus other administrative (intra-domain) expenses amounted to another 5,000 kan. What is of particular interest here is the remaining 2,000 kan transferred to the special account, *buikugata*, the fund for industrial development, which was established by Lord Shigetaka.[6]

The samurai of the domain also had their own retainers (rear vassals, or *baishin*) in proportion to their stipends. The samurai numbered almost 5,700; the baishin about 6,200 (Suematsu, 1921). The former group expended some 4,000 kan from their own income on the support of the baishin. Because the BFC was a survey of the economic life of the commoner population, it does not include information on the sumptuary life of the samurai. Therefore, the three entries in column Cw are no more than my speculations.[7] In particular, there is a strong probability that

---

5) The *kan* was originally a unit of weight (1 kan = 3.75 kilograms; 1,000 momme = 1 kan). Silver money was basically money by weight, and so kan and momme were used to denote the value of silver domainial note, or *hansatsu*, even after silver coins were later introduced by the shogunate. The figures in Table 1 are measured in domainial note. One domainial paper kan was worth a bit more than 800 silver momme in Chōshū (see Nishikawa and Tanimura, 1980).

The *ryō* was a unit of gold coin, *koban*, the weight and quality of which were decreased considerably by several debasements throughout the Tokugawa period, while the official exchange rate between gold and silver money had been kept constant (1 ryō = 60 momme) since the late 17th century. The market rate however varied around the official rate.

6) According to Akimoto (1977, Figure 2), this fund was actively used during the latter half of the 18th century, but was largely hoarded after the beginning of the 19th century, so that by the 1840s it has grown up to roughly 60,000 kan. Seifū Murata, leader of the Tempō reform of the domain, used some 10,000-20,000 kan to redeem a part of the domainial debts. Since then the fund had grown and eventually reached 80,000 kan before the Restoration. In 1867-68 around 20,000 kan was used to support domainial forces in the civil war and 30,000-40,000 kan was donated to the Emperor.

7) In Nishikawa (1985, Table 3-3), this rear vassal consumption (1,000 and 3,000 kan) were aggregated into those of commoners.

the 1,000 kan of residual (R, Cw) is the result of an underestimation of total samurai consumption expenditures.

The BFC is a series of reports from "individual" villages, therefore it contains little on commerce or financial transactions between villages, much less on exports from the domain. The figure for exports of agricultural products (A, E) is based on Meiji-era recollection by former han officials. The volume of exports gradually rose, and fluctuated to some extent year by year, but 100,000 koku appears to be about a good annual average in the first half of the 19th century. Non-agricultural exports (M, E) were largely comprised of paper, salt, and cotton. The han exercised an official monopsony on paper, and thus paper exports, like those of rice, were controlled by the han and/or the agent merchant.

Trade in cotton and salt was in the hands of merchant guilds, *kaisho* or *ton'ya*, and shipowners who exported goods northward along the coast of the Sea of Japan. There are no reliable data on the volume of goods exported by these merchants. The figure presented here is also a conjecture based on fragmentary evidence. The last trade entry involves imports (F, M), but only includes imports of dyestuffs, iron, cotton, and so forth, which were the raw materials for handicraft and manufacturing industry. For example, it is noted in one volume of the BFC that shipowners imported rice for consumption by saltworkers and others, but no figure is given. Thus the estimated value of imports must be an underestimate of actual magnitude.

The data entered in column U would represent, in a usual input-output table, capital formation. However, because of the paucity of the data our figures for consumption and for imports and exports include some errors; consequently, what this column shows is that the eventual disposition of non-agricultural products with a value of some 5,000 kan is simply unknown. Therefore I have refrained from labelling column U as "Capital Formation." The BFC records stocks of fixed capital such as draft animals, ships, and irrigation works, but not rates of increase therein. In all likelihood the real rate of net investment was lower than 5,000 kan. If we assume that the ratio of capital to output was 5, then 5,000 kan of capital investment would produce additional output worth 1,000 kan. The domestic product, as shown in the next section, totalled 95,000 kan, so that the economic growth rate was more than 1%. The population growth rate was .3%, making the annual per capita economic growth rate .7%, or almost twice the growth rate seen from the mid-18th to early 19th centuries. A rate so high is quite dubious.[8]

Moreover, according to the BFC there were in Chōshū a total of 1,032 ships, with a capacity of 158,000 koku (equivalent to 15,800 tons). According to Ishii (1968, pp. 174–176), assuming a lifetime of 12 years, an annual amortization of 15 (gold) ryō per 10 koku of capacity gives a figure of roughly 1,500 kan. If this were so, then net investment must be reduced to 3,500 kan, and the rate of growth falls accordingly. Additionally, the depreciation of buildings such as homes and warehouses must be figured in. Unfortunately, the data necessary for such a calculation are nowhere to be found in the BFC. It is certain that the share allocated to "reinvestment" or

---

8) Akimoto (1981) estimated the higher growth of capital stocks in the saiban along the Inland Sea coast (see Figure 1) during the mid-18th and mid-19th centuries, but it is not certain whether such growth continued after the 1840s.

replacement was more considerable,[9] and it seems likely that "net investment" was therefore at most 3,000 kan or much less.

Total surplus (R, T) amounted to 7,000 kan.[10] However, the 2,000 kan of han savings was, from the late 18th century onward, simply hoarded in the han coffer (see note 6 above). Therefore the amount of capital formation (actually "Unallocated") amounted to only 5,000 kan. Moreover, investment opportunities for big merchants and rich farmers were even less so numerous; most salient among them were land reclamation and the purchase of cropland and salt fields. Such investment, particularly land purchase, does not constitute any physical capital stock increase. It simply raised the asset value of cropland and salt fields.

3. The Structure of Production

The first two columns of Table 1 show the input-output relationships in the agricultural and non-agricultural sectors. That is:

(1) Agricultural output = intermediate input + value added,
      (64)   (2 + 4)   (28 + 30)

(2) Non-agricultural output − material imports = intermediate input + value added.
      (58)   (6)   (5 + 10)   (36 + 1)

(The figures in parentheses below the items are the values from Table 1, in thousands of kan.)

The intermediate input in the agricultural sector amount to only 9.4% of sectoral output, which means that the ratio of value added to output (or income ratio) is high. As we have already seen, more than half of the value added in this sector was absorbed into the form of the land tax, and became the income of the ruling class. The income ratio in the non-agricultural sector is a little lower, at 63.8%. This is because for this sector both domestic product (15,000 kan) and material imports (6,000 kan) are used as intermediate input.

Combining equations (1) and (2), and deleting intermediate and imported input, we have the domestic product in the domain:

(3) Output of both sector − (intermediate input + material imports)
    (64 + 58)   (2 + 4 + 5 + 10)   (6)

                                         = domestic product.
                                            (95)

The sum of intermediate inputs and material imports equals 28.4% of the domestic product. In

---

9) Interestingly enough, the depreciation of draft animals and farm tools is given in the BFC. This is included, as a current agricultural input (sector *A*), in the first two figures recorded in row *A* of Table 1. In some saiban, this information is combined into the value of fertilizer purchased and/or consumption expenses of household, and it is difficult to calculate it separately as reinvestment.

    The depreciation rate for draft animals was 7% per annum, which suggests a useful life of 14 years was assumed. The value of depreciation of farm tools was 13 momme per household, and that of draft animals 16 momme.

10) Those familiar with the national accounting are probably aware that in an open economy—which Chōshū was, at least vis-à-vis the rest of Japan—total saving may be calculated as (capital formation) and (export) less (import).

the input-output table for Yamaguchi Prefecture in 1980 this proportion was 62.5%, which reveals that the "roundaboutness" of production was quite short-cut and limited to 140 years ago.

The ratio of agricultural to non-agricultural output is 52 : 48 in terms of the domestic product, while in terms of value added it is 61 : 39. Obviously agriculture is of greater importance here. Parenthetically, the 1980 ratio between the primary sector, and the secondary and tertiary sectors was 3 : 97, showing the industrialization has proceeded since the late- and post-Meiji period. This is not, however, to slight the importance of the protoindustrial and other non-agricultural sector 140 years ago, since it occupied almost 40% of output even then.

Table 2 presents data on the non-agricultural sector, broken down more finely into industrial categories. Of the output of almost 58,000 kan, material production such as manufacturing, forest products, quarrying, and fishing accounted for 62% and the remaining 38% was service income from commerce, transportation, and other occupations. Construction is not included here because investment expenditures are not recorded in the BFC. In the BFC for certain sai-ban, expenditures on maintenance and repair cost of houses are included under "consumption," but there are no data on new construction of houses or other types of buildings. For net- and boat-owners (*amimoto*) only estimated profits are recorded. Since ships and buildings were built wholly of wood, it is certain that shipbuilders, carpenters, plasterers, thatchers, and other crafts-men must have been at work, but in their case also only estimated income is recorded. Further, there are substantial numbers of sawmill workers among the artisans but they, like construction and shipyard workers, are ignored in the data; thus the "Forestry" includes only a comparatively small volume of commodities such as firewood and charcoal.

Table 2   The Structure of "Industry" in Chōshū

Type of business	Output (in *kan*)	Share (in %)
Manufacturing[a]	27,945	77.4
Paper	3,865	10.7
Salt	6,833	18.9
Sake	6,368	17.7
Cotton weaving	7,947	22.0
Handicrafts[b]	2,932	8.1
Forestry and quarrying	4,600	12.8
Fishing and marine products	3,547	9.8
Total 1	36,092	100.0
Transportation	3,557	16.3
Commerce	12,147	55.5
Services	1,154	5.3
Other occupations	5,001	22.9
Total 2	21,859	100.0

Notes: a) Sum of the following five categories of manufacturing.
b) Half of total. The remaining half is included under "Other occu-pations" below.
Source: Nishikawa and Akimoto (1977, Table 2).

215

The "Quarrying" includes construction materials such as clay, mortar, and oyster shell ash. It also includes a small quantity of coal, produced in Funaki Saiban and used for fuel in the evaporation process of salt manufacturing. However this coal was virtually strip-mined immediately below the surface of cropfields by farmers during the agricultural off-season and amounted to very little. The required quantity of coal was supplied from the coal fields of northern Kyūshū and brought to Chōshū in small cargo ships.

In analyzing the geographic distribution of the manufacturing industry one should look back at the map (Figure 1). Papermaking was concentrated in mountainous districts such as Oku- and Mae-Yamashiro Saiban and in parts of Oku-Abu and Tokuchi Saiban. The natural environment of the villages in these districts was so harsh that only a poor harvest, especially in rice, was possible. The han found that paper produced by farmers in the villages in the wintertime was a more favorable article for merchandizing outside the domain, and thus, from the mid-17th century on, purchased an assigned amount at a lower than market price. The "price" was paid in the tax rice which otherwise would be collected from the villages, and sometimes with a little addition of paper money. Therefore one may call it a pseudo-monopsony, or may regard that the land tax of papermaking villages was largely paid in paper.

It might at first seem strange to include salt production under the heading of manufacturing, but in Japan this production did not involve simply exploitation of rock salt formations. The standard process began with sunlight evaporation of sea water over the sand field, the residue was collected and dissolved again in water, and this concentrated brine was boiled to obtain salt crystals. The producers of the salt field—in many cases they were tenants of the merchant owners of the fields—employed several saltmaking artisans, plus supplementary laborers. The boiling process required special skills, and was done for the most part by seasonal artisans who came for six months, usually from the third to the eighth month, from Oshima and Kaminoseki Saiban. These island and peninsular villages from which they came had little cropland or water resources so many of their residents made a living as sailors or fishermen. Thus seasonal salt work was an important employment opportunity for the other (peasant) residents, and served to alleviate the food shortage in these saiban. Additionally, the wives and daughters of the seasonal workers augmented family income by weaving cotton. Weaving was concentrated in the two saiban mentioned, and was widespread in the saiban along the Inland Sea coast such as Mitajiri, Funaki, and Ogōri, through putting-out system. Being the side work for women, there is a tendency to underestimate the importance of weaving but, as shown in Table 2, it accounted for the major share of manufacturing output.

Sake was made from rice. Brewers were allowed to purchase tax rice from the han, (the payment including a brewing tax) for their production. It is also likely that brewers bought rice from farmers via merchants, but there are no reliable data on this quantity. Sake brewing was also a wintertime activity, and provided a by-employment opportunity for farmers.

Thus all four of the major manufactured commodities were produced through by-employments of farmers and their families, a point which firstly demanded our attention by Smith (1969) based on the Kaminoseki BFC. With the exception of sake, the above output figures are based exclusively on the totals of the data in the BFC of all saiban, and therefore errors in our "estimates" are probably small. The input coefficients for these three industries are also obtained from the BFC and relevant materials, and may be considered free of major errors (Nishikawa, 1976).

By contrast, our estimates of service income—as is even the case today—probably contain considerable errors. Commercial profits account for the greater part of service income, but they are calculated as the per family income (which must have varied greatly from salt and cotton guild profits to peddling) times the number of families or individuals involved.

Transportation includes overland transport by pack animal, but sea transport shares for the most part. Since merchant ships were "merchant" enterprises, the profit therefrom also has commercial quality to it. If we were to subsume it under the heading of commerce, this category would account for an even greater share of the total.

In contrast to the above, one gets the impression that service occupations play a very small role. If one adds income from "Other occupations" the share increases somewhat, but part of this "other" income is accounted for by the half of the artisan's income attributed to repair services, and another part represents the wage income of day laborers. The point here is that day labor, overland transport, peddling, and so forth were also by-employments of farmers.

4. Occupational Structure and Household Income

The BFC includes data on the occupational distribution of the Chōshū work force. The task of this section is to classify them by industry and compare them with the industry-specific structure of output. The unit of measurement of the occupational statistics is the household. Oridinarily the BFC first present the number of households in each village and then record the distribution of households across occupational categories. However, there are villages in which the total of the latter does not equal the former.[11] The question of whether the number of households was miscounted or whether there are omissions or miscountings in the occupational categories was addressed by referring to data on population, cropland, and other matters such as craft-licence etc. Table 3 presents the distribution with the "Other" (*i.e.*, unknown) category thus reduced as much as possible.

The first point in Table 3 which draws our attention is the overwehlming 80% of households engaged in agriculture. According to theories of economic development, this attests to the backwardness of the Chōshū economy. But the reality is hardly so simple. We have already noted that the manufacture of paper, sake, cotton cloth, and salt were done by farm family by-employments. Of more than 85,500 farm families, some 27,000 were landless tenants, or *modo-*

---

11) The number of households is given in the BFC as both numbers of "houses and households." In most saiban, however, the number of houses equals the number of households (literally, "ovens" or "hearths"), and therefore only one set of figures is given. In Mitajiri and Yoshida the two are differentiated, with the latter being more numerous. This gap is particularly large in the towns. It is because of rental housing and boarding houses, in which one building sheltered several households (or "hearths"). By contrast, in rural villages there seems to have been one house per household. For the most parts, total figures on occupational distribution too accord with the one of households. So far as the towns and villages of Mitajiri, and in Imaura-gaisaku Village (in Yoshida Saiban) are concerned, I have used the household figures. Finally, only household figures are given in the BFC of Mae- and Saki-Ōtsu Saiban, and so they have been used.

Table 3 Occupational Distribution, by Households

(Units: households or individuals)

Total households	106,925	100.0%
Farming	85,531	80.0
Fishing and hunting	3,567	3.3
Artisans	5,840	5.5
Transportation	1,349	1.3
Commerce	7,518	7.0
Day labor	2,680	2.5
Services	347	.3
Unknown	93	.09
Outcasts	2,209	
Doctors	148 (individuals)	
Clerics	4,306 (individuals)	

byakushō; the rest were landed farmers or *hon-byakushō*.[12]

Table 4 gives the total and per-household incomes by occupations of the household. The after-tax household income of farmers is shown in row 1, column 3, which amounts to only 327 momme, indicating the harsh domainial exploitation. Given an average commoner family size of 4.4 persons and an average consumption expenditure of 128 momme per capita, the household expenditures amount to 563 momme.[13] Apparently the farm household could not survive without any supplementary earnings. In the case of, *e.g.*, papermaking farm families (row 2, column 3), their income from paper was 291 momme which, when added to their farm income that was presumably lower than the average (327 momme), gives a total income nearly equal to the above consumption expenditures (563 momme).

Participations in many other by-employment was so complicated that it was hardly discernible like in the papermaking. The following observations by occupation are able to suggest the pattern of by-employment. A total laborer population is 2,680. Mitajiri Saiban accounted for 1,048, or 39% of these.—Additionally, its population included 821 persons engaged in peddling and petty trade. The total population of the two towns and 29 villages of the saiban was almost 31,300 persons, in 7,760 households. As a proportion of households, the day labor-petty trade proletariat accounted for 24%. There were a further 641 persons in this sort of proletarian stratum in Yamaguchi Town, and 283 in the vicinity of the castle town of Hagi. There were also those who engaged in day labor "along with" or "in the intervals between" farming, to use the BFC's terms.

---

12) Calculated from the social status statistics given in the BFC. Almost all of those from fishermen to day laborers were landless. In the towns of Yamaguchi, Mitajiri, and Miyaichi there was no farm population. The merchants and artisans of these towns—a total of 2,324 households—may have been categorized as *chōnin* (townspeople). The term "townsman" however is not used in the BFC, and I have categorized them according to Shimomura (1934). Excluding them, 56% of the remaining 104,601 families were landed and 44% were landless.

13) Commoner population was approximately 470,000 in 107,000 families, and their consumption expenditure is estimated to have been 60,000 kan (Column 3 in Table 1).

Such persons are listed in the enumeration of industrial income given in the Mitajiri BFC (although not in the other saiban's). Even estimating conservatively, they numbered more than 1,350, 30% of which were presumably engaged in packhorse transportation.

Table 4 Income Per Household

Occupation	Total income	Number of households	Income per household
Agriculture	28,000 kan	85,500	.327 kan
Papermaking	3,865[a]	13,300	.291
Fishing	3,547	3,551[b]	.999
Handicrafts	5,864[c]	5,840	1.004
Transportation	3,557	1,349	2.637
Commerce	12,147	7,518	1.616
Services	1,154	347	3.326
Day labor	2,069[d]	2,680	.772

Notes: a) Costs, aside from those of purchasing a part of raw materials, were almost zero. The figure to the right is the number of farm households in Yamashiro and Tokuchi Saiban.
b) Excludes 33 hunters.
c) The half of the income of this group which was included under "Other occupations" in Table 2 is restored to this category.
d) Excludes the half of the artisans' income included under "Other occupations" in Table 2.

A further 215 women—16% of the total—occupied in collecting the evaporated sea salt and preparing the salt fields are included in the above 1,350 figure. Men were also employed in the salt industry, but most of them were classified as "steady" day laborers,[14] who worked at other jobs during the off-season of the salt industry and whose wages thus are included under a variety of other occupational categories.

Therefore, the wages paid to day laborers in the salt industry, as shown in Table 2, are also entered in the category of "Other occupations," and there is thus unquestionably some double counting. However, for the following two reasons this double counting does not pose a serious problem. In the first place, the wages of salt workers were high, while those of day laborers were low. Second, the income of outcast groups is not included in Table 2. There were 2,209 households of such persons in Chōshū (see Table 3), with a total population of 10,300, but regarding their income there are almost no data in the BFC. Only in the Mitajiri BFC are there such estimates. In this saiban there were 1,081 members of outcast groups in 209 households; a total income of 53 kan is recorded for 914 of them (in 171 households). Income from the weaving of salt mats is also included in this figure, so that one cannot exclude the possibility of double counting again, but the total figure of 53 kan is more or less equivalent to wages of day laborers in the salt industry. Thus in the case of Mitajiri the exclusion of outcasts' income offsets the double accounting. In other saiban, where salt was of little importance, we may dismiss the effects of double counting.

---

14) Brokers were classified as "steady" day laborers. Because of this consolidation, it is not possible to calculate their numbers separately.

There are several reasons for the low figure for total income in the service sector. The 347 households shown in Table 3 as being in the service industries—most of them in the towns—were concentrated in "entertainment" such as inns, restaurants, teahouses, bathhouses, brothels, streetwalking, hair-dressing, massage, and so forth.[15] Forty-nine doctors are included here also, although there were an additional 99 doctors and veterinarians that are recorded in addition to the household statistics. Nevertheless, their incomes are not recorded, even in the Mitajiri BFC.

Finally, as shown in the bottom row of Table 3, there was a sizable population of monks, nuns, and priests. There were unquestionably some shrine and temple lands in Chōshū, but their kokudaka is not known. It is very likely that they were relatively small. These clerics and their families (and their servants, numbering 1,429) probably subsisted on the donations of the faithful. In the estimation of per capita income and consumption expenditures the outcasts, doctors, clerics and their families, and samurai are included in the total population. To make the argument consistent, one should add up all of their service income.[16] If one does so, the output of the non-agricultural sector of the economy becomes much larger.

Rows 3 through 8 of column 3 of Table 4 present data on per household income for non-agricultural occupations, excluding manufacturing, forestry, and quarrying. The first noteworthy aspect of the data is the higher average income in the service sector. One reason for this is that, as noted above, doctors and entertainers—many of whom were outcasts—and some other occupations were omitted from the household figures. The second is that although there were among the day laborers some who worked also in trades and services, their wages were included in the "Other" category in Table 2. If, for convenience sake, we combine services and "other occupations" and re-calculate the per household income, we get a figure of 1.66 kan, which is much closer to the income of artisans.

The next item of interest is fishermen's household income, which is roughly 1 kan. As noted above, the average household consumption is 563 momme, leaving a surplus of over 400 momme in the case of fishermen. However, the fishing population includes net- and boat-owners, and it is into their purses that most of this surplus went. The income of workers on whaling boats and single-line fishermen was probably on a par with that of day laborers and farmers. The "high" level of income in transportation and commerce also reflects the high level of income of ship-owners and guild members. The wage income of ordinary seamen and petty traders was probably also under 1 kan.

Farm households were forced by the Tokugawa revenue system which was heavily skewed toward the land tax into by-employments to augment their income. Nevertheless, it is likely that they were on an income position much inferior to that of non-farm families. If the level of non-farm household income was roughly 1 kan, and that of farm households merely some .6–.7 kan, one wonders whether one should not expect an even greater movement away from agriculture.

---

15) The Mitajiri BFC records 23 streetwalkers, with per capita incomes ranging from 230 to 460 momme. The former is probably an underestimate, while the latter an overestimate. In Kaminoseki, 54 prostitutes and 5 male shop-clerks are added into the number of outcasts.

16) It is probable that there were a large number of servants in the homes of samurai and townsmen, but there are almost no data on their number and their income. This may be because such services were done for either paying debts or getting only a nominal wage.

To this inquiry the following reply is possible: first, roughly 20% of the total population were landless "peasants" who had in fact stopped farming and were engaged almost exclusively in non-agricultural occupations. Second, where by-employment opportunities existed, farm families—both landed and landless—were able to earn income which was essentially untaxed. Third, restrictive guild organizations and the small scale of markets prevented the emergence of larger number of specialized merchants, and the technology and organization of protoindustry too prevented the exploitation of economies of scale. Household enterprises and the labor force in by-employments were sufficient to meet the needs of the economy. The elimination of these restrictive conditions awaited the introduction of modern technology, which came after the opening of Japan to foreign trade in 1859, and the institutional reforms which followed the Meiji Restoration, which allowed free choice of crops and occupation.

5. Conclusion: Chōshū and Yamaguchi Prefecture in the Late Nineteenth Century

The economy of Chōshū in the early 1840s was clearly preindustrial. Fully 80% of the commoner households were agricultural, but this does not mean that Chōshū's was a "backward" agrarian economy. Both the producers and workers in the protoindustries which developed during the 18th century—especially in its latter half—were from the farming class. Half of the landless peasants were already engaged in commerce, transportation, and other non-agricultural occupations. And even those who were occupied in agriculture turned, due to the land-tax-based revenue system, to non-agricultural by-employments to supplement their farming income.

Because of this, it is a mistake to conclude that the majority of commoners lived in extreme poverty. As calculated from Table 1, the Engel coefficient for Chōshū was high—almost .70 (= 42/60). On the other hand, per capita food consumption from grain was almost 1,700 calories per day, and if one adds other foodstuffs such as fish, meat, and fruits and vegetables, it was nearly 2,000 per day. This figure is only 20% lower than the food intake in 1960 (Nishikawa, 1986). Because the commoner population increases only at an annual rate of .3% from the mid-18th to mid-19th century, it is obvious that Chōshū did not fall into a Malthusian trap.

The savings rate in commoner households was 6.25% (= 100 · (4/64)) in Table 1. It reflects, however, the rate of "net" savings, exclusive of the depreciation of tools and draft animals (see note 9). If we add a depreciation allowance (approximately 2,600 kan) to both the numerator and denominator of the above calculation the "gross" savings rate becomes 6.8% (= 100 · (6.6/97.6)). Most savings were probably concentrated in the hands of high-income merchants, landlords, sake brewers, shipowners, and amimoto. They had to have money sufficient to replace their capital assets of ships, nets and warehouses, and moreover to have some money available for new capital formation.

How such new capital was used is unclear, but there are at least three possibilities. First, since we may have "underestimated" consumption, perhaps such money was either non-existent or very scarce. Second, it was used to buy cropland and salt fields. These two alternatives hardly contributed to economic growth, either. According to Umemura (1981), there is evidence to suggest that local entrepreneurs elsewhere, stimulated by the gradual inflation and profits expectation which occurred from the 1830s on, began to invest their savings in irrigation facilities and ships, which contributed to some increase in productive capacity.

If this third possibility did take place in Chōshū, and if we assume net capital formation of 3,000 kan, then the domestic product would have increased by 600 kan (= 3,000/5), which means an aggregate growth rate of .6% and a per capita rate of .3%. This is roughly equivalent to the growth rate during the mid-18th and early 19th centuries. In the 1850s and 1860s did the growth rate become higher? During the 1860s, Chōshū got herself involved in the war against the European fleet and in the civil war, which probably deterred economic growth in the domain. Moreover, Chōshū was far from the major ports opened for foreign trade (especially Yokohama), and did not produce any major export goods such as silk or tea. Rather, it "exported" political talent in the persons of Kido Takayoshi, Ito Hirobumi, Inoue Kaoru, and Yamagata Aritomo to the Meiji government. The talents which remained in Chōshū (then Yamaguchi Prefecture) such as those of Kasai Junpachi (the founder of Onoda Cement) and Watanabe Yūsaku (the president of Ube Mining) did not bear fruit until after 1890. During the 1870s and 1880s Yamaguchi seems to have experienced a "de-industrialization" (see Nishikawa, 1979).

(Keio University)

REFERENCES

Akimoto, H. (1977) "Hagi Han Zaisei Shūshi to Keizai Seisaku [Fiscal Balance and Economic Policy in Hagi Han]," *Shakai Keizai Shigaku*, Vol. 42, February, No. 4, pp. 341–363.
_____ (1981) "Capital Formation and Economic Growth in Mid-19th Century," *Exploration in Economic History*, Vol. 18, January, No. 1, pp. 40–59.
Barna, T. (1975) "Quesnay's Tableau in Modern Guise," *Economic Journal*, Vol. 85, September, No. 3, pp. 485–496.
Craig, A. M. (1961) *Chōshū in Meiji Restoration*, Cambridge, Mass.: Harvard University Press.
Ishii, K. (1968) "Sengoku Bune" [Merchant Ship], in Sudō, R., ed., *Fune*, Tokyo: Hōsei University Press, pp. 150–182.
Ishikawa, T., ed. (1968) *Yamaguchi-ken Kinsei-shi Yōran* [Manual of Early Modern History of Yamaguchi Prefecture], Tokuyama: Matsuno Shoten.
Nishikawa, S. (1976) "1840-nendai Bōchō Ryōgoku ni okeru Hi-nōsanbutsu 3-pin no Sanshutsu-daka to Tō'nyū-keisū" [Output and Input Coefficients of the Three Major Manufactured Commodities in 1840s Chōshū] *Mita Shōgaku Kenkyū*, Vol. 19, April, No. 1, pp. 1–31.
_____ (1979) "Chōshū-Yamaguchi-ken no Sangyō Hatten" [Industrial Development of Chōshū-Yamaguchi Prefecture], in Shimbo, H., and Y. Yasuba, eds., *Kindai Ikōki no Nihon Keizai*, Tokyo: Nihon Keizai Shimbunsha, pp. 29–48.
_____ (1981) "18-19 seiki ni okeru Chōshū Han no Saiban-betsu Jinkō Zōka" [Population Growth by Saiban in Chōshū during 18–19th Centuries], *Mita Shōgaku Kenkyū*, Vol. 24, April, No. 1, pp. 1–16.
_____ (1985) *Nihon Keizai no Seichō-shi* [Japanese Economic Growth in Historical Persepective], Tokyo: Toyo Keizai Shinposha.
_____ (1986) "Grain Consumption: the Case of Chōshū," in Jansen, M. B. and G. Rozman. eds., *Japan in Transition, from Tokugawa to Meiji*, Princeton, N.J.: Princeton University Press, pp. 421–446.
_____ and Akimoto, H. (1977) "Bōchō-ichien Keizai-hyō: Josetsu" [A Tableau Economique in 1840s Chōshū: A Preliminary Version], in Shakai Keizaishi Gakkai, ed., *Atarashii Edojidaishizō o motomete*, Tokyo: Toyo Keizai Shinposha, pp. 101–125.
_____ and Tanimura, K. (1980) "Hansatsu-ron Saikō [Domainial Note Revisited]," *Mita Gakkai Zasshi*, Vol. 73, June, No. 3, pp. 91–114.
Shimomura, F. (1934) "Kinsei Nōson no Kaikyū Kōsei" [Class Structure in the Early Modern Chōshū Villages], *Rekishigaku Kenkyū*, Vol. 3, December, No. 2, pp. 114–138.
Smith, T. C. (1969) "Farm Family By-employment in Preindustrial Japan," *Journal of Economic History*, Vol. 29, December, No. 4, pp. 687–715.

Suematsu, K. (1921) *Bōchō Kaiten-shi* [Revolution by Chōshū], rev. ed., reprinted (1980), Tokyo: Kashiwa Shobō.

Umemura, M. (1981) "Bakumatsu no Keizai Hatten" [Economic Upsurge in the Bakumatsu Period], in *Bakumatsu-Ishin no Nihon: Nempō Kindai Nihon Kenkyū*, Vol. 3, Tokyo: Yamakawa Shoten, pp. 1–30.

EXPLORATIONS IN ECONOMIC HISTORY 15, 69–83 (1978)

Productivity, Subsistence, and By-Employment in the Mid-Nineteenth Century Chōshū*

SHUNSAKU NISHIKAWA

Keio University

Thanks to the ample information contained in the *Bōchō Fūdo Chūshin-an* (census-like survey of the Chōshū, now called Yamaguchi Prefecture, at about 1840s), marginal productivity in agriculture can be successfully estimated. (1) It is higher than or at the very least equal to the subsistence level at the time, and (2) it is almost identical with the wages of employment in salt manufacturing and of other by-employment in the area. These findings, though limited with respect to the period and region under consideration, cast some doubts about the plausibility of the Lewis' model and similar theories of dualistic development, as applied to the modern development of Japanese economy. A useful step, suggested by this study, for finding a more reasonable explanation, would be to incorporate an appropriate analysis of by-employment into the model.

1. INTRODUCTION

Arthur W. Lewis' (1954) theory of dualistic development has, on occasion, been applied to the Japanese economy. One such attempt, by Fei and Ranis (1964) identifies the 1910s as the watershed marking the transition from a classical stage of labor surplus to the neoclassical stage of the economy which was characterized by no labor surplus. An alternative attempt by Minami (1970) claims that the switch from the first of these stages to the second occurred later and not before the 1960s. Apart from these wide differences in dating, both investigations are limited to observations made of the first half of the twentieth century and to nation-wide data. In this paper we explore the validity of these theories as applied to mid-nineteenth century Chōshū data as contained in the *Bōchō Fudo Chūshin-an* (hereafter abbreviated *BFC* for convenience).[1] Although the use of the *BFC* data restricts our exploration to the region

---

* The author wishes to acknowledge contributions made by Mr. Hiroya Akimoto and Mrs. Shōko Ishibe as part of their collaboration on portions of this study. Professor Thomas C. Smith also spent many hours supervising the original draft and made many valuable suggestions. None of these people are, of course, responsible for the views presented by the author, or any errors which may appear in this paper.

[1] A part of it was once utilized by Smith (1969).

0014-4983/78/0151-0069$02.00/0

consisting only of the two provinces of Suwō and Nagato (now the Yamaguchi Prefecture), an additional advantage accrues from viewing the question in a longer historical perspective. Indeed, many economists and economic historians who have investigated the Japanese economy before and after the Meiji Restoration and throughout the nineteenth century have developed theories similar to Lewis'.[2]

Chōshū *han* (domain), well-known for the leading role it played in the Meiji Restoration of 1868,[3] is well represented by the data contained in the *BFC*, a census-like survey of more than 300 villages which in addition describes the geography, land and forest, sea resources, weather and soil conditions, rivers, and irrigation facilities. More specifically, it also lists such information as average-yield-basis outputs in agriculture, other nonagricultural outputs or incomes, costs of production, taxes, food and nonfood consumption requirements as computed by village officials, and the stocks of existing factors such as population, animals, ships, and boats in the villages.[4]

In section 2 we have estimated the marginal productivity of labor in agriculture and compared it with the subsistence level of people estimated from the *BFC* data (in section 3). If the economy actually is in a state of labor surplus, the marginal productivity of labor must be, to some extent, below the subsistence level, or in extreme cases where the marginal productivity of labor is not more than zero, a substantial fraction of the labor force may be regarded as being in a state of disguised unemployment. We shall show, however, that estimates of the marginal productivity of labor either exceed or at the very least coincide with subsistence levels. Moreover, in section 4 it is shown that the marginal productivity of labor per day was approximately equal to the daily money wage for nonagricultural work, at least in salt-making at Mitajiri *saiban* (county).[5] This suggests that a competitive wage or income prevailed among forms of agricultural self-employment and nonagricultural by-employment in this region. Lewis' and similar theories are therefore inapplicable toward a true understanding of the structure of the Chōshū economy. Thus, the dating given by Fei and Ranis and Minami should be reconsidered in light of our new findings.

[2] For instance, the *Kōzaha* economist developed a similar model, though the similarity was to some extent skin-deep, as noted by Yasuba (1975); in addition, Ohkawa (1967, 1975) presented a variant yielding "excessive (self-) employment" in the indigenous sector, i.e., mainly agriculture.

[3] About the political role as well as the contemporary economy of Chōshū, see Craig (1961).

[4] The *BFC* is published in 21 volumes by the Prefectural Archive of Yamaguchi.

[5] A *saiban* (county) was a local administrative unit in the Chōshū *han*. There were some seventeen *saiban* in Chōshū around the 1840s. The magistrate and his officials in every *saiban* were appointed by the *han* government from the *samurai* class (warriors). The location and demarcation of *saiban*, and of the fief as well, are shown on the Map.

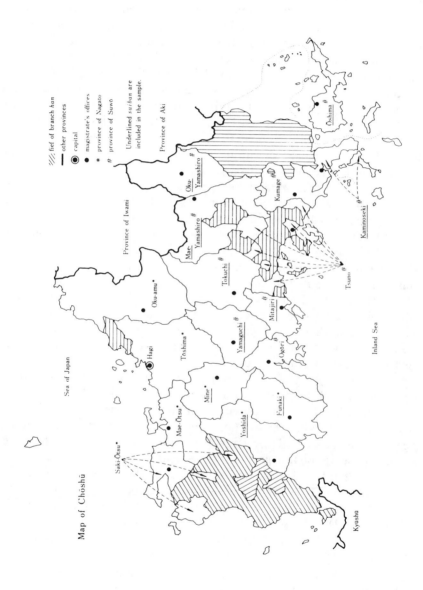

Map of Chōshū

//// fief of branch *han*
—— other provinces
◉ capital
● magistrate's offices
* province of Nagato
# province of Suwō

Underlined *suihan* are
included in the sample.

Province of Aki

Province of Iwami

Sea of Japan

Inland Sea

Kyushū

Oshima

Kumage #

Kaminoseki #

Oku-Yamashiro #

Mae-Yamashiro #

Tokuchi #

Tsuno #

Mitajiri #

Yamaguchi #

Ōgōri #

Oku-amu *

Toshima *

Hagi

Mine *

Funaki *

Yoshida *

Mae-Ōtsu *

Saki-Ōtsu *

227

2. AVERAGE AND MARGINAL LABOR PRODUCTIVITY[6]

The sample used for estimating the average and marginal productivity of labor consists of selected villages in the 10 underlined counties on the Map. The six nonunderlined counties were excluded for one or another of the following reasons. First, Mae- and Saki-Ōtsu and Oku-amu in the northern coastal area along the Sea of Japan represent essentially different climatic and soil conditions and therefore a different type of farming. Also, the compilation of their *BFC* was delayed until about 1845–46, while the others' had been completed a few years earlier. Second, three counties in the southern coastal area along the Inland Sea were excluded because of deficiencies in their accounts. The six excluded counties contained some 115 villages; in addition, some 40 villages in the included counties had to be deleted because of various data limitations. In all, our sample then consists of about 160 villages.

It is a natural presumption that geographic conditions determine the type and mode of farming in a given village. Table 1 shows the relevant input–output variables, and on lines 1 and 2 the figures are given for coastal lowland villages and inner upland villages. The most conspicuous differences may be observed in the first and last columns, where the average yield per *tan* (cf. the note to Table 1) of land is larger in the lowland villages and the input of purchased fertilizer is larger than in upland villages. The figures in lines 3 and 4 were obtained by subdividing the sample into villages with and without purchased fertilizer input. Obviously the villages with such inputs achieved higher yields than those without. Thus the two breakdowns show that purchased fertilizers were more widely used in lowland than in upland villages.

It is interesting to note that labor input per *tan* of land was substantially higher in the villages without purchased fertilizer and that these same villages also had lower oxen per *tan* of land than the villages with purchased fertilizer. While the ox–horse ratio was nearly equal to 1 in the villages with purchased fertilizer, it reached 6.3 in the other villages. These preliminary observations suggest that some consideration should be given to factor inputs other than labor in estimating labor elasticity of output, $\alpha_L = (\Delta Y/\Delta L)(L/Y)$, where Y stands for the value of agricultural output, L for farm population, and Δ for change in the value of the variables.[7]

The Cobb–Douglas production function is generally accepted as a good approximation of input–output relationships, especially in agriculture. In this context the production formula may be written as

[6] To a degree this section is based upon the results in Akimoto and Nishikawa (1975).

[7] For readers who may want to skip econometric details, we may note that we estimate α_L as 0.5 (see footnote 9), and thus marginal productivity $(\Delta Y/\Delta L)$ in farming is estimated as the product of α_L and average productivity Y/L, which can be calculated from the figures given in Table 1; e.g., $0.5 \times 298.4 = 149.2$ (*momme*) for lowland villages, and $0.5 \times 162.4 = 81.2$ (*momme*) for upland villages.

TABLE 1

Output–Input per *Tan* of Land[a]

Sample	Y/A (momme)[b]	L/A (person)	S₁/A (head)	S₂/A (head)	F/A (momme)
Lowland villages	151.0	0.506	0.030	0.052	12.27
Upland villages	95.8	0.590	0.090	0.025	1.31
With commercial fertilizer	136.1	0.493	0.048	0.047	9.04
Without commercial fertilizer	85.2	0.714	0.101	0.016	—

Note: Figures are not $\Sigma(X_i/A)$, but $\Sigma X_i/\Sigma A$, where X_is stand for Y, L, S_1, S_2, and F. Σ denotes summation over villages in the samples.

[a] *Tan* = unit of square measure, about 0.25 acre.

[b] *Momme* = unit of local currency. Silver was used as money by weight, and *momme*, originally a unit of weight, was still used for the unit of paper money issued by the *han* government. The Chōshū currency is known to be exchanged for silver coin, exclusively issued by *Bakufu* (Shogunate), at a rate of nearly 80%. One thousand *momme* is called *kwan* and is equal to 3.75 kg.

$$Y/A = e^{\alpha_0}(L/A)^{\alpha_L}(S_1/A)^{\alpha_{S_1}}(S_2/A)^{\alpha_{S_2}}(F/A)^{\alpha_F}, \qquad (1)$$

where A = land, i.e., paddy and field, Y = agricultural output in terms of local currency, L = farm population, S_1 = oxen (and cows), S_2 = horses, $S = S_1 + S_2$, F = purchased fertilizer in terms of local currency, and e is the basis of the natural logarithm. The αs are the respective factor elasticities estimated by the conventional least squares regression technique. (The sum of αs, except α_0, is assumed to be 1.)

A technical difficulty appears, however, in applying the above equation to the sample in cases where an input is zero, since this renders the logarithmic transformation impossible. This case occurs in a few villages without either oxen or horses, and in such cases we have deleted the village from the sample. The hazard in doing so is greatest for villages without purchased fertilizer, since their omission would substantially reduce the size of the sample and thus apparently bias it in favor of commercial lowland farming.

To cope with this difficulty we applied the following two abridged functions,

$$(Y/A) = e^{\alpha_0}(L/A)^{\alpha_L}(F/A)^{\alpha_F} \qquad (2)$$

and

$$(Y/A) = e^{\alpha_0}(L/A)^{\alpha_L}(S_i/A)^{\alpha_{S_i}}, \quad (i = 1, 2), \qquad (3)$$

to the reduced sample of the villages without purchased fertilizer and to the whole sample, respectively. Table 2 gives the results of Eq. (2), in which regressions were run for subsamples of lowland, peninsular and

TABLE 2

Regression Results of Eq. (2)

Sample	α_A	α_L	α_F	$\bar{R}^2$
Lowland villages	0.361	0.462 [4.21]	0.177 [3.76]	0.355
Peninsular and island villages	0.565	0.400 [4.05]	0.035 [0.90]	0.569
Upland villages	0.291	0.548 [3.89]	0.161 [4.00]	0.701
All villages (with commercial fertilizer)	0.407	0.473 [10.20]	0.120 [5.95]	0.516

Note: $\alpha_A = 1 - (\alpha_L + \alpha_F)$. Figures in brackets are t-statistics.

island, and upland villages with purchased fertilizer. Peninsular and island villages, 24 in all, were identified by reason of their different ecological conditions. Our result, specifically the insignificant fertilizer elasticity in peninsular and island villages, apparently reflects the peculiar geographic conditions which enabled them to get dried fish as fertilizer more cheaply and readily than other villages.

Labor elasticity α_Ls were estimated to be similar in considering the associated sampling errors, and hence α_As, computed as $1 - (\alpha_L + \alpha_F)$, were also similar among the samples. By contrast, when taking animal inputs into account, the estimated α_Ls in Table 3 seem significantly smaller

TABLE 3

Regression Results of Eq. (3)

Sample	α_A	α_L	α_{S_1}	$\bar{R}^2$
Lowland villages	0.496	0.604 [4.55]	−0.100 [2.64]	0.265
Upland villages	0.726	0.202 [1.39]	0.072 [0.56]	0.040
	α_A	α_L	α_{S_2}	$\bar{R}^2$
Lowland villages	0.413	0.322 [2.40]	0.264 [2.63]	0.268
Upland villages	0.484	0.293 [3.19]	0.223 [6.48]	0.395

Note: See the note to Table 2.

TABLE 4

Regression Results of Eq. (4)

i	α_L	α_{S_i}	γ_i	$\bar{R}^2$
1, Ox	0.544 [3.93]	−0.107 [0.94]	0.173 [5.43]	0.315
2, Horse	0.494 [5.21]	0.083 [1.85]	0.085 [4.28]	0.514

Note: See the note to Table 2.

than the α_As in Table 2. But the results obtained from regressions on ox input and labor input are poor (in coefficient of determination) and provide unrealistic and insignificant coefficients of animal input. The results of regressions on horse input yield better results, though the coefficients of determination still remain insignificant.

The results may reflect the different roles of oxen and horses in relation to purchased fertilizer and geographic conditions. First, oxen may have been more important in manure production and a better mode of transportation in upland villages, whereas the horses would have been more useful than oxen for transportation as well as for farming in lowland villages. In the *BFC* there is a record for several counties of the amount and kinds of feed used throughout the year. According to these records horses consumed twice as much crop fodder as did oxen during the peak season. In the slack season the amount of crop fodder given horses was halved, while oxen were fed upland grass. Horses were, therefore, much more expensive to feed than oxen. We also note from scattered references[8] in the *BFC* that the sale price of horses was about twice that of oxen. Thus oxen, which were cheaper to buy and feed but were also less productive, were used in upland farming, and horses, which though more productive and also more expensive, were used in lowland farming. The contribution of animals to cultivation and manure production should be given more careful consideration in the model, as restated by the formula

$$(Y/A) = e^{\alpha_0}(L/A)^{\alpha_L}(S/A)\alpha_{S_i} + \gamma_i E, \quad (i = 1, 2), \qquad (4)$$

where E is a dummy variable that takes the value of zero if any purchased fertilizer was used and of unity if none was used (i.e., reversely valued). The coefficient γ_i measures the interaction between inputs of animal manuring and purchased fertilizer. If it is positive, animals contribute

---

[8] A few records of transactions tell the relative prices, which are confirmed by referring to the allowance for animal depreciation in the village. The annual rate of depreciation was equal for both animals, i.e., 7%, and the sum of the values of both animals, which were obtained, respectively, as the product of the number and of the price, are nearly identical with the amount of depreciation given in the *BFC*.

not only to ploughing and transportation but also to manuring. Table 4 gives the regressions which were run for the entire sample. As expected, γ_1 in the ox regression is significantly larger than γ_2 in the horse regression. The elasticities α_{S_i}s were insignificant in the ox regression and less so in the horse regression, thus emphasizing the importance of both animals in manure production.

Estimated labor elasticities range from 0.4 to 0.55 in Tables 2 and 4. These figures were calculated separately according to different formulations, and no combined formula was applied because of the technical difficulty mentioned above. We may, however, choose 0.5 as an approximate (and convenient) value of labor elasticity,[9] and as already described in footnote 7, the marginal productivity of labor is estimated straightforwardly as the elasticity times the average productivity of labor.

3. SUBSISTENCE AND CONSUMPTION

The food requirement per man-day in cereal equivalents[10] of every village was calculated by village officials. On the average, annual per capita food requirements for all *saiban* ranged from 1 to 1.5 *koku* (nearly 0.25 cubic yard), the monetary value of which was about 70 to 80 *momme*. The unit price of food, therefore, was about 60 *momme* per *koku*.[11]

We observe here that the above estimate of the subsistence level, 80 *momme*, is almost identical with the marginal labor productivity of upland villages. But this estimate includes food only, and some allowance should be made for nonfood necessities. The Engel coefficients among the several *saiban* studied[12] ranged from 0.6 to 0.8. Adjusting the food requirement by the median figure of the coefficients, we have another estimate for subsistence income including nonfood items of 100 to 114

---

[9] We assumed the value of 0.55 instead of 0.5 assumed in Akimoto and Nishikawa (1975). In addition, another amendment is made in this paper regarding the value of the average productivity of the upland village. This value which was specified as 205.4 *momme* in the 1975 paper, is now shown as 162.4 *momme*. The latter value is the one obtained by deflating the former by the participation ratio of 0.79.

[10] Wheat and other cereals were the basic food stuffs of the villagers, but rice after taxes was also eaten. The mixture of cereals differed from place to place, and different formulas were used in different *saiban* to calculate the food requirement. For example, some village officials, in figuring the food requirements per capita took into account the age and sex structure of the population as well as migratory movements, while others counted several noncereal items such as *daikon* (long radish) after converting the amounts into their cereal equivalents.

[11] The price of rice, 75 *momme* per *koku*, dominated the estimated value of food. After examining several typical cereal mixes, we chose the value of 60 *momme* per *koku* of food stuffs. This means that the villager ate 0.5 *koku* of rice and 0.75 *koku* of other cereals, the price of which was assumed to be roughly 50 *momme* per *koku*. However, it is not inconceivable that all 1.25 *koku* was made up of nonrice cereals.

[12] Except in the two *saiban* cited in the text and a few not mentioned here, most *saiban* neglected to record either the estimated village requirement or the actual consumption of nonagricultural products.

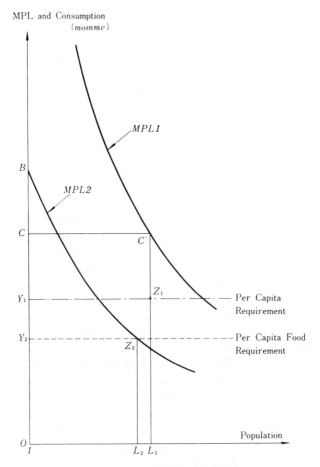

FIG. 1. Comparison of MPL with Subsistence.

momme. These figures exceed by 20 to 30 the marginal labor productivity estimate for the poorer counties, but the higher figure is still identical to the average of marginal labor productivity estimates for upland and lowland villages, i.e., 115.6 *momme*.

Both of the subsistence estimates are relevant for the whole region. But if we look for minimum subsistence, we obtain a third estimate. Mae-Yamashiro *saiban*, possibly one of the poorest counties in the inner hilly district, had food requirements per capita estimated at barely 59 *momme* (by village officials) and per capita consumption was enumerated at merely 78 *momme* (from the *BFC* data).[13] These two figures, especially

[13] Consumption of some home-made items such as soy paste and sauce, cotton cloth, and so forth, was imputed in making our estimates that included nonfood expenditures in both Mae-Yamashiro and Mitajiri.

233

the latter which includes nonfood items, when taken as the minimum level of subsistence, suggest that they are almost identical with the marginal productivity or labor in the upland villages. On the other hand, the marginal productivity of labor in the relatively wealthy counties obviously far exceeds our third estimate of subsistence.

It is interesting to note that the per capita food requirements computed in the *BFC* seemed to be positively associated with the corresponding levels of marginal productivity of labor in agriculture. For example, the food requirement for Mitajiri *saiban* was set by the village officials at one hundred *momme*. The county, situated on the coast of Inland Sea, flourished not only in agricultural activities, but also in salt-making and other activities such as trade, transportation, and various services. We found the average per capita consumption to be 156 *momme* for the entire county.[14] This is slightly above the higher marginal productivity estimate for lowland villages. Since the village officials responsible for the compilation of the report were very well acquainted with the level and structure of agricultural and nonagricultural production, they may have adjusted the (standard) estimate of the cost of living to the level of total output (or income). Presumably this is the reason why per capita consumption in Mitajiri was set so much higher than it was in Mae-Yamashiro. Still, it is conceivable that the people in Mae-Yamashiro could live on 80 *momme* or less.

The foregoing discussion can be summarized by Fig. 1, in which the curves labeled MPL1 and MPL2 stand for the marginal productivity of labor curves in lowland and upland villages, respectively. The dotted line Y_2Z_2 shows the per capita food requirement and the broken line Y_1Z_1 the per capita consumption requirement. The former is almost equal to the upland marginal productivity L_2Z_2, while the latter is also equal to the averaged marginal productivities of labor. However, that curve is not shown explicitly in Fig. 1. The third estimate of minimum subsistence, derived from the *BFC* of Mae-Yamashiro, is slightly below the line Y_2Z_2, whereas the per capita consumption at Mitajiri is somewhat above the line Y_1Z_1.

Consequently, the three estimates of subsistence income are likely to be smaller than, or at least equal to, the corresponding estimates of marginal productivity in Chōshū of the 1840s. Obviously this result is not expected in the model of a labor surplus economy. Disguised unemployment and surplus of labor were hardly discernible in those times. Unless taxes were extremely heavy, the ratio was approximately 40% of agricultural outputs, the peasants could enjoy some residuals even after paying the costs of production. This was not, however, the rule. Often-

---

[14] Interestingly enough, upon averaging the per capita consumption in both Mae-Yamashiro and Mitajiri, we come up with an average of 117 *momme*, which is again nearly identical with the *averaged* marginal productivity.

times income available after taxes scarcely covered the villages' food requirement even in wealthy Mitajiri. The peasants and their families were obliged to engage in supplementary employment at night and/or during slack seasons to earn extra income. Furthermore, the *BFC* tells us that nonagricultural by-employment was also prevalent during cultivating seasons and that this income was an essential supplement for covering the deficit in the family budget. The importance of this source of income was enhanced by the fact that it was usually either tax-free or taxed quite moderately.

4. EMPLOYMENT AND THE WAGE IN SALT MANUFACTURING

The significance of nonagricultural by-employment in preindustrial Japan has been attested to by Smith (1969), using the *BFC* of Kaminoseki *saiban*. He estimated the ratio of nonagricultural earnings to agricultural (after-tax) income to be 55:45[15] and argued that the farm family by-employment in nonagricultural activities tended to detach labor from agriculture and village life and to encourage the spread of new disciplines and attitudes favorable to emerging factory employment, not only in Japan but also in Western countries during the early stages of their industrial development. Yasuba (1975) has also emphasized the significance of nonagricultural by-employment and incorporated it explicitly into a modern theory of dualistic development. Here, the wage rate in the nonagricultural sector will equal the marginal productivity of labor in agriculture.[16] Support for this theory by this new data is discussed below.[17]

Thanks to the *BFC* of the Mitajiri *saiban*, particularly those from four salt-making villages, we have a wealth of data on wages and working days. Such data is seldom found in the *BFC* of other *saiban*, where only the amounts of wage earnings are given, with no indication of the man-days worked. Salt paddies in this county had been developed by the *han* government since the middle of the preceding century. There were two hundred paddies, most of which were 1.5 *cho* (10 *tan*) in size, each theo-

[15] A similar ratio in Mitajiri is 47:53. Imputing the service income of priests, *samurai*, and entertainers as Smith did, the ratio would approach 50:50. Nevertheless we have the impression that the ratios, to an unknown extent, exaggerate the proportion of by-employment earning, since the ratio is 28:72 for the 24 agricultural villages in Mitajiri, while it is 89:11 for the other, which is combined with two towns, four salt-making villages, and one adjacent village. Thus the relative proportion of by-employment earning in the farm family budget seems to be roughly 30%, or less than that of the Chōshū as a whole.

[16] According to Yasuba (1975), if the family heads of farm households consciously or coercively behaved so as to exploit the possibility of increasing family income through by-employment, the dualistic development model would apparently be reduced to the neoclassical one, even though the heads persuaded their families to work in *dekasegi* in a paternalistic manner.

[17] The discussion below is the revised version of my contribution, "Seisansei, Seizon Suijun, Hi-nō Chingin [Productivity, Subsistence, and Non-Agricultural Wage]" in H. Simbo, A. Hayami, and S. Nishikawa (1975). See also Nishikawa and Ishibe [1975].

retically being owned by a producer, but at the time of our study, some actually being owned by salt merchants with some producers having become merely tenants or hired managers.

Whatever his status, owner or tenant, the producer would hire six skilled craftsmen and five daily laborers to help with production. The skilled craftsmen consisted of four *hamako* (salt-making craftsmen) of different grades and two *kamataki* (boiler-men). Usually the first four constituted a team and were employed from villages with poor land resources in Kaminoseki, Oshima, and elsewhere, while the boiler-men seem to have been recruited from the salt-making and surrounding villages within the county. Both groups were engaged in salt production throughout the season, from the third to the eighth month of every year.[18] One should note that the season for salt production overlapped the cultivating season, and thus craftsmen and boiler-men could be identified as specialized workers engaged exclusively in this work. (Of course, this included their engagement in alternative employment during the slack season.) In fact, they earned from 450 to 800 *momme* per 6-month period, as well as some payment in kind, customarily a daily ration of food. The level of money wages among these craftsmen presumably was dependent on their respective differences in skills and the jobs for which they were employed. However, on the average it was equal to the annual income of other skilled craftsmen like carpenters, blacksmiths, thatchers, stone cutters, and so forth. Assuming three or four dependents in a family, our estimate of consumption per household is from 440–550 to 624–780 *momme*.[19] Thus, these skilled salt workers were able to support their families from work in the salt paddies alone.

The five daily laborers consisted of two males and three females, all of whom were recruited from nearby villages. According to the record, one of the male workers was paid 4.6 *momme* per day. If he was hired throughout the production season, about 150 days, he received 690 *momme*, a sum almost equal to the amount paid the skilled workers. He was in fact referred to as a *Jō-hiyō*, which meant steady employment on a daily basis. We regard him as a skilled worker like the craftsmen and boiler-men above.

One of the females, paid only 0.4 *momme* per day, was also an exceptional case. She was engaged in miscellaneous tasks in which she could be, and frequently was, replaced by a child. Deleting these two extremes, the remaining three positions for one male and two females represent the common unskilled jobs available to a laborer from a farm family. There were wage differentials between male and female: The daily wage for a male was

---

[18] Since the end of the preceding century, the producers, with the permission of the *han* government, had limited the operating period in order to avoid the decline in price.

[19] The former are derived as an overall estimate of 110 *momme* times 4 or 5, while the latter as Mitajiri estimates of 156 *momme* times 4 or 5. The average size of a household was estimated in the *BFC* to be four or five.

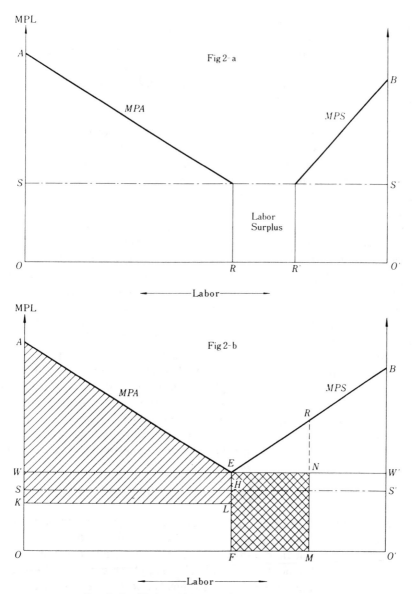

FIG. 2. Equilibrium with and without Labor Surplus.

1.6 *momme* and for a female was 0.8 *momme*, giving a weighted average of nearly 1 *momme* per day.

On the other hand, the marginal productivity of the lowland village, if divided by 200 days, was equal to the above female wage. However, as this estimate was made with respect to farm population per se, it might be considered more appropriate in such a comparison to use the estimate in terms of the actual labor force instead of population, although the ratio of labor force (aged 13 and over) to population is known for only one county, Oku-Yamashiro. If this ratio, set at 0.79, is applied to the above estimate of 0.8 *momme*, the revised estimate appears to be about 1 *momme*. Clearly, it is almost identical to the average wage of unskilled workers in salt production.

The implication of our findings may be seen clearly in Fig. 2, where *OO'* denotes available labor (or population) in appropriate efficiency units, and wages and productivities are measured on the vertical axis in terms of monetary values. The lines labeled by MPA and MPS (running from right to left) stand for the marginal productivity curves of labor in agriculture and salt production, respectively. Fig. 2-a depicts the equilibrium with labor surplus RR', in which OS represents the subsistence wage.

Nevertheless, our picture of mid-nineteenth Chōshū seems quite different: we found no labor surplus as depicted in Fig. 2-b, where the marginal productivity of labor in agriculture EF coincided with the competitive wage WO of unskilled salt workers, i.e. of farm family by-employment. Also, both EF and WO exceeded the subsistence OS. The "feudal" tax on agricultural output, the shaded area AKLE, was often so burdensome that not only the product surplus was exhausted, but some portion of subsistence stores as well. The peasant and his family therefore would migrate or engage in by-employment in salt manufacturing or domestic industries, cotton weaving for example,[20] to fill the deficit in the household's budget. Interestingly enough, the *daimyō* (lords) usually levied a nominal tax on such incomes. Therefore, the doubly shaded portion EFMN was possibly larger than the lost income WKLE in most families. Thus peasants were not severely limited to a "minimum" subsistence but adjusted their supply of labor between other opportunities according to changes in wages and other work conditions.[21]

5. CONCLUDING REMARKS

We have found little evidence indicating that the labor surplus equilibrium existed in Chōshū around the middle of the last century. Considering the limitations of time and locality, we do not claim that the theory of dualistic development is completely inapplicable to the Japanese economy as a whole, particularly in reference to this century. Still, we

---

[20] Needless to say, weaving was the work of women. It was widely prevalent in the coastal area of Suwō. In Mitajiri 10 *tan* (a module of cloth one foot wide and 10 yards long) were produced per household per year. In Kaminoseki this quantity was nearly twice that of Mitajiri, presumably making it the largest producer in the area. The average price per *tan* was ten *momme*, 30% of which was paid out as wage cost. Unfortunately no information is given in the *BFC* about man-hours required per *tan*.

[21] According to Yasuba's explanation (1975), *Kōzaha* economists have a different equilibrium, in which competitive wage coincides with subsistence, but the marginal productivity is somewhat larger. However, this possibility is not supported by our findings.

have some doubts about the plausibility of the explanations given by those proponents of the theory mentioned at the beginning of this paper.[22] On the basis of our data, we conclude that the by-employment factor, *kengyō* or *dekasegi*, which has been observed and documented throughout the country during the twentieth century, should somehow be incorporated into the theory.[23] Comparative studies of other less developed domains would be highly desirable, since Chōshū is believed to have been one of the most well-developed domains of its time, an impression which is confirmed by a general survey of *BFC* data which is beyond the scope of this paper. Also, any further exploration of the evolution of the Chōshū economy would certainly be useful in revealing the interdependence of underdeveloped and relatively well-developed domains,[24] although excellent quantitative data like that contained in the *BFC* is largely unavailable.

REFERENCES

Akimoto, H., and Nishikawa, S. (1975), "Jūkyū Seiki Chūyō Bōchō Ryokoku no Nōgyō Seisan Kansū [Agricultural Production Function in the Mid-Nineteenth Century Chōshū]." *Keizai Kenkyū* [*The Economic Review*] 26, 302–311.

Craig, A. M. (1961), *Chōshū in the Meiji Restoration*. Cambridge, Mass.: Harvard University Press.

Fei, C. H., and Ranis, G. (1964), *Development of the Labor Surplus Economy: Theory and Policy*. Homewood, Ill.: Richard D. Irwin.

Lewis, A. W. (1954), "Economic Development with Unlimited Supplies of Labour." *The Manchester School of Economics and Social Studies* 26, 1–32.

Minami, R. (1970), *Nihon Keizai no Tenkanten* [*Turning Point of Japanese Economy*]. Tokyo: Sōbunsha.

Nishikawa, S., and Ishibe, S. (1975), "1840-nen dai Mitajiri Saiban no Keizai Keisan [Regional Accounting of Mitajiri *Saiban* in the 1840s]." *Mita Gakkai Zasshi Mita Journal of Economics* 68, 663–732.

Ohkawa, K. (1967), *Nōgyō no Keizai Bunseki* [*Economic Analysis of Agriculture*]. Tokyo: Taimeido.

Ohkawa, K. (1975), *Kajō Shugyo: Sairon* [*Excessive Employment: Reconsidered*]. In Ohkawa and Minami (Eds.), *Kindai Nihon no Keizai Hatten* [*Economic Development of Modern Japan*]. Tokyo: Tōyō Keizai Shimpō-sha.

Simbo, H., Hayami, A., and Nishikawa, S. (1975), *Sūryō Keizaishi Nyūmon* [*An Introduction to Quantitative Economic History*]. Tokyo: Nihon Hyōron-Sha.

Smith, T. C. (1969), "Farm Family By-Employment in Pre-Industrial Japan." *The Journal of Economic History* XXIX, 687–715.

Yamamura, K. (1973), "Toward a Re-examination of the Economic History of Tokugawa Japan, 1600–1867." *The Journal of Economic History* XXXIII, 509–546.

Yasuba, Y. (1975), "Anatomy of the Debate on Japanese Capitalism." *The Journal of Japanese Studies* 2, 63–82.

---

[22] Including Fei and Ranis, Ohkawa and Minami, and even the representative of the Kōzaha theory.

[23] See Yasuba (1975). Though our findings do not lend support to his model which concerns *dekasegi*, it is admittedly an alternative formulation.

[24] Yamamura (1973).

EXPLORATIONS IN ECONOMIC HISTORY 15, 101–124 (1978)

The Tokugawa Monetary Policy in the Eighteenth and Nineteenth Centuries*

TAKEHIKO OHKURA AND HIROSHI SHIMBO

Fukui Prefectural College and Kobe University

1. INTRODUCTION

With the reestablishment of diplomatic and trade relations with the Western Powers in the late 1850s, which terminated more than two centuries of seclusion, the Japanese economy changed from a closed system to an open system. This entry into the world economy had varied and wide-ranging effects on the Tokugawa economy. One result of the opening of Japanese ports was a drastic reform of the Tokugawa monetary system in the recoinages of Ansei-Man'en (1859–1860). In this paper we shall attempt to examine the causes and results of the Ansei-Man'en monetary reforms and to discuss the historical significance of these reforms as an important turning point in the monetary history of Tokugawa Japan.

Before we analyze the monetary reforms of 1859 and 1860, it will be necessary to review briefly the Tokugawa monetary system. The traditional system is generally called "*sanka seido*" (three-monies system), for it consisted of three kinds of money, that is, gold coin, silver currency by weight, and copper coin. Each money circulated on the basis of its own unit and had its own sphere of circulation.[1] All three kinds of

---

* This is a revision of our paper presented in December, 1976, to Daisankai Sūryō-keizai-shi Kenkyūkaigi [The Third Conference of Quantitative Economic History].

We are grateful for the comments from Professor M. Umemura, Professor Y. Sakudō, Professor S. Nishikawa, Professor T. Takeoka, Professor T. Kamiki, Professor Y. Yamamoto, and Professor M. Iwahashi. We particularly appreciate valuable suggestions from Professor K. Yamamura and Professor E. S. Crawcour which led to revision of our earlier draft.

[1] Gold coins circulated according to *ryō, bu,* and *shu* denominational units, with one *ryō* being equivalent to 4 *bu* or 16 *shu*. Silver currency by weight was put into circulation by *kan* and *momme* units of weight. The units of copper coins were *kan* and *mon* denominational units, with one *kan* being equal to 1000 *mon*. The circulation sphere of each kind of money was as follows. First, in eastern Japan, primarily gold coin was used and the prices were expressed by the gold money unit, while in western Japan, silver currency by weight circulated and the prices were expressed by weight unit of silver. Second, gold coin was used in wholesale transactions among merchants, while copper moneys were used in small transactions. Silver currency by weight was used in both wholesale and small transactions. Third, the *daimyo,* upper class of retainers, and merchants had access to gold coins, but peasants or urban commoners had little chance to obtain gold coins.

0014-4983/78/0151-0101$02.00/0

money were all legal tenders which could circulate without restraint. Copper coin (*zeni*), being a petty coinage, was virtually subsidiary to gold and silver. The three kinds of money were exchanged at the market rate. While there was, as we will note, no free bullion market,[2] there was a limited and closely controlled market for precious metals for nonmonetary purposes in which the relative value of gold and silver approximated the international ratio. The market rate of exchange between gold and silver money, while it reflected this international ratio between the metals to some extent, usually diverged from it under the influence of other factors.

This divergence was possible because Japan was a closed economy with no free bullion market. Besides gold, silver, and copper money there were *hansatsu* (paper money issued by *han* authority) and *tegata* (private promissory notes and bills of credit), the supply of which was beyond the direct control of the Shogunate. With the transition to an open economy this divergence could have been corrected by a simple quantitative adjustment. The situation was, however, complicated by the progressive introduction of subsidiary coinage in gold unit denominations but in fact made of silver after 1772. These silver coins came to assume the character of token coinage. As token subsidiary coinage, its value was linked to the standard gold unit (*ryō*) and was independent of the intrinsic value of its silver content. By the time Japan was opened to foreign trade, this token subsidiary coinage, mainly silver one-quarter *ryō* pieces (*ichibu-gin*), made up about 40% of Japan's gold unit coinage.

In negotiating Treaties of Amity and Commerce with Japan, first the United States and then the remainder of the five Powers insisted on treating these *ichibu-gin* as though they were silver standard coinage like the silver dollar. Under the treaties, export of Japanese coins (gold and silver), circulation of foreign coins in the domestic market, and exchange of Japanese coins for foreign coins (on terms of exchanging coins of similar metal and fineness on a weight-for-weight basis) were allowed in 1858. On this basis, three pieces of Japanese *ichibu-gin* (silver coin equivalent to a quarter of one *ryō*) would be equivalent to one dollar silver coin (American or Mexican), or 100 pieces of one dollar silver coin would be exchanged for 311 pieces of Japanese *ichibu-gin*. At the same time the foreign powers insisted that within Japan the *ichibu-gin* continue to exchange for gold coin at its face value as subsidiary token coinage, that is to say, as one quarter of a *ryō*. As the Japanese coinage then stood, this represented about three and a half times the international value of its silver content.

A foreigner who obtained 311 pieces of Japanese *ichibu-gin* in exchange for 100 silver dollars could then exchange them for 77.75 *ryō* in Japanese

---

[2] The primary reason why there was no bullion market is that the Shogunate exclusively owned the gold and silver mines and the bullion produced there was sent to the mint which was completely controlled by the Shogunate. In addition, free transactions in bullion were not permitted.

gold coins. The gold/silver ratio in this transaction (1/4.5) was much higher than the international gold/silver ratio (1/15.5). This extraordinary arrangement made foreign merchants' trade very profitable in importing silver and exporting gold. The profit from exchanging silver for gold in this manner must have been more than 100%.[3] As a consequence a large quantity of silver was brought to Japan and a correspondingly large amount of gold flowed out. Despite official Japanese efforts to keep exchange of silver dollars for *ichibu-gin* to a minimum, the outflow of gold coin in the first year is estimated at 500,000 *ryō*.[4] Clearly the only way to deal with this situation brought about by the demands of the foreign powers was to bring the nominal and bullion ratios between *ichibu-gin* and gold coins into line with each other. The Shogunate was well aware of this and took steps to bring about this reconciliation by debasing the gold coinage in the Ansei-Man'en monetary reforms of 1859–1860.

These monetary reforms of 1859–1860 were quite different in kind from the recoinages of 1736 and thereafter which had resulted in the introduction of *ichibu-gin* and similar token coinage. While the latter were in response to internal economic and fiscal conditions, the reforms of 1859–1860 were carried out to cope with pressure from the foreign powers. The Ansei-Man'en reforms represent the creation of a system viable in the context of an open economy yet within the restrictions imposed by foreign demands, on one hand, and by the existing Japanese currency system, on the other.

This essay focuses on the *ichibu-gin*—the silver coin which was subjected to the anomalous demands of the foreign powers and which was the pivot of the negotiations and monetary policies of the end of the Tokugawa period. We shall examine how this coin came to occupy such an important position in the Japanese money supply as a result of a series of recoinages, especially those after 1818. We shall then see how the monetary situation created in this way was reconciled with the opening of international transactions. For these reasons it will be useful to divide our discussion into two parts: first, the monetary policy in the latter part of Tokugawa Japan and, second, the monetary policy in 1859–1860 immediately after the opening of foreign trade.

2. MONETARY POLICY IN THE LATTER HALF OF THE TOKUGAWA PERIOD

The monetary reforms of 1736 built up the fundamental framework of the monetary system which was effective in the latter half of Tokugawa Japan, and it is within this framework that the recoinages in the second half of the eighteenth century and the first half of the nineteenth century took place. In

[3] Ishii (1952), pp. 3–8; Ono (1958), pp. 1–17; Shinjo (1962), pp. 9–10.
[4] Ishii (1940), pp. 411–415.

its recoinages the Shogunate had two aims. First, the Shogunate intended the acquisition of the profit from recoinage to solve the financial problem of the government. Second, through the recoinage the Shogunate intended to influence prices by responding to the increasing demand for money that accompanied commercial development.[5]

It should be noted that these two aspects are not unrelated, since much of the Shogunate's tax revenue was in the form of rice and the price of rice was therefore an important factor in its financial situation. We should therefore examine the recoinages of Tokugawa Japan in regard to both aspects. Whether one aspect is more important than the other in any particular recoinage depends on the economic conditions under which that recoinage was carried out.

The aim of recoinage or debasement in 1736 was to raise the rice price through the extension of effective demand by means of the increase of currency in circulation. The acquisition of profit was not the direct objective of this recoinage. In the Kyōho period (1716–1735) the relative price of rice dropped remarkably.[6] The fall in the relative price of rice was, needless to say, unfavorable to the revenue of the Shogunate, whose major resource was land tax in rice. Faced with this problem the Shogunate tried to raise the rice price through a variety of means which aimed to increase the effective demand for rice.[7] But these means were not very effective. The Shogunate ultimately resorted to increasing the money supply in the recoinage of 1736. In this recoinage the Shogunate conceded that the exchange of the old money for the new should be done with a premium. Thus, most of the premium was realized by the owners of the old money, and the sum gained by the Shogunate was small. The rate of profit in the recoinage of 1736 was only 2.7%, in comparison with about 20% in the case of the debasement of the Genroku-Hōei period (1688–1710).[8]

After the recoinage of 1736 the rice price rose rapidly, as Fig. 1 shows, and the balance of the Shogunate's budget went into the black by a large margin. Although the wholesale price index at Osaka is not available before 1754, we can observe the rise in the relative price of rice if we look at the movement of the consumers' price index at Kyoto. The rise in the relative price of rice associated with an increase of land tax revenue in terms of rice contributed to a surplus in the Shogunate's budget.[9] In a debasement like the recoinage of 1736 in which the exchange of old money for new is put into

---

[5] Professor Sakudō in particular has pointed out the importance of this aspect. See Sakudō (1958), p. 59.

[6] Yamazaki (1963a), pp. 107–117.

[7] On these points, see Shimbo (1972a), pp. 17–19.

[8] The exact amount of the premium acquired by the Shogunate in this period is not available, but the profits gained through the debasement of silver currency by weight is estimated at more than 4 million ryō. Taya (1963), p. 191.

[9] On the problem of the increase in land tax revenue in the Kyōho period, see Furushima (1965), pp. 20–22.

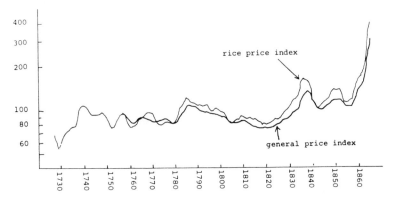

Fɪɢ. 1. Movement of general price index and rice price index (1840–1844 = 100; 5-year moving average). For source, see Table A1.

effect with a premium, the increase in the money supply is nothing but the augmentation of the assets held in money by the owners of the old money. The increment of money assets with the highest liquidity was additional income for money owners. Then, since a large part or all of it flowed into the commodity market, the effective demand expanded. In the case of the recoinage in 1736, the demand for rice was relatively great as compared with other commodities, because the income elasticity of the demand for rice was high in those days.[10] As a result, the relative price of rice began to rise. The movement in the relative price of rice was crucial to the revenue of the Shogunate in real terms as long as the Shogunate imposed the land tax in rice. The recoinage of 1736 had the positive effect of strengthening the fiscal base of the government through raising the relative price of rice.

We must note here the effect the recoinage policy adopted by the Shogunate had on its samurai retainers. The economic position of the upper class of retainers was the same as that of the Shogunate, because they received their stipends in rice. On the other hand, most of the retainers received their stipends in money at a rate of commutation set by the Shogunate.[11] This rate was intended to reduce fluctuations in their real income, but it also had some relation to the market price of rice and so these retainers benefited when the rice price went up. Therefore, the recoinage of 1736 was performed not only to solve the financial problems of the Shogunate itself, but also to protect the economic position of the retainers.

The effects of the recoinage could not, however, continue for very long. As a matter of fact, from the time of this recoinage until the 1760s, the Shogunate's budget stayed in the black by the greatest margin of the Tokugawa period and the reserves of gold and silver in its treasury reached

[10] Akimoto (1975), p. 43.
[11] Yamamura (1974), p. 36.

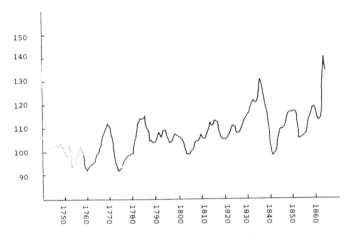

F IG. 2. Index of the relative price of rice (1840–1844 = 100; 5-year moving average). For source, see Table A1.

3 million *ryō*.[12] This implies that the Shogunate withdrew money from the market, so that money in circulation decreased. This had more or less an opposite effect from that of the increase in the money supply brought about by the recoinage. This represents the downward phase in a cyclical process. Around 1760, general prices, as well as the rice price and the relative price of rice, began to fall (see Fig. 2), the surplus of the Shogunate's budget shrank rapidly, and the balance of the budget eventually turned to a deficit.

The measures employed by the Shogunate to cope with such a situation were the *goyōkin* (forced loan from merchants) policy of 1761 and the issue of the *An'ei nishu-gin* (two-*shu* silver coin) in 1772. Leaving aside for the moment the *goyōkin* policy,[13] we shall try to explain the *nishu-gin*, the first token subsidiary coinage which would later come to have a close relationship with the reforms of the monetary institution that took place in the last decade of Tokugawa Japan, the main subject of our discussion.

Nishu-gin was a silver coin which was denominated in a gold unit, "*nishu*" (one-eighth *ryō*). Its value was determined by the fact of its being a token for one-eighth *ryō*. Thus it was quite different from silver currency by weight. Though *nishu-gin* was made of silver, it was treated entirely the same as a gold coin in circulation and came to circulate before long as normal gold-unit currency. Thereafter, such silver coins became the principal component of the monetary system in Tokugawa Japan, alongside the gold coin and silver currency by weight, both of which had been the

[12] Furushima (1965), p. 28.

[13] The loans raised by the Shogunate in 1806, 1809, and 1813 totaled about 1.4 million *ryō* which was used mostly as a fund for purchase of rice in the market to raise the price of rice: *Osaka-shi Sanjikai* (1913), pp. 240–277; Takeuchi (1965), p. 213.

standard money from the beginning of the Tokugawa monetary system. *Isshu-gin* (one-sixteenth *ryō*) and *ichibu-gin* (one-quarter *ryō*) followed *nishu-gin* successively, and their introduction increased the proportion of silver coin in the total amount of the money circulated (see Table 1).

The aims of the issue of *nishu-gin* appear to have been not only to acquire the profit of recoinage but also to increase the supply of small-denomination money. In the monetary system of 1736, the smallest unit of the gold coin was *ichibu* (a quarter of one *ryō*), equivalent to approximately

TABLE 1

Amounts and Shares of Gold and Silver Money[a]

Year	Kinds of money	Amount of money (unit: 1000 *ryō*)	Shares (%)
1695	Gold coin	10,627	76.1
	Silver currency by weight	3,333	23.9
	Total	13,960	100.0
1710	Gold coin	15,050	58.3
	Silver currency by weight	10,755	41.7
	Total	25,805	100.0
1714	Gold coin	13,570	42.8
	Silver currency by weight	18,120	57.2
	Total	31,690	100.0
1736	Gold coin	10,838	51.5
	Silver currency by weight	10,204	48.5
	Total	21,042	100.0
1818	Gold coin	19,114	65.3
	Silver currency by weight	4,208	14.4
	Silver coin	5,933	20.3
	Total	29,255	100.0
1832	Gold coin	23,699	51.7
	Silver currency by weight	5,361	11.7
	Silver coin	16,804	36.6
	Total	45,864	100.0
1858	Gold coin	28,315	53.7
	Silver currency by weight	3,902	7.4
	Silver coin	20,536	38.9
	Total	52,750	100.0
1869	Gold coin	74,321	57.1
	Silver currency by weight	3,512	2.7
	Silver coin	52,392	40.2
	Total	130,224	100.0

[a] Source: Iwahashi (1976), p. 258.

15 *momme* of silver currency by weight or 1000 pieces of *zeni* (copper coin). The currencies employed in petty transactions were the silver currency by weight and copper coin. As commercial development, in particular the commercialization of agriculture and the monetization of the rural economy, continued,[14] the shortage of small-denomination currency became serious. The rise of the exchange rate of copper coin in the 1760s had clearly indicated a shortage of a small currency.[15] It is quite clear that the issue of *nishu-gin* was a measure adopted to ease the shortage of small currency.

Let us now examine the acquisition of premium in this recoinage of 1772. While the silver content of Ganbun silver currency by weight per one *ryō* value equivalent was 27.5 *momme*, that of *nishu-gin* as token currency was naturally less. It was, in fact, 21.6 *momme*. The coinage of *nishu-gin* resulted in the acquisition of a premium of 5.9 *momme* silver bullion per *ryō*. The appearance of this silver coin, however, did not mean the abolition of silver currency by weight; the latter (*chō-gin* and *mameita-gin*) still kept the position of a basic money. It is quite clear that the silver coin was no more than token subsidiary money, playing the role of the quarters and dimes of today. This subsidiary money played a leading part in the recoinages throughout the nineteenth century and also in the outflow of gold coin immediately after the opening of Japanese ports.

Although the Shogunate earned a premium by the issue of *nishu-gin* and the balance of the budget took a temporary turn for the better, it did not last long and the Shogunate once again became involved in financial difficulties. By this time the Shogunate could no longer break the deadlock on finance by imposing an additional land tax in rice or raising the rice price, both of which were rooted in the system of payment of land tax in rice. Why did such a situation occur? We can identify two reasons.

As long as the fiscal base of the lords (the Shogunate and daimyo) under the Tokugawa regime was taxation on land in terms of rice, the lords could not fully participate in the fruits of the commercial development which was increasing throughout the period under consideration. Under such a taxation system as that of Tokugawa Japan, it was not easy for the lords to tax commercial crops, and it was still more difficult in the case of industry and commerce. It is extremely difficult to assess the magnitude of the flow of income and then to levy tax on it unless the notion of "capital" and "profit" in industry and commerce has been established. Even if these had been established, it is not possible to impose tax on the income without "an administrative revolution," in Hicks' words.[16] This revolution, however, would have required the abolition of the system of land tax in rice and

---

[14] There are numerous books and articles on this problem. Here we would like to refer to Yamamura (1973).

[15] Shimbo (1976), pp. 13–14.

[16] Hicks (1965), pp. 99 and 162.

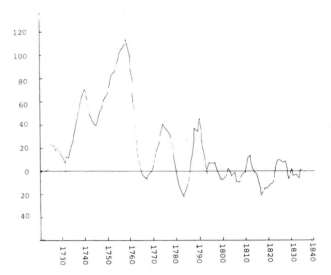

FIG. 3. Balance of shogunate's income and expenditure (unit: 1000 ryō; 5-year moving average). For source, see Table A2.

implied the fall of the system of government by Shogunate and daimyo (*bakuhan* system).

The second difficulty the Shogunate faced was that of assuming the function of a modern centralized government responsible for increasing expenditures on defense against threats from overseas and on investment in developing a social infrastructure.[17] The finances of the Shogunate were clearly inadequate to respond to these increasing demands. The base of the Shogunate's revenue was still confined to its own domain, which was essentially the same as the daimyos' territory (*han*), and for this reason the balance of the Shogunate's budget inevitably worsened. Needless to say, the Shogunate could no longer finance heavy deficits from its revenues. The only means by which the Shogunate's government could escape from continuous financial difficulties under these conditions was to exploit its exclusive right of coinage. The Shogunate began a series of recoinages, that is, the debasement of various kinds of gold and silver coin, in 1818 (Bunsei 1). These recoinages were carried out in the context of a long-term falling trend in general prices that began in the last decade of the eighteenth century (see Fig. 1). The recoinage in the Bunsei period (1818–1829) thus had two aims. One was to reverse the declining movement in general prices

[17] Although the data for expenditures of the Shogunate are much more scarce than those for revenues, we have access to fragmentary information about the nature of expenditures since the end of the eighteenth century. This information suggests an increasing share of expenditure for national defense and social infrastructure. The data is available in Sakiyama (1958) and Katsu (1928).

and the relative price of rice, through expansion of effective demand brought about by a sharp increase in the money supply associated with increased Shogunate expenditure. The second aim was the acquisition of a premium or profit by debasement in order to finance this increased expenditure.

In contrast to the recoinage of 1736, the premium in these later recoinages was not given to the old money owners, but poured mostly into the Shogunate's treasury.[18] As a result, the balance of the Shogunate's finance swung upward and remained in the black for a time (see Fig. 3). The recoinage of the Tempo period (1830–1843) which aimed at the acquisition of profit by debasing coins had to be carried out soon after the Bunsei debasement. The recoinage of the Tempo period produced enormous additional revenues to the Shogunate's budget, but it had direct repercussions in the general rise of prices, which led to an increase in government expenditure in terms of money. Moreover, there was a sharp drop in tax paid in rice due to poor harvests from 1736 to 1738, and the Shogunate still faced financial difficulties.

In these respects, it seems that the recoinage of Tempo was in essence the same as that of Bunsei. There is, however, a difference between these two recoinages. The recoinage of Bunsei was put into operation in a deflationary phase which continued for about 20 years. By means of this recoinage the amount of money in circulation increased sharply and the general price level rose quickly and continuously, but the rise in prices was no more than a recovery to the 1790 level which may be considered normal since the influence of the Temmei famine on prices had almost disappeared (see Table A1). On the other hand, the recoinage of Tempo was performed in the context of the post-1818 inflation. Thereafter the rise in general prices passed through and beyond the phase of recovery from a decline, as Fig. 1 shows, and it is likely that a fiscal inflation occurred. Looking at the movement of the general price index from 1830 to 1858, prices fluctuated considerably in consequence of the serious Tempo famine from 1836 to 1838 and the deflationary policy in the 1840s, but the general price index sustained a high level during these years. It seems to us to be beyond dispute that there were inflationary tendencies within the economy caused by large-scale expansion of the money supply associated with the emergence of *ichibu-gin* as a major component of the Japanese currency. Moreover, these inflationary tendencies became increasingly strong during the 1850s.[19] It was against this backdrop that the recoinages of Ansei-Man'en appeared on the stage of monetary history in the Tokugawa period.

---

[18] The amount of premium acquired by the Shogunate in the Bunsei period is estimated at nearly 6 million *ryō*. Taya (1963), pp. 396–397.

[19] In addition to the recoinages of gold and silver money, a large quantity of Tempo *hyakumon-sen* (copper coin of 100 *mon* unit) was issued. Yoshida (1925) Vol. 1, pp. 358–359.

TABLE 2

Movement of the Parity of Gold and Silver[a]

Period	Gold coin vs silver currency by weight	Period	Gold coin vs silver coin
1736–1817	Ganbun Koban vs Ganbun Chōgin (1:11.5)	1773–1817	Ganbun Koban vs Anei Nishu-gin (1:7.3)
1818–1836	Bunsei Koban vs Bunsei Chōgin (1:10.2)	1824–1836	Bunsei Koban vs Bunsei Nishu-gin (1:7.2)
			Bunsei Koban vs Bunsei Isshu-gin (1:4.8)
1837–1855	Tempo Koban vs Tempo Chōgin (1:8.4)	1737–1855	Tempo Koban vs Tempo Ichibu-gin (1:4.5)
			Tempo Koban vs Kaei Isshu-gin (1:3.8)
1856–1859	Ansei Koban vs Ansei Chōgin (1:5.0)	1859	Ansei Koban vs Ansei Nishu-gin (1:17.2)
			Ansei Koban vs Ansei Ichibu-gin (1:5.1)
1860	Man·en Koban vs Ansei Chōgin (1:14.8)	1860	Man·en Koban vs Ansei Ichibu-gin (1:15.3)

[a] Source: Taya (1973), pp. 35–39.

3. MONETARY POLICY IN THE ANSEI-MAN'EN PERIOD

In the first half of the seventeenth century, the gold/silver ratio in Japan was very close to that in Europe because the import and export of bullion or specie were permitted.[20] After the Shogunate adopted the seclusion policy, however, a difference arose between the gold/silver ratios of Japan and Europe,[21] and as time went on the difference became wider. Looking at Table 2, we find that in the period under observation the parity between the gold bullion content of gold coin and the silver content of the same value of silver currency by weight rose gradually, and at the same time the parity between gold coin and silver coin was always higher than the parity between gold coin and silver currency by weight. The process may most likely be described as follows.

The Shogunate issued new silver coin, the *nishu-gin* of 1772, of which the ratio versus gold coin was much higher than the current gold/silver ratio of gold coin versus silver currency by weight. Next, the government debased in some degree the silver currency by weight, while gold coin and silver

[20] Okurashō (1931), pp. 19–20, 31–36.
[21] Okurashō (1931), pp. 19–20, 31–36.

coin remained unchanged or were debased to a lesser degree. Consequently, the gold/silver ratio between gold coin and silver currency by weight rose, and came close to the gold/silver ratio between gold coin and silver coin. In turn, using the silver acquired by the above operation, debased silver coin was issued in large quantities. Through this recoinage the Shogunate enjoyed a big gain, and the share of silver coin in total money issues became larger. At the same time, the gold/silver ratio between gold coin and silver coin underwent another great rise. After all, the profit on recoinage in the last century of Tokugawa Japan was acquired for the most part through the issue of a large amount of silver coin, which was virtually a subsidiary money for gold coin as a standard money.

Why then, did the Shogunate stress silver coin rather than gold coin in the debasement? The answer to this question is probably as follows. Since silver was relatively scarce as an initial condition because of the outflow of silver and a drop in silver production, there was a rise in the relative value of silver.[22] This made the debasement of silver currency by weight both possible and necessary. Furthermore, debasement of gold coin required the use of silver as an admixture[23] and since sufficient silver was not otherwise available, the debasement of silver money was also necessary to secure silver for recoinage of gold coin. Finally, the debasement of silver currency by weight and the decreasing share of it among the money in circulation, as seen in Table 1, had little influence on the Tokugawa economy itself. Silver currency by weight did not circulate as normal currency in the last quarter of the Tokugawa period, although it retained its status as a basic money standard under the Tokugawa monetary system.[24] Thus the gold/silver ratio was a cardinal point in the recoinages of the late Tokugawa period, and the ratio, as Table 2 indicates, rose steadily after 1772. This was possible only because, under the policies of the Shogunate, the currency was virtually isolated from bullion markets both at home and abroad.

The Treaties of Amity and Commerce contracted with Western Powers in 1858 provided, as mentioned already, for the exchange of the Mexican (or American) dollar for *ichibu-gin* on terms of weight for weight. The implication of this fact was that the silver coin, despite the fact that it had by then become virtually token subsidiary money, was treated as standard money for payments in foreign trade. This caused the difference between the domestic gold/silver ratio and the international ratio to become much greater and a sudden and tremendous outflow of Japanese gold coin occurred. The Shogunate considered the outflow of gold coin to be perilous

[22] On the export of silver in the seventeenth century, see Tashiro (1976), pp. 223–239.

[23] The proportion of silver contained in gold coin increased successively through recoinages in the nineteenth century, see Satō (1933), pp. 780–784.

[24] Crawcour and Yamamura (1970), p. 492. Shimbo (1974), pp. 1–7.

TABLE 3

Amounts of Gold Coinage and Its Export[a]

Year	Coinage	Export
1871	2,668,920	
1872	23,659,740	142,646
1873	19,348,549	2,013,602
1874	3,760,344	7,597,753
1875	822,785	6,058,281
1876	381,744	5,591,343
1877	1,066,714	1,905,614
1878	357,578	4,641,969
1879	460,365	5,323,859
1880	469,429	5,308,805
1881	490,585	1,864,042
1882	803,645	1,463,795
1883	429,570	1,129,525
1884	494,840	1,053,898
Total	55,250,808	44,095,132

[a] Unit: yen. Source: Okurashō (1931), Vol. 13, p. 112.

and strove to attack this urgent problem. Why was the Shogunate so afraid of the outflow of Japanese gold coin? The outflow of Japanese gold coin meant the influx of foreign silver coin into Japan. The quantity of silver inflow quickly reached the point where it forced the domestic gold/silver ratio to decline to the prevailing level of the international gold/silver ratio. Then, the monetary system would undoubtedly turn to the silver standard with abundant silver reserves. Since the silver standard was common in East Asian countries at that time and international payments were made in silver, it might even have been favorable to shift to the silver standard. In addition, it is also a historical fact that the Meiji government changed the monetary system to a *de facto* silver standard, when in the 1870s Japanese gold coins flowed out in even greater amounts than in the Ansei period, due to failure of the Meiji government to keep the domestic gold/silver ratio in line with the international ratio (see Tables 3 and 4).[25] Why did the Shogunate adopt a monetary policy different from that of the Meiji government, when both regimes faced the same problem? The Shogunate could not accept such a drastic institutional change as the abolition of gold coin as standard money because it believed that this would undermine the foundation of the Shogunate. The monetary policy of the late Tokugawa period, which played a vital role in the overall economic policies of the Shogunate, was deeply rooted in the "*ryō*" gold coin standard system which had gradually replaced the "three-monies" system

[25] Patrick (1965), pp. 196-197.

TABLE 4

Movement of the Parity of Gold and Silver in the First Half of the Meiji Period[a]

Year	Legal parity in Japan	Parity in London market
1868	15.58	15.59
1869	15.58	15.60
1870	15.58	15.57
1871	16.01	15.57
1872	16.01	15.63
1873	16.01	15.92
1874	16.01	16.17
1875	16.01	16.59
1876	16.17	17.88
1877	16.33	17.22
1878	16.33	17.94
1879	16.17	18.40
1880	16.17	18.05
1881	16.17	18.16
1882	16.17	18.19
1883	16.17	18.64
1884	16.17	18.57
1885	16.17	19.41
1886	16.17	20.78
1887	i6.17	21.13
1888	16.17	21.99
1889	16.17	22.10
1890	16.17	19.76
1891	16.17	20.92
1892	16.17	23.72
1893	16.17	26.47
1894	16.17	30.06

[a] Source: Okurashō (1931), pp. 46–47.

as a result of forcing silver coin into the role of subsidiary money.[26] This monetary policy had been effective to some degree in strengthening the fiscal base of the Shogunate. Therefore, an abandonment of the "ryō" gold coin standard did not become possible until the monetary authority was transformed into a solid and effective modern central government based on an adequate fiscal base. Thus, the Shogunate could not choose any other policy.

The Shogunate attempted to adjust the domestic parity to the international parity, while maintaining the "ryō" gold coin standard. The measure which the Shogunate took as the first step was to raise the quality of silver coin, that is, to devalue silver against gold. This was achieved by

[26] Mikami (1975), pp. 59–84.

the issue of the new *nishu-gin* of 1859 (Ansei 6).[27] The gold/silver ratio between the current gold coin and this new *nishu-gin* was 1 to 17.2, somewhat lower than the international gold/silver ratio. The Shogunate, however, had to stop the coinage of new *nishu-gin* at only 90,000 *ryō*, because of vigorous opposition from the Western Powers.[28]

In response to this pressure the Shogunate reverted to the debased *ichibu-gin*.[29] The outflow of gold coin, of course, did not cease, and the Shogunate adjusted the parity by debasing gold coin by a large margin in the reform of the monetary system in 1860 (Man'en 1). As an emergency interim measure, the Shogunate "called up" the face value of the existing gold coins (Tempo and Ansei gold coins) two to three times larger at one leap in the so-called revaluation decree of 1860.[30] Four months later, the new smaller Man'en gold coin came into circulation. As a result, the outflow of gold coin completely stopped.[31] What we must notice here is that the three *ichibu-gin* per dollar exchange rate was applied only to transactions with foreign governments, and exchange rates for private transactions were negotiated between the parties involved.[32] Therefore, when the demand for *ichibu-gin* by foreign merchants increased, the rate of exchange rose, the arbitrage profit fell, and the incentive for gold speculation diminished. Nevertheless, the monetary reform of Man'en was necessary since there appears to have been some leakage between the official rate of three *ichibu-gin* per dollar and the private rates which remained much higher than the international gold/silver parity. It was not the rise of private exchange rates but the monetary reform of 1860 that eventually stopped the outflow of gold coins.

Why was it that the devaluation of silver coin met with opposition from Western Powers and the revaluation of gold coin did not? It is evident that both means would be equally effective in bringing to a close the acquisition of profit through the exchange of Mexican dollars for Japanese gold coin. The devaluation of silver, however, meant the devaluation of foreign money against Japanese money. According to the principle of exchanging the same kind of money on a weight for weight basis under the terms of the Treaties of Amity and Commerce, the purchasing power of the Mexican dollar for Japanese goods fell to one-third at a single blow. Thus devaluation of silver necessarily influenced foreign trade, as payment was

---

[27] Tempo *ichibu-gin*, which was circulated before the issue of Ansei *nishu-gin* contained 2.3 *momme* of fine silver. Ansei *nishu-gin* was a coin of 3.6 *momme* of fine silver, although the face value of the latter was half that of the former.

[28] Crawcour (1968), pp. 278–282.

[29] The new *ichibu-gin* issued in 1859 had the same weight as Tempo *ichibu-gin* but the quality was slightly lower.

[30] Taya (1963), pp. 457–458.

[31] Ishii (1940), pp. 405–409.

[32] Frost (1970), pp. 31–32.

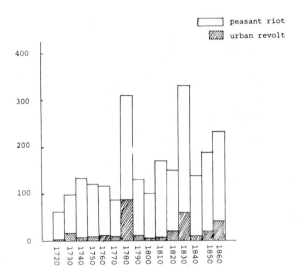

FIG. 4. Number of peasant riots and revolts per decade. Source: Aoki (1967).

made by silver coin in East Asia. Revaluation of gold coin, on the other
hand, did not lead to a change in the exchange rate, although it had great
effect on the domestic economy. For this reason foreign countries did not
oppose the revaluation of gold coin.

In the end, however, the monetary reform of 1860 greatly affected not
only the domestic economy but also foreign trade. Let us first examine the
impact on the domestic economy. In this particular recoinage the
Shogunate could not obtain the profit, for the exchange of old money for
new was carried out with a premium. Consequently, it was of no help to thè
Shogunate's deteriorating finances. Hence the Shogunate had no
alternative but to undertake the *goyōkin* (forced loans from merchants)
policy on a large scale.[33] This recoinage was put into operation in the
already inflationary situation brought about by the debasement of the
Tempo period, and caused a very sharp increase in the amount of currency
in circulation (see Table 1). The increment of money did not flow into the
market through the expansion of the Shogunate's expenditures, but
immediately became an increase in money assets of the owners of the old
gold coin. This was largely responsible for a rapid and sharp rise in general
prices from 1860 on. The general price index of 1865 was three times higher
than the level of the mid-1850s (see Table A1).

The hyperinflation in the last decade of Tokugawa Japan had a
destructive impact on the economy, affecting not only growth but also
distribution. In the case of the recoinage of 1860, redistribution took a turn

---

[33] On the *goyōkin* of this period, see *Osaka-shi Sanjikai* (1913), pp. 742–750, 786–799,
914–925, 936–954.

to an increase in the money assets of owners of gold coin, not those of silver coin, since the recoinage affected exclusively gold coin. In contrast, peasants and urban commoners, who held little or no gold coins, were hit expecially hard by this sharp fall in the relative value of their silver and copper coins. This was a major cause of the peasant riots and urban revolts during the 1860s which were, as seen in Fig. 4, more numerous than at any other time in Tokugawa Japan, except for the Temmei period of the 1780s and the Tempo period of the 1830s, both of which were famine years. We can also observe that the proportion of urban revolts was extremely high. The disturbances of the 1860s were clearly due to the rapid rise in the relative price of rice[34] and the fall in real wages.[35]

Lastly, we should note the effect of the 1860 monetary reform on foreign trade. Naturally enough the terms of trade were affected by these monetary policies. Once the exchange rate was adjusted by the Man'en reform it remained virtually unchanged and thereafter changes in the terms of trade were the results of changes in internal Japanese prices. The domestic price level rose by leaps and bounds and the competitive power of domestic goods against imported goods weakened markedly, while the prices of exportable goods in Japan quickly rose to the international level. This led to drastic changes in the relative prices of commodities, which had repercussions in the transformation of the whole structure of the Tokugawa economy.[36] If the issue of Ansei *nishu-gin*, that is to say, devaluation of silver, had been successful, the hyperinflation with its destructive effects on the Japanese economy would not have occurred and even the impact on foreign trade might well have been milder. Initial conditions for Japan's modern economic development would certainly have been different from what they actually were. Whether the ultimate effect on Japan's modern economic growth would have been by and large more favorable or not is an extremely complicated question. To answer it would involve detailed counterfactual investigation of the whole economic and even political history of Japan since that time.

4. CONCLUSION

From our discussion in this paper we conclude that the monetary reforms of Ansei-Man'en were undertaken to achieve equilibrium in the international arena at the expense of equilibrium in the domestic economy These recoinages threw the Tokugawa economy into disorder in various ways, and the social unrest in the last few years of the Tokugawa regime

---

[34] Social unrest and poor harvests in the last several years amplified the rise in the relative price of rice.
[35] On the fall of real wages, see Umemura (1961), pp. 173–174; Sano (1962), pp. 69–71; Saito (1973), pp. 54–58.
[36] On this problem see Shimbo *et al.* (1975), pp. 244–248.

was in part due to them. Furthermore, the recoinages meant the end of the monetary system which had supported for a long time the political and economic system of Tokugawa Japan. Under the original Tokugawa monetary system, the money supply was not unified, efficient, and elastic. The coinage of gold denomination silver money such as *nishu-gin* and *ichibu-gin* had opened the way to a unified money supply, though the silver currency by weight remained in the background as legal tender and a quasi-standard money. The recoinage of Man'en made the silver currency by weight null and void in fact, and the *"sanka seido"* (three-monies system) basically came to an end. In regard to the control of the money supply, the Tokugawa monetary system was not efficient and elastic because the Shogunate lacked control of credit creation through a central bank.[37] Thus, the Shogunate could control the money supply only through the coinage of gold and silver money and the budget balance. There is no doubt that the lack of efficient and elastic control over the money supply led to the drastic hyperinflation after 1860 and establishment of a system of efficient and elastic money supply became an urgent problem.[38]

. The new coinage act in 1871 finally dissolved the Tokugawa monetary system. By this act, *"yen"* took the place of *"ryō"* and this action played an integral part in the modern economic development of Japan. It was not until the establishment of the Bank of Japan as the central bank that the government could efficiently and elastically control the money supply. We may conclude that the monetary reforms in 1859 and 1860 were the beginning of the end of the Tokugawa monetary system.

APPENDIX

TABLE A1

Osaka Indexes of Rice Price, General Price, and Relative Price of Rice: 1733–1867[a]

Year	Rice (A)	General price index (B)	Relative price of rice (A/B)	Year	Rice (A)	General price index (B)	Relative price of rice (A/B)
1727	66.6			1800	96.9	91.2	106.3
1728	59.8			1801	95.0	90.4	105.1
1729	54.7			1802	90.9	88.7	102.5
1730	60.1			1803	84.7	85.4	99.2
1731	66.1		(84.9)	1804	80.7	81.7	98.8
1732	68.9			1805	80.0	80.2	99.8

[37] One might cite the sophisticated credit creation by *"ryōgae shō"* (merchant bankers) at Osaka, but it was not directly linked to the central monetary authority of the Shogunate. See Crawcour (1961), pp. 342–360.

[38] Patrick (1965), pp. 187–188.

TABLE A1 (*Continued*)

Year	Rice (A)	General price index (B)	Relative price of rice (A/B)	Year	Rice (A)	General price index (B)	Relative price of rice (A/B)
1733	71.0			1806	81.7	80.5	101.6
1734	75.4			1807	85.0	81.4	104.5
1735	76.5			1808	85.6	81.8	104.6
1736	76.8			1809	90.8	84.6	107.4
1737	88.8			1810	88.7	84.2	105.4
1738	99.7			1811	86.7	82.2	105.4
1739	105.0			1812	86.6	80.0	108.3
1740	106.7			1813	88.4	78.6	112.5
1741	103.4			1814	84.7	76.1	111.3
1742	98.2			1815	86.7	76.3	113.6
1743	94.6		(102.0)	1816	85.4	75.6	113.0
1744	92.9		(101.8)	1817	82.3	75.1	109.5
1745	93.4		(102.6)	1818	79.7	75.3	105.8
1746	93.5		(103.5)	1819	80.2	76.0	105.6
1747	94.2		(102.6)	1820	79.4	75.2	105.5
1748	94.4		(103.4)	1821	79.9	75.1	106.5
1749	92.3		(102.2)	1822	82.1	75.3	109.0
1750	88.2		(100.0)	1823	84.4	76.3	111.1
1751	81.3		(97.2)	1824	86.3	77.9	110.7
1752	75.9		(102.9)	1825	85.5	79.1	108.1
1753	77.0		(93.6)	1826	87.9	81.1	108.4
1754	82.0		(93.9)	1827	93.6	84.2	111.1
1755	87.7		(96.7)	1828	96.6	85.4	113.0
1756	92.3		(98.4)	1829	99.7	86.7	114.9
1757	95.2	93.5	101.9	1830	103.9	89.1	116.5
1758	90.2	91.1	99.0	1831	111.6	93.1	119.9
1759	81.6	87.7	93.0	1832	117.7	96.6	121.8
1760	76.8	83.5	92.0	1833	118.9	98.5	120.7
1761	76.0	81.3	93.4	1834	128.1	103.9	123.2
1762	76.5	81.0	94.5	1835	156.0	119.5	130.6
1763	79.7	83.5	95.4	1836	162.3	126.4	128.4
1764	84.1	85.5	98.3	1837	159.5	129.7	123.0
1765	87.4	87.7	99.7	1838	157.5	132.1	119.2
1766	91.6	88.4	103.6	1839	144.6	129.0	112.1
1767	94.5	88.1	107.2	1840	117.1	114.7	102.2
1768	95.7	87.2	109.8	1841	104.6	106.0	98.7
1769	96.0	85.5	112.2	1842	100.0	100.0	100.0
1770	93.1	83.6	111.3	1843	104.0	99.1	104.9
1771	87.0	82.8	105.0	1844	109.6	99.7	109.9
1772	81.9	83.2	98.5	1845	111.9	101.7	110.1
1773	78.7	83.7	94.0	1846	115.8	104.7	110.7
1774	78.6	85.3	92.1	1847	120.1	107.8	111.3
1775	80.6	86.9	92.7	1848	130.2	112.7	115.5
1776	83.0	87.3	95.5	1849	135.9	115.9	117.3
1777	83.1	85.8	96.8	1850	135.3	115.8	116.9

TABLE A1 (*Continued*)

Year	Rice (A)	General price index (B)	Relative price of rice (A/B)	Year	Rice (A)	General price index (B)	Relative price of rice (A/B)
1778	81.0	82.7	98.0	1851	137.1	116.7	117.5
1779	80.0	80.7	99.1	1852	136.7	116.9	116.9
1780	80.7	81.1	99.5	1853	122.5	111.1	110.3
1781	88.7	83.6	106.1	1854	111.6	105.4	105.9
1782	100.7	89.7	112.3	1855	111.7	104.3	107.2
1783	106.5	93.5	113.9	1856	115.3	106.4	108.3
1784	110.3	96.9	113.7	1857	118.2	105.9	111.7
1785	120.5	104.3	115.6	1858	132.1	114.9	115.0
1786	118.7	107.0	110.9	1859	153.4	129.0	119.0
1787	112.3	106.7	105.3	1860	164.4	137.5	119.5
1788	111.4	106.4	104.7	1861	169.1	144.7	116.8
1789	109.5	105.0	104.3	1862	180.4	157.9	114.2
1790	106.7	101.5	105.2	1863	214.3	183.7	116.6
1791	107.5	99.1	108.4	1864	358.9	254.0	141.3
1792	104.4	97.9	106.6	1865	419.6	311.0	134.9
1793	104.7	96.2	108.9				
1794	107.0	97.6	109.6				
1795	101.1	94.8	106.7				
1796	96.6	92.9	103.9				
1797	98.0	93.3	105.1				
1798	100.7	93.7	107.5				
1799	99.0	92.4	107.1				

a 1840–1844 = 100; 5-year moving average. Note: The sources of data are Nakai (1952), pp. 6–79; Yamazaki (1963b), pp. 144–150, 154–157; Tsuruoka (1972), pp. 114–207. The original data are expressed in silver currency by weight, but we have converted it to units of gold coin, using the current exchange rate of gold units and silver units. Our general price index is the weighted mean of 14 commodity price indexes, namely, rice, wheat, soy bean, rape seed, ginned cotton, rapeseed oil, cottonseed oil, sake, soy sauce, sugar, cotton cloth, firewood, charcoal, and wax. The weights are as follows: rice = 30.0, manufactured goods (rapeseed oil, cottonseed oil, sake, soy sauce, sugar, and cotton cloth) = 32.3, and the rest as a whole = 37.7. The price indexes of the latter two are, respectively, the unweighted means of the components of each group. We cannot give the relative price of rice before 1754, because the general price index for Osaka is not available in this period. We show as the substitute for it the relative price of rice as against the Kyoto consumers' price in parentheses. For details of our general price index, see Shimbo (1972b) and Shimbo's forthcoming book, *Yedojidai kōki no bukka to keizai*.

TABLE A2

Balance of the Shogunate's Income and Expenditure[a]

Year	Balance	Moving average (5-year)	Year	Balance	Moving average (5-year)
1722	−134		1781	−143	−126
1723	243		1782	−173	−194
1724	293	154	1783	−386	−219
1725	107	227	1784	−259	−180
1726	262	220	1785	−133	−124
1727	232	168	1786	52	46
1728	206	198	1787	105	134
1729	32	156	1788	466	360
1730	262	107	1789	479	339
1731	46	68	1790	700	451
1732	−11	132	1791	−55	222
1733	11	113	1792	3	138
1734	352	198	1793	−18	−7
1735	166	274	1794	61	63
1736	471	368	1795	−24	59
1737	371	488	1796	292	62
1738	481	595	1797	−16	8
1739	950	649	1798	−3	−30
1740	702	707	1799	−207	−67
1741	739	632	1800	−218	−68
1742	664	485	1801	109	−55
1743	104	446	1802	−21	23
1744	217	396	1803	63	1
1745	505	390	1804	−34	−35
1746	491	469	1805	−112	−20
1747	632	540	1806	−72	−95
1748	500	588	1807	56	−98
1749	573	629	1808	−312	−46
1750	745	667	1809	−48	−17
1751	693	774	1810	146	−23
1752	826	828	1811	74	106
1753	884	847	1812	26	134
1754	992	932	1813	331	37
1755	841	989	1814	94	−18
1756	1,115	1,049	1815	−338	−37
1757	1,114	1,075	1816	−203	−135
1758	1,183	1,136	1817	−67	−195
1759	1,122	1,080	1818	−160	−148
1760	1,148	934	1819	−205	−146
1761	835	712	1820	−103	−130
1762	384	469	1821	−196	−117
1763	70	213	1822	12	−96
1764	−92	31	1823	−93	34
1765	−130	−26	1824	−98	94
1766	−75	−58	1825	364	92

TABLE A2 (*Continued*)

Year	Balance	Moving average (5-year)	Year	Balance	Moving average (5-year)
1767	96	-65	1826	286	67
1768	-90	-39	1827	1	81
1769	-85	-9	1828	-216	20
1770	-41	67	1829	-30	-74
1771	74	157	1830	61	12
1772	476	219	1831	-188	-39
1773	363	294	1832	2	-26
1774	222	403	1833	-41	-62
1775	337	365	1834	35	13
1776	618	345	1835	-119	
1777	283	317	1836	189	
1778	267	248			
1779	81	95			
1780	-11	4			

a Unit: 1000 *ryo*. Source: Sakiyama (1958), pp. 220–256.

REFERENCES

Akimoto, H. (1975), "Jūkyū seiki chūyō Suō Ōshima saiban no shōhi kansū" [Consumption Function of Oshima District in Suo Province at the End of the Tokugawa Period]. *Mita Gakkai Zasshi* 68, No. 11–12, pp. 31–50.

Aoki, K. (1967), *Hyakushō ikki no nenjiteki kenkyū* [Chronological Study of Peasant Riots]. Tokyo: Shinseisha.

Crawcour, E. S. (1961), "The Development of a Credit System in Seventeenth Century Japan." *Journal of Economic History* 21, No. 3, pp. 342–360.

Crawcour, E. S. (1968), "Bakumatsu no kahei mondai ni tsuite" [On the Currency problem at the End of the Tokugawa Period]. In Ōtsuka, T. Matsuda, Y. Ando, and H. Sekiguchi (Eds.), *Shihon shugi no keisei to Hatten* [The Genesis and Development of Capitalism]. Tokyo: Tokyodaigaku, Shuppankai.

Crawcour, E. S., and Yamamura, K. (1970), "Tokugawa Monetary System: 1789–1868." *Economic Development and Cultural Change* 18, No. 4, Part 1, pp. 489–518.

Frost, P. (1970), *The Bakumatsu Currency Crisis*. Cambridge, Mass.: Harvard University Press.

Furushima, T. (1965), "Bakufu zaisei shūnyū no dōkō to nōmin shūdatsu no kakki" [Trends in Bakufu Income and the Periodization of Peasant Exploitation]. In Furushima (Ed.), *Nihon keizaishi taikei* [Japanese Economic History Series], Vol. 4, Tokyo: Tokyodaigaku, Shuppankai.

Hicks, J. R. (1965), *A Theory of Economic History*, Oxford: Oxford University Press.

Ishii, T. (1940), "Bakumatsu kaikō to kinka ryūshutsu mondai" [The Opening of Ports and the Problem on the Outflow of Gold Coins at the End of the Tokugawa Period]. *Rekishi Chiri* 76, No. 5, pp. 17–41; No. 6, pp. 15–32.

Ishii, T. (1952), "Bakumatsu kaikō-go ni okeru kahei mondai no shuppatsuten" [The Starting Point of Currency Problem after the Opening of Ports]. *Shakai Keizai Shigaku* 18, No. 4.

Iwahashi, M. (1976), "Tokugawa jidai no kahei suryō" [The Amounts of Currencies in Circulation during the Tokugawa period]. In M. Umemura, H. Shimbo, A. Hayami, and S. Nishikawa (Eds.), *Suryō keizaishi ronshū 1:nihon keizai no hatten* [Collected

Papers on Quantitative Economic History 1:Development of Japanese Economy].
Tokyo: Nihonkeizai shinbunsha.

Katsu, K. (1928), "Suijin roku" [Dusty Tomes from the Past], *Kaishū zenshū* [Complete Works of Katsu Kaishū], Vol. 4, Tokyo: Kaizosha.

Mikami, R. (1975), *Yen no tanjō* [The Birth of Yen]: Toyokeizaishinposha.

Nakai, N. (Ed.) (1952). *Kinsei koki ni okeru shuyō bukka no dōtai* [Movements of Major Commodity Prices during the Late Tokugawa Period]. Tokyo: Nihon Gakujitsu-shinkōkai.

Okada, S. (1955), *Bakumatsu ishin no kahei seisaku* [Monetary Policy in the Late Tokugawa and Restoration Periods]. Tokyo: Moriyamashoten.

Okurashō (Ministry of Finance) (Ed.) (1931), *Meiji zenki zaisei keizai shiryō shūsei* [Collected Materials on the History of Finance in the Early Meiji Period], Vol. 12, Tokyo: Kaizosha.

Ono, K. (1958), "Nihon ni okeru mekishiko-doru no ryūnyū to sono kozai" [The Influx of Mexican dollars into Japan and Its Merits and Demerits]. *Keizai Ronsō* **81**, No. 3, pp. 1–17; No. 4, pp. 34–52; No. 5, pp. 24–37; No. 6, pp. 37–55.

Osaka-shi Sanjikai (Osaka Municipal Government) (1913), *Osaka-shi shi* [History of Osaka City], Vol. 2, Osaka: Osaka-shi Sanjaiku.

Patrick, H. T. (1965), "External Equilibrium and Internal Convertibility: Financial Policy in Meiji Japan." *Journal of Economic History* **25**, No. 2, pp. 187–213.

Saitō, O. (1973), "Nōgyō chingin no sūsei" [Trends in Real Wages of Agricultural Labourers]. *Shakai Keizai Shigaku* **39**, No. 2, pp. 50–69.

Sakiyama, G. (1958), "Seisai zakki" [Seisai's Memorandum], *Edo sōsho* (Edo Series), Vol. 8, Tokyo: Edo-sāsho kankokai.

Sakudō, Y. (1958), *Kinsei nihon kaheishi* [History of Currencies in Tokugawa Japan]. Tokyo: Kobundo.

Sano, Y. (1962), "Kenchiku rōdōsha no jisshitsu chingin: 1830–1894" [Real Wage of Construction Labourer: 1830–1894]. *Mita Gakkai Zasshi* **55**, No. 11, pp. 49–76.

Satō, C. (1933), "Kyū kahei hyō" [Compendium of Old Currencies]. In Mitsui (Ed.), *Kyū kahei nenpyō narabini soba hyō* [Chronological Table of Old Currencies and the Rate of Exchange]. Tokyo: Iwanamishoten.

Satō, J. (1930), "Kahei hiroku" [The Secret Record of Currency]. In Takimoto (Ed.), *Nihon Keizai Taiten* [Collected Japanese Writings], Vol. 45. Tokyo: Keimeisha.

Shimbo, H. (1972a), "Hansatsu ni tsuiteno ichi kōsatsu" [A Study of Paper Money Issued by *han* Authority]. *Kobe Daigaku Keizaigaku Kenkyū Nempō*, No. 19, pp. 1–37.

Shimbo, H. (1972b), "Tokugawa kōki no bukka suijun" [The Price Level in the Late Tokugawa Period]. *Kokumin Keizai Zasshi* **127**, No. 2, pp. 18–39; No. 3, pp. 1–18.

Shimbo, H. (1974), "Tokugawa Jidai kōki nishi-Settsu ni okeru kahei ryūtsū" [Currencies Circulated in the West-Settsu District of the Late Tokugawa Japan]. *Hyōgo-ken no Rekishi* [History of Hyōgo Prefecture], No. 11, pp. 1–7.

Shimbo, H. (1975), "Bakumatsu no bukka hendō, 1830–67" [Movements of Prices, 1830–67]. *Keizai Kenkyū* **26**, No. 4, pp. 289–301.

Shimbo, H. (1976), "Zeni sōba no hendō: 1736–88" [Zeni Market: 1736–88]. *Kokumin Keizai Zasshi* **133**, No. 6, pp. 1–17.

Shimbo, H., Hayami, A., and Nishikawa, S. (1975), *Sūryō Keizaishi Nyūmon* [Introduction to Quantitative Economic History]. Tokyo: Nihon hyoronsha.

Shinjo, H. (1962), *History of the Yen*. Kobe: The Research Institute for Economics and Business Administration, Kobe University.

Takeuchi, M. (1965), "Bakufu keizai no hendō to kinyū seisaku no tenkai" [Changes in the Bakufu Economy and the Development of Financial Policy]. In T. Furushima (Ed.), *Nihon Keizoishi taikei* [Japanese Economic History Series], Vol. 4. Tokyo: Tokyo-daigaku Shuppankai.

Tashiro, K. (1976), "Tokugawa jidai ni okeru gin yushitsu to kahei aridaka" [Silver Export and the Volume of Currency in Circulation in Tokugawa Japan]. In M. Umemura, H. Shimbo, A. Hayami, and S. Nishikawa (Eds.), *Sūryō keizaishi ronshū 1: nihon keizai no hatten* [Collected Papers on Quantitative Economic History 1: Development of Japanese Economy]. Tokyo: Nihonkeizaishinbunsha.

Taya, H. (1963), *Kinsei ginza no kenkyū* [Silver Mint in Tokugawa Japan]. Tokyo: Yoshikawa Kōbunkan.

Taya, H. (1972), "Bakumatsu kansai no ryūtsū kahei" [Currencies Circulated in Kansai District at the End of the Tokugawa Period]. *Rekishi Kenkyū*, No. 14, pp. 1–17.

Taya, H. (1973), "Edo jidai kaheihyō no saikentō" [Re-examination on the Compendium of old Currencies]. *Shakai Keizai Shigaku* **39**, No. 3, pp. 21–39.

Tsuruoka, M. (1972), "Kinsei beikoku shijō to shiteno Ōtsu" [Ōtsu as the Rice Market in the Tokugawa Period]. *Shiryōkan Kenkyū Kiyō*, No. 5, pp. 19–208.

Umemura, M. (1961), "Kenchiku rōdōsha no jisshitsu chingin: 1726–1958" [Real Wage of Construction Labourer: 1726–1958]. *Keizai Kenkyū* **12**, No. 2, pp. 172–176.

Yamamura, K. (1973), "Towards a Re-examination of the Economic History," *Journal of Economic History* **33**, No. 3, pp. 509–546.

Yamamura, K. (1974), *A Study of Samurai Income and Entrepreneurship*. Cambridge, Mass.

Yamazaki, R. (1963a), "Genroku-Kyōho ki no bukka hendō ni tsuite" [On the Movements of Prices in the Genroku-Kyōho Period]. *Keizaigaku Zasshi* **48**, No. 4, pp. 96–118.

Yamazaki, R. (1963b). "Kinsei kōki ni okeru nōsanbutsu kagaku no dōkō" [Movements in Prices of Agricultural Products in the Late Tokugawa Period]. *Osaka Shiritsu Daigaku Kenkyū Nempō*, No. 19, pp. 109–168.

Yoshida, K. (Ed.) (1925). *Dai nippon kaheishi* [History of Japanese Currency], Vol. 1. Tokyo: Chōyōkai.

EXPLORATIONS IN ECONOMIC HISTORY 15, 84–100 (1978)

The Labor Market in Tokugawa Japan: Wage Differentials and the Real Wage Level, 1727–1830*

OSAMU SAITO

Keio University

Tokugawa economic history provides quite an interesting example of the workings of the labor market: In the Tokugawa period a contraction in occupational wage differentials occurred concurrently with a rise in real wages. This paper deals with these aspects of wage change and a general set of problems which has arisen about them. The first section sets out these problems; the second deals with the evidence on wage differentials and real wages in Kinai from 1727 to 1830. The third provides a theoretical framework to explain the findings; finally the last section examines the implications of the findings.

I

Narrowing trends in wage differentials between skilled and unskilled workers have been observed in many advanced countries.[1] A tendency for the skill differentials to contract in periods of labor shortage has also been noted.[2] These facts have been the subject of various theoretical investigations, but a most important model is that of Reder (1955). According to his model, during boom years employers try to adjust to changes in labor requirements by upgrading unskilled workers so that the lower-skilled and finally the reserve labor forces, from which most of the lowest-grade workers are recruited, are exhausted. This raises the wage level for the least-skilled and, hence, makes the skill differentials contract.[3] According to this theory, however, there is the important proviso that

---

* An earlier version of this paper was presented at the conference held by the Institut für Japanologie, Universität Wien, in May 1976. The author is grateful to the editors of this issue for their suggestions, to the Matsunaga Science Foundation for financial support for the research on which this paper is based, and to Peter Grey for his assistance in making stylistic revisions of the manuscript.

[1] See Reynolds and Taft (1956), part 2.

[2] The American evidence is summarized in Reder (1955); for pre-war Japan, see Odaka (1976). However, there does not seem to be a general agreement that the short-term behavior of wage differentials has affected the secular trend. Reder emphasises that a contraction during the boom years was more or less irreversible, while Reynolds and Taft do not think that the slope of the trend line has been affected by fluctuations in employment (pp. 363–4).

[3] When the boom is over, on-the-job training which the upgraded workers have undergone will prevent the reestablishment of the previous differentials. Thus, the long-term narrowing trend will be created.

0014-4983/78/0151-0084$02.00/0

this hypothesis holds true, as Reder (1955) says, "only when labor demand increases sufficiently to adsorb the labor reserve." If, for instance, the rural sector continuously supplied a number of out-migrants because of a higher level of fertility, or if a quick substitution of less for more skilled workers were prevented by rigid social systems such as apprenticeship, the contraction in skill differentials would not occur.[4] Indeed, these conditions are what Hicks (1969) thought relevant to preindustrial societies. Except for the case of new countries where land is abundant, therefore, it is quite unlikely that preindustrial economies exhibit a narrowing movement of skill differentials even in times of industrial or commercial expansion.

Tokugawa economic history, however, provides evidence against this conclusion. Tokugawa Japan was by no means a country of ample land; nevertheless, there occurred a general rise in real wages accompanied with narrowing skill differentials. This fact calls for attention. Did industrial or commercial expansion, contrary to the above conclusion, raise the general wage level? Or, have Reder and Hicks failed to incorporate other important factors in their models?

Most specialists in Tokugawa history would agree with the former conclusion; in fact, contemporaries attributed the rise in wages to a "pull" by the nonagricultural sector. Smith (1959) summarizes the contemporary view as follows:

> Labor was in short supply after about 1700 because capital in trade and industry was growing faster than population (p. 111).

> The rising cost of labor was a trend that lasted throughout the last half of the Tokugawa period and beyond, drawing complaints all the while from those who found the rise painful. Administrative officials and village headmen, both speaking on the whole for the larger holders, variously claimed that the rising cost of labor was ruining, had ruined, or would soon ruin agriculture (p. 120).

Many Japanese historians also share this view, and Nakamura, (1968) in particular has commented that wage differentials observed between towns and rural areas were narrowing *pari passu* with the rise in agricultural real wages.[5]

Yet it has hardly been discussed if this observation is consistent with the "pull" explanation. If the demand for labor in towns continued to be so strong, why did urban craftsmen fail to raise their wages at the same rate as agricultural wages rose? The question is partly answered by pointing out that "trade and industry were by no means exclusively urban

----

[4] Reder was well aware that this implication becomes important especially when we turn to historical cases. He suggested that in England the skill differentials may have widened during the industrial revolution despite the rapid expansion of production, because the increase in population which had begun in the late eighteenth century created a pool of unskilled workers (p. 852).

[5] Nakamura (1968), p. 275.

phenomena"; the growth was to some extent "rural-centered".[6] This argument appears correct but if a similar phenomenon is also observed in the rural areas, which is, as we shall see, true, that is not a sufficient explanation. What has been neglected is the role of agriculture. Agricultural productivity is important in determining the lowest wage level on which the whole wage structure was based, because it was from the agricultural sector that most of less-skilled workers were recruited. As we shall see, this can easily be shown by using simple tools of microeconomics. An increase in agricultural marginal productivity has by itself the effect of narrowing the differentials and, hence, of raising the general level of wages.

Apart from this general problem, there still remains an empirical question on the economic history of the Tokugawa period: Is the chronology of wages, so far presented, indisputable? With regard to the trend from 1820 onward, when the real wage curves began to move downward, we have sufficient grounds for accepting it. For urban builders in particular, there exists a set of good series of wage data for the period even before 1820, which has been compiled from the business records of a draper in Kyoto.[7] Although these are not continuous series, they give sufficient information about long-term movements of the money wage-rates and retail prices in one of the biggest cities in the Tokugawa period.

Is there similar quantitative evidence for rural areas? As shown in the quotation from Smith (1959, p. 120), the evidence has largely been drawn from nonquantitative sources such as village officials' or landlords' complaints about the rising cost of labor, although, as he rightly emphasises, "they give us a very inadequate idea of how great the rise actually was."[8] There is, however, an important exception which has often been quoted, that is, Kamikawarabayashi's data. Kamikawarabayashi is a village near Osaka. This village gives exceptionally good time-series information about wage rates, not only for various farm laborers but also for builders employed by the Okamoto family, the largest landholder in the village. The former has already been compiled in Imai and Yagi (1955); unfortunately, however, their figures for agricultural wages are presented as 20-year averages, which are of course inadequate for the purpose of discussing the course of change in detail.

An attempt to redo the estimates of the Kamikawarabayashi agricultural wage series has been made, and the wages for builders have also been collected from the same source material. These data enable us to compare wages, not only between farm day laborers and urban builders,[9] but also between rural and urban builders, between different occupations in the

---

[6] Smith (1959), p. 111; the term "rural-centered" is found in Smith (1973).

[7] Mitsui Bunko (1952), pp. 68–74.

[8] Smith (1959), p. 120.

[9] Nakamura's generalization is based on this comparison.

building trades, between farm laborers and builders within the rural area, and finally between town and farm day laborers, both of whom comprised the unskilled classes in the wage structure.

The results of these calculations are given in Table 1 and Figs. 1 and 2. Before going on to examine them, however, two points should be noted. First, conclusions drawn from these series are limited to the Kinai region, i.e., the area around Kyoto and Osaka. Both cities were two of the largest commercial centers in the Tokugawa period. By the beginning of the eighteenth century the Kinai region had reached the most developed and commercialized level of economy in Japan. It would be easy to assume that the Kinai figures reflect those which are to be found in the rest of the country, and this might be realistic in the case of some commodity prices. However, such an assumption would be unwise in the case of the labor force, partly because of the paucity of data in other areas and partly because of the well-known fact that the labor market tends to be more localized than the commodity markets. Moreover, it should be kept in mind in this connection that Kinai began to face competition, although not too severe as yet, from other districts in the second half of the eighteenth century. Indeed, the Kinai economy may have been stagnant, but this does not necessarily mean that the rest of the country failed to grow. The significance of this point will be understood when we touch on an argument put forward by Yamamura (1973), which implies a widening gap between the advanced areas (Kinai and Chūgoku) and the less developed ones in the latter half of the Tokugawa period.

Second, this paper is mainly concerned with the period before inflation began. After about 1820, prices began to move up and real wages down. This commencement of inflation has often been attributed to the Bunsei debasement in 1818–20. But, whatever the cause was, it is quite clear that it was a period of inflation on which the movement of real wages was largely dependent.[10] Thus, it would be better at the moment to limit our scope to the period in which the role of monetary change was less decisive.

II

Wage Differentials

Our first task is to look at changes in wage differentials between occupations. Table 1 presents the basic wage series for carpenters and day laborers in Kyoto and for carpenters and farm day laborers in Kamikawarabayashi.[11] Of the four, only the agricultural wage series is a

---

[10] See for example Shimbo, Hayami, and Nishikawa (1975), Chap. 11.

[11] Tables 1 and 2 and Figs. 1–3 are reprinted from Saitō (1975) by permission of the editors of *Shakai-kezaishigaku*. Details of the calculations will be found there; however, the theoretical consideration given in this paper is new. It should be noted that farm laborers did not form an occupational class. They were employed, to supplement their income from

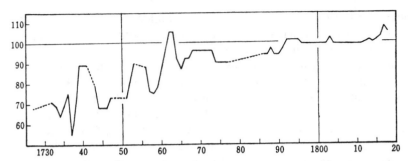

FIG. 1. The wage differential index between farm day laborers and carpenters in Kamikawarabayashi. Wage differential index = (wage index of farm laborers/wage index of carpenters) × 100 (for 1802–1804 = 100).
Source. Table 1 below.

composite index, where three or four job rates and male and female rates are, if available, taken into account.[12]

Let us first compare the two Kamikawarabayashi series. Figure 1 shows the movement of the index of the ratio of agricultural to carpenters' wages. Note that, since all the series are given in index form, the movement is also shown in that way with base years of 1802–04. For example, the figure of 67 in 1727 does not mean that the money wage-rate for farm laborers was 67% of that for carpenters; rather, it indicates a relative level of the differential which is standardized by the ratio in the base years, when the rate was 2.6 *momme* for carpenters and 1 *momme* for the male springtime farm workers. Year-to-year fluctuations are not small, but since they are less reliable, let us take a longer view. The movement began with a sharp rise, and the rise gradually slowed down. To put it in a schematic way, the whole period is divided into two phases; in the first phase, up to the early 1760s, the differential index changes from less than 70 to about, or a little less than, 100, whereas in the second it shows neither an upward nor a downward trend. In other words, while no marked change took place in the second phase, the rate of increase in agricultural wages in the first was about 50% higher than that in carpenters' wages in the rural area.

The occupational differentials observed in the building trades, however, followed a different course. The wage rates for carpenters and thatchers[13] in Kamikawarabayashi show that there was no secular change in the differential between the two building occupations in the rural area

---

farming, usually in busy seasons by their landlords, but by other farmers as well. In the rice planting season in particular, girls often formed a work gang and went round among farmers in neighboring villages.

[12] This is a linked series of those for 1727–61, 1759–92, and 1790–1830. Three job rates are examined for the first and second periods and four for the third.

[13] Many of the thatchers did farm work for the Okamotos as well; probably thatching was a part-time job.

TABLE 1

Wage Indices in Kyoto and Kamikawarabayashi (1802–04 = 100)

	Kyoto		Kamikawarabayashi	
	Carpenters (1)	Day laborers (2)	Carpenters (3)	Day laborers (4)
1727	69	—	(64)ᵃ	43
28	69	—	—	—
29	69	—	—	—
30	69	—	—	—
1731	69	—	—	—
32	62	—	(58)	41
33	—	—	58	40
34	—	—	(58)	37
35	—	—	(58)	40
36	—	—	74	56
37	—	—	111	62
38	—	—	88	62
39	—	—	88	79
40	—	—	88	79
1741	—	96	88	79
42	—	108	—	68
43	—	91	87	68
44	—	102	96	66
45	—	91	(96)	66
46	97	96	96	66
47	—	91	96	70
48	—	108	(96)	—
49	—	102	(96)	—
50	97	130	(96)	—
1751	100	125	96	71
52	97	91	96	79
53	97	91	88	79
54	145	91	—	89
55	145	91	—	89
56	(145)	91	100	89
57	145	91	(100)	76
58	97	91	100	75
59	97	91	100	77
60	—	91	100	87
1761	—	91	(100)	96
62	—	91ᵇ	(100)	105
63	—	—	100	105
64	—	—	100	92
65	—	—	100	87
66	—	—	100	92
67	—	—	100	92

TABLE 1 (*Continued*)

	Kyoto		Kamikawarabayashi	
	Carpenters (1)	Day laborers (2)	Carpenters (3)	Day laborers (4)
68	—	—	100	96
69	—	—	100	96
70	—	—	(100)	96
1771	—	—	100	96
72	—	—	100	96
73	100	—	100	96
74	100	—	(100)	90
75	(100)	—	(100)	90
76	(100)	—	(100)	(90)
77	100	—	100	90
78	100	—	—	90
79	100	—	—	89
80	100	—	—	—
1781	100	—	—	96
82	100	—	—	—
83	100	—	—	—
84	100	—	—	—
85	100	—	—	89
86	100	—	100	94
87	(100)	—	100	94
88	(100)	—	(100)	97
89	(100)	—	100	94
90	(100)	—	(100)	94
1791	(100)	91	100	97
92	100	108	(100)	101
93	100	102	100	101
94	(100)	91	100	101
95	(100)	96	(100)	(101)
96	(100)	91	(100)	99
97	100	91	(100)	99
98	100	96	(100)	(99)
99	100	91	(100)	99
1800	100	102	(100)	99
1801	(100)	91	(100)	99
02	100	91	(100)	99
03	100	91	(100)	102
04	100	119	100	99
05	100	85	(100)	99
06	(100)	68	(100)	99
07	(100)	68	(100)	(99)
08	100	74	(100)	(99)
09	100	96	(100)	(99)
10	100	102	(100)	99

TABLE 1 (*Continued*)

	Kyoto		Kamikawarabayashi	
	Carpenters (1)	Day laborers (2)	Carpenters (3)	Day laborers (4)
1811	100	96	(100)	99
12	100	102	(100)	100
13	100	108	(100)	101
14	100	119	(100)	100
15	100	119	(100)	101
16	100	108	(100)	103
17	100	96	(100)	108
18	(100)	102	(100)	105
19	(100)	96	—	104
20	(100)	96	—	102
1821	100	133[b]	—	101
22	100	—	—	101
23	100	—	—	102
24	100	—	—	102
25	100	—	—	97
26	100	—	—	100
27	100	—	—	—
28	100	—	—	—
29	100	—	—	99
30	100	—	—	106

[a] Figures in parentheses are those interpolated or, for column 3, estimated from the wage rate for plasterers.
[b] Spring only.
Sources: See text and footnotes 7 and 11–12.

throughout the whole period. The latter series is not given in Table 1, because in the original material all of the entries are given in a different monetary unit, i.e., *sen*. Using rates of conversion, we obtain the percentages of thatchers' to carpenters' wage rate: 67% in the early 1730s, 69% in the 1760s, and 62% in the base years, 1802–04 (note that these are not index numbers). The differential between rural and urban carpenters shows basically the same tendency. The differential indices, as the denominator of which Kyoto's is taken, are 94 in 1732, 99 in 1746, and 100 in the base years. Although the rural–urban differential seems to have narrowed in the earlier years, it would be difficult to say that it was a substantial change. Thus we may conclude that wages for farm laborers rose in the earlier decades faster than those for building craftsmen as a whole, whether rural or urban, and that this tendency continued until the early 1760s.

Turning to the comparison between wages for urban casual workers and for farm day laborers (Fig. 2), we notice two facts, despite the long break in

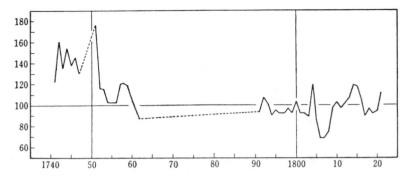

FIG. 2. The wage differential index between town and farm day laborers. Wage differential index = (wage index of Kyoto day laborers/wage index of farm day laborers) × 100 (for 1802–1804 = 100).
Source: Table 1 above.

the differential index series. One is that from the 1740s to the next decade the level of agricultural wages caught up with that of town laborers. This pattern parallels the one observed between agriculture and the building trades. The other is that during the period from 1791 to 1830 there was neither an upward nor a downward secular trend, although short-term fluctuations were not small. In 1802–04 the wage rate in Kyoto was at the 80% level of the male rate for springtime farm work. In farming there were several pay grades (although even its highest rate was low by urban standards) and the lowest grade was also set at the 80% level of the springtime rate. Putting these two findings together strongly suggests that the town rate for casual workers was equilibrated with the lowest level of agricultural wages throughout the period after the 1770s. This relationship indicates that the Kinai labor market had reached a new equilibrium position. To put it in a different way, the first phase might be regarded as a process during which the unification of rural and urban labor markets in Kinai was going on with respect to the unskilled labor force, so that the regional variations in their wages were to be reduced. The rigidity in the wage differential structure of the building trades could be seen from this point of view. With regard to skilled building craftsmen, perhaps the unification process had nearly been completed by the earlier years of the eighteenth century.

To sum up the whole period of 1727–1830, two phases exhibit a sharp contrast. The first was a period of narrowing wage differentials, whereas the second was not. The turning point appears to have been in the early 1760s. This dating may not be entirely conclusive, but it is certainly earlier than Nakamura (1968) supposed. In the first phase, however, not every aspect indicated a narrowing trend. In the building trades, whether rural or urban, the stability of the wage structure was evident throughout the first and second phases. The narrowing tendency itself consisted of two types of

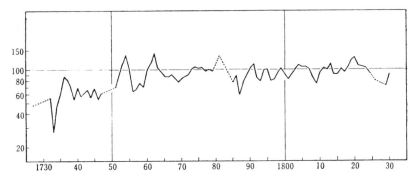

FIG. 3. The real wage index of farm day laborers (for 1802–1804 = 100).
Sources: Table 1 above. See also text.

change. One was geographical, the leveling of wages between town and farm day laborers belonging to this type. The other was occupational; a case in point is the one observed between farm laborers and building craftsmen. Now it is clear that it was agriculture, rather than other sectors, that was the prime mover of the major changes in the first phase. This conclusion is confirmed even further by an analysis of the course of real wages.

Real Wages

In order to estimate real wages, a suitable deflator is needed. But, as far as premodern times are concerned, there is little choice of price series. Here we use two different price series, both of which cover the whole period in question. One is the unbroken series of rice price in Osaka compiled in Yamazaki (1963a). The other is the Kyoto retail price index estimated in Umemura (1961) from the Mitsui records. This covers eleven commodities, although there are some breaks in the series.

Fig. 3 shows the course of real wages in agriculture, deflated with the Osaka rice price index. Taking a long view again, we notice that a steady rise in the real wage index took place in the earlier decades, during which it doubled. This continued up to the early 1760s and then the rise began to slow. The agricultural real wages, therefore, followed a course similar to that of wage differentials.

To confirm this point, annual rates of change in wages for carpentering and farm labor in Kamikawarabayashi have been calculated along with the Kyoto retail prices for two periods, 1730–1762 and 1762–1820.[14] Table 2 gives a measure of the contrast between the two phases. The rates of change, each of which can be approximately calculated by subtracting a rate of change in prices from that in money wages, are as follows: 1.6% for

[14] These dates are chosen to minimize the bias because they are peak years in the cyclical movement.

TABLE 2

Annual Rates of Increase in Wages and Prices

	Rates of increase (%)	
	1730–1762	1762–1820
Kamikawarabayashi		
Carpenters	1.6	0
Farm laborers	2.6	0.1
Kyoto		
Retail prices	1.0	−0.03

Sources: Table 1 above. See also text.

farm laborers and 0.6% for carpenters in the first phase, as against 0.1% for the former and a very small percentage change for the latter in the second phase. The rise in the first phase was a striking one. Although we have no direct evidence of when it actually began, it is likely that it dated from before 1730 and that it lasted at least for half a century. An annual rate of 1.6% compounded over 50 years means a more than twofold increase in wage earnings of peasant families, whose sons or daughters might otherwise have left the land to work elsewhere. It is in this context that the contraction in wage differentials took place.[15] It should be stressed, however, that this rising trend was not a sustained one. As far as the period up to 1820 is concerned, this does not mean that their wage earnings fell in real terms. But, this stagnant phase of the Kinai economy seems to have been ignored. This will be examined later when we address Yamamura's model of the late Tokugawa period.

III

Now that it is clear that agriculture played the primary role in the course of wage change, our next task is to provide a theoretical explanation.

We assume that there are two sectors: agricultural and nonagricultural. In the latter, the labor force is divided into various grades according to skill, and only unskilled workers can be recruited directly from the agricultural sector. For convenience, regional variations and the heterogeneity of labor in agriculture will not be taken into account. We also assume that the population and family size does not grow. In the Hicks model, although the rate of natural increase in rural population is supposed to be positive, the age composition would remain stable because of a constant outflow to

[15] This does not imply that when real wages began to move downward, wage differentials also began to widen. From 1820 to the late 1850s, both agricultural and building wages show little variation in money terms, so that the wage differential structure remained stable; see Saitō (1973) and Umemura (1961).

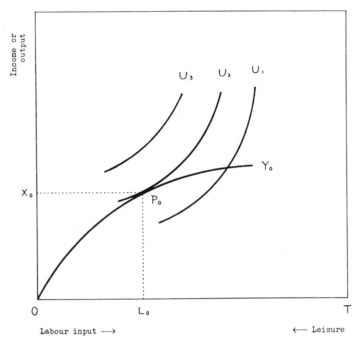

FIG. 4. Determination of output and labour input.

towns. In our model, however, since those who are drawn off from farming are not always emigrants to other places but may have employment at home, the assumption of static population and family size is necessary to keep constant the family's preference between income and leisure.[16] Fortunately enough, it seems realistic to make this assumption, because the Kinai population did not grow at all throughout the period in question.[17]

In general, the unit of analysis of the labor supply should be the family, not the individual in isolation who is supposed to behave by taking only changes in wages into consideration. In agricultural societies in particular, self-employed families characterize the supply side of the labor market. Thus the farm family is regarded here as a unit of production as well as consumption.

Suppose first that the farm family has no outside employment opportunities. In this case, there are two factors to be considered for the family to decide how many days should be worked in the course of the year: a preference between income and leisure and the output curve in farming.

[16] For the effects of population change, see my unpublished paper (1977) on eighteenth-century England. The effects on labor force participation of families are demonstrated.

[17] According to the *bakufu* population "censuses," the trend was rather a declining one; see Sekiyama (1958), pp. 140–1.

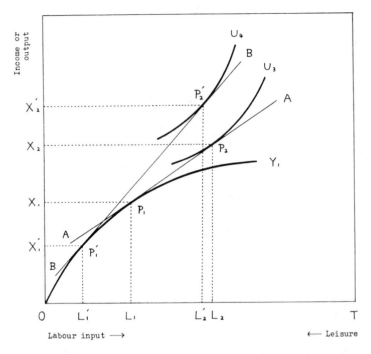

FIG. 5. Determination of the amount of labour supplied to the nonagricultural sector and effects of a change in wage rate.

In Fig. 4 income or output is measured along the vertical axis. OT represents the family's total time available, which consists of working days and leisure time. The family's preference function is given as U_0, $U_1, \ldots , U_n$; each indifference curve represents a locus of combinations of labor input and leisure time, which yield an equal amount of satisfaction. Y_0 shows how the total output varies with labor input per acre. The equilibrium point is P_0, where the slope of the output curve, the marginal productivity of labor, is equal to the slope of the indifference curve, and OL_0 represents the optimum working days for the family.

If a job which does not require special skill is offered from the outside, whether rural or urban, a third factor should be introduced, working conditions of the job offered. Let us assume that they are well reflected in the wage rate, which is indicated by the slope of line AA in Fig. 5. P_1 and P_2 are the optimum points, at which the wage-rate line is tangent to both the output curve and an indifference curve. OL_1 is devoted to farming and L_1L_2 to nonagricultural activities. Note that the wage rate for the nonagricultural unskilled is equal to marginal labor productivity in farming.[18] If the

[18] This proposition has been verified by Nishikawa for Chōshū-*han* in 1840. His observation is based on the comparison between the marginal labor productivity in the lowland, derived

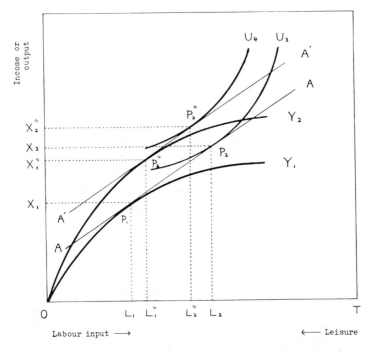

FIG. 6. Effects of increased agricultural productivity on labour supply.

agricultural wage is also determined according to marginal productivity of labor, then we will get the result that the wages in both sectors are set at the level of marginal labor productivity in agriculture.[19]

For any family there must be a certain wage level below which the family members would not work outside. This wage rate is called the "minimum supply price of labor." Now, imagine that the wage rate offered to the family members has raised above the minimum supply price (from line AA to line BB in Fig. 5). This will decrease the working days in farming and, probably, increase those devoted to the nonagricultural activity (OL_1 to OL_1' and L_1L_2 to L_1L_2', respectively).[20]

Finally, the effects of an increase in agricultural output owing to technical progress are illustrated in Fig. 6. The shift of the output curve reflects an increase in productivity. It is not difficult to see that the greater

from the estimated Cobb–Douglas-type agricultural production function, and the average wage rate for unskilled workers in salt farms; see Akimoto and Nishikawa (1975), and Shimbo, Hayami, and Nishikawa (1975), pp. 162–3.

[19] There is no need to suppose that the family is self-employed, if only this proposition is to be established.

[20] I say "probably" because, strictly speaking, whether or not the total amount of labor supply increases is dependent on the slope of the indifference curve.

the shift is, the higher the supply price of labor becomes. In other words, when their income from agriculture is sufficient enough, there will be no need for them to supplement their income by taking by-employment or by sending their children into service. Provided that the wage rate remains unchanged (which is indicated by the slope of line $A'A'$ that is parallel with line AA), a rise in agricultural productivity will be followed by a decline in the amount of labor supplied to the outside activity (L_1L_2 to $L_1''L_2''$ in Fig. 6), or if the amount of labor input in the commercial and manufacturing sector is to be maintained, the wage level will inevitably rise.

So far the emphasis has been on how important agricultural labor productivity is in determining the wage level for the unskilled; also examined are the effects of a rise in the wage rate offered, which can be interpreted as an indicator of the growth of industry and commerce and of a shift in agricultural productivity. Now, we turn to the application of these considerations to the actual situation.

IV

There can be no doubt that the effects of both industrial and commercial expansion and agricultural progress were intertwined. Commercialization of the Kinai agriculture was under way and its productivity was rising in the first half of the Tokugawa period.[21] Along with these developments, processing industries of agricultural products, such as *sake* brewing, rapeseed oil pressing, and cotton weaving, whose demand for labor was limited mainly to lower-grade workers, expanded outside Kyoto and Osaka. Building and its related trades, on the other hand, may not have been so flourishing, for Kinai's stagnant population seems to suggest that building activities in this region had reached a zenith by the end of the seventeenth century. Thus, the evidence is not inconsistent with the findings in section II.

On the other hand, the importance of agricultural growth should be emphasised. First, the dominance of agriculture in this period imposed a difficult task on industry with respect to the absorption of labor. The nonagricultural sector was so scattered that its fairly high rate of growth may have had a relatively small effect on the demand for labor in comparison with the vast agricultural population and, hence, a small effect on the general wage level and the wage structure.

Second, if the effect of a "pull" by industry had outweighed that of a rise in agricultural productivity and if the latter had been negligible, the total value of agricultural produce, despite the rise in marginal productivity, would have decreased, as is shown in Fig. 5 (OX_1 to OX_1'); this means that there would have been a substantial transformation in the Kinai economic structure, which would have made the whole Kinai region specialize in

[21] For a very brief summary, see Yamazaki (1963b), pp. 337–340.

industry and commerce and become a net "importer" of agricultural products. But this is not what actually happened; Kinai remained the most advanced agricultural region throughout the Tokugawa period.

Third, the rise in agricultural productivity may have made the Kinai industries less competitive compared with the same industries in other districts. Since most of these processing industries were not those characterized by massive investment in fixed capital, a further growth of these industries depended largely on the availability of cheap labor. Probably agriculture undermined this ground by raising the Kinai farm families' supply price of labor, hence making the cost of labor in the industrial sector higher. In-migration from areas outside Kinai could have made up for this; indeed, in the Nada *sake*-brewing industry this shift occurred to some extent. But, the stagnant Kinai population suggests that the flow of immigrants was not increasing.

This brings us to the final point. There is no serious question about the fate of industry and commerce in the Kinai economy after the second half of the eighteenth century, for both, having faced competition from other areas, could no longer enjoy relative prosperity.[22] Moreover, the static real wages and wage structure seem to suggest that even agriculture began to stagnate in the second half of the eighteenth century. This may be controversial, but again Kamikawarabayashi gives us some evidence on average land productivity. Although it was rising until 1830, the rate of increase was gradually decreasing,[23] and behind this phenomenon, the *rate of increase* of marginal labor productivity may have been moving toward zero.

Yamamura's two-region model of the Tokugawa economic development should be reexamined in this respect. According to him, development in the advanced region was accelerated during the late Tokugawa period, while the backward region grew but at a slower rate. He stresses the importance of the backward region's growth, having taken for granted the acceleration in the advanced region. As far as Kinai is concerned, however, what he took for granted is not true. Since there is scattered but unmistakable evidence for development in some less developed areas,[24] my picture of the Kinai labor market suggests that interregional wage differentials between the most advanced and other regions were narrowing, rather than widening, during the second half of the eighteenth century and after.[25]

[22] See, for example. Yagi (1962), Chap. 6, and Yasuoka (1959), Chaps. 1 and 5. Needless to say, Kinai was by no means a homogeneous region. It is, therefore, not surprising that in Izumi, a relatively backward province in Kinai, cotton weaving began to grow in this period.

[23] Imai and Yagi (1955), p. 105.

[24] With regard to real wages, see Saitō (1973) for the Suwa region and Yamamura (1973) for Morioka-*han*. Of course, there must have been regions where the rise in real wages did not occur. Musashi, the area around Edo, was likely one of such regions; see Saitō (1973), p. 181.

[25] This lends support to H. Shimbo's remark; see Shimbo, Hayami, and Nishikawa (1975), p. 278.

Perhaps, this becomes important when we discuss the continuity and discontinuity in the late Tokugawa and Meiji periods.

REFERENCES

Akimoto, H., and Nishikawa, S. (1975), "19-seiki chūyō Bōchō ryōgoku no nōgyō seisan kansū." *Keizai Kenkyū* **26**, 302–311.

Hicks, J. R. (1969), *A Theory of Economic History*, Oxford: Oxford University Press. Chap. 8.

Imai, R., and Yagi, A. (1955), *Hōken Shakai no Nōson Kōzō*, Tokyo: Yūhikaku.

Mitsui Bunko. (1952), *Kinsei-kōki ni okeru Shuyō Bukka no Dōtai*. Tokyo: Nihon Gakujutsu Shinkokai.

Nakamura, S. (1968), *Meiji Ishin no Kiso Kōzō*. Tokyo: Miraisha.

Odaka, K. (1976), "Kita-Kyūshū ni okeru kahei chingin no hendō." In Umemura, M., Shimbo, H., Nishikawa, S., and Hayami, A. (Eds.), *Nihon Keizai no Hatten: Kinsei kara Kindai e*. Tokyo: Nihon Keizai Shimbunsha.

Reder, M. W. (1955), "The Theory of Occupational Wage Differentials." *American Economic Review* **45**, 833–852.

Reynolds, L. G., and Taft, C. H. (1956), *The Evolution of Wage Structure*. New Haven: Yale University Press.

Saitō, O. (1973), "Nōgyō chingin no sūsei." *Shakai-keizaishigaku* **39**, 170–189.

Saitō, O. (1975), "Tokugawa chūki no jisshitsu chingin to kakusa." *Shakai-keizaishigaku* **41**, 449–466.

Saito, O. (1977), "The Demographic Impact on Labour Force Participation of Families in Eighteenth-Century England." Unpublished manuscript. Available from the author, Faculty of Economics, Keio University.

Sekiyama, N. (1958), *Kinsei Nihon no Jinkō Kōzō*. Tokyo: Yoshikawa Kōbunkan.

Shimbo, H., Hayami, A., and Nishikawa, S. (1975), *Sūryō Keizaishi Nyūmon*. Tokyo: Nihon Hyōronsha.

Smith, T. C. (1959), *Agrarian Origins of Modern Japan*. Stanford: Stanford University Press.

Smith, T. C. (1973), "Pre-Modern Economic Growth: Japan and the West." *Past and Present* **60**, 127–160.

Umemura, M. (1961), "Kenchiku rōdōsha no jisshitsu chingin, 1726–1958." *Keizai Kenkyū* **12**, 172–176.

Yagi, A. (1962), *Kinsei no Shōhin Ryūtsū*. Tokyo: Hanawa Shobō.

Yamamura, K. (1973), "Toward a Reexamination of the Economic History of Tokugawa Japan." *Journal of Economic History* **33**, 509–546.

Yamazaki, R. (1963a), "Kinsei-kōki ni okeru nōsanbutsu kakaku no dōkō." *Keizaigaku Nenpō* **19**, 109–168.

Yamazaki, R. (1963b), "Edo kōki ni okeru nōson keizai no hatten to nōminso bunkai." *Iwanami Kōza Nihon Rekishi* **12**, 331–374.

Yasuoka, S. (1959), *Nihon Hōken Keizai Seisaku Shiron*. Tokyo: Yūhikaku.

Bonner Zeitschrift für Japanologie, Vol. 8
Bonn 1986

SAITŌ OSAMU

SCENES OF JAPAN'S ECONOMIC DEVELOPMENT AND THE 'LONGUE DURÉE'

The purpose of this paper, as its title suggests, is quite ambitious. Starting with the beginnings of the Tokugawa regime, it covers about four centuries of economic change. At the same time, however, what I aim at in this paper is rather modest. Certainly it is not 'the causes of Japan's modern economic development', nor is it 'why Japan has succeeded'. The paper merely attempts to make an overview of changing scenes of Japan's long-term economic development and underlying tendencies characterising the scenes. By 'changing scenes' I mean shifts of the engine of growth from agriculture to rural handicraft, and from handicraft to factory, especially to that of heavy, chemical industry.and what is meant by 'underlying tendencies' is chiefly relationships between economic spurt and living standards of the population. In so doing, an attempt will also be made to place the so-called 'age of high economic growth', a rather unique period from, say, 1955 to 1975, in a very long-term, historical perspective.

I

Whenever an economist turns his (or her) eyes from year-to-year or decade-to-decade fluctuations of economic indicators to very long-term changes, he (or she) faces the question of periodization. The stage theory, be it Marxian, Rostovian, or that of the German historical school, is often suggested as a solution to this problem. But any stage-theoretic scheme has repeatedly been refuted and rejected by empirical works of historians. A recent alternative to the stage theory, the one which has increasingly become influential, is the approach by the *Annales* school. In 1958 Fernand Braudel brought three concepts of time into historical writings: *longue durée, conjoncture,* and event.[1] For the European economy, for instance, Braudel regards a long period from the fourteenth century to the mid-eighteenth as structurally coherent and resistant to change, so maintaining more or less the same position over several centuries. In short, the *longue durée* is 'a history of constant repetition, ever-recurring cycles'. Thus, half-century to full-century cycles, *conjonctures,* observable in price and population series in conjunction with other economic indicators and even in social and mental aspects during this long period, are likened to sea tides, observation of which enables us to investigate in detail the structure of the economy over the long period. A salient feature of the structural traits has often been described in terms of Malthusian economic demography. If, therefore, we turn to very long-term economic development in Japan, we, too, ought to think of it in terms of either *longue durée* or *conjonctures*.

Then a question arises: are we right in supposing that the *longue durée* from, say, 1600 was terminated with the Meiji Restoration of 1868, and that *conjonctures* in this long period were identifiable, upswings being in the seventeenth century and in the period after about 1820, with a stable and saturation period in-between, but without any clear-out downswing phase ?

Probably the periodization for the Tokugawa era poses little problem, as it is clear from recent historiography on price movements. In addition, the shift from the seventeenth-century to the eighteenth-century phase has long been recognized as an important epoch in many aspects of Tokugawa history other than price movements. However, Shimbo Hiroshi's book in 1978, as well as Umemura Mataji's article in 1981,[2] draw our attention to an equally important shift, which occured after the Bunsei debasement of 1818. They claim that in the 1820s and 1830s, not only inflation began due to increase in money supply, but that real economy also started to pick up. In other words, in the period after 1820 too, we can see changes in many aspects of the economy other than price movements. Their hypothesis, in my opinion, has increasingly gained support.

What ought to be questioned is, therefore, whether or not the Meiji Restoration can be considered a watershed in Japan's economic history. In fact the textbooks of Japanese history are still dominated by Restoration-watershed theory. However, recent works by some economic historians and history-oriented economists suggest that this theory is no longer tenable. Indeed, the arguments by Shimbo and Umemura did suggest that the roots of modern economic growth can be traced back to the 1820s and 1830s. The increase in the size of economy at that time was not simply a repetition of the seventeenth-century expansion, which was characterised by increases in both land reclamation and population, which led not only to an expansion of arable farming, but also to the construction of castle towns. Whereas the period after 1820 also saw growth in reclamation and population, their rates of increase were far lower than those in the seventeenth century; the annual rates of increase in population and arable land are less then 0.05 percent and about 0.1 percent, respectively, for the early nineteenth century, whereas those for the seventeenth are estimated as about 0.7 and 0.3 percent respectively.[3] What Shimbo and Umemura have made clear is that the engine of growth in the 1820s and 1830s was not arable farming, but the proliferated production of non-food commodities for various markets. It is important to note here that this change was marked in the countryside, and that this trend of what we would call rural industrialisation, or to use the term publicized in recent debates on European economic history, 'proto-industrialisation', is historically-linked to the modern economic growth which started in the Meiji era.

Thi. argument is strengthened by the findings concerning the size and structure of the traditional and modern sectors of Meiji and Taishō economy. By 'modern industry' I refer to those whose technology and business organisation were introduced from the West after about 1850. According to Nakamura Takafusa's painstaking estimates based on the first census of 1920,[4] of the working population engaged in the secondary and the tertiary industry, the share of the 'modern' sector was no more than 30 percent; the percentage did not exceed 40 percent even if the manufacturing sector was singled out. In this 'modern' sector computation includes all those employed in workshops (*kōjō*) with five or more operatives. Evidently the majority of workshops employing only five workers could not be genuine 'modern factories'. It is clear therefore, that the weight of the traditional, or *zairai* industry was much greater than we had once imagined.

Another evidence supporting this argument is provided by looking at the introduction of mechanical power in the course of industrialisation. In 1909, of all the workshops with five or more operatives only 28 percent were power-driven, and of total horsepower only 13 percent was accounted for by electric motors, 70 percent by steam engines and 11 percent by water wheels. The proportion of power-driven workshops rose rapidly since then; five years later, it was 46 percent, and by 1930, it reached the 80 percent line. As is well known, this process was accompanied by electrification. However, in early stages it was steam engines that electric power substituted for, while water wheels, a traditional form of motive power, increased in number. In fact, horsepower of water wheels quintupled from 1909 to 1921, equivalent to the rate of increase in total horsepower, although the number of water wheels dropped precipitantly after 1921.[5] Thus, by 1920, when the unprecedented boom occasioned by World War I collapsed, small workshops of traditional character had not yet been replaced by 'modern' factories.

These findings suggest, therefore, that despite much celebrated developments of borrowed technology-based, factory-type industry in the Meiji era, the size of the traditional sector was expanding at a steady, if not rapid, speed, up to 1920. It was not until the 1920s and 1930s, as Nakamura noted,[6] that the traditional sector began to change.

However, there still remains one problematic point: neither can we ignore the Western impact, nor do we dismiss adverse effects on domestic industries, especially on cotton textiles, of the opening of the Treaty ports in 1859. It is true that silk producing areas gained enormously from entering into world trade; but if cotton was hit hard and damaged by imports from the West, why could the traditional sector as a whole grow in the Meiji period ? Here it should be remembered that there are a minority of historians, albeit a growing minority,[7] who argue that the impact of cotton imports on domestic producers was hardly devastating. The Western impact was not a straightforward one; it was felt only through the intra-Asian trade networks, in which Chinese and other Asian merchants played a dominant role. And for cotton in particular, it is contended, domestic cloth was so thick and had so different a touch that imported cloth could not be a substitute for the traditional one.

At this stage of research it is premature for us to draw a conclusion. But I think it is fair to say that not a few industries of various parts of the country, whose commodities were, directly or indirectly, affected by the influx of imports, faced difficulties as a result of the entry into foreign trade, and had to go through the stirring years of the 1860s and 1870s. On the other hand, however, it is also true that while some rural industrial areas went into decay during this period, some others emerged as new centres, keeping their traditional outlook more or less intact. Indeed this supposition is consistent with what we know about cotton weaving in the first half of the Meiji period. In Mōka, Shimotsuke (part of present-day Tochigi-prefecture), and some Hōki areas (part of present-day Tottori-prefecture), for example, cotton cloth had been widely produced in the Tempō period (1830-1843), but disappeared after the commencement of foreign trade. On the other hand, southern parts of Senshū and Enshū (parts of present-day Ōsaka- and Shizuoka-prefectures), to name but a few, were new weaving centres that emerged after the late 1880s. Of course, weaving had been carried out from Tokugawa days in these areas, but they became known as major centres only in the mid-Meiji period.[8] Moreover, it is interesting to note, their growth was not achieved by establishing themselves as factory industries, but accomplished on a traditional, putting-out basis. In fact, the putting-out system was predominant in weaving, whether cotton, silk, or other fabrics, until around 1910 for several major centres, and until the 1920s for the rest of many, many weaving districts of the country.[9]

Finally, demography also points to a similar conclusion about the modern/premodern divide in economic and social history. Modernity in the demographic sense is featured by the widespread, deliberate control of fertility within marriage; and a shift from a state of 'no birth control whatsoever' or practising unconscious control through taboos and customs, to that of deliberate control, is called fertility transition. According to computation of measures of deliberate fertility control, the fertility transition did not take place until the 1930s; and a more sweeping break with the traditional pattern seems to have occured as late as the 1950s. Before this period, as a recent monograph by Carl Mosk suggests,[10] there existed an interlocking structure observable in terms of natural fertility (i.e. marital fertility for a couple showing no deliberate control), mortality (especially infant mortality), age at first marriage, and the standard of living. When the level of living standards rises, argues Mosk, there will occur an increase in natural fertility and a decline in infant mortality, on the one hand, and a rise in age at marriage, on the other; so that the age at marriage will be related positively to natural fertility, and negatively to infant mortality. Based on cross-section, county-level data in the interwar period, he provides us with findings that precisely exhibit the expected pattern of interrelationship.

This important observation indicates that before World War II, some kind of homeostatic mechanism was operating within the demographic system— 'homeostatic' in the sense different from that which is supposed to have functioned in 'pre-modern' Europe over several centuries up to the nineteenth century.[11] The mechanism observed for traditional Japan kept the rate of population increase lower than otherwise, nonetheless allowed population to grow as an improvement in living standards took place. In fact, what population history shows is that the country's population exhibited an upturn in the 1820s, the tempo of growth rising gradually towards the end of the Meiji era, then to the interwar period. What functioned behind this general trend in population is characteristically called a 'pre-modern' demographic regime.

II

Thus there seems no a priori reason to suppose that the Meiji Restoration was the great watershed in Japan's economic and social history. So, let us turn back to *'conjonctures'*, not in the Tokugawa period only, but for the moment in the entire period from Tokugawa to World War II.

For this long period we may identify three major phases of expansion of the economy. The first phase and the second are the seventeenth century and the period after 1820, to which I have already referred; the interwar period may be regarded as the third phase of expansion. By 'expansion' here is meant that of the size of economy as a whole; it should not be interpreted as anything measured in *per capita* terms. Each of those three, as suggested earlier, cannot be seen as a mere repeat of the previous one. While the seventeenth century was marked by the expansion of arable farming, the other two phases were featured by growth in non-agricultural and industrial activity: rural industry for the second phase, and heavy, chemical industry for the third. Parallel to this shift in the engine of growth is the change of the scene on which factors of growth played their parts. In the seventeenth century it was the increase in population and paddy fields in the fertile floodplains of major rivers that contributed most. This debouchment of the population onto the plains enabled small peasant families to depend more on arable farming, a change which has so far given Tokugawa peasantry the appearance of 'subsistence' economy. The early nineteenth century saw a proliferation of non-agricultural economic activity in rural areas,[12] not only in the plains this time, but sometimes in remote, mountainous areas also. Each region now tended to have its own specialities: sake, soy sauce, various kinds of textiles, and so forth, a good part of which were 'exported' to other regions through the commercial centre of Ōsaka.

This process of rural industrialisation, a more or less parallel one to European proto-industrialisation in the eighteenth century, was thus matched by both a geographical expansion and a penetration of the market in provincial areas, on the one hand, and by mobilisation of more human resources from the farm household sector, be entrepreneurial resources or out-workers as cheap labour, on the other (both of which, characteristically, took the form of farm family 'by-employment'). While this change is regarded as 'industrialisatton before industrialisation , the industries which started to grow in the interwar period were very different in nature from their precursors. Those which newly emerged were far larger in size, factory-based, and technologically far advanced, their labour force thus being more or less disciplined, internalised, and separated from land. Their products were not merely consumers' goods, but also producers' goods, which after World War II were increasingly substituted for imports. It is these industries that played a leading part in the postwar epoch of rapid economic growth.

Of course, the roots of each industrialisation process may be traced back beyond the epoch in question, thus one may come across, already at the beginning of the eighteenth century, a number of examples of locally manufactured goods sent to Ōsaka, while efforts levelled at import substitution by transplanting factory industry from the west were found in the *shokusan kōgyō* policies of the new Meiji government. Yet quantitatively there can be no doubt that full-fledged industrialisation gained momentum after World War I, and it seems probable, though based on scanty quantitative evidence, that an expansion of the size of rural industrial production in the eighteenth century was, if any, a very gradual one.

On the other hand, each of the epochs specified above was not necessarily the end of the previous cycle. It is certainly true that both agriculture and traditional industry were at a low ebb in the very same period of heavy, chemical industry's spurt. But such a coincidence was not always the case for the whole period before 1920. In fact, while the reclamation of arable land virtually came to an end at the beginning of the eighteenth century, that century saw a gradual, but steady rise in productivity in farming, especially in the Kinai, and the next century gradual diffusion of improved farming methods originated in the Kinai to provincial areas, then finally a general rise in land productivity again in the period from the Russo-Japanese War to World War I, after which it showed almost a sudden stop and stagnation. Similarly traditional industry exhibited a long life cycle, although its life course was much more volatile than agriculture's. In the 1820s and 1830s, by which Kinai agriculture had already reached its saturation phase, growth of local industry was observed in various parts of the regions outside the Kinai, which, as noted earlier, took the form of by-employment of the peasant farm household. Despite a geographical reshuffle occasioned by the opening of the Treaty ports and various institutional reforms in early Meiji years, followed by the so-called Matsukata deflation, the traditional sector as a whole seems to have, with tendencies of more regional specialisation, kept growing well into the twentieth century. It was indeed not until the interwar period when the structure of the national economy began to transform, traditional industry had either to decline, to come under control of big businesses, or to make a desperate effort to become factory industry itself.

Slicing the long period in this way is certainly a different approach from that of stage theory; and also, it should be stressed, it is somewhat different from the *Annales* school's. Cycles in the foregoing description are not just alternating patterns of upward and downward phases; they are 'life cycles' of dominant economic activity, whose time spans were different from each other, so that they sometimes overlapped one another. There is some merit in describing *conjonctures* in such a manner; it makes easier to understand some important topics in Japanese economic history. Take two examples as cases in point.

One is the question of why and how rural industrialisation gathered momentum in the 1820s, without any external stimuli such as an opening up of new international markets and transfers of high-level technology from the West. There is, at this stage of investigation, no ready-made answer to this interesting question. However, it is possible to work out one hypothesis.[13] The starting point is the eighteenth century, in which, as noted earlier, agricultural improvements and, hence, rises in living standards of peasants were attained in the Kinai. This had two effects. One was an increase in Kinai's demand for manufactured goods, especially those popularly priced goods such as cotton cloth dyed with indigo. The other effect was to raise levels of supply price of Kinai peasant labour to manufacturing like cotton weaving. The latter meant that even Kinai's rural putting-out industry tended to become less competitive in the inter-regional market. Against this background the Bunsei debasement of 1818 took place. It increased money supply enormously; but, according to Shimbo's argument, money was not simply thrown out onto the market, it was brought out through the *bakufu*'s expenditure. This had a Keynesian effect on the private sector of economy, creating an inflation gap. Equally important was the follow-up by various *han* governments, who increased the supply of paper money (*hansatsu*) in this period in the hope to finance local industry and commerce to 'export' their own specialities for inter-regional trade.[14] With this stimulus from above, rural industrialisation started in company with inflation. This process was also accompanied by shifts of industrial location from the Kinai and other advanced regions to provincial areas such as the new weaving centres in the Hokuriku and Kantō and silk reeling districts in central and eastern Japan, were peasant labour was still cheap. And inflation prevented real labour costs from increasing, so that substantial profits accrued to local entrepreneurs – substantial enough, probably, to keep rural industrialisation going.

Another example concerns scenario-writing for economic history of the whole period from Meiji to World War II. The conventional scenario is a uni-linear evolution of 'capitalism' or industrial society from early Meiji onwards. Yet the foregoing narrative of overlapping cycles does not suggest such an evolution. Rather it indicates a different story. In Meiji, or more precisely in the period from the late 1880s to 1920, both agriculture and traditional industry grew, as noted already, at a steady speed, while influences, be good or bad, of the spurt of full-fledged industrialisation were not yet fully felt. As for the interwar period situations were in marked contrast. It was the period in which heavy, chemical industrialisation started; at the same time, it was the period in which agriculture and traditional industry had to face a lot of difficulties. Admittedly, many textbooks still refer to the 'industrial revolution' in the mid-Meiji period. It is true that in the late 1880s there was a sudden increase in the number of joint stock companies, a substantial proportion of which were in cotton spinning. Since joint stock company is regarded as one indicator of economic modernity, and since cotton mills were one of the leading sector of the English industrial revolution, one might call the upswing in the late 1880s an 'industrial revolution'. However, it is also evident that the only modern industry whose products got a substantial share in total manufacturing output   was cotton spinning (with weaving sections run by the same cotton spinning firms). Of course, its share increased gradually, but it was not until 1914 that the percentage reached 10 percent.[15] This fact, together with the already noted finding that virtually no traditional industries were replaced by modern counterparts during the Meiji period, seem to suggest that the word 'industrial revolution' may be inappropriate for any period before World War I.

III

Now let us introduce one more factor, which has so far been excluded deliberately from the consideration of 'conjonctures'. That is changes in the level and differentials of living standards of the population, or to use readily available measures, wages and earnings. Throughout the European longue duree up to about 1750, an improvement in living standards and an increase in the size of production (and hence a general rise in prices) were not compatible. An examination of half-century, or even full-century cycles in the price and wage series reveals that price rises took place in conjunction with production expansion, but that population grew at the same time, so that money wages lagged behind. The consequence was thus a decline in real wages. This was indeed the case for the sixteenth century for almost all regions across Western Europe.

Historical data on wages were not ample for the Japanese case. Yet works so far done by Umemura Mataji, Odaka Kōnosuke, myself, and others, provide sufficient information to draw a rough sketch of the general course of wage changes over two centuries or more. Here I should like to pay as much attention as possible to changes in wage differentials and earnings inequality, as well as to changes in the general level of wages and earnings. In so doing, I hope, a little more will be added to our understanding of the relationship between economic expansion and living standards of people.

As to the seventeenth century, no usable series for wages are available, but it seems certain that agricultural wages hardly improved in real terms, since rice prices rose at a fairly rapid rate during the century, and since the rate of increase in grain output is estimated as 0.6 percent per annum,[16] a little lower than that of population. On the other hand, the next century, in which the total farm land area virtually stopped expanding, saw a rise in the general level of real wages together with a contraction in wage differentials. Probably in the Kinai, the change had already started in the late seventeenth century and by the 1760s and 1770s it reached a saturation phase. Indeed, this is the finding that I made by comparing a Seisetsu series for agricultural day labourers with those for building craftsmen in both a Seisetsu village and Kyōto.[17] There, marked contractions in wage differentials between skilled and unskilled, as well as urban and rural, took place in conjunction with an increase in agricultural real wages of 1.6 percent per annum, which compounded over 50 years, meant a more than twofold increase in peasant families' wage earnings. Although evidence for other regions is not yet sufficient, in the Kantō area, for example, similar changes were likely to have taken place from the late eighteenth to the early nineteenth century. However, as inflation started in the 1820s, so real wages started declining. Unfortunately, no analysis is available for trends in wage differentials from the 1820s to the Restoration. Yet as far as real wages are concerned, the downward tendency was unmistakable and ubiquitous.[18] Perhaps it was after the Matsukata deflation that recovery in the real wage series became recognizable. From the late 1880s onwards, the general level of wages seem to exhibit a slow rise in real terms up to the first decade of the twentieth century. Choice of occupation, deflator and time periods to be compared, however, makes a subtle difference. Umemura Mataji, for example, suggested 0.7 percent as an annual rate of increase in manufacturing wages for 1882 to 1914;[19] Yasuba Yasukichi gives 0.4 percent for four unskilled occupations from 1885 to 1905,[20] whereas Minami Ryōshin suggests a slightly negative figure for agricultural wages from 1893/99 to 1907/13.[21] At any rate, it may be safe to conclude tentatively that improvements, if any, were slight before World War I. On the other hand, there is concensus for the period after 1914, and for the general course of change in wage differentials from the 1880s to the 1930s. Real wages, after a sharp upturn during the war boom in the late 1910s, became stagnant, then started declining slightly, from the 1920s to the 1930s. As for wage differentials,[22] there occured no widening of gap between skilled and unskilled, and between industrial and agricultural occupations until the 1920s. It is from this decade that wage differentials and income inequality tended to become large, not only between agriculture and manufacturing, but also between large-scale and small-scale manufacturing industries. The so-called 'dual structure' took root firmly in the national economy. This structure emerged again in the 1950s, viz. at the very early stages of postwar rapid economic growth. However, after about 1960, as the annual rate of improvement in real wages recorded eight percent or more, there took place a sweeping contraction in wage and earnings differentials. Indeed, income-levelling was a consequence of the realisation process of 'income-doubling'.

Putting the foregoing chronology of long-term wage changes and changing scenes of economic development together, we may find some interesting patterns concerning *'conjonctures'* in the long period up to World War II.

291

1) In the phases of expansion in the size of production, whether it was agricultural expansion, proto-industrial growth, or spurt of factory-based industrialisation, either a decline in real wages and earnings or widening of wage and income differentials took place.

2) It was in a matured economy of the eighteenth century that wage differentials (and probably inequality in earnings also) contracted concurrently with rising levels of wages and income in real terms – 'matured' in the sense that growth in size of economy had virtually stopped, while productivity levels were kept reasonably high.

3) During the long period in question, therefore, economic spurt – not in *per capita* terms – was incompatible with substantial improvements in living standards at the lower sections of population, which could go on over, say, one generation or more.

There is one era which could have been an important exception to the above conclusions: that is the Meiji period. Of course, Meiji cannot be considered a matured economy; it was in a stirring state. GNP grew at a fairly high rate of, on average, about three percent per annum. Nonetheless, any pressures which the spurt of full-fledged industrialisation would have exerted were not felt yet. As we have seen, neither a substantial decline in real wages, nor a widening of earnings was recorded. Perhaps the fact that population was still in the 'pre-modern' demographic regime, so that the rate of its natural increase was lower than we had once imagined, and another fact that a very strong foreign demand for raw silk stimulated industrial activity in areas which had been (economically) 'backward' in Tokugawa times, contributed most. Anyhow, Meiji was a rare age in which 'balanced growth' was achieved – 'balanced', not only in that both agriculture and non-agriculture, and both modern and traditional sectors grew side by side, but in that the labour market, both inter-sectoral and intra-sectoral, was in equilibrium.[23]

As far as phases of expansion are concerned, therefore, the Japanese pattern of *'conjonctures'* is not inconsistent with that found in pre-industrial Europe. Of course, the mechanism by which such an empirical regularity concerning the relationship between economic spurt and living standards was shaped may be different. The mechanism suggested especially for the pre-industrial European continent (but not for England) is Malthusian,[24] while the eco-demographic system in the Japanese past is non-Malthusian.[25] Moreover, within the time span of the Japanese long period, the mechanism for one phase of expansion may well differ from that for another. Indeed, the ways in which income distribution and wage differentials became more unequal during the interwar period seem to have been similar to what Alexander Gerschenkron postulated in relation to the industrial spurt of 'late comer' countries,[26] while for proto-industrial growth in the 1820s and after market forces operating in inter-regional trade may have been important in responding to monetary stimuli. And in the seventeenth-century agricultural expansion, no doubt, ecology and *daimyō*'s effort played a leading part. Demography, too, may have played a different part in each phase of expansion. Nonetheless, it seems unwise to dismiss the observed 'repetitive and 'recurring' pattern of relationship between economic expansion and people's living standards as a mere coincidence.

IV

It is in this context that the age of high economic growth calls for special attention. This age was one of the phases of expansion. In fact, the performance of this phase was extraordinary. During one decade and a half real GNP quadrupled. And particularly for the decade from 1960, the year that inaugurated a new era in the banner of the Ikeda Cabinet's 'Income-doubling plan , it seems probably unique in that the spurt in economic growth did not exert pressure on people's living standards and inequality, but brought about b o t h a considerable rise in earnings and a marked contraction in earnings differentials, which in the past, as we have seen, were observed only in the eighteenth-century phase of shift to maturity.

The consequence of this growth was enormous and far-reaching in various aspects of our economic and social life. During the course of change, the proportion of working population engaged in agriculture and forestry dropped from more than one-third to less than one tenth. Agriculture could no longer occupy an important place in national economy. Thus, high economic growth has not only made people, especially those at the lower sections of society, rich, but has changed their life styles, work patterns, and relations with the natural environment.

Of course, this extraordinary growth cannot be a never-ending story. As a matter of fact, signs of the shift to slow growth are already visible. As the Nobel prize winner economist Sir John Hicks remarked, scarcity of labour can be the cause of the exhaustion of 'impulse' generated by technological invention, the 'mainspring of economic progress'.[27] Being rich per se, therefore, causes the scarcity of labour, which will in turn act as a brake upon economic growth. It may well be that, as Hicks himself noted at the end of the 1930s, with respect to the 'whole Industrial Revolution of the last two hundred years', the postwar 'high economic growth' of one decade or so was 'nothing else but a vast secular boom' and hence 'a disappointing episode in human history'.[28] Nevertheless, if we turn our eyes from the 'mainspring' and mechanism of economic growth to its economic and social consequences, no doubt, the 1960s was a great epoch, an epoch which probably terminated one long period in our history.

Notes

1)   F. Braudel, 'History and the social sciences', in P. Burke, ed., *Economy and society in early modern Europe: essays from Annales* (London, 1972). Originally published in *Annales: E.S.C.*, XIII (1958). See also his *The Mediterranean and the Mediterranean world in the age of Philip II* (London, 1972-73), preface.

2)   Shimbo, *Kinsei no bukka to keizai hatten* (Tōkyō, 1978); Umemura, 'Bakumatsu no keizai hatten', *Nenpō kindai Nihon kenkyū*, No. 3 (1981).

3)   Based on Shimbo Hiroshi, Hayami Akira and Nishikawa Shunsaku, *Sūryō keizai-shi nyūmon* (Tōkyō, 1975), ch. 3; and Miyamoto Matao, 'Hitori atari nōgyō sanshutsu-daka to seisan sho-yōso hiritsu', in Umemura Mataji, et. al., eds., *Nihon keizai no hatten*, QEH ronshū 1 (Tōkyō, 1976).

4)   Nakamura Takafusa, *Meiji Taishō-ki no Nihon keizai* (Tōkyō, 1985), ch. 8.

5)   Based on Minami Ryoshin, *Dōryoku kakumei to gijutsu shimpō* (Tōkyō, 1976), pp.222-226.

6)   Nakamura, op. cit. in note 4, pp. 183-185.

7)   See articles by Sugihara Kaoru and Kawakatsu Heita, in Special Issue on 'The Trading World of Asia', *Shakai keizai-shi gaku*, Vol. 51. No. 1 (1985).

8)   T. Nakamura, *Economic growth in prewar Japan* (New Haven, 1983), p.52.

9)   See Saitō Osamu, 'Zairai men-orimono-gyō ni okeru kōjōsei kōgyōka no sho-yōin', *Shakai Keizai-shi gaku*, Vol. 49, No. 6 (1984).

10) Carl Mosk, *Patriarchy and fertility: Japan and Sweden, 1880-1960* (New York, 1983).

11) For this contrast see my 'Population and the peasant family economy in proto-industrial Japan', *Journal of Family History*, VIII, No. 1 (1983); and also *Puroto-kōgyōka no jidai: Seiō to Nihon no hikaku-shi* (Tōkyō, 1985).

12) According to Nishikawa Shunsaku's pioneering quantitative analysis of the Chōshū-han economy, as much as 48 percent of the total product was non-agricultural. See his *Edo jidai no political economy* (Tōkyō, 1979), ch. 1.

13) This hypothesis has not yet been stated anywhere. The following is what I am currently outlining.

14) For han's development policy and hansatsu supply, see a recent piece by Nishikawa Shunsaku: 'Han senbai-sei no fukyū ni tsuite', *Keizai kenkyū*, XXXVI, No. 3 (1985).

15) Calculation is based on Shinohara Miyohei, *Kō-kōgyō*, Vol. 10 of *L.T.E.S.* (Tōkyō, 1972), pp. 142-143; and Fujino Shozaburō, et. al., *Sen'i kōgyō*, Vol. 11 of *L.T.E.S.* (Tōkyō, 1979), p. 243.

16) Based on Nakamura Satoru's estimates of 'Jisshū koku-daka' : *Meiji ishin no kiso kōzō* (Tōkyō, 1968), p. 170.

17) O.Saitō, 'The labor market in Tokugawa Japan: wage differentials and the real wage level, 1727-1830', *Explorations in Economic History*, XV, No. 1 (1978).

18) See for example Umemura Mataji, 'Kenchiku ródósha no jisshitsu chingin, 1726-1958'. *Keizai kenkyū*, XII, No. 2 (1961); and Shimbo, op. cit. in note 2, pp. 150-163.

19) Umemura, 'Meiji nenkan ni okeru jisshitsu chingin to ródō no kyōkyū', *Shakai keizai-shi gaku*, Vol. 27, No. 4 (1962), p. 21.

20) Yasuba, *Keizai seichō ron* (Tōkyō, 1980), p.160.

21) Minami, *Nihon no keizai hatten* (Tōkyō, 1981), p. 250.

22) The following account is based mainly on Umemura, loc. cit. in note 19, pp 34-35; Minami, op. cit. in note 21, pp. 257-263; and in particular, Odaka Kōnosuke, *Rōdō shijō bunseki: Nĳū kōzō no Nihonteki tenkai* (Tōkyō, 1984).

23) 'Balanced growth' is the term chosen by Nakamura Takafusa for the period before World War I, in his *Economic growth* (op. cit. in note 8).

24) See for example E. Le Roy Ladurie's statement in his inaugural lecture: 'L'histoire immobile', in *Le territoire de l'historien* (1973, 78).

25) For various models of the eco-demographic system and their relevance, see Saitō, op. cit. in note 11, ch. 4 and pp.243-246.

26) A.Gerschenkron, *Economic Backwardness in Historical Perspective* (Cambridge, Mass. 1976), especially ch. 1 and postscript.

27) J.R.Hicks, *Economic Perspectives: Further Essays on Money and Growth* (Oxford, 1977), p. 15.

28) J.R.Hicks, *Value and Capital* (Ofxord, 1939), p. 302n.

Note : I should like to thank my colleague Odaka Kōnosuke for his comments and suggestions offered during the preparation of this paper. Of course, I alone take full responsibility for the views expressed.

Journal of Banking and Finance 13 (1989) 487–513. North-Holland

FORWARDS AND FUTURES IN TOKUGAWA-PERIOD JAPAN

A New Perspective on the Dōjima Rice Market

Ulrike SCHAEDE*

Universität Marburg, 3550 Marburg, Federal Republic of Germany

Received May 1988, final version received March 1989

The first thoroughly organized futures exchange that fulfilled all the technical criteria specified by modern research in finance can be traced back to 18th century Japan. The Dōjima rice market in Ōsaka developed as a trading center for rice in the 17th century, and the futures market materialized according to the traders' needs; differences to modern futures exchanges can be observed in early mark-to-market procedures and margin requirements. If the role of rice in the pre-modern Japanese economy is acknowledged to be monetary, rice bill futures can also be regarded as financial futures.

1. Introduction

According to the most widely accepted view, the first thoroughly organized futures exchanges were those established at the end of the 19th century in Frankfurt (1867) and London (1877). To be sure, the Chicago Board of Trade was founded in 1848, but because of the Great Fire there are no records that show the exact nature of futures transactions in Chicago prior to 1871. In 1872, the New York Cotton Exchange was incorporated; it did not, however, provide for clearing facilities before 1892 [Seki (1985, p. 10), Kaufmann (1984, p. 11), Kolb (1985, p. 3)].

In Japan, an organized exchange with a standardized futures clearing system was officially permitted in Dōjima, a section of the city of Ōsaka, as early as in 1730. Various authors have suggested that this was a fully-fledged futures market [e.g., Sansom (1964, p. 126)]; some have even claimed that it was a financial futures market [Shimamoto (1969), Sakudō (1961, p. 345)]. However, it is not clear to what extent the Ōsaka market can be characterized as a futures market in the technical sense used in the modern literature of finance.

*This paper was written while the author was a Visiting Researcher at the Institute for Monetary and Economic Studies, The Bank of Japan. She is highly indebted to Dr. Shinji Takagi, Dr. Adrian E. Tschoegl, Professors Matao Miyamoto, Shunsaku Nishikawa, Kazui Tashiro, Hidekazu Eguchi and Erich Pauer for their insightful comments, and to the Japan Foundation for financial support. However, the author alone is responsible for the opinions expressed and all remaining errors.

0378/4266/89/$3.50 © 1989, Elsevier Science Publishers B.V. (North-Holland)

This paper will examine the exact operations of the Dōjima rice market during the Tokugawa-period (1603–1867) and evaluate how closely the Ōsaka market corresponded to what we now understand a futures market to be. It will show that, while Dōjima indeed can be evaluated as a futures market, it had a few characteristics that slightly differentiated it from its modern theoretical counterpart. Likewise, it requires some qualifications to characterize the Dōjima market as a financial futures market.

There are two fundamental questions to be raised. First, what would be the economic implications of the difference in practice, if any, between the Dōjima market and its modern counterpart? Dōjima developed without any guidance from financial authorities. Thus, this was a market that materialized solely in response to the needs of market participants, who made up their own rules in a way that best suited their needs. This contrasts sharply with today's markets. Differences between contemporary trading practices and those in the 18th century might either imply that the Dōjima market was imperfect or that contemporary rules do not meet the economic needs of market participants.

Secondly, what was the reason for futures trading practices to develop at all? As Telser and Higinbotham (1977) pointed out, it may be that the major motive for the introduction of an organized futures exchange is that of minimizing transaction costs. This issue will be dealt with briefly.

For an evaluation of Edo-period trading practices, the following criteria, necessary components of a futures market today, are used as a standard:

(1) only exchange members can participate in the market;
(2) contracts traded are standardized;
(3) for each position, a 'good-faith' money (margin) has to be deposited at the clearinghouse;
(4) trading is not bilateral, but the clearinghouse enters each transaction as a third party and guarantees the fulfillment of all contracts;
(5) the contract runs for a certain trading period and open positions are reassessed daily in accordance with price fluctuations (mark-to-market); and
(6) positions dissolved before the end of the trading period are cleared by cash settlement.

The paper will show that the Dōjima market practices generally satisfied these criteria except that it had different margin rules, different mark-to market mechanism, and several clearinghouses. The margin rules and the mark-to-market mechanism, modified when a new system was introduced in the 1860s, are probably of little substantive importance.

The analysis relies on primary materials [as reprinted in Shimamoto (1969, 1970)] as well as on early Japanese research [Suzuki (1940), Shimamoto (1953), Tanaka (1910)] that is based on such primary sources as merchants' notebooks. The paper builds on the pioneering work of Miyamato (1972, 1977a, b, 1982, 1986), by analyzing in greater detail the crucial role of rice bills as forwards or futures contracts as well as the clearing procedure in the whole trading system. The lack of reliable data, however, did not allow for a more quantitative examination of these issues.

The paper is organized as follows. Section 2 describes the evolution of Ōsaka as the so-called 'kitchen of the country' [Dohi (1981, p. 69)]. Section 3 presents the organization of the Dōjima market. Sections 4 and 5 describe the trading systems in forwards and futures respectively. Section 6 deals with the question of market efficiency and categorizes trading practices in Dōjima according to whether they were commodities or financial, traded as forwards or futures; it will argue that, if rice is considered to have had the function of money in the broadest sense during the Tokugawa period, futures traded on the rice market can be characterized as financial futures. Section 7 will give some final concluding remarks.

2. The emergence of Ōsaka as a trading center

In the 250 years of the Tokugawa period, Japan's population is estimated to have been remarkably stable at roughly 30 million people. Of this total, 87% were farmers, 5% were 'warriors' (*bushi*), who actually were the public servants of feudal domains (*han*), and 8% were merchants and artisans living in the cities [Sekiyama (1957, p. 247)]. The population of the city of Ōsaka was an estimated 200 000 in 1609; it doubled to 400 000 by the 1750s [Dohi (1983, p. 18)].[1]

The city became the 'kitchen of Japan' during the reign of Toyotomi Hideyoshi, the second of the three great unifiers of the country, who placed his castle in Ōsaka. In his attempt to unify the then divided country, Hideyoshi faced strong opposition from the nearby city of Sakai which had been a free town and the dominant trading city since the 14th century. Hideyoshi made an effort to make his castle town, Ōsaka, into the principal commercial base of the country in order to lure merchants away from independently-minded Sakai. He improved the infrastructure of the city by building a closely-knit channel system and requested the merchants to gather on a single spot right in the center, called Senba. An active market soon evolved in Senba and attracted Sakai merchants, thus eventually contributing to the fall of the former trading center.

Ōsaka became the most important rice market not only because of its already existing merchant community and distribution systems, but also because of its physical characteristics. Although Ōsaka was located on the

---

[1]Throughout the paper, dates are given in accordance with the primary sources, some of which are based on the old Japanese calendar. However, this differed only slightly from the Western calendar.

arterial roads connecting the east and the west of the country, it was even more important as a port. As losses were high when transporting rice on horseback through the mountainous and untraversed country, territorial (feudal) lords (*daimyō*) built their own ships, which they could easily unload in Ōsaka because of its many rivers and channels; warehouses were built along the waterfront.

Hideyoshi also began to unify Japan's currency system. In the 17th century Japan used gold coins, quantities of silver, and copper or iron coins [on the monetary system of Tokugawa-period Japan, see Crawcour (1961), Crawcour and Yamamura (1970), and BOJ (1974)]. Silver money was not coined, but had to be weighed for each transaction. As weighing was a great bother, silver went out of circulation in the 18th century. It remained as an accounting unit, however, because the silver system used decimal division.

Of equal importance with money was rice. Because rice was the most important product of an agrarian economy and largely homogeneous, it was the basic unit for taxation by the bakufu[2] and the feudal domains, i.e., the basis of national income. The size of a parcel land was measured in *koku* of rice producable on it, taxes were levied in rice, and emoluments to the *bushi* were disbursed in rice. However, it was only in the very beginning of the Tokugawa-period that rice was used as a means of payment.

Farmers had to pay a certain percentage of their annual harvest as tax to their feudal lords. What was left after the farmers' own consumption they sold to rice merchants on local markets. The local rice merchants in turn brought the rice to Ōsaka where all the large merchants were located. Similarly, the feudal lords used the rice they levied as tax to pay their retainers and for their own consumption, and sent the surplus to Ōsaka. The rice sent to Ōsaka was stored in warehouses (*kurayashiki*) until the sellers' trading agents in the city could bring it to the market.

In addition to the Ōsaka merchants, Ōsaka already had money changers (*ryōgae-ya*). Because the feudal lords needed to smooth out expenditures throughout the whole year out of annual shipments of rice, they developed a special relation with the money changers, who became the financial agents of the feudal lords and supplied credit against future rice transport.[3]

All important feudal lords had their own warehouse in Ōsaka in the 1670s. They sold rice by issuing a certificate of title to a certain amount of rice in the warehouse in exchange for money. The certificates were called rice bills and initially were traded in an occasional fashion in front of the house

---

[2]The bakufu or shogunate was the military government in Edo (present-day Tōkyō) as distinct from the court in Kyōto which had no political power.

[3]The city of Edo, which had become the seat of the bakufu in 1603, only started to develop when Ōsaka was already a fully-fledged trading center. In the 18th century, Edo began to catch up with Ōsaka in its size and role as an important rice market, because rice harvests of bakufu-owned domains and from some of the nothern domains were sent there. However, advanced trading practices as known in Ōsaka were never officially permitted in Edo.

of Yodoya, the outstanding trading house at the time. Because Yodoya was situated on the main road to Kitahama in the northern part of the city and the crowd of merchants who would gather there daily disturbed the traffic, in 1688 the authorities asked the merchants to gather in Dōjima, a small island at the delta of the three main rivers in the northern part of the city. In 1697, Yodoya himself moved to Dōjima, establishing the island as the central trading place, In 1730, the authorities officially acknowledged the market place as an exchange. It was at the same site that a modern commodities exchange was established in 1871[4].

3. Organization of the market

3.1 Warehouses

Ōsaka had 91 warehouses in 1673, and 124 in 1730 [Suzuki (1940, p. 6)]. The functions of a warehouse belonging to a particular domain were:

(1) to sell goods on hand (most importantly rice);
(2) to buy goods not available in the domain; and
(3) to arrange credit to the domain.

Management was in the hands of the warehouse superintendent (*kuramoto*). Initially, the warehouse superintendent was a *bushi* sent from the domain. As early as the 1660s, however, Ōsaka merchants took over the tasks of the superintendent (*chōnin-kuramoto*, merchant superintendents). The superintendent was responsible for organizing auctions in order to sell the rice and for selecting those merchants permitted to take part in his auction.

In addition, the warehouses had a special financial agent (*kakeya*, lit. 'money raiser') whose business very closely resembled that of a modern bank. The financial agent kept the books on all transactions, by recording such items as assets obtained from selling rice, credits granted to the feudal lord, and money transfers to the government in Edo on behalf of the domain. These were standing orders, i.e., they were automatic credit extensions to the domain. Furthermore, raising fees and delivering certificates became the task of the financial agents who expeditiously took over all of the auction proceedings [Suzuki (1940, p. 7–8), Miyamoto (1982, p. 53)].

3.2 Rice bills

While in most of Japan, including Edo, rice dealings were exclusively done

---

[4]Ōsaka also functioned as a trading place for numerous other goods at the time. An investigation of trading practices on such other markets is left for future research.

on a spot basis in the cash commodity, the dealing in Ōsaka was made through rice bills. In the 17th century, these bills were paid for immediately after the auction and changed into rice within a few days.

Rice bills (*kome-tegata* or *kome-gitte*) were introduced as a means to minimize the transaction costs of trading large volumes of rice that arrived in Ōsaka during a short period of time. Without the securitization of rice trading, it would have been more difficult to smoothe out rice consumption over the year and over Japan, and large temporal price fluctuations could have resulted. When brokers began to deal in bills until their maturity, maturities were soon extended up to 18 months – in spite of repeated bakufu reprimands (see section 3.3). The warehouses did not mind in the least, but began to issue unbacked bills and did not charge storage fees [Suzuki (1940, p. 86)]. Eventually, rice bills took the form of futures contracts as futures trading in rice emerged in the latter half of the 17th century.

In the beginning, the rice bill was a warehouse receipt. The issuer of a warehouse receipt in general cedes right of ownership to the purchaser and remains in charge of storage only. The receipt also defines the commodity in detail; along with the ownership, the bearer of the receipt takes the risk of damages and losses of the goods in storage. In Dōjima, however, the question of who bore the responsibility for safe storage was not generally settled until the beginning of the 18th century, when a fire burnt down the warehouses of the domains Kaga and Murakami (Echigo), two of the leading domains. While Murakami tried to maintain its reputation by declaring all bills written on its warehouses eligible, the Kaga domain insisted that no guarantee was given in case of losses due to fire or flood. Holders of Kaga bills protested sharply, putting the domain's political prestige at stake. In the event, the Kaga domain replaced the non-guarantee clause on its bills by a full guarantee [Miyamoto (1982, p. 54)].

As time went by, the rice bill came to acquire a new dimension that was independent of the underlying commodity. Whereas rice bills originally transferred the entitlement to a certain amount of rice at a certain warehouse from the issuer to the purchaser, they changed into more of a promissory note. The rice bills, however, differed from what we normally associate with contemporary promissory notes in that the bill carried a promise of delivery of physical commodities rather than a repayment of debt. In order to facilitate trading, these bills were standardized in terms of 10 *koku*[5] of rice counted in number of rice bales at around 1700. Moreover, some of the warehouses began to issue interest-bearing bills, i.e., the initial payment for the bill was one third of the face value plus interest on the remaining two thirds [Suzuki (1940, p. 10)].

With the issuance of unbacked rice bills and the further development of the market, bills with different rights and features appeared. One way to

[5]1 *koku* = 10 *to* = 180 litres.

categorize bills is a division into two types according to inscription. Bills that were issued after the arrival and immediate sale of rice, i.e., the backed and wholly paid-for bills, were called 'delivering bill' (*dashi-kitte*). They gave the running number of the bill, name of the buyer, number of bales, name of the auctioneer (financial agent), date of the auction and name of the warehouse. Bills that were issued without rice being on stock, i.e., unsecured bills, were called 'monk bills' (*bōzu-kitte*). The monk bill derived its name from the Buddhist practice of tonsure that resembled the practice of not inscribing the name of the purchaser, nor the date on the unsecured bills. Thus, monk bills are analogous to bearer bonds.

In general, securities can be divided into debt securities (such as bonds and mortgages) and ownership securities (such as stock certificates and titles to marketable assets). Depending on the manner in which they were issued, the rice bills traded in Tokugawa-period Dōjima took the shape of either a debt security or an ownership security.

'Delivering bills' and 'monk bills', together referred to as auction bills (*rakusatsu-kitte*), were sold by way of auction and were in effect ownership securities. Auction bills were delivered upon paying a 'good-faith' deposit, the amount of which varied according to the respective warehouse's rules and to the kind of bill issued. Such a bill represented evidence of a property right in a certain amount of rice which was stored in the warehouse.

On the other hand, 'prepayment bills' (*sennō-kitte*), issued without auction on payment, were closer to debt securities. These bills were also called 'empty (rice) bills' (*kūmai-kitte*), overdraft bills (*kamai-kitte*), or financial bills (*chōtatsu-kitte*, lit. '(money) raising bills'), each implying that they were issued without connection to the issuing warehouse's inventory. Neither the issuer (the warehouse) nor the purchaser regarded them as titles to physical rice. Instead, these bills were more like a note evidencing a credit extended by a merchant to a warehouse. In case the warehouse was not able to pay the credit back after one year the bill was converted into an auction bill, with the interest being payed either independently or added to the total sum [Miyamoto (1982, p. 54), Suzuki (1940, p. 200), Shimamoto (1953, p. 15)].

According to the Hachiboku-chō, a notebook on rice prices, bills in circulation represented more than 110,000 bales of rice in 1749, whereas the inventory at that time only amounted to approximately 30,000 bales [Hachiboku-chō, April 17th 1749, in: Shimamoto (1970)]. That is to say, the oustanding balance of rice bills represented almost four times the actual quantity of rice available for physical delivery.

These differences in the type of rice bills mean differences in the way the bills were traded. If the buyer had to furnish the whole amount of money on the day he bought a bill that was unbacked, he actually bought a bond. On the other hand, if the rice merchant bought a backed rice bill, he entered a forward contract. If this rice bill was standardized and being traded on the futures market, he effectively entered into a futures contract.

3.3 Government rice policy

As rice played the paramount role in the economy of the Tokugawa period, it is understandable that the bakufu in Edo pursued an active rice policy by issuing official decrees (*o-fure*) from time to time. The earliest of the recorded decrees were issued in the 1650s, discouraging the extensive issue of unbacked rice bills. Because the bakufu – rightly or wrongly – considered the expansion of unbacked rice bills to be the main cause of inflation, it prohibited unbacked rice bills in 1652[6]. In 1660, the bakufu altogether prohibited trading in rice bills and limited the maximum term of a bill to 30 days. In 1663, it further shortened the term to 10 days. The decrees, however, did not have the desired effect: the merchants now paid the total amount of the bill within 10 days, while the rice continued to remain in the warehouses and bills were traded as actively as before [Sakudō (1961, p. 348), Miyamoto (1972, p. 207)]. The bakufu seems to have abandoned the 10-day restriction a few years later.

Since decrees were of no effect, the bakufu looked for other ways to influence the rice market. The new scapegoat for rising prices was soon to be found in futures trading, the market in 'book transactions' (*chōaimai-akinai*), i.e., the trading in front of Yodoya's house that was said to be nothing but gambling[7]. In 1705, Yodoya's house was closed, his credits to feudal lords were declared void, and his impressive wealth was confiscated. The official reason for these actions was Yodoya's violation of sumptuary restrictions. However, the actual reason was the hope that dissolving the 'fictitious' gambling would stop the increase in rice prices [Sugie (1984, p. 17)]. In spite of these restrictive bakufu measures, book trading kept flourishing under cover in front of Yodoya's closed house.

The Kyōho era (1716–1735) under Tokugawa Yoshimune, who was also called the 'rice shōgun', saw a 180 degree reversal in government rice policy. The so-called Kyōho-reforms consisted, among others, of attempts to increase tax revenue by undertaking or encouraging additional rice land cultivation, a revision of the tax system and sumptuary regulations. Furthermore, the bakufu revalued the currency so that one *koku* of rice which sold for 200 *monme*[8] in 1714 sold for about 30 *monme* in 1718 [Sugie (1984, p. 24)]. Rice prices fell not only in nominal terms, but also in real terms because of a series of good harvest years. What the bakufu aimed at now was to reduce the general price level and to raise rice prices at the same time. Because the bakufu regarded the trading practices of the Dōjima rice

---

[6]One of the most important decrees at that time was issued in 1654, when the word bill (*tegata*) was mentioned by the officials for the first time. According to the decree, these bills were issued on payment of only a part of the total sum and 'passed through more than ten hands a day' [Ōsaka-shi Shiyakusho (1972, vol. 3, p. 47)].

[7]Coincidentally, midwestern American farmers tried for years to close down the Chicago Board of Trade on the argument that futures trading violated antigambling statutes.

[8]1 *monme* of silver was 17,36 grains.

merchants to be 'fictitious' and 'price-hiking', it officially authorized prolonged transactions in 1728; in 1730, the Dōjima rice market became the only officially acknowledged and organized futures exchange in Japan.

In recognizing the futures market, the decree of 1730 specifically stated [Shimamoto (1953, p. 9–10), emphasis added]:

(1) the aim of officially allowing the market was to increase rice prices;
(2) 'book transactions' must be conducted only *according to conventional practices* [to be explained later];
(3) clearing business was restricted to the 50 clearinghouses that *had been active in this business before* [1730];
(4) exchange members had to follow market rules; and
(5) only Dōjima, and no other market, could deal in book transactions.

As these suggest, book transactions had already been in existence as an established system with well-defined trading patterns by this time. Also, the authorization of an organized 'rice futures' market was meant to be temporary, because the bakufu initially intended to prohibit trading on the book as soon as rice prices rose again. However, once the market was formally established, the bakufu could not close it.

In the 1770s, the bakufu gave up its futile attempts to regulate the size of the rice bill market and decided to use qualitative measures. In 1773, it introduced 'suing-days' that made it possible for the merchants to bring suits in connection with fraud or default in rice bill trading to the governor of Ōsaka (*Ōsaka machi-bugyō*). If the suit was justified, the government paid out the claims. The bills were also safe even if the government confiscated the possession of a merchant or financial agent[9], because the merchant's rice bill holdings were transferred to his wife or children [Shimamoto (1953, p. 19, 22)]. The bakufu probably gave this guaranty in order not to topple the entire credit system. Because of these guaranties, rice bills were in effect equivalent to local bonds or bakufu-backed bonds, except that the rice bills were denominated in rice, whether or not physically defined. This distinguishing feature of rice bills has some crucial implications for the final evaluation of the trading practices.

3.4. Rice merchants

There were two types of rice merchants: so-called rice traders or rice wholesalers (*kome-donya*), and rice brokers (*kome-nakagai*). Whereas brokers (or retailers) in Edo typically bought their goods from the wholesalers and sold them on the market, brokers in Ōsaka followed totally different

---

[9]This happened quite often for several reasons, one being that a feudal lord or the bakufu itself was heavily indebted to a merchant.

practices. When Dōjima was officially acknowledged as a rice exchange in 1730, rice merchants were registered. In order to keep the number of rice merchants within controllable limits, the bakufu sold licenses (*kabu*): 500 in 1731, another 500 in April 1732, and 300 in November 1732. The first 500 licensed merchants obtained the most privileged position of rice traders (*tonya*), the remaining 800 became brokers [Shimamoto (1953, p. 57), Honjo (1954, p. 591)].

Tonya had the legal right to deal on the spot market as well as on the futures market. Some of the *tonya* were also active in warehouse rice delivery or rice transportation, even though most of them specialized in one field or another. Although we do not know how traders were divided into dealers and brokers on the exchange, it is clear that those traders permitted by the warehouses to participate in their auctions were elected among those 500 *tonya*. In this function, they were called *kura-namae*, lit. 'warehouse names'.

The so-called brokers, who bought the exchange license in 1732, were confined to only one of the activities in the market. On the exchange in Dōjima, they dealt in the rice bills previously bought at auction by the *tonya*.

Both types of merchants were required to pay an annual fee for the license, called *myōgakin* (lit. 'thanks-money'). This fee was in effect a trading license tax. The bakufu in return granted controlled market access in rice trading and especially in futures transactions. Issuing these licenses also enabled the bakufu to exercise close surveillance over the Ōsaka rice market.

More important than bakufu legislation, however, was the rice merchants' self-regulation. In the 1730s, the rice merchants formed groups or guilds (*kumiai, nakama*) based on the ward they lived in. The merchants of the same area and business who would not join the group were required to close their shops. The guilds were divided into those made up of licensed rice merchants (*kabu-nakama* 'licensed guild') and those not officially acknowledged (*nakama*) [Matsuyoshi (1932, p. 157)].

3.5. The exchange

The development and formalization of trading practices was not a government-led process but emanated from the market's own dynamics. The exchange was an autonomous, voluntary, non-profit association of its members, and its main function was supervising everyday trading, so it regulated brokers and auctions, settled disputes, registered official daily closing prices, and collected fees for its operations. Originally, exchange members were supposed to bear these expenses collectively, but payment was soon taken over by particular warehouses [see section 5.2, Tanaka (1910, p. 29)].

The staff of the exchange consisted of five so called 'annual directors' (*nengyōji*), five 'monthly directors' (*tsukigyōji*), 14 'watermen' (*mizukata*, whose function will be explained in section 5.3) and other officials with such special responsibilities as superivising rice transportation and daily trading practices. The board of directors was elected annually by the exchange members. During their honorary term of office, directors were not allowed to trade by themselves and had to leave business to their secretaries. Before the exchange building was completed in 1783, the house of the head of the board served as the office building. However, even though the annual directors enjoyed several benefits (e.g., tax exemption), the cost of being a director probably outweighed the benefits; it was a rather unpopular job. Directors often reported sick, or else engaged themselves in active trading precisely because this would result in suspension from the board. In 1774, the system was revised by making re-election possible and by abandoning the voting system; the directors in office began nominating their successors [Suzuki (1940), p. 57, Shimamoto (1953, p. 52)].

The exchange members of every ward (i.e., the members of the licensed guild) elected a head each month. Out of approximately 35 such heads, the five representing the largest groups made up the board of 'monthly directors'. These directors were intermediaries between the rice merchants and the board of 'annual directors'.

The clearing center (*keshiai-ba*, lit. 'settlement place') was near the market place. There were several clearinghouses which registered the open futures positions of their customers and settled them on liquidation days (see section 5.4). The cost of maintaining the central clearing place was paid for by the clearinghouses. Thus, the clearing center was an association of individual clearinghouses, and clerks at the clearing center were actually employees of the clearinghouses.

3.6. Clearinghouses

The original function of clearinghouses (*komegata-ryōgae* or *yarikuri-ryōgae*, lit. 'rice-merchants' money changer' or 'matchmaking agents') was to change rice into money and keep the deposits of rice merchants. The more actively rice bills were traded, the more difficult it was for a merchant to keep an eye on all his open interests in the futures market and settle all his transactions with a huge number of different trading partners. Therefore, he entrusted his daily market operations to his special money changer.

In 1731, 50 special licenses (*kabu*) were issued for these specialized money changers and another 10 in 1746. These houses were not permitted to trade in their own interest, but they could only fulfil orders. Their clientele was restricted to the licensed exchange members for whom they settled open trading positions. Moreover, on receiving margin payment, they took responsibility for the fulfillment of the contract [Suzuki (1940, p. 79)]. Thus, the merchants paid a margin and fees on their open positions and could in turn settle their positions at the clearinghouse without regard to the creditworthiness of the ultimate counterparty. In this interpretation, the clearinghouse provided intermediation services for futures market participants. This intermediation service is one of the key features of a modern futures exchange.

We can only guess what the exact margin requirements were. They seem to have fluctuated around 30% of the value traded, depending on the credit standing of the client as well as on prevailing market conditions[10]. Commissions were regulated by the exchange. The clearinghouses were not allowed to charge for clearing of daily trading positions. Probably because daily clearing constituted a highly labor-intensive business, the houses suffered a loss in daily clearing; of the original sixty houses that were established in the first half of the 18th century, only four survived into the 19th century. However, it is still remarkable that Ōsaka had four clearing institutions towards the end of the Tokugawa-period, while a modern exchange has only one clearinghouse.

4. The forward market

The eastern part of the Dōjima market place was designated for two kinds of transactions: *shōmai-akinai*, lit. 'dealings in real rice', and *nobemai-akinai*, lit. 'prolonged transactions'. Although the name 'dealings in real rice' is suggestive of spot transactions, the transactions so designated were in fact forwards.

4.1. 'Prolonged transactions'

Forward transactions, called prolonged trading (*nobeuri-nobegai*, lit. 'prolonged selling – prolonged buying'), developed as early as in the 1620s. Two parties contracted to exchange a certain amount of rice while extending delivery as well as payment to a specified future time. In other words, such a transaction was an agreement to complete trade at a future time and price specified when the agreement was made. The bills used for this kind of transaction were called 'prolongation bills' (*nobe-tegata*). They were drafts drawn on the buyer by the seller, but were not presented for payment before the contract matured [Honjo (1954, p. 1293)].

Prolonged transactions were 'empty' dealings, that is, the seller did not necessarily have the rice on hand at the time of the forward sale. This kind of transaction is said to have originated in an incident that happened during the years 1616–1621. A rice merchant from Nagoya frequently met a

[10]An entry in *'ina no ho'* ('On rice') evidences that margin requirements were lowered to one to two *monme* of silver per *koku* of rice in 1770 (Ōsaka-shi Shiyakusho 1927/V). This means 200 to 300 *monme* per trading contract of 100 *koku*, hence a minimal margin requirement of only 5%. This suggests that margin practices were not standardized, at least not over the entire Tokugawa-period.

colleague from Sendai on his business trips to Edo and exchanged information on harvest, weather conditions etc., in their hometowns. One day the Nagoya merchant learned of an impending bad harvest in the northern parts of Japan which would reduce rice shipments to Edo by about 50%. At the same time he knew that the Nagoya area would have a good harvest. Recognizing the potential profit opportunity, the Nagoya merchant bought the future harvest of his region by paying approximately 10% to the farmers and writing drafts for the rest of the negotiated amount. These drafts were not to be presented for payment before the rice was actually sold. When the harvest came in, he stored it and after three or four months sold it with a profit of 30–40%, as prices had climbed in the meantime [Sugie (1984, p. 5)]. The benefit for the seller (i.e., the farmer) was the advance payment of 10% and the guarantee he had about the future revenue he would receive from the known buyer. In other words, he could hedge his future income against rice price fluctuations. Soon other merchants copied the system, which became the prevailing trading practice and remained so until the 1650s.

This practice of buying in advance, i.e., taking a long position on unharvested rice without the money to pay for it, is the earliest form of forward transactions in Japan. Although it was a widespread trading method in the 17th century, prolonged transactions gradually lost much of their importance with the development of rice bills. It is improbable that prolongation bills were traded independent of the actual transaction.

4.2. The trading system

When rice bills came to be traded in the early 17th century, they were a receipt on the delivery of a certain amount of rice to be made within 30 days. The receipt was delivered upon payment of a fraction of total value as a good-faith deposit, which varied according to the rules of the various warehouses and to the kind of bills issued. An initial payment of 30% seems to have been the usual practice from the 1650s onward. In time, the scope of rice bills expanded to cover any bill written on any rice, and the bills' period of validity was extended from 30 days to more than a year.

In the first half of the 17th century, the basic pattern of rice trading appears to have been as follows:

For instance, a rice broker (*tonya*) would buy a bill on seven *koku* rice from a warehouse by paying about 30% (i.e., the margin) of the market price of the auction day. If the maturity of the bill (promise of delivery) was, for example, 25 days, the balance of the price would be due in 25 days from the day he purchased the bill at the latest. Thus, the bill represented a contract between two trading partners on the delivery of seven *koku* rice in 25 days at the price of the day on which the contract was made with an advance payment of 30%. This type of rice trading was thus a forward transaction. Such trading was already a forward transaction even during the

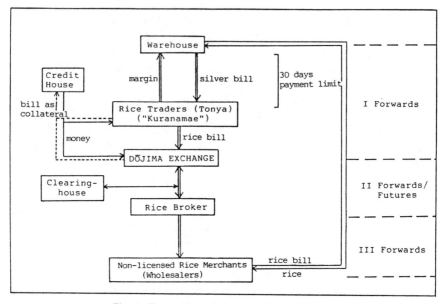

Fig. 1: Forward and futures market transactions.

first third of the 17th century, when the margin requirement was customarily 100%, i.e., when the full amount had to be paid on the day the agreement was made. The so-called 'dealings in real rice' probably derived their name from the fact that the underlying price of the contract was the current rice price of the day the contract was made, even if 'real rice' was not necessarily traded.

In the second half of the 17th century, the trading system became more intricate. With the standardization of rice bills, trading in futures became common. Fig. 1 will help to clarify the system.

As mentioned in section 3.4, there were two types of merchants: the *tonya* who were admitted to warehouse auctions, and the *nakagai* who did not have this right. The *tonya* deposited 30% of the total sum as 'good–faith' and for this received a receipt called silverbill (*gin-gitte*), which quoted the total price of the transaction in silver units. The *tonya* had to pay the 70% balance due within the next 30 days and received the rice bill (phase 1 in fig. 1), which he could then sell on the futures market in Dōjima (phase 2 in fig. 1)[11]. At some point, an exchange member might buy the rice for resale to

---

[11]Another kind of receipt issued at the auction against a margin payment was the 'defining receipt' (*sashi-gami*), which quoted the actual amount paid to the warehouse and was probably not traded.

a wholesale rice merchant who, in contrast to the exchange members, would buy the bill with the intention of taking possession of the underlying rice (phase 3). As the maturity of the rice bill was extended to more than one year, the bill could remain on the market for some time.

The *tonya* could, of course, trade their silverbills (margin receipts) before maturity and thus speculate on daily price fluctuations. A fully-fledged trading system emerged out of such practice, with so-called credit houses developing into financing institutions.

4.3. Credit houses and margin transactions

Credit houses (*irikae-ryōgae*, lit, 'pay and convert'-money changers) resemble today's securities financing firms (*shōken-kinyū-gaisha*) which finance margin transactions. The credit houses were wealthy money changers who extended credit against rice bills, silverbills or commodities as collateral. There were 20 houses of this kind, although only the largest six took part in volume business where credit sums exceeded 100 *koku* rice. In addition to charging interest, the credit houses earned profits by trading the bills which they had accepted as collateral. For this reason, the credit houses only accepted bearer bills (monk bills) as collateral [Shimamoto (1953, p. 35, 25–26); Honjo (1954, p. 69)].

The credit houses financed and traded with participants in the futures markets as well as the *tonya* depicted in phase 1 of fig. 1. The *tonya* would deposit his silverbills at the credit house and in turn receive a credit. The credit house would either give the bill back on.repayment of the credit sum or pay the outstanding balance to the financial agent and receive the rice bill itself. Thus, the credit house would lend either the face amount of the bill minus interest or just the margin. The actual amount of lending could also have been smaller than 70% of the face value of the silverbill (the margin certificate) by the amount of interest to be paid to the credit house.

The advantage of this type of credit financing for the *tonya* was as follows. Suppose that the *tonya* was convinced that rice prices would climb within the maturity of his silverbill. He would then ask a credit house for money, giving his first long (=buying) position to the house as collateral and opening up a second long position in the forward or futures market. If prices were indeed higher in a few days, the *tonya* could make a profit by selling his second long position. He would subsequently run to his credit house, buy back his silverbill and make a second capital gain by selling this one as well. Alternatively, if he had just borrowed the margin, he could sell the bill, repay the loan for the margin, and take the profit. In contrast to the contemporary practice of margin transactions, however, there is no evidence that credit houses in the Tokugawa period furnished securities; credits were given in money only.

311

5. The futures market

The further development of the original spot and forward market into a rice bill futures market was accomplished by

(1) the emergence of a fully-fledged secondary market for rice bills,
(2) the increased issues of standardized bearer bills, and
(3) the centralization of a clearinghouse in the trading process (phase 2 in fig. 1).

Trading futures was called '(rice) book transactions' (*chōaimai-akinai*). It can be reasonably assumed that trading on the book (i.e. settling positions without delivering contracts or goods) emerged in order to reduce transaction costs: having an organized exchange where all transactions in standardized contracts were settled by a central clearing institution allowed participants on the market to trade without regard for the credit standing of the counterparty (Telser and Higinbotham 1977).

5.1. The mechanics of trading

Trading periods. A year was divided into three periods: January 4–April 8, April 17–October 8, and October 17–December 24[12]. The market was closed for about 10 days between two succeeding trading periods in order to make a rollover of open positions to the following period impossible. The last day of every trading period was the liquidation day (*kiri-ichi*, lit. 'closing the market'), when all positions had to be settled. During the last three days of a trading period no new positions could be taken.

Standard rice (tatemono-mai). The rice traded in futures contracts changed with every period. The so-called 'winter-standard' (*fuyu-tate*) and 'spring standard' (*haru-tate*) were chosen from the harvest of the feudal domains of Chikuzen, Higo, Chūgoku, and Hiroshima, depending on which of the four had the best harvest. The 'summer standard' (*natsu-tate*) was rice from Kaga (or, if the harvest was poor, Yonago). A feudal domain benefited from furnishing the standard rice, because the standard commanded a premium price and the domain enjoyed a number of privileges during the period when its rice was used as the standard. In turn, the domain was willing to bear the expenses of the exchange for the period.

Trading unit. In principle, one contract (*ichi-mai*, lit. 'one sheet (of paper)') was written on 100 *koku* rice. It is not clear whether a contract could be

---

[12]Various sources give different dates for the three trading periods. The other dates are January 8 – April 27, May 7 – October 8, and October 17 – December 23.

written on higher amounts in 10 *koku* units, such as 130 *koku*. 100 *koku* rice was quoted by the number of rice bales which differed in size from region to region, such as 200 bales of 5 *to*, 250 bales of 4 *to*, or 300 bales of 3 *to*. Trading was quoted by the number of contracts. For example, '3 *mai* (bills) for 23' would have been 300 *koku* rice for 23 *monme* per *koku*.

Tick. Minimum price movements were measured in the market price for one hundredth of a unit of the standard contract, hence the price for 1 *koku*.

Margin. For taking a futures position, the trader had to deposit up to one third of the total amount traded as good-faith at a clearinghouse. This margin was not an individual deposit with the broker at the clearinghouse which would have varied in line with his positions; instead, the margin was traded with the contract, i.e., it was taken over by the next purchaser. The reason for this seems to be that, in the formative years of the system, the bilateral element in each transaction was still prevalent and only later did margin practices change into what they are today. Nevertheless, the underlying function was the same: in return for the margin, the clearinghouse guaranteed the fulfillment of the contract.

Accounting. There was no central book in which all transactions were registered. Instead, each exchange member had his own 'trading notebook' (*baibai-techō*), in which he made an entry on every contract detailing the amount traded. Every evening exchange members would pass the notebooks on to their clearinghouses, which would then collectively register all transactions of the day.

5.2. Price fixing

Trading began at 8 a.m. for futures and at 10 a.m. for forwards and spots. The futures price at 10 a.m. was written on a board and was the opening price for forward transactions. At 12 a.m., the exchange closed for a lunch break.

The closing price at the end of the afternoon trading session was fixed in a sophisticated method called the *ruiyō* system (lit. 'establish and use'[13]). A wooden box containing a fuse cord was hung at the ridgepole of the exchange building. Exchange officials put fire on the cord and allowed trading to continue as long as the box was on fire. The prevailing price at the moment the fire went out became the day's official closing price, called the 'fuse cord price' (*hinawa-nedan*). However, traders were little impressed

---

[13]The original meaning of this word is not clear. It could as well be interpreted as 'to burn out and use'.

by the official closing of the market and had to be stopped from continuing their transactions by the 'watermen' (*mizukata*) who splashed water all over the market place in order to disperse the trading crowd. Because splashing was also of limited effectiveness, in their second attempt the watermen would dash whole buckets of water over the crowd, which usually stopped the day's trading. The prevailing price at this time, the 'bucket price' (*oke-nedan*), was the actual daily trading price which was registered in the books and used for mark-to-market or settlement. On the other hand, the official fuse cord price became the opening price of the following day's session [Shimamoto (1953, p. 41), Suzuki (1940, p. 100–101)].

This price fixing system included a settlement obligation: if no price was found at the time the fire went out, or if the box did not burn down completely by itself for some reason, all transactions of the day were declared void and open positions that had been kept overnight had to be cleared by the fuse cord price of the preceding trading day [Sugie (1984, p. 46)].

This rule had both positive and negative effects. On the positive side, the clearing obligation made hoarding or dumping practices almost impossible. For example, if a broker engaged in hoarding purchases and other market participants became aware of this, they simply stopped trading and left him standing alone on the market place. No fuse cord price could be found, as there was no trading, and all transactions of the day were nullified. In this way, the *ruiyō*-system ruled out cornering.

On the negative side, the clearing obligation encouraged riotous behavior. A broker who had suffered great losses during the day could certainly try to disturb trading at the market closing time, e.g. by charging through the market place on a horse. Or else, he could try to extinguish the fire before the box had burnt down. Brokers who had a 'big day' certainly wanted to see the box burn down without interference and have a fuse cord price established for the day, so that they could finalize their gains. It is not difficult to imagine how two groups of brokers – not unlike two basketball teams – would end up fighting over the burning wooden box at the ridgepole of the exchange building at the end of the afternoon session.

Market disturbances of this type became more and more frequent during the second half of the Tokugawa-period, and then became the rule at the end of the period. It was often the case that the market could not establish a fuse cord price for several days in a row, leading to the final breakdown of the system. It should be stressed, however, that the system of fixing exchange prices by use of a wooden box was very effective in preventing market manipulation and hoarding for a substantial period of time. The obligation to register all positions at the end of the trading day at the clearinghouse at the bucket price was equivalent in function to today's mark-to-market mechanism, i.e., the daily reassessment of all open positions.

5.3. The clearing system

Evidence suggests that, for a substantial period of time, traders settled all positions at the end of each trading day. If this was impossible, they could hold a position at the clearinghouse only overnight. In the course of time, it became more common to retain positions over longer periods, as evidenced by the system of '10-day-clearing' (*keshiai-hi*, lit. 'liquidation day').

Every evening brokers went to their clearinghouses and transcribed their transactions of the day into the trading book of the house. Every ten days the secretaries of the clearinghouses met at the central clearing place and assessed the positions of their customers. If they found a customer's position not balanced, they asked for settlement on the following day. In particular, those who had suffered losses were asked to pay the difference (maintenance margin) and those who had gained profits received disbursements from the clearing center [Shimamoto (1953, p. 73), Tanaka (1910, p. 421), Suzuki (1940, p. 103–104)]. This system thus represented a ten-day mark-to-market mechanism.

A special system, here called 'cash-or-carry' (*shōgin-shōmai*, lit. 'real silver–real rice'), was introduced for settling all positions at the end of the trading period in 1737. This system allowed for settlement by physical delivery as well as in cash during the last three days of each trading period. As the standard rice changed with every period, the purpose of the close-of-trading day was to clear all positions, close the exchange and then start again with new rice. Although positions were supposed to be settled according to the ten-day pattern, those traders who had kept open positions or had not yet paid for their losses had to clear all obligations during the last three days of the period either in cash or in rice [Tanaka (1910, p. 52), Miyamoto (1982, p. 55). In practice, only few contracts were settled by physical delivery except at the very end of the Tokugawa-period.

It is worth mentioning that futures transactions without clearing at the central place, 'in-house' or 'retail' futures, also existed. 'In-house' futures were possible because of the existence of four clearinghouses (and even more in the first half of the 18th century). A clearinghouse could settle futures transactions of its own clientele without taking it to the market or contacting the other clearinghouses [cf. for details Tanaka (1910, p. 42), Suzuki (1940, p. 107)]. Although these 'in-house' transactions, which were not settled at the central clearing place, comprised only a small fraction of the total value of all futures transactions, they are important in that they cast a new light on the existence of multiple clearinghouses which allowed such 'in-house' transactions that are not usually associated with the current characterization of a futures market.

5.4. The 'small futures' market

What was called small futures or '*koku* futures' (*ko-akinai, kokudate-*

315

akinai, lit. 'trading per *koku*) began as early as book-rice transactions, but did not come into widespread use before the end of the Tokugawa-period. The *koku* futures market derives its name from the fact that in contrast to book transactions, the standard contract was written not on the usual 100 but on 20 (later 10) *koku*.

According to early-18th century records, the trading year was divided into six trading periods; trading in the following period's contract began 15 days before the running contract matured. Thus, the strict division of periods as known in the book-rice market was abandoned. The settlement price was the mean of the forward closing prices of the preceding three days. If the small futures prices deviated from forward prices by more than 15 *monme*, all open positions had to be settled by taking up reverse positions or by physical delivery. Thus, the system provided for a price limit which, in contrast to present-day practices, was linked to price movements on the cash market[14]. Daily transactions were registered at the clearing center and mark-to-market was done the next morning, with margins being disbursed or replenished. Unlike book transactions, the margin was not traded. As known today, the margin was a 'good-faith' deposit of one market participant with his clearinghouse [Sugie (1984, p. 55), Shimamoto (1953, p. 47)]. The reason for this change in system might be that market participants realized an opportunity for reducing transaction costs by keeping individual margins.

The system went through several modifications over the years, but was not very active between 1750 and 1850. The Tenpō-years (1830–1843) saw an economic downturn resulting from a series of bad harvests, rice riots, and an increasing indebtedness of the bakufu and domains to the merchant class. Although the spot and forward prices of rice rose along with the general price level, futures prices did not rise because the *ruiyō*-system made regular price fixing impossible, creating a wide spread between spot and futures prices (cf. fig. 2); the market in book transactions collapsed altogether. Also, clearinghouses raised commissions and margin requirements in order to minimize the risk of guaranteeing futures positions. By April 1866, the authorities had to close the market for forward and book-rice transactions [Sugie (1984, p. 56), Shimamoto (1953, p. 56, 49)].

Meanwhile, the small futures system had been revised and simplified in 1863: the trading unit was 10 *koku*: a trading period lasted for one month; settlement day was the last day of the month; and all remaining open positions were cleared at the price valid ten days before settlement [Shimamoto (1953, p. 49)]. Small futures trading under the new system was active between 1866 and April 1869, when the authorities closed the Dōjima rice market following the Meiji-Restoration. The significance of the small futures market lies not so much in the actual trading during this period as in its

---

[14]It is noteworthy and probably worth further study in the context of futures markets in the 1980s that, in a period of economic deterioration, price limits were introduced to the market.

impact on the new trading rules adopted for the Dōjima commodities exchange opened in 1871.

6. Evaluation of the market

It was not because of abstract insight or prior economic reasoning that the rice bill market in Dōjima was organized. Rather, the market was a natural result of the given economic necessities of the time and its evolution was shaped in a trial-and-error manner by the market participants, who traded bills in order either to speculate on price fluctuations or to shift the risk of price fluctuations onto those who were willing to bear it.

A trader who auctioned rice at the warehouse and intended to sell it in a few weeks could hedge his assets in rice bills against a possible decline in prices by simultaneously taking a futures position. A rice wholesaler who signed a contract to deliver rice at a future date without having the rice at hand could hedge against a possible increase in prices by simultaneously taking an opposite futures position.

Successful risk shifting requires that there be speculators who are willing to take the risk. There was no lack of profit-seeking rice brokers in Ōsaka, especially because the seasonality of prices made rice an ideal object for speculation. Furthermore, rice is an agricultural product whose output is much more vulnerable to natural conditions (weather, floods, plagues, etc.) than to the marketing strategies of its producers. Thus, the variability of price changes increased the need for hedging by some traders and also created ample scope for speculation by others.

In a series of papers, Miyamoto (1977a, b, 1986) demonstrated a high correlation between spot prices and futures prices from 1751 through to the 1830s on the basis of annual and quarterly average price fluctuations, and concluded that the market was efficient until around 1830, when the hedging function of the market began to deteriorate[15] (see fig. 2). Although the lack of reliable data precludes a more vigorous testing of the efficiency hypothesis, the very fact that the Dōjima futures market showed a constant high trading volume for more than 100 years must indicate that the market fulfilled its purposes.

Regarding the mechanics of trading, one can classify the different types of transactions on the Dōjima rice market into forwards and futures according to the system of fig. 3.

(1) The issue of a rice bill by the warehouse represented a promise to

---

[15]An analysis based on annual data seems to be deficient in one important respect: it includes the liquidation days on which spot and futures prices are equal; because the 'liquidation day' in fact covered a period of about 14 days (three days of liquidation procedures and ten to eleven days of exchange holidays), use of annual average data must bias the result toward higher correlation.

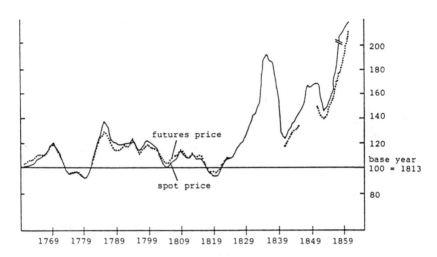

Fig. 2: Spot and futures prices between 1731 and 1859.
Source: Miyamoto (1977, p. 181).

deliver a specified amount of rice at a certain time in the future at the price of the day of settling the contract; this was a forward transaction.

(2) Trading (standardized) rice bills on the exchange, with a clearinghouse in charge of the settlement procedure and guaranteeing fulfillment of contracts, was a futures transaction.

(3) A rice bill that served as collateral at a credit house became a collateralized credit bill, but it regained its original character as a rice bill if it was then traded on the market; trading such a bill was thus a forward.

(4) The settlement of trading in credit bills, financing bills, or silverbills on the exchange was entrusted to clearinghouses; thus these were futures transactions.

Because the bills traded at the exchange were not bought (sold) in order to buy (sell) rice, there was hardly a connection to actual rice. However, the underlying commodity of all these bills, i.e., the commodity the bills were written on and priced in, was rice[16]. In this sense, the Dōjima rice market was a market for commodities forwards and futures.

Shimamoto (1953, 1969) and Sakudō (1961, p. 345) claim that the

---

[16]This is true for silverbills also, because they were written on a certain partial payment (margin) in relation to a certain amount of rice.

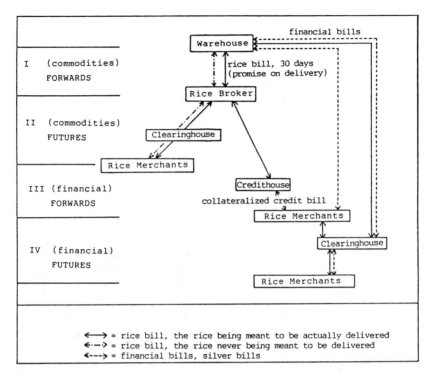

Fig. 3: The division of trading practices on the Dōjima exchange into forwards and futures.

Tokugawa-period Dōjima market was not a commodities exchange but was in fact a securities exchange. This claim is based on the assumption that no bill traded at Dōjima had any connection to its underlying commodity, and especially so the financing bills that made up the greater part of the contracts. As a logical extension of this assumption, trading practices in Dōjima would have to be divided into financial forwards and financial futures.

However, because it remains a fact that the underlying commodity of all contracts was rice, a more fundamental question concerns the extent to which the rice upon which the bills were written was in fact nothing but a commodity, or the extent to which rice can be considered to have functioned as 'money' in the Tokugawa-period. In the 17th and 18th century, rice played a unique role in the Japanese economy: size of land was measured in 'output of rice' (*kokudaka*), taxes were for the most part levied in rice, emoluments to *bushi* were paid in rice, and the wealth of merchants was mainly evaluated according to their holdings of rice bills. At the same time, there was a bona fide currency system with gold and copper (iron) coins and silver money as well as, in the second half of the period, government notes

319

and special notes and coins issued in each domain. This leads to two questions:

(1) Can a conventional currency system coexist with 'money in kind' (such as rice)?
(2) Can such 'money in kind' function both, as 'money' and as a non-monetary commodity?

In modern monetary theory, money must serve as

(1) a general (nationwide) medium of exchange,
(2) a store of value, and
(3) a unit of account.

According to these criteria, rice was never money in the strictest sense of the word. Although rice was used as a medium of exchange in local transactions at the very beginning of the Tokugawa-period, it was not used as a nationwide means of payment. Rice is also badly suited for storing valuables, except in its form as a rice bill. Rice, however, was used as the basic unit of account, particularly for fiscal purposes. If we want to fully capture the role of rice in Tokugawa-period Japan, a new concept of money may be needed, which allows for an object that is neither rare nor durable, neither quantitatively limited nor controllable, but nevertheless is the basic measuring unit of the economy and of economic policy.[17]

If rice in the Tokugawa-period is acknowledged to be monetary, rice bills can be categorized into commodity bills and securities, according to the way they were used. Fig. 3 then has to be divided into trading in commodities forwards and futures and trading in financial forwards and futures. In particular, financial forwards and futures would include transactions based on financial, credit, and silverbills as well as all unbacked bills (phases 3 and 4 in fig. 3). Under this interpretation, the Dōjima market was both, a commodities exchange and a securities exchange that offered forwards and futures in both parts of the market.

7. Summary and conclusions

Futures trading in rice, i.e., trading a certain kind of rice 'on the book'

---

[17]The ambiguous role of rice both as 'money' and as a commodity can be regarded as a reflection of the nature of financial systems prior to high degrees of specialization and the developments of fiat money replacing metals. The very same ambiguity can be observed in recent discussions as to whether gold should be considered simply as a commodity or as a monetary asset, and, accordingly, as to whether futures on gold are to be classified as commodities or financial futures.

based on a cash settlement system, materialized soon after the domains began to build their rice warehouses in Ōsaka. Rice bills were perfectly suited for futures trading, because

(1) the increased size of rice shipments to these warehouses in the mid-17th century provided market liquidity, and
(2) there were sharp seasonal fluctuations in these rice shipments.

Feudal lords who were typically in constant financial need, obtained financing in Ōsaka in two ways. One was the direct credit of an Ōsaka merchant. The second, indirect, was the issue of 'unbacked' rice bills that were empty promises of rice delivery. Because of the crucial role of this credit system in the economy, the bakufu began guaranteeing all rice bills in 1773, effectively changing the deficit financing bills of domains into bakufu-backed bonds.

In the 17th century, rice bills were traded as forwards. Maximum maturity was gradually extended to 18 months from the officially prescribed three weeks. When traders standardized bills in order to facilitate transactions, it sufficed to write all commitments in a personal trading book instead of exchanging the actual bill with each transaction. As trading became less and less bilateral, the merchants entrusted accounting and settlement procedures to one of the special settlement institutions, the clearinghouses. These houses in turn constituted an interdealer-market with a central clearing place and charged for registering, clearing and guaranteeing the fulfillment of the contracts. The margin requirement was between 5 and 30% of the total trading sum. The features of the trading system officially admitted in 1730 were as follows:

(1) one year consisted of three trading periods of a little less than four months each;
(2) the number of participants was confined to 1300 licensed rice merchants, i.e. exchange members;
(3) all contracts (i.e., rice bills) traded as futures were standardized;
(4) contracts were written on a certain brand of standard rice which was designated for each period;
(5) on the last day of the period all positions had to be cleared, either in cash or by physical delivery;
(6) the central clearing place, which was an institution made up of a number of individual clearinghouses, assumed contract obligations when a default occurred.

Judged against the integral features of a present-day futures market (see the introduction), 'book-rice' trading in Dōjima was undoubtedly trading in futures. However, the Dōjima market had three features that distinguished the market from contemporary markets. First, daily reassessment of positions entailed settlement of the entire position, at least in the 18th century. Second, the margin differed from the later 'small' futures system and current practices in that a margin was not an individual account of a client at his clearinghouse, but was traded along with his specific position. Third, the price fixing system, connected with a clearing obligation, was originally designed to discourage market manipulations. However, in the very long run the system proved to be unfeasible because it allowed market participants to influence the very existence of a closing price.

'Small futures' were traded during the last five years of the Tokugawa-period. The trading system meets all the criteria of a modern futures market and had an important influence on the Meiji-period Dōjima commodities exchange.

It is important to recognize that the spontaneous development of an organized exchange at which standardized contracts were traded seems to support the view that there is an economic need for such a standardized market as a mechanism to reduce transaction costs and provide market liquidity. Also, the development of the Dōjima rice market is a reflection of the sophistication and ingenuity of Tokugawa-period Japanese merchants.

References

Bank of Japan, Research Department (BOJ, Nihon ginkō chōsa-kyoku), 1974, Nihon no kahei, 3: Kinsei heisei no hatten (The currencies of Japan, 3: The development of a currency system in the Tokugawa period) (Tokyo-keizai shinpō-sha, Tokyo).

Crawcour, E.S., 1961, The development of a credit system in seventeenth century Japan, Journal of Economic History 21, No. 3, 342–360.

Crawcour, E.S. and K. Yamamura, 1970, The Tokugawa monetary system: 1787–1868, Economic Development and Cultural Change 18, No. 4, 489–518.

Dohi, Noritaka, 1981, Edo no Komeya (Rice merchants in Edo), 'Edo'-sensho 7 (Yoshikawa-kōbunsha, Tokyo).

Dohi, Noritaka, 1983, Kome to edo-jidai – kome-shōnin to torihiki no jittai (Rice in the Edo-period – Rice merchants and rice trading), 3rd ed. (Yūsankaku-shuppan, Tokyo).

Hara, Makoto and I. Arai, eds., 1986, Sakimono-torihiki (Futures transactions) (Yūhikaku-bijinesu 9, Tokyo).

Honjo, Eijiro, 1954, Nihon keizai-shi jiten (Dictionary of Japanese economic history) (Nihon-hyōron shinsha, Tokyo).

Kaufmann, P.J., ed., 1984, Handbook of futures markets – Commodity, financial stock index, and options, (Wiley, New York).

Kolb, R.W., 1985, Understanding futures markets (Glenview/Illinois, London).

Matsuyoshi Sadao, 1932, Nihon ryōgae-kinyū-shi ron (History of money changers and finance in Japan) (Bungei-shunjū-sha, Tokyo).

Miyamoto Matao, 1972, Kinsei Ōsaka-kurayashiki ni okeru haraigome-shihō (Rice payment methods in Tokugawa-period warehouses in Ōsaka), Kōbe daigaku keizaigaku-kenkyū nenpō 19, 188–219.

Miyamoto Matao, 1975, Kinsei-kōki Ōsaka ni okeru beika-hendō to beikoku-torihiki kikō–shōmai-kakaku to chōaimai-kakaku no ugoki (Rice price fluctuations and mechanisms of rice trading in Ōsaka in the late Tokugawa period – Fluctuations of spot and futures prices), Keizai-kenkyū 26, No. 4, 359–368.

Miyamoto Matao, 1977a, Kakaku to shijō no keisei (Prices and market formation), Keizai-shakai-shi gakkai, ed., Atarashii Edo-jidai-shizō o motomete (In search for a new perception of Tokugawa-period history), (Tōyō-keizai shinpō-sha, Tokyo), 199–223.

Miyamoto Matao, 1977b, Ōsaka kurayashiki no kome-gitte kyōkyū-kansū (Demand and supply functions for rice bills of the Ōsaka warehouses), in: Hidemura Senzo et al., eds., Kindai-keizai no rekishiteki kiban (Historical Foundations of the Modern Economy) (Minerva-shobō, Tokyo), 29–44.

Miyamoto Matao, 1982, Edo-jidai no kome-shijō – sono kōzō to kinō (The rice market in Edo-period Japan: Its structure and function), Kikan-Gendai-keizai, Spring, 48–63.

Miyamoto Matao, 1986, Emergence of National market and commercial activities in Tokugawa Japan – With special reference to the development of the rice market, Ōsaka Economic Papers 36, Nos. 1,2.

Ōsaka-shi Shiyakusho (Osaka City Office), 1927, Ōsaka-shi shi (History of the city of Ōsaka) (Seibundō, Ōsaka).

Ōsaka-shi Shiyakusho (Osaka City office), 1980, Ōsaka-shi shi (History of the city of Ōsaka) revised and reprinted edition (Seibundō, Ōsaka).

Sakudō Yōtarō, 1961, Nihon no kahei-kinyū-shi no kenkyū (Research on the history of Japanese currencies and finance) (Miraisha, Tokyo).

Sansom, G., 1964, A History of Japan, 3: 1615–1867 (The Cresset Press, London).

Seki Kaname, 1985, Saiken-sakimono-torihiki to zaimu-senryaku (Bond futures trading and financial strategies) (Kinyū-zaisei, Tokyo).

Sekiyama Naotaro, 1957, Kinsei Nihon no jinkō-kōzō (The population of Japan during the Tokugawa period) (Yoshikawa Kobunkan, Tokyo).

Shimamoto Tokuichi, 1953, Tokugawa-jidai no shōken-shijō no kenkyū (Research on the Tokugawa-period securities market) (Sangyō-keizai, Ōsaka).

Shimamoto Tokuichi, 1969, Dōjima kome-kaisho kobunken – sekai saiko no shōken-shijō (Early records on the Dōjima rice exchange – the oldest securities market of the world, Kinki daigaku sekai-keizai kenkyūjo, Sekai-keizai mondai kenkyū-sosho 9 Ōsaka).

Shimamoto Tokuichi, 1970, Dōjima kome-kaisho kobunken (Early records on the Dōjima rice exchange).

Sugie Masahiko, 1984, Tōki to sakimono-torihiki no riron (The theory of speculation and futures) (Chikuma Shobō, Tokyo).

Suzuki Shohei, 1940, Dōjima kome-shijō-shi (History of the Dojima rice market) (Nihon hyōron-sha, Tokyo).

Tanaka Tashichiro, 1910, Nihon-torihikijo ron (On exchanges in Japan) (Yūhikaku-shobō, Tokyo).

Telser, L.G. and H.H. Higinbotham, 1977, Organized futures markets: Costs and benefits, Journal of Political Economy 85, No. 5, 969–1000.

Both a Borrower and a Lender Be

From Village Moneylender to Rural Banker in the Tempō Era

RONALD P. TOBY

ELL before opening its ports to unlimited foreign trade and the advent of the Meiji industrialization, Japan had entered an 'age of protoindustrialization' in the late eighteenth and early nineteenth centuries.[1] A money economy was so far advanced that in some regions even rural households derived half or more of their income from wage labor, cottage industry, and other non-agricultural pursuits.[2] Indeed, a money-and-market orientation had progressively altered rural economic and social

THE AUTHOR is professor in the departments of History and East Asian Studies, University of Illinois, Urbana-Champaign. He is grateful for support from the Fulbright-Hays Faculty Research Abroad Program, a Hewlitt Summer Research Fellowship from the Office of International Programs and Studies, and generous research support from the Faculty Research Board of the University of Illinois at Urbana-Champaign; and the hospitality of the Faculty of Economics, Keio University, where he conducted most of the research for the present study.

[1] The notion of 'protoindustrialization' was articulated by Franklin Mendels in 'Proto-industrialization: The First Phase of the Industrialization Process', in *Journal of Economic History* [JEH], 32:1 (1972), pp. 241–61. It proposed a model characterized by 'the rapid growth of traditionally organized, but market-oriented, principally rural industry', whose production is destined for distant, as opposed to local markets, mediated by merchants and long-distance trade.

The fully articulated model also entails socio-demographic changes of the sort adumbrated in the work of Thomas C. Smith, *Agrarian Origins of Modern Japan*, Stanford U.P., 1959; 'Premodern Economic Growth, Japan and the West', in *Past & Present*, 60 (1973), pp. 127–60, etc. As Osamu Saitō notes in his review essay of Smith's work over the last thirty-five years, although 'Smith never used the term,' he may be credited with 'the discovery of proto-industrialization.' Saitō, 'Bringing the Covert Structure of the Past to Light', in JEH 49:4 (1989), pp. 992–99.

Following Saitō Osamu 斎藤修, *Puroto-kōgyōka no Jidai: Seiō to Nihon no Hikakushi* プロト工業化の時代：西欧と日本の比較史, Nihon Hyōronsha, 1985, I take 'protoindustrialization' here to characterize an era, rather than seeking some particular industry organized in a 'proto-industrial' manner.

[2] Thomas C. Smith, 'Farm Family By-employments in Pre-industrial Japan', in JEH 29:4 (1969), pp. 687–715, reprinted as Chapter 3 in Smith, *Native Sources of Japanese Industrialization, 1750–1920* University of California Press, 1988, estimated that 55% of farm-family income in one Chōshū county in the 1840s derived from non-agricultural pursuits. Using a

325

structure, promoting a differentiation of primarily agricultural villages from increasingly industrial ones. The latter relied on the market for ever-larger proportions of their income, for a growing portion of the raw materials essential to production, and for their consumption needs in food, fuel, and fiber. These changes favored smaller farm and household size, increased use of purchased materials and labor, and cash-crop outputs; as employment opportunities in the villages grew more numerous and attractive, urban centers began to lose population to the countryside.[3]

By the early nineteenth century the advancing rural industrial production, and long-distance trade brokered by rural merchants and destined for distant urban markets, demanded concentrated accumulations of capital to which nascent entrepreneurs might turn to finance their enterprises. Yet the place of credit and credit institutions in the age of protoindustrialization has yet to be systematically examined in either Japan or the West.[4] Here we will examine the operations of rural credit and creditors in rural Mino province (modern Gifu prefecture) in the years 1828–1844 to see how creditor organization and behavior changed in the protoindustrializing heartland.[5]

My discussion will be based on an examination of the banking ledgers of the Nishimatsu 西松 house, hereditary headmen of Nishijō, a peasant village in the polders of lowland Mino, some dozen kilometers southeast of Ōgaki, the nearest castle town, and thirty kilometers west of Nagoya, the city on which the economy of the Nōbi region was focused.[6] This examination will show that in the years under review the Nishimatsu credit enterprise was dramatically

---

broader, Chōshū-wide data set, Shunsaku Nishikawa, in 'The Economy of Chōshū on the Eve of Industrialization', in *The Economic Studies Quarterly*, 38:4 (December 1987), p. 335, arrived at a slightly lower figure, but his definitions are different from Smith's, so their conclusions may not be commensurable.

[3] Smith, 'Premodern Economic Growth'.

[4] Remarkably, neither credit nor credit institutions are part of Mendels's model or the general discussion of protoindustrialization, despite their importance to some earlier models of industrialization, especially Joseph Schumpeter, *The Theory of Economic Development: An Inquiry into Profits, Capital, Credit, Interest, and the Business Cycle*, Harvard U.P., 1936.

[5] On the economic geography of the nineteenth-century Nōbi region, see Hayami Akira 速水融, *Edo no Nōmin Seikatsu-shi: Shūmon Aratame Chō ni Miru Ichi Nōson* 江戸の農民生活史：宗門改帳にみる一農村, NHK Bukkusu, 1988, and Iwahashi Masaru 岩橋勝, 'Chihō Keizai Kōzō no Chirigaku: "Kōki Nōbi Chihō-ken" no Bunseki' 地方経済構造の地理学：「後期濃尾地方圏」の分析, in Shimbo Hiroshi 新保博 & Saitō Osamu 斎藤修, ed., *Nihon Keizaishi* 日本経済史, 2: *Kindai Seichō no Taidō* 近代成長の胎動, Iwanami, 1989, pp. 219–66. Hayami's study focuses on Nishijō.

Of particular importance in characterizing the Nōbi region as 'protoindustrial' in the late eighteenth and early nineteenth centuries is expanding production of striped cotton cloth, an industry that depended on long-distance trade for both raw materials and final markets. See especially Hayashi Hideo 林英夫, *Kinsei Nōson Kōgyō-shi no Kiso Katei* 近世農村工業史の基礎過程, Aoki, 1960, and Niwa Hiroshi 丹羽邦男, *Jinushi-sei no Keisei to Kōzō: Mino Shima Chitai ni okeru Jisshōteki Bunseki* 地主制の形成と構造：美濃縞地帯における実証的分析, Ochanomizu Shobō, 1982.

[6] For an introduction to the social ecology of the Edo-period Mino polders, see Thomas C. Smith, *Nakahara: Family Farming and Population in a Japanese Village, 1717–1830*, Stanford U.P., 1977, esp. Chapter 3; Hayami, *Edo no Nōmin Seikatsu-shi*. Smith's 'Nakahara' is a few kilometers west across the Ibi River from Nishijō.

transformed. Although the family had been lending on a modest scale locally since at least 1764, they seem to have relied almost entirely on their own funds for loan capital until 1837. Loan capital was thus limited to personal surpluses—the returns from land rents, interest from previous loans, and profits from other enterprises in which the family may have engaged.

Beginning in 1837, however, the Nishimatsu family relied increasingly for their loan capital on borrowing from a network of other local rural creditors like themselves. Where, as far as we can tell from their ledgers, virtually all their loan capital prior to 1837 was internally generated, borrowed capital thereafter accounted for an increasingly large proportion of total lending, rising from 10% in 1837 to as high as 77% in 1841, and it seems to have remained at levels of 60% or more from then on.

The Nishimatsu ledgers show that this change reflects broader developments among rural credit institutions—moneylending headmen such as Nishimatsu— in the Mino lowlands as a whole. More and more, local lenders relied on the growing network of interbank wholesale credit to finance their own local, retail lending. Whereas the Nishimatsu and their peers had up to then heeded half of Polonius's advice, lending but not borrowing, they now turned that advice on its head and became both borrowers and lenders. By doing so, each network participant had access to larger pools of capital than he would have had on his own. Consequently local borrowers had more efficient access to credit, at lower interest rates, than might have been the case had lenders been forced to continue relying on internally generated loan capital.

These pages present a picture of a hitherto unrecognized development of signal importance in Japanese economic history. The emergence of rural interbank networks in the protoindustrial countryside substantially increased the efficiency, mobility, and liquidity of the money supply in their regions, which in turn kept capital costs low and thus promoted rising investment in the secondary sector.[7] The significance of these developments lies principally in two

[7] I have seen no other study proposing wholesale credit networks in either urban or rural pre-Meiji Japan. There are examples of large urban ryōgae 両替 (moneychangers) such as the Kōnoike 鴻池 of Osaka, engaged in the packaging of funds from several lenders, for the specific purpose of so-called daimyō-gashi 大名貸 (lending-to-daimyo); in such cases, however, the Kōnoike acted as the pooling agent, but the risk was shared, as in a joint investment: the Kōnoike were not at risk to their fellow-creditors, but commonly, with them.

I am not aware of any instances in the English- or Japanese-language literature arguing the sort of wholesale interbank network of moneylenders-as-borrowers proposed here, where creditors used other people's money, capital borrowed at interest, to finance the operation and expansion of credit-supplying activities. Sakudō's data suggest that the Kōnoike also lent to village leaders near Osaka, who in turn re-lent these funds, while Kalland suggests in passing that by the late eighteenth century Fukuoka merchants were borrowing from public relief funds to re-lend at higher rates, but they do not pursue the implications of this point.

Sakudō Yōtarō 作道洋太郎, Kinsei Hōken Shakai no Kahei Kin'yū Kōzō 近世封建社会の貨幣金融構造, Hanawa, 1971, pp. 457, 515 & 520ff; Arne Kalland, 'A Credit Institution in Tokugawa Japan: The Ura-tamegin of Chikuzen Province', in Gordon Daniels, ed., Europe Interprets Japan, Paul Norbury, Tenterden, 1984, pp. 3-12 & 245-251; Arne Kalland, 'Rural Credit Institutions in Tokugawa Japan', unpublished, 1982.

areas, economic history and business history. Economically, as has been suggested here, the emergence of wholesale interbank credit networks helps explain how the protoindustrial expansion was financed, how (to follow W. G. Beasley's suggestion) Japan was able to generate sufficient capital to proto-industrialize in the early nineteenth century and to industrialize later without resort to foreign borrowing.[8] There is little doubt that the rural sector held substantial potential capital accumulations, for rural savings rates in some parts of the country approached 7%,[9] but it is unclear whether these accumulations were available for entrepreneurial investment, and if so, how they were made accessible to entrepreneurs.

From this perspective the economic importance of interbank networks is paralleled by their significance as a new mode of business organization and operation in the countryside, and by the willingness of credit entrepreneurs to undertake higher levels of risk in pursuit of new banking opportunities and more rapid growth. For it will be seen below that by entering into a regional interbank network of credit merchants, the Nishimatsu were able to effect a fourfold increase in the size of their lending operations within a decade; they transformed their business from a simple moneylending operation into something better characterized as a bank, while also freeing up sufficient capital to take up new forms of enterprise as well. Further, the Nishimatsu's experience suggests the high degree to which, by the Tempō era, 1830–1844, entrepreneurial activity, theirs and their customers' included, was dependent on borrowed capital.

Late Edo-period Credit and Creditors
Students of preindustrial Japan often see the local creditor as an exploitative usurer, reducing, rather than enhancing, peasant liquidity and economic opportunity. Village leaders, they say, charged 'high', 'outrageously high', or even 'usurious' interest rates on loans to desperate peasants. Many too readily accept E. H. Norman's assertion that borrowing was no more than the last resort of the peasant who 'turn[ed] in desperation to the userer', while credit relations were a prime mechanism for the expropriation of land, and the ultimate reduction of the peasantry to destitution in the face of 'conditions of life often below the subsistence level.'[10]

---

[8] W. G. Beasley, 'Foreword', in Shinya Sugiyama, *Japan's Industrialization in the World Economy, 1859–1899*, Athlone, London, 1988, p. xiii.

[9] Nishikawa, 'The Economy of Chōshū'.

[10] E. Herbert Norman, *Japan's Emergence as a Modern State*, Institute of Pacific Relations, New York, 1940, pp. 21–24.

A recent historian in this tradition is Herbert P. Bix, *Peasant Protest in Tokugawa Japan*, Yale U.P., p. 10: 'Under such circumstances [as "tribute exploitation" by fiefs and "a rigid status system"], the increased exposure by the poor to merchant moneylenders accelerated a debt cycle in villages and defaults on land, hence social poverty.' See also Anne Walthall, *Social Protest and Popular Culture in Eighteenth-Century Japan*, University of Arizona Press, 1986, pp. 7ff; Stephen Vlastos, *Peasant Protests and Uprisings in Tokugawa Japan*, University of California Press, 1986, p. 87.

William Jones Chambliss, *Chiaraijima Village: Land Tenure, Taxation, and Local Trade,*

Many who borrowed were surely the desperate poor, but others borrowed too. How else could peasant entrepreneurs gain access to capital accumulated as savings? In order for petty savings to be available to finance entrepreneurial activities, they must be packaged through institutions such as banks and made accessible to borrowers. Some of these functions were already performed on a small scale in the early nineteenth century by *mujinkō* 無尽講, voluntary mutual-aid associations in which peasants pooled savings and rotated the use of the pool among their members.[11] Another and larger source of credit was peasant moneylenders of the sort to be examined here, who lent their own savings, their surplus land rents, or accumulated profits from their other enterprises.[12]

Yet neither the *mujinkō* nor the village moneylender appears to add greatly to liquidity or greatly to increase the efficiency of the money supply in the rural economy: the former concentrated and assigned to one the funds of all, while the latter accumulated his own profits from land, lending, and other enterprises, and re-lent them at interest. Neither was capable of increasing its lending at a rate that exceeded its own (or the group's) profits. If credit was to grow faster than the ambient profit margins of preexisting enterprises, thus adding to the liquidity of the economy, reducing the cost of capital, and promoting new investment and growth, lenders—entrepreneurial lenders—had to find new ways to increase their lending beyond their personal capital and accumulated profits. Somewhere there had to emerge an institution capable of having a multiplier effect on the local money supply, something analogous to banks, which cumulate the petty savings of others, or otherwise direct available capital through loans to the investments of the entrepreneur.

In the towns, nascent bankers 'were accepting deposits [as well as] making loans in the 1640s and probably considerably earlier,' it has been argued, and in Osaka, Kyoto, and Edo, 'moneychangers were well on their way to becoming bankers by the 1680s.'[13] Some of these urban moneylenders, such as the

1818–1834, University of Arizona Press, 1965, pp. 36–38, takes the opposite view—that without credit and commercialization, 'the degree of wealth and standard of living in Chiaraijima would have been much closer to a subsistence level,' but later, p. 50, reverses himself to suggest that it was the 'hard pressed peasant' who turned to credit.

[11] For a brief analysis of *mujinkō*, or *tanomoshikō* 頼母子講, see Fukuyama Akira 福山昭, *Kinsei Nōson no Kin'yū Kōzō* 近世農村の金融構造, Yūzankaku, 1975, Chapter 3, or Sakurai Tokutarō 桜井徳太郎, *Kō Shūdan Seiritsu Katei no Kenkyū* 講集団成立過程の研究, Yoshikawa, 1962. For a fuller treatment, Yui Kennosuke 由井健之助, *Tanomoshikō to sono Hōritsu Kankei* 頼母子講と其の法律関係, Iwanami, 1935. See also Kalland, 'Rural Credit Institutions', pp. 11–14. Such institutions continue to function today in Japan and Korea (where they are called *kye*), and among Japanese- and Korean-American communities in the U.S.

[12] Most scholarship sees these as the principal sources of loan capital. Representative is Uemura Masaharu 植村正治, *Kinsei Nōson ni okeru Shijō Keizai no Tenkai* 近世農村における市場経済の展開, Dōbunkan, 1986, who finds, working from loan contracts, that the village lender he studied in Harima used exactly these sources of loan capital.

[13] E. S. Crawcour, 'The Development of a Credit System in Seventeenth-Century Japan', in JEH 21:3 (1961), pp. 348–49.

Crawcour is not explicit about the distinction between moneychanger and banker. See Henry Rosovsky, *Capital Formation in Japan*, Free Press of Glencoe, 1961, p. 75.

Kōnoike 鴻池 of Osaka, operated on a massive scale toward the end of the Edo period, lending sums exceeding the annual revenues of major daimyos.[14] But the rural moneylender in the historiography was a pure creditor who lent but did not borrow, who had capital at hand to lend in the form of accumulated profits from his land rents, other enterprises, and earlier loans-at-interest, but neither held deposits nor borrowed from others.[15] The rural creditor depicted in the historiography in the pre-Meiji countryside was a 'landowning-usurer' (Norman's term) in his countinghouse, but not yet, nor on his way to becoming, a banker. Histories of credit institutions, moneylending, and moneychanging in the Edo period abound; histories of 'banking' begin with the Meiji Restoration.

The present article distinguishes between the simple 'moneylender', or 'moneychanger', on the one hand, and the 'banker' on the other. The former relies exclusively on personal wealth and surplus revenues either from prior loans or from other entrepreneurial activities; since he 'has only his profits to reinvest . . . [he] is unable to . . . create a system of moneylending greater than his ordinary source of capital.' Bankers, by contrast, 'borrow from some in order to lend to others, and this process is regular and ordinary.'[16] By relying extensively on other people's money, which they borrow or accept on deposit, at interest, and relending it at higher rates of interest, bankers are indeed able to 'create a system of moneylending greater than [their] ordinary source of capital.' This transformation, as we have noted, has both organizational and socio-economic implications.

The changes in rural credit examined here are important not only in understanding economic change in protoindustrial Japan, but in the broader context of the protoindustrialization model itself. For although the role of credit has occupied the attention of both theoreticians and historians of economic change, it has been remarkably absent from the protoindustrialism debate itself. Schumpeter argues that credit is the essential catalyst enabling entrepreneurs to create 'new combinations' of production and to 'outbid' owners of older forms of 'combination' for the 'required means of productions'.[17]

---

[14] Sakudō, pp. 520ff, for example, finds the Kōnoike making loans to peasant capitalists averaging more than 2,500 *kan* (totalling more than 37,000 *kan*) of silver in the 1860s.

[15] For this nearly universal view, see Fujita Teiichirō 藤田悌一郎, 'Shōka no Shihon Chikuseki' 商家の資本蓄積, in Miyamoto Mataji 宮本又次 & Nakagawa Keiichirō 中川敬一郎, ed., *Edo Jidai no Kigyōka Katsudō* 江戸時代の企業家活動, Nihon Keizai Shimbun, 1977, pp. 118–44; Nagano Hiroko 長野ひろ子, *Bakuhansei Kokka no Keizai Kōzō* 幕藩制国家の経済構造, Yoshikawa, 1986; Nakayama Tomihiro 中山富広, 'Kinsei Kōki ni okeru Kashitsuke Shihon no Sonzai Keitai: Bingo Fuchū Nobuto-ke no Jirei' 近世後期における貸付資本の存在形態：備後府中延戸家の事例, in *Hiroshima Daigaku Shigaku Kenkyū*, 172 (1986), pp. 1–20; Sakudō, *Kinsei Hōken Shakai*; Yasuzawa Mine 安沢みね, 'Kinsei Kōki ni okeru Nōmin Kin'yū ni tsuite' 近世後期における農民金融について, in Hidemura Senzō 秀村選三 et al., ed., *Kindai Keizai no Rekishiteki Kiban* 近代経済の歴史的基盤, Minerva Shobō, 1977, pp. 63–76.

[16] Frank T. Melton, *Sir Robert Clayton and the Origins of English Deposit Banking, 1659–1685*, Cambridge U.P., pp. 9ff.

[17] Schumpeter, p. 71.

Some have even questioned 'whether Europe would have known an "Industrial Revolution" had not a "Financial Revolution" preceded it,'[18] while Alexander Gerschenkron, although questioning the significance of banks in Britain's industrialization, argues that elsewhere the role of finance may be crucial to explain the industrialization of 'backward' countries, including even continental Europe.[19] Yet students of protoindustrialization largely ignore the role of credit and finance in their analyses. Mendels, as noted above, did not include credit in his model; Hans Medick, with whom Mendels collaborated at times, sees credit as a hindrance to capital accumulation, investment, and economic advancement, and, as if borrowing indeed dulled the edge of husbandry, says that it 'functioned as an impediment to the productive use of potential income in the form of investment capital.'[20]

Recent students of the late-Tokugawa economy, beginning with Shimbo Hiroshi, have proposed a Keynesian argument, that a major stimulus to protoindustrial growth in the mid-nineteenth century was the bakufu's recoinage policies of the Bunsei period, 1818–1830, effectively an expansionary monetary policy. This new money entered the economy as bakufu expenditures, stimulating the economy at large. Entrepreneurial propensity to invest in new or expanded ventures, they argue, was stimulated by the resulting growth in the money supply and the slow secular inflation trend it initiated. The inflationary expectations of the age made investment in protoindustrial activity attractive, they conclude.[21] Similarly, as Hayashi Hideo has shown,[22] the

[18] Geoffrey Parker, 'The Emergence of Modern Finance in Europe, 1500–1750', in Carlo Cipolla, ed., The Fontana Economic History of Europe, Fontana Books, 1973, pp. 531ff.

[19] Alexander Gerschenkron, Economic Backwardness in Historical Perspective, Harvard U.P., 1962, pp. 11–16.

[20] Hans Medick, 'The Proto-industrial Family Economy', in Peter Kriedte et al., ed., Industrialization before Industrialization: Rural Industry in the Genesis of Capitalism, Cambridge U.P., 1981, p. 49.

Medick takes a dim view of the intelligence of peasant borrowers, suggesting that their borrowing dulled the edge of husbandry, as they wasted borrowed capital so that less was invested in production, capital formation was hindered, and the peasant family was driven 'into a vicious circle' of reliance on credit that prevented them from taking new occupational opportunities.

I don't wish to suggest that no Japanese peasants borrowed in desperation; many did, and many fled their bankruptcy, even in Nishijō. The borrowers in desperation, however, then as now, formed a different market segment, and generally went to different lenders. The issue of market segmentation in nineteenth-century Japanese credit, however, is complex and must be left to a separate discussion.

[21] Shimbo Hiroshi, Kinsei no Bukka to Keizai Hatten: Zen Kōgyō e no Sūryōteki Sekkin 近世の物価と経済発展：前工業への数量的接近, Tōyō Keizai Shimpōsha, 1978, pp. 58 & 74, calculates a 57% growth in coinage in circulation, 1818–1832; 8.4%, 1831–1836, an annual growth rate of slightly under 3%, and credits this growth in the money supply with instigating what Nishikawa Shunsaku has called the 'inflationary half-century' (infure no hanseiki), 1820–1870. Nishikawa Shunsaku 西川俊作, Edo Jidai no Poritikaru Ekonomii 江戸時代のポリティカル・エコノミー, Nihon Hyōron, 1979, p. 114. See Umemura Mataji 梅村又次, 'Bakumatsu no Keizai Hatten' 幕末の経済発展, in Bakumatsu-Ishin no Nihon: Nempō Kindai Nihon Kenkyū 幕末維新の日本：年報近代日本研究, Yamakawa, 1981, 3, pp. 1–30. See also Kozo Yamamura, Samurai Income and Entrepreneurship, Harvard U.P., 1974, p. 55.

[22] Hayashi, Kinsei Nōson, finds that merchants at all product chain stages, from raw materials to final market, in the shima-momen 縞木綿 (striped-cotton cloth) industry were

shima-momen 縞木綿 (stripe-woven cotton cloth) industry, whose development is central to the characterization of the Nōbi region in the late eighteenth and early nineteenth centuries as protoindustrial, depended heavily on various forms of credit. Thus a finding of local or regional networks of interbank credit that kept credit readily available and capital relatively cheap, would enhance the power of the Shimbo thesis to explain the protoindustrial age in Japan.

Gombei, Nishijō, and the Mino Polders

Nishijō was a medium-size farming village in the polder region of the lower Kiso-Nagara-Ibi watershed in Mino province, bounded on two sides by rivers diked to heights that loomed above the housetops, and on two sides by the fields of neighboring villages. A ferry connected Nishijō with Nakamura across the Nakamura River. Villagers raised several varieties of rice, wheat, barley, coarse grains, and beans, as well as rapeseed and cotton, which were cash crops. There was no oilpress in the village, so the rapeseed had to be sold as raw material or shipped out for pressing, in either case further enmeshing the village in market relations and the money economy. By the 1830s there was a *sake* brewery in the village as well, using 100 koku of rice a year, nearly one-third the village's production. Nishijō was a polder village, so fuel and lumber were scarce, and were bought from mountain villages upriver; some commercial fertilizers, bought with cash, were also used. Neighboring villages in the same polder housed carpenters, blacksmiths, sawyers, coopers, masons, oil pressers, and a physician.[23]

The women of Nishijō wove, but it is not clear whether this was subsistence weaving for home use or participation in the *shima-momen* industry. The emergence of regional specialization in the production of *shima-momen* is important in the characterization of late eighteenth-century to early nineteenth-century Japan as 'protoindustrial'. The degree of Nishijō's direct participation in *shima-momen* weaving, however, is not clear. As noted, the *mura meisai-chō* for the 1830s record weaving as a common occupation for women, but do not make it clear what they wove, or whether it was destined for home consumption or the market. But Nishijō was located almost exactly on the border between a major area of *shima-momen* production to the east across the Nagara and a principally agricultural area to the west. Several of the Nishimatsu's borrowers, lenders, and depositors were in the area that produced

plagued by collection difficulties, and that much of the industry operated on consignment or other forms of credit transactions. He also finds the industry dependent on long-distance trade for raw materials and markets, and capital relations as well increasingly interregional, for example, the Owari peasant-entrepreneur who bought raw materials (dyed cotton yarn) produced in Kii from a Kyoto merchant, had them processed in Owari, and sold the finished goods to a merchant in Matsuzaka (pp. 67ff).

[23] Wanouchi Chōshi Hensan Iinkai, comp., *Wanouchi Chōshi* 輪之内町史, 1981, pp. 855–75, contains *meisai-chō* 明細帳 from the 1830s for several villages in the polder. For the 100-koku production of the brewery, *Goyō Nikki* 御用日記, MS, 1835, in Nishimatsu-ke Monjo, Rikkyo University Library.

shima-momen.[24] It is just such regional specialization, with the industrial *shima-momen* production sector growing east, but not west, of the Nagara, that prompts Saitō and others to characterize this as a protoindustrial age.

Nishijō's population in the period 1820–1850 fluctuated widely between 277 and 330 persons, and 66 and 76 households, partly owing to mortality and migration during the Tempō famine, 1837–1839.[25] Located within a half-day walk of Ōgaki (Nishijō was a *tenryō* 天領, or shogunal fisc, village, administered by Ōgaki han as agent for the bakufu) and about a day's walk from Nagoya, Gifu, or Kuwana, where it delivered its tax-rice. Lacking its own sources of fuel, fertilizer, and construction materials, Nishijō was early enmeshed in the market and the money economy.[26] For some administrative purposes, Nishijō was joined with its neighbor to the south, Niremata, although each had its own headman (*shōya* 庄屋); further, the east part of Nishijō had a separate informal name, Jūrembō, which occasionally appears in the records.

The heads of the Nishimatsu house, who all took the name Gombei 権兵衛, were hereditary headmen of Nishijō and its wealthiest residents from at least the 1770s; they had been engaged in moneylending as a distinct business enterprise from at least the mid-eighteenth century. Their ancestors had been village officers and major landholders since the early seventeenth century and appear to have been descended from local samurai who were residing in Nishijō by 1588.[27] Although most residents of Nishijō were Jōdo Shinshū adherents affiliated with temples in the village, the Nishimatsu main and branch houses were affiliated with a Rinzai Zen temple in another village a few kilometers south, and the family graves were located there as well.

The history of the headship of both the village and the Nishimatsu house may be relevant to an understanding of Gombei's behavior as a local creditor during the period under examination. Gombei I had succeeded his father to become head of both the house and the village in 1804, governing the village, overseeing his tenants, and managing his moneylending operations. Especially in the decade beginning in 1811 there had been a rapid turnover in land titles in Nishijō, leaving Gombei I and a village priest with much larger holdings than a few years earlier. The priest, who had possessed no registered land previously, appeared with 26 koku in 1811, and 29 in 1814; Gombei's holdings had gone

---

[24] Niwa, p. 17, maps the principal *shima-momen* area of Mino, which is essentially east of the Nagara. Only three villages in Anpachi-gun, which includes Nishijō, are shown as *shima-momen* producers, and Nishijō is not among them. In 1888 this region produced 98.5% of Gifu-ken's *shima-momen*; Anpachi-gun, almost none.

[25] *Mino-no-kuni Niremata-mura no uchi Nishijō-mura Shūmon Ninbetsu On-aratame Chō* 美濃国俟村之内西条村宗門人別御改帳 [SAC], MS, 97 volumes, 1773–1869, in Nishimatsu-ke Monjo, Rikkyo University Library. Precise titles vary slightly from year to year.

[26] As early as 1620, for example, Nishijō's taxes were due partly in cash, although calculated in kind. *Chōshi*, p. 806.

[27] SAC, 1773 & 1774; *Chōshi*, p. 805; *Nayosechō* 名寄帳, MS (1660), Nishimatsu-ke Monjo, Ōgaki Municipal Library; '[*Ichihashi-ke Monjo*] *Chigyō Mokuroku*' 知行目録, 1588, Ichihashi-ke Monjo, in *Chōshi*, p. 75.

from 49 koku in 1773, to 86 in 1801, and 120 in 1825.[28] As the Nishimatsu land-holdings more than doubled, their share of total village arable rose from less than one-sixth to more than one-third (38%); by 1833 the main and branch Nishimatsu houses held nearly half the village farmland, although they made up only one-twentieth of the households.[29] Yet after 1833, Nishimatsu land-holdings in Nishijō did not rise significantly through the end of the Edo period.

The rapid concentration of village arable in the hands of the headman and the priest may merely reflect changes in the way landholding was registered; the village also saw a large increase in the number of formerly landless (*mizunomi* 水呑) listed as holders for the first time.[30] But the accumulation of land by head-man and priest likely represents the results, either delayed or immediate, of foreclosures on bad loans. At the least, it was resentment against Gombei I for abusing his position as headman and principal source of credit that provoked a village protest led by the second-largest landholder, forcing him to retire from office in 1818. Although he appears to have retained the name Gombei, the headship of the Nishimatsu house and management of its land and business interests until his death in 1837, headship of the village was transferred to his eighteen-year-old son, Kitasuke 喜多助, under the supervision of a headman from a neighboring village.[31] Gombei I may well have been chastened in his greed by this experience. But some of the most significant changes in the organization of the Nishimatsu credit operation appear in 1837, after Gombei I had died, and they probably reflect an infusion of new ideas introduced by a new generation of leadership, as Kitasuke succeeded as Gombei II and began to manage the family enterprises.

Sources
The principal sources for this study are the moneylending and banking ledgers of the Nishimatsu family,[32] which form a nearly complete annual series from

[28] SAC. The landholding figures in SAC are not identical to those in the *Menwarichō* 免割帳, but are adequate to show changes in the patterns of land registration.

[29] Nishimatsu diaries, lawsuit documents, and other sources, show that they held land in other villages as well, and SAC shows both *irisaku* 入作 (outsiders holding land in Nishijō) and *desaku* 出作 (villagers with land elsewhere). The Nishimatsu, although *nōmin* 農民 (legally peasants), were not farmers themselves, but purely landlords, entrepreneurs, and adminis-trators. All their land was tenanted.

[30] Most of these new holders (*takamochi* 高持) were listed with tiny parcels that were probably houselots, reflecting a new degree of independence (self-dependence; precariousn···) of the sort documented by Smith in *Agrarian Origins*; they do not signify a trend toward more even distribu-tion of land.

[31] Such headmen-in-receivership were apparently common in this polder, especially in cases of disputed succession, village protest against the headman, or a young, inexperienced head-man. Here, two of the three conditions prevailed. Cases of each sort are found in SAC and other Nishimatsu papers. Kitasuke (Gombei II after 1837) became a talented headman-overseer, and was often called on to serve as such in the 1830s, '40s and '50s.

The name Gombei went with household headship and dated at least from the mid-eighteenth century; it is unclear how many generations of men called Gombei precede our examination; we deal here with only two Gombei, whom we will call I and II.

1764 to 1925, missing only a few years in the 1850s and 1860s. With rare exceptions, the Nishimatsu archives do not include individual loan contracts, which are not part of the ledgers, and this makes certain kinds of tests (types of collateral, default penalties, etc.) impossible. These are strictly enterprise records, distinct from both landholding records and rent receipts, and from records of personal or household operations.

The Nishimatsu Credit Operation
The Nishimatsu credit operation changed rapidly in scale, in nature, and in complexity in the years under review. As credit demand increased, both Gombei I and Gombei II responded to the new environment by entering into new kinds of transactions that enabled them to keep pace with a growing volume of lending. What we witness, therefore, is not merely the growth of a lending enterprise, but its metamorphosis into a more intricate and highly ramified enterprise. Moreover, the relationship between the Nishimatsu finance operations, their landholdings, and other entrepreneurial activities may signal a new stage in their development as country bankers and rural entrepreneurs.

In order to understand the nature of these transformations, we will look at the changing volume of credit business, at interest rates, and at the kinds of financial transactions in which the Nishimatsu family engaged.

Volume of Credit and Demand for Credit
Nishimatsu credit operations both within and outside Nishijō expanded markedly in the years of the Tempō period, 1830–1844. Indeed, the ledgers show that period as having the most rapid growth in overall scale of operations in the final century of the Edo period. Whereas Gombei I had made 138 loans in 1833, by 1837, the worst year locally for the Tempō famine, he had 217 borrowers, a 57% increase in activity. Total volume of lending likewise rose rapidly: the balance of loans outstanding at year's end rose from an average of 396 ryō in 1829–1832, to an average of 1,547 ryō for the years 1837–1842, an increase of 391%.

The data in the Nishimatsu ledgers strongly suggest that local demand for credit in lowland Mino (Gombei I and II lent to borrowers in several nearby, and increasingly distant, villages and towns) grew rapidly in the mid-Tempō years. The credit climate was sufficiently attractive that, when Gombei II took over, he was willing, even eager, to capitalize on the expansion of credit, and was prepared to rely ever more extensively on borrowed capital to finance his moneylending activities. The Nishimatsu lending volume, as measured by year-end balances, increased nearly fourfold from the late 1820s to the mid-1840s. The ability to meet this rising demand and expand operations in this fashion was almost entirely dependent on the availability of outside sources of loan

---

[32] *Kingin Taishaku Chō* 金銀貸借帳, MS. 1764–1925, 161 vols., Nishimatsu-ke Monjo, Rikkyo University Library.

Figure 1.
Total volume of lending activity (in ryō of gold) for selected years,
as shown in Gombei's year-end totals.

Year	Volume lent (A)	Loan volume index (1828-1831=100)	Price index (Note ID)	Deflated loan volume
1828	G 349.00	91	80.9	112
1829	G 432.50	109	112.7	97
1830	G 491.00	124	101.1	123
1831	G 442.75	108	105.3	103
1832	G 260.00	66	93.2	71
1837	G 1152.75 B 121.00 N 1030.50 [sic]	292	178.9	163
1838	G 1157.00 B 234.50 N 881.00 [sic]	293	141.3	207
1839	G 1218.00 B 509.00 N 709.00	308	114.4	269
1840	G 1074.00 B 375.00 N 698.00 [sic]	272	76.2	357
1841	G 1007.75 G' 118.75 B 776.25 B' 8.75 N 231.50	255	82.0	311
1842	G 1481.00 B 918.25 N 563.00 [sic]	375	96.4	389
1843	*	521*	91.5	581*
1844	G 1639.50 B 1162.00 N 477.50	415	96.4	430

A=volume excludes minute amounts recorded in silver monetary units.
G=gross lending volume
G'=(?) loans written off as uncollectible (*jigoku*, 'hell')
B=gross sum borrowed (excludes sums held for depositors' accounts)
B'=another category of borrowed money, meaning unclear
N=net asset value of loans (G-B)
ID=index computed on basis of arithmetic average of spring, summer, and autumn Osaka wholesale rice prices as per Yamamura (1974, p. 52), with 1828-1834=100. 'Deflated loan volume' is nominal volume deflated by this price index.
*amounts recorded in private code; G, B both appear to exceed 2,000 ryō, with B under 2,100 ryō; index curve computed as G=2,100. Assume G=2,100, since we know that B≦2,100, and N≧1. Totals for 1833-1836 are not recorded in the ledgers.

Figure 2.
Gombei's lending: volume and index, 1828–1844.

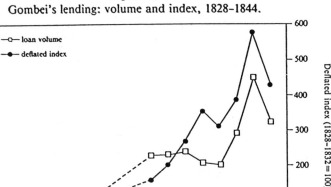

capital—wholesale credit that could be re-lent at higher rates of interest. This finding differs significantly from the pattern that Uemura noted in Harima province, where, he argues, the lender's principal source of loan capital was profits from prior lending and his other enterprises.[33] This pattern of increased reliance on borrowed capital was apparently introduced by Gombei II when he succeeded to household headship and management of the Nishimatsu enterprises. In 1837, the year in which he took over, only 10.5% of his lending was financed by borrowed capital, but by the following year the proportion had doubled to more than 20%. In the following year, it had doubled once more to nearly 42%; and by 1841, more than three-quarters of his lending activities were financed by borrowed capital.

This pattern of increasingly highly leveraged lending is remarkable. It indicates a willingness to take new financial risks in pursuit of expanded enterprise and greater profit. With all, or nearly all, his loan capital internally generated, Gombei I could survive a fairly high level of default or a decline in land (collateral) values; even Gombei II, initially financing only one-tenth of his lending with borrowed capital, was fairly safe. But when he was borrowing three-fifths to three-quarters of the capital for his loans, his own financial survival could be endangered by even a small increase in the default rate.

Still more important, this pattern of increasing reliance on borrowed capital indicates fundamental transformations in the nature and behavior of rural credit institutions in lowland Mino. First, as will be noted below, Gombei II's wholesale, or interbank, creditors were, like him, local financiers in the Mino polders; they were his counterparts as lenders, entrepreneurs, and headmen in

---

[33] Uemura, p. 221. Note that Uemura uses loan contracts, not ledgers, so other sources of capital may be hidden from view.

Figure 3.
Gombei's Leverage, 1837–1844.

Year	Borrowings as % of loan volume	Gross lending as multiples of personal capital
1837	10.50%	1:1.12
1838	20.27%	1:1.25
1839	41.79%	1:1.79
1840	34.92%	1:1.54
1841	77.03%	1:4.72
1842	61.99%	1:2.63
1844	70.83%	1:3.43

Figures for 1843 not available.

nearby villages. They also appear in Gombei's ledgers from time to time as his debtors, borrowing from him at wholesale, just as he borrowed from them. Several of them also appear in his books as depositors.

Gombei II, that is, had turned to what appears to have been an already existing network of cross-transactions among local financiers, rather than being himself the originator of a new form of financial behavior. It is here that he made the transition from moneylender to banker. One can readily imagine the young Kitasuke: seeing the volume of business of other local creditors growing through the exploitation of this network of wholesale credit, he was eager to join it to expand the Nishimatsu moneylending operation, and impatient at the old-fashioned unwillingness of Gombei I to get with the times. In this regional interbank market, when one member was temporarily short of loan capital, he turned to another; a few months later, the situation might well be reversed. In effect, interbank wholesale credit was short-term money, while retail credit was

Figure 4.
Gombei's leverage rates, 1837–1844.

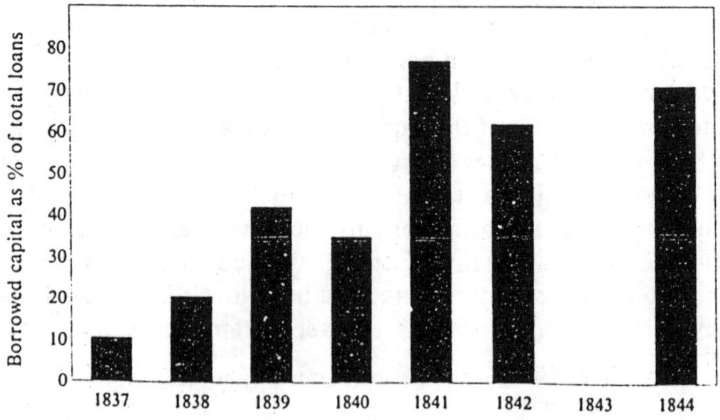

longer term. Thus, for example, while in 1837 Gombei's retail loans turned over on an average of 1.68 times per year (average term was 7.2 months), his wholesale borrowings turned over 2.61 times per year (average term, 4.6 months). It was not unusual for Gombei II to be both creditor and debtor vis-à-vis the same person simultaneously, or to hold deposits to the account of a borrower.

Figure 5.
Loans as multiple of capital, 1837–1844.

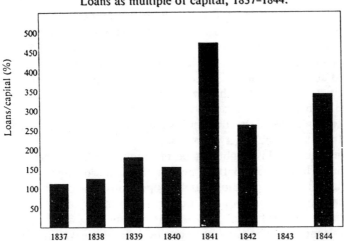

The implications of this point are quite substantial. Gombei II was taking out loans to finance a banking enterprise that was, by 1841–1843, lending an average of 3.6 times its capital (not correcting for deposit liabilities). If lenders were willing to supply him with short-term capital for that purpose, as he was to supply them, there must have been a high level of confidence in the soundness of local financial institutions and the general stability of the financial climate. Lenders had to be confident of repayment from retail borrowers, both their own and, in this case, Gombei's, to justify the risks involved in lending other peoples' money and in being overexposed by a factor of three to four. This suggests a highly developed network of faith in the institutions of finance, and of financiers in each other, which is what, at root, 'credit' means. Several factors may account for this advancement of 'faith' credit, but the arguments of Naomi Lamoreaux about the importance of kinship networks to the development of banking in early national New England are highly suggestive. There, she argues, 'The operation of . . . banks was shaped primarily by kinship networks—alliances . . . cemented by ties of marriage and consanguinity,' which enhanced stability and flexibility, enabling merchants to raise considerable capital while reducing risks.[34] And indeed, among Gom-

[34] Naomi R. Lamoreaux, 'Banks, Kinship, and Economic Development: The New England Case', in JEH 46:3 (September 1986), pp. 648 & 653.

bei's clients—as borrowers, lenders, and depositors—were several of his relatives among the elite of nearby villages.

Beyond the institutional points just noted, moreover, what we have found here has important implications for the broader sweep of Japanese economic development in the Tempō era. Gombei I had acted primarily as a simple moneylender, mostly lending from his own capital, supplementing it, as the Kondō family of Harima apparently did also, with profits from other Nishimatsu enterprises.[35] Using other people's capital, however, Gombei II was able to change the nature, and increase the scale, of his moneylending operations, while *reducing* the amount of his own capital involved. At the end of 1837, total loans outstanding were only 1.12 times his banking capital, which stood at 1,030.5 ryō (before adjusting for his liabilities to depositors). Within five years, he was able to effect a 28.5% increase in the size of his lending operation while reducing the amount of his own capital involved by 45%; he lent an average of 3.6 times the 'net asset value'[36] of the banking operation as shown in his year-end balances; if we subtract his liability for depositor's funds (as he does not), the deposit multipier is even higher.

The significance of this ought not be misunderstood. Gombei II was not unique in his behavior, but participated in a regional network of interbank lending and borrowing of substantial proportions. He went regularly to a half-dozen others in his own and nearby districts for loans at wholesale, interbank rates of interest, and they came to him in the same fashion. Thus, they were able more efficiently to move capital from those who held it to those who needed it at retail, while keeping the retail risks local. When Gombei was short of loan capital, he borrowed it from others at short-term, wholesale interest rates (see 'Interest Rates', below) to meet local retail demand; when others were short of loan capital, they came to him in similar fashion. They did not demand repayment of Gombei's interbank debts to them, which were not yet due, nor did they withdraw their deposits with him (*azukari* 預り). Rather, Gombei and his peers were simultaneously borrowers from, lenders to, and depositors with, each other.

By joining and exploiting this network of wholesale credit, Gombei and his peers were able effectively to increase efficiency of the money supply in the local economy. This increased efficiency probably worked to keep the cost of credit relatively low, encouraging the establishment of local petty enterprises and facilitating the operation of enterprises already in existence, thus fostering industrialization in the region.[37] This institutional reorganization of rural

---

[35] Uemura, p. 221.

[36] Gombei's term is simply *hiite* 引テ, 'subtracting', or the difference between total loans outstanding and total borrowings due to others. Given Gombei's rapidly rising reliance on borrowed capital, it is unlikely that one could find a meaningful modal leverage rate (dependence on borrowed capital) among the participants in this interbank network. Even a half-century later, under modern Japanese banking laws, capitalization rates varied widely from bank to bank. See Teranishi Jūrō 寺西重郎, *Nihon no Keizai Hatten to Kin'yū* 日本の経済発展と金融, Hitotsubashi Daigaku Keizai Kenkyū Sōsho Bessatsu, Iwanami, 1982, p. 54.

credit in the Nōbi lowlands, transforming moneylenders into bankers operating at deposit multipliers of three-to-one or four-to-one, increased the efficiency of the behavior of money in the local and regional economy. If the pattern found here in the Nōbi region, and inferred from Sakudō's Kōnoike data also to be true of the Osaka region, as well holds true elsewhere, it may increase the power of the Shimbo-Uemura thesis, of recoinage and bakufu spending sparking growth in the money supply and slow long-term inflation, to explain the advance of protoindustrialization that reversed the flow of population into the towns, bringing a relative decline in castle-town populations and a rural revival.[38]

Interest Rates

Interest rates varied widely in the late Edo period, from interest-free loans sometimes provided as relief measures by the shogun or daimyo in times of crisis,[39] and even between private creditors and borrowers,[40] to commercial retail rates of 30% per annum or higher.[41] These have been variously described in the Western-language literature as 'high interest rates', 'outrageously high rates', or 'usurious interest rates'.[42] But to judge whether these characterizations are warranted, we need to know what interest rates actually were, and consider whether they existed in the context of a local, regional, or national credit market. It would also be useful to make empirical comparisons with interest rates in other pre- or protoindustrial societies. Ideally we would like to make calculations of variables such as likelihood of repayment, collateral, anticipated effects of inflation, enforceability of debtor's obligation, etc.

In the early-modern Ottoman Empire, where Koranic proscriptions on usury ought to have eliminated lending-at-interest, 'an interest rate of 20% per

[37] Gombei's ledgers do not identify the uses to which his borrowers put their funds, but several were located in important centers of the *shima-momen* trade, such as Okoshijuku, east of the Kiso in Owari province, and Fuwa Isshiki, between the Kiso and the Nagara. The borrower in Okoshi, however, is not known to have been involved in the *shima-momen* trade, but is listed in the Okoshi SAC as a miso manufacturer in the 1840s and 1850s. *Okoshi-mura Shūmon Ninbetsu Aratame Chō*, MS, 37 vols., 1827–1869, Hayashi-ke Monjo, Rikkyo University Library; see Hayashi, p. 122.
Gombei himself entered the *sake*-brewing business in 1837 or 1838, probably acquiring the brewery by foreclosure from a villager caught bootlegging in 1835. See below, p. 000.
[38] Smith, 'Premodern Economic Growth', shows that such rural industry drew population away from urban centers in the last decades of the Edo period. It was employment opportunities offered by petty industrial operations such as Gombei's, and those that operated on credit he supplied, that were responsible for this population shift, visible in Nishijō too, after mid-Tempō.
[39] See Dan Fenno Henderson, *Village Contracts in Tokugawa Japan*, University of Washington Press, 1975, document 16, pp. 100–01.
[40] *Gifu Kenshi Shiryō Hen*, 20 vols., Gifu-ken, 1966–1973, *Kinsei*, 3, pp. 295–315.
[41] Henderson, document 21, pp. 110–11; Yosaburo Takekoshi, *Economic Aspects of the History of the Civilization of Japan*, Macmillan, London, 1930, 3, p. 72.
Interest rates continued to vary widely well into the Meiji period as well. See, for example, Asakura Kōkichi 朝倉孝吉, *Meiji Zenki Nihon Kin'yū Kōzō-shi* 明治前期日本金融構造史, Iwanami, 1961.
[42] Walthall, p. 7; Eijiro Honjo, *The Social and Economic History of Japan*, Institute of Economic Research, Kyoto, 1935, p. 78; Vlastos, p. 87.

year was accepted by the entire religious community as in accordance with [religious law].[43] Interest rates in early-modern Antwerp ran even higher, sometimes as high as 25%. In England in the 1570s rates of 10% were common; even after the passage of the usury laws there in 1571, lenders used surcharges and other devices (analogues of the 'points' in modern mortgages in the U.S.) to keep effective rates well into double digits.[44] All such rates would have been 'outrageous' by comparison to the rates on public debt in Britain around 1800, which averaged just over 5%.[45]

Indeed, it is even open to question whether the rates cited by Takekoshi, or those in Henderson's loan contracts, were usual in Tokugawa Japan. Sakudō's classic study of the banking activities of the Kōnoike house reports that it charged rates of 10–20% in the 1670s, but that rates then fell below 10% in 1685, and never again rose above that figure for loans to daimyos. Even loans to peasants were at single-digit rates in Sakudō's small sample of fifteen cases from the 1860s where the interest rates were recorded; the highest rate (and the most common: ten of the fifteen cases) was 8.5%.[46]

Yasuzawa Mine has examined a sample of forty loans, using records from a village west of Edo (and now part of Tokyo) between 1791 and 1868. Principal amounts in her sample ranged from 1 to 32 ryō, and loan periods from five months to ten years (with three open-term loans to mutual-aid societies, three with term unspecified, and one 'on demand'). Rates on the interest-bearing loans ranged from 10% (three cases) to 20% (three cases), with the rate unrecorded in seven cases, and one at 'market'. Yet even here, the most common rate was only 12% (12 cases), and in fully 75% (21 of 28) of the cases where the rate was both fixed and recorded, the rate fell in a range between 12% and 12.8%. The average interest rate for all loans was 12.92%. In two other retail loan samples from the same village, average interest rates were slightly higher, but with one exception (21.7%) the range was the same.[47]

In Fukuoka *han*, in northern Kyushu, Arne Kalland found 'normal' interest rates on loans made from publicly sponsored credit funds ranged from 10% to 15% in the late Edo period.[48] He calls these 'very low interest rate[s]' that would be attractive to merchants who could borrow from the fund, while

---

[43] Ronald C. Jennings, 'Loans and Credit in the Early 17th Century Ottoman Judicial Records: The Sharia Court of the Anatolian Kayseri', in *Journal of Economic and Social History of the Orient*, 16:2–3 (1973), p. 184.

[44] Parker, p. 17; G. C. A. Clay, *Economic Expansion and Social Change: England 1500–1700*, II: *Industry, Trade and Government*, Cambridge U.P., 1984, p. 233.

[45] L. S. Presnell, *Country Banking in the Industrial Revolution*, Oxford U.P., 1956, pp. 450ff. The 5% limit on interest rates set by the nineteenth-century British usury laws was honored largely in the breach. Presnell, p. 285.

[46] Sakudō, pp. 457, 515 & 520–21. The Kōnoike appear in these cases to have been wholesalers, lending to retail lenders in the villages, who were themselves wealthy farmers like Gombei. Although Sakudō does not draw inferences of a transition to banking from this, it would appear that the Kōnoike were here supporting debt-financed bankers.

[47] Yasuzawa Mine, '*Kinsei Kōki ni okeru Nōmin Kin'yū no Hatten*' 近世後期における農民金融 の発展, in *Kōbe Jogakuin Daigaku Ronsō*, 26:3 (1980), pp. 266ff & 270–73.

lending their own funds 'at an interest rate of 15–30 per cent per annum.' In private lending agreements, Kalland admits great difficulty in determining the level of interest rates, noting, 'The interest varied according to the social relationship between the creditor and the debtor, the risk involved, the type of contract. . . , etc.' Still, Kalland concludes, 'Nonetheless it seems safe to say that short-term loans to farmers carried the highest interest, usually 20 or 30 percent in Fukuoka.' Fukuoka *han* had authorized interest rates of 25% to 30% in 1771, and these limits still stood in the mid-nineteenth century.[49]

By these standards, Gombei appears to have lent at more or less normal market rates. Furthermore, he does not seem to have taken exceptional advantage of rural distress during the Tempō famine to extract greater profits. I examined the interest rates he charged his retail customers, those he paid his depositors, and those he paid his wholesale credit suppliers, for three separate years, 1829, 1833, and 1837, for all loans where the rate was recorded or could be calculated from the recorded data. Because Gombei himself made such a distinction, I differentiated among loans to fellow-residents of Nishijō, residents of Jūrembō, residents of Nakamura, and all others.[50] The results are summarized in Figure 6 on p. 502.

Gombei charged his borrowers interest rates varying from a low of 5% to a high of 17%.[51] Those loans extended to borrowers outside Nishijō at rates lower than 10% seem to have been to 'agents' (*toritsugi* 取次) re-lending for Gombei, or wholesale loans to other country bankers. As in Yasuzawa's sample, the 'normal' retail interest rate was between 12% and 15%. The rates paid were fairly stable over the years under study, more so than pawnshop rates in Osaka, but like the latter, Gombei's rates on retail loans, interbank borrowings, and deposits were lower in 1841 than they had been at any time in the previous dozen years.[52]

It is also clear that Gombei differentiated among his customers by place of residence. He seems to have charged slightly lower interest rates on loans to his immediate neighbors, whom he administered and who were his main source of tenant labor. The average rates charged 'outsiders' were marginally higher, and the modal rate for outsiders was also higher. Yasuzawa also found differences in the nature of loans made locally and those made to people in

---

[48] Kalland, 'A Credit Institution', p. 13; 'Rural Credit Institutions', p. 5.

[49] Kalland, 'Rural Credit Institutions', pp. 10ff. If Fukuoka merchants were using borrowed capital to finance their moneylending, as Kalland infers, they too were effecting a transition to banking.

[50] *Kingin*. Gombei noted 'Jūrembō' next to a few loan entries; later, he began segregating his ledgers by place of a borrower's residence.

[51] One exceptional loan appears, by calculating back from the interest amount, to have carried a 30% rate, but that is probably payment of two years' interest at once.

[52] Saitō Osamu, '*Tokugawa Kōki ni okeru Rishiritsu to Kahei Kyōkyū*' 徳川後期における利子率と貨幣供給, in Umemura Mataji *et al.*, ed., *Suryō Keizai-shi Ronshū* 数量経済史論集, 1: *Nihon Keizai no Hatten: Kinsei kara Kindai e* 日本経済の発展：近世から近代へ, Nihon Keizai Shimbunsha, 1976, pp. 281–97.
Saitō finds that the interest rates of Osaka pawnshops varied inversely with inflation, particularly after 1860, but the inverse correlation is less striking in the Tempō era.

Figure 6.
Interest rates charged by Gombei in 1829, 1833 & 1837.

Interest per annum	Number of loans to borrowers in:			
	Nishijō	Nakamura	Jurembō	Other
	1829 (Bunsei 12)			
0.00–9.99	7 (22%)	9 (30%)	0 (0%)	1 (9%)
10.00–14.99	13 (41%)	5 (17%)	0 (0%)	5 (45%)
15.00	10 (31%)	14 (47%)	2 (100%)	4 (36%)
15.01–17.00	2 (6%)	2 (7%)	0 (0%)	1 (9%)
Total cases Average a.p.r.	32 (100%) 12.12%	30 (100%) 12.30%	2 (100%) 15.00%	11 (100%) 12.51%
	1833 (Tempō 4)			
0.00–9.99	11 (23%)	5 (28%)	1 (25%)	0 (0%)
10.00–14.99	14 (29%)	7 (39%)	0 (0%)	1 (17%)
15.00	20 (42%)	5 (28%)	3 (75%)	3 (50%)
15.01–20.00	3 (6%)	1 (6%)	0 (0%)	2 (33%)
Total cases Average a.p.r.	48 (100%) 12.36%	18 (100%) 11.84%	4 (100%) 13.33%	6 (100%) 14.69%
	1837 (Tempō 8)			
0.00–9.99	8 (16%)	7 (18%)	0 (0%)	2 (22%)
10.00–14.99	27 (55%)	9 (23%)	0 (0%)	4 (44%)
15.00	15 (31%)	20 (51%)	2 (100%)	2 (22%)
15.01–20.00	0 (0%)	3 (8%)	0 (0%)	0 (0%)
30.00	0 (0%)	0 (0%)	0 (0%)	1 (11%)
Total cases Average a.p.r.	46 (100%) 12.86%	39 (100%) 12.92%	2 (100%) 15.00%	9 (100%) 13.14%*

*Average rate including loan with nominal 30% rate. Average if that loan is excluded: 9%. These tables include only those loans for which interest rates are recorded or for which data permit calculating a putative rate.

other villages, noting that the former tended to be for smaller amounts than loans where borrower and lender lived in different villages.[53] Still, she did not find the sort of interest-rate differential seen in Nishijō.

Why Gombei offered more favorable interest rates on local loans is unclear, for we are working from ledgers, not a statement of banking philosophy. The differentials may reflect his greater enforcement power over peasants under his jurisdiction, where his ability to calculate risk and enforce collection was more direct. Also, if a loan to a local borrower was secured, no other headman would block Gombei's access to the collateral. He may also have been constrained by his own sense of obligation to his Nishijō neighbors, for he forgave

[53] Yasuzawa, 1977 & 1980.

interest in some cases when borrowers were in distress, and, as has been noted, appears to have ceased using loan foreclosures as a means of acquiring new land at about the time of the Tempō famine. Indeed, after 1833, he stopped increasing his landholdings at all. Further, the memory of the premature transfer of village headship in response to local protest may well have encouraged Gombei I and II to moderate the rates they charged when dealing with close neighbors.

Nishimatsu interest rates seem to have been generally consistent with rates in the local, regional, and national money markets. In a ledger from another village, dating from 1840, rates on wholesale loans made to other Mino villages in the shogunal fisc ranged from the rare interest-free loan to the more common rate of 10%.[54] This was at the high end of the range that Gombei paid on borrowed funds and charged for interbank money.

Moreover, the markup between the interest Gombei paid to depositors (*azukari*) and wholesale-market creditors (*kari* かり, 借り), and the rates he charged retail customers on their loans (*kashi* かし, 貸し) do not seem exceptionally high. Certainly, his rates are in line with the contemporary national market, judging from comparison with the data that Sakudō, Yasuzawa, Kalland, and others have found. If the lender has to recover through interest his anticipated losses owing to defaults, and offset the effects of the secular inflationary trends of the day,[55] these will be reflected in higher interest rates; this is independent of whether such recovery is 'fair' or 'exploitative'.[56] Gombei I paid an average of 8.15% on borrowed funds in 1829, and charged an average of about 12.5% on his retail loans. For the four years tested, the differentials are set out in Figures 7 & 9, below.

The Nishimatsu family was charging markups of between 3.12 and 4.58 percentage points (15% to 54% markups) over wholesale on retail loans. Whether these interest rates are 'normal' or 'outrageous' depends on the factors noted above, many of which are impossible to compute. But in a decade when both commodity prices and the relative values of specie were unstable, our comparison with known interest rates elsewhere in the country suggests that they were at least consistent with the contemporary market.

[54] *Gifu Kenshi Shiryō-hen Kinsei*, 3, pp. 295–315.
[55] See n. 21, above.
[56] Besides inflation and profit, the margin between wholesale and retail rates will reflect factors such as term, risk, collateral, and the relatively higher unit transaction cost on smaller loans.

The Mitsui house likewise had a sliding scale of interest rates varying with the amount of principal in the funds that it lent to branch shops. In the early 1700s, rates ranged from 7% per half-year for loans over 1,000 ryō, to 10% for loans under 500 ryō. Fujita, p. 131.

More informally, a series of telephone calls to local Illinois banks in 1988 found that they were operating with almost exactly the same spread between wholesale and retail money as Gombei did. If Kalland's Fukuoka merchants were indeed borrowing at 15% to relend at 25–30%, they were operating at margin levels undocumented elsewhere.

Figure 7.
Interest rates paid by Gombei on borrowed funds.

%	1829	1833	1837	1841
2.25	—	—	—	1
2.50	—	—	—	2
3.30	—	—	—	1
3.75	1	—	1	—
4.50	—	—	—	1
5.00	1	—	—	—
5.80	—	—	—	2
6.00	—	—	1	1
6.30	—	—	—	1
6.37	—	—	1	—
6.40	—	—	1	—
6.70	—	—	1	—
7.00	1	—	—	—
7.76	—	—	1	—
8.00	3	2	—	—
8.30	—	—	—	1
9.00	2	1	—	1
10.00	4	4	4	—
average a.p.r.	8.15%	9.29%	8.37%	5.11%

Who Borrowed?

The Nishimatsu family's immediate environment was populated mostly by farmers, so, naturally, most of their borrowers were farmers—but some were not. Other than local farmers, and farmers and rural entrepreneurs in nearby towns and villages, the Nishimatsu also extended loans to urban merchants and rural temples. In 1837, for example, during the Tempō famine, they lent 5 ryō to a nearby Zen temple. But Nishimatsu lending was not entirely local; it was regional and, even, inter-regional in scope. Indeed, the Nishmatsu extended loans to merchants in Ōgaki and Nagoya, more than twenty-five kilometers to the southeast, and to a small-town entrepreneur in Okoshijuku, in the heart of the *shima-momen* district; occasional loans were made to borrowers as far away as Sakai, a suburb of Osaka, more than 150 km to the west. These loans far beyond the confines of village and polder, across province and domain boundaries, and even to the commercial heartland of Osaka, further suggest how deeply the Nishimatsu and Nishijō had become enmeshed in a regional, and even national, credit market. And in the last three decades of the Edo period, the family began 'lending' (loans never repaid) to the office of the shogunal representative in Ōgaki. This may have been the price of its elevation (return?) to samurai status in 1861.

But most Nishimatsu borrowers—more than 90% in 1829, with the percentage rising through the Tempō era—were local peasants, either from Nishijō itself, or from Nakamura, the village immediately north across the river. These were neither daimyos nor merchants in distant towns, whose credit needs provided Gombei with lending opportunities that tempted him, as has been suggested of headman-creditors, to exploit his peasant charges. He was not lured into 'taking all surplus from the peasants . . . extracting taxes from [his] subordinates and neighbors, [while keeping] enough for [himself] to initiate'[57] loans 'to daimyo, villages, irrigation districts. . . .'[58] This is not to say that Gombei did not extract 'surpluses from the peasants', but whether he did or not, peasants were also his principal customers for credit.

Although Nishijō and Nakamura peasants formed the largest group of borrowers, residents of many other villages also turned to the Nishimatsu for loans; in addition (although obviously not visible in the Nishimatsu ledgers), some local peasants went outside the village for credit, or even to others within the village, such as the priest noted above whose landholdings grew rapidly in the 1810s.[59] Some of their borrowers were fellow members of the local elite, members of the Nishijō governing council as well as headmen and other officials from nearby villages. A regular Nishimatsu customer throughout the Tempō years was a village headman a few kilometers to the west; he happened to be Gombei I's father-in-law (or his successor).

But it is unlikely that, at least after the mid-1830s, Gombei was lending actively to the poorest peasants. For example, his average loan was 7.4 ryō in 1833, 8 in 1837, and 13.7 in 1841.[60] These were considerable sums in a decade when a carpenter could be hired for an annual wage of 2.5 ryō in Kazusa province, the average annual wage of a maidservant in one Harima village was between 1.6 ryō (one-year contract) and 2.08 ryō (short-term contract), and the annualized wage of planting-season agricultural labor at day rates in the Osaka area (assuming, unrealistically, a 300-day work year) was 6.29 ryō.[61]

We have seen that the Nishimatsu lending operation encompassed a wide geographical and social reach—to Nagoya, Okoshi, Ōgaki, and even Sakai—and we find Gombei himself entering the business of *sake* brewing by 1838.

[57] Walthall, p. 7.

[58] Smith, *Agrarian Origins*, p. 168.

[59] The moneylending ledgers of the Tanabashi, hereditary headmen of Niremata, show regular loans in the mid-Tempō period to peasants in both Nishijō and Jūrembō. *Yorozu Oboe Chō* 万覚帳, MS (1834), 1838 & 1839, in Tanabashi-ke Monjo, Gifu Kenritsu Shiryōkan.

[60] *Kingin*. Since many people borrowed more than once during a year, the averages per borrower are somewhat higher: 11.2 ryō (1833), 16 (1837), and 24.9 (1841).

[61] Henderson, p. 7 (Kazusa); Uemura, p. 182 (Harima); Saitō Osamu, '*Tokugawa Chūki no Jisshitsu Chingin no Kakusa*' 徳川中期の実質賃金の格差, in *Shakai Keizai Shigaku*, 41:5 (1975), p. 457 (Osaka area).

The increasing size of the Nishimatsu's average loan suggests that most of their borrowers were not desperate members of the peasantry, the sort envisioned by Medick as borrowing merely to sustain themselves in the struggle for survival; they seem to have been instead middling peasants seeking capital to participate in the economic expansion that, Shimbo and Uemura argue, characterized these decades. This pattern is consistent with the findings of Nakayama in Bingo province, where the lender he studied altered his business activities so that, 'After about the Tempō era, peasant producers and the Fuchū urban lower classes were excluded as the object of loans, which were increasingly limited to commercial capitalists in all areas [of endeavor].'[62]

To be sure, poorer peasants, too, must have borrowed from somewhere, for then as now the poor often fell into 'a vicious circle of permanently having to live on credit.'[63] But neither the Nishimatsu, nor the Nobuto family that Nakayama studied, was interested in this low-volume, high-risk market. What we witness, rather, is a market segmentation and specialization of creditors, with houses such as the Nishimatsu and the Nobuto concentrating on the lower-risk, lower-interest premium market, that included rural entrepreneurs and left the riskier low-end market to others.

Types of Transactions
The rapid growth of Gombei's credit operation, and his transformation from moneylender to banker, in late Tempō came about because he defied both sides of Polonius's advice, engaging in an ever more varied range of transactions. We will now examine that range of transactions as it appears in the Nishimatsu ledgers, looking first at where the Nishimatsu placed their loans, then at the sources of their lending capital.

Uses of Funds
Collateralized retail loans at interest made up the bulk of Nishimatsu lending activity and consumed most of their available loan capital. But, as noted above, foreclosure on collateralized land seems to have ceased after about 1833. At least, the Nishimatsu landholdings did not grow after that date, although they may have been selling foreclosed land for cash. Loans at interest without collateral were a smaller part of the business; these loans were smaller and carried higher rates of interest (as best can be seen from the ledgers) because of higher risk.

Gombei II seems to have engaged in two principal types of interbank lending. First, loans placed wholesale through agents (*toritsugi*) in other villages, who lent the funds locally at retail but on the Nishimatsu account. In these cases, the *toritsugi* appear not to have been at risk to the Nishimatsu and were paid a handling fee. In villages where Gombei had few local contacts, these agency loans would offer better assurances than if he had dealt directly with unknown retail customers. Second, Gombei lent substantial sums wholesale to

---

[62] Nakayama, p. 18.   [63] Medick, p. 49.

other rural bankers like himself, who in turn lent the money locally on their own account.

Sources of Funds

Like other rural moneylenders, Gombei II surely used personal capital, that is, accumulated profits from land rents and other enterprises, including money-lending, as sources of lending capital. These, however, are only implicit and not immediately evident from the ledgers; hence they are not quantifiable with the data in hand. Yet until Gombei II began heavy wholesale borrowing, land rents were likely his major source of loan capital. Most scholarship sees this as the principal, and often the only, source of loan capital for the village moneylenders in the Edo period.[64]

Funds borrowed (*kari*) from other rural capitalists in nearby villages, a source of only minor loan capital prior to 1837, became increasingly important until, by 1841, they were Gombei II's principal source of banking funds. It is worth reiterating that some of the people from whom Gombei borrowed were also people to whom he simultaneously lent large sums. These were the other rural bankers who comprised the emerging interbank wholesale credit network that Gombei II had joined. They had formed this network perhaps to spread their risks, as well as to be able to respond more flexibly and immediately to retail loan on demand. The appearance of Gombei II's wholesale suppliers of credit simultaneously as his wholesale credit customers, moreover, suggests that, at least in the Nōbi lowlands, Gombei was neither unique nor anomalous, but representative of an emerging class of village bankers who participated in an informal, but sophisticated, regional network of interbank cross-credit arrangements.

Funds Held on Deposit

Gombei II's heavy reliance on borrowing from this interbank network for loan capital was augmented by his acceptance of interest-bearing deposits, either for fixed terms or on demand, from local individuals and institutions, who placed with him savings they wished to protect and increase without the risks attendant on engaging directly in moneylending or other entrepreneurial activity. Depositors' funds (*azukari*, also the modern term) are clearly differentiated from borrowed funds (*kari*) in the ledgers; 'deposits', 'borrowing', and 'loans' are separately labeled and separately recorded. By 1837 total deposits were nearly 100 ryō, and these and borrowed capital accounted for more than 21% of all Gombei's loan capital. In 1838, the largest single depositor was the headman of a nearby village, a maternal kinsman of Gombei II, to whom he also lent funds at the same time (see above). Other borrowers included a widow who was an affinal relative of Gombei II, and a group of parishioners (*kō* 講) at a nearby Zen temple.[65] Interest rates on deposits were, naturally, lower than

---

[64] For example, Uemura, p. 221.

[65] It is not clear from the Nishimatsu ledgers whether this *kō* was simply the temple's parishioners, setting aside joint funds for a specific common purpose, or a revolving-loan group of the *tanomoshikō/mujinkō* type.

Figure 8.
Interest rates paid by Gombei
on funds held for depositors.

rates	1837	1841
4.0%	—	1
6.0	—	6
6.6	1	—
7.5	—	1
10.0	1	3
average a.p.r.	8.3%	7.04%

rates charged on loans out, and a standard notation on new deposits was that the deposit was 'received on [date], but interest accrues only from the first of the following month.'

Figure 9.
Differential between interest charged and interest paid.

Year	Interest charged to borrowers	Interest paid to creditors	Interest paid to depositors
1829	12.33%	8.150%	none recorded
1833	12.41%	9.290%	none recorded
1837	12.95%	8.370%	8.30%
1841	10.41%	5.113%	7.04%

Agency Funds

Funds were also accepted as agent for other local bankers to be lent on their account. Details from the ledgers are unclear and so we do not know just how Gombei profited from these transactions (probably a handling fee), but these *toritsugi* funds mirror monies that Gombei placed with others as agents for him. Agency placements were a minor source of funds, and it is not certain that they should be counted as part of Gombei's loan capital at all.

   Another set of transactions appearing in the ledgers is a major non-lending use of Nishimatsu funds in the later Tempō years, not directly noted in the banking ledgers as an account, but which may help explain the rapid increase in reliance on borrowed capital during the second half of the Tempō era. This was the takeover (or less likely, the founding) and financing of a local *sake* brewery in Nishijō, which had been operated illegally by another local peasant until it was officially licensed in 1835.[66] The bootlegger was head of an old elite house in the Jūrembō section, a longtime member of the Nishijō governing council, who had a history of declining landholding and growing indebtedness

---

[66] *Goyō Nikki*, MS (1835).

to Gombei I. It had been he who led the protest against Gombei I in 1819. After 1835 he disappears from the rolls of the council, after more than sixty years' nearly continuous service by his family.[67] The brewery is noted in the official inventory of village economic activity by at least 1838,[68] and by 1841 was clearly in Gombei's hands; his ledgers note that the brewery was producing revenues of 130 ryō by that year, and in 1844 they had grown to 464 ryō. When brewing revenues were first noted in the ledgers (simply as an addendum at year end, not as part of the banking business), they amounted to 33% of the net asset value of Gombei's banking business; by 1844 they were equal to 72%.[69] There is no indication that the *sake* revenues were used in the banking business.

It had puzzled me why the rapid increase in money-lending activity, and the change from moneylender to banker and the move into brewing, were not reflected in an increase in Gombei's landholdings, which had risen by 75% from 1801 to 1833, but did not rise significantly thereafter. But Gombei was no longer principally interested in land. We are therefore witnessing not merely the transformation of a village moneylender into a rural banker but also that of a landlord into a general rural entrepreneur. By the 1870s the Nishimatsu augmented their farming, banking, and brewing activities with textile operations that became the mainstay of the family's considerable wealth in the Meiji, Taishō, and early Shōwa periods.[70] But it is important to note that it is during the 1830s that Gombei began to make a rudimentary year-end balance sheet, and to calculate the capital value of his banking operations. For many years Gombei I had recorded total loans outstanding at year end, but in 1837, for the first time, Gombei II recorded his total borrowings, as well as total loans, outstanding. Although he did not use terms such as *shihon* 資本 (capital) or *shisan* 資産 (assets), from 1837 on, at the end of each year's ledger he closed the books by calculating the difference between these two sums, constituting in crude form a calculation of the net worth of his banking business. At this stage, Gombei II was not treating deposits as a liability for this purpose, as he did borrowings, but we can nevertheless see this as a primitive capital account. It became a permanent feature of Gombei's bookkeeping, reflecting a new stage of entrepreneurial consciousness in transition to capitalism.

Furthermore, it is precisely at this time that Gombei II ceased to accumulate additional landholdings. This was not the case for the Tanabashi 棚橋 family in Niremata, who continued to invest in land until the end of the Edo period, adding 104 koku to their landholdings within Niremata (they also held land in Nishijō) between 1853 and 1868, an increase of 49%. Yet Gombei II was

---

[67] *Goyō Nikki*; *Kingin*; SAC.

[68] *Meisaichō*, in *Chōshi*, p. 869.

[69] As noted, one management and accounting advance Gombei II introduced was a year-end balancing of the books, and rudimentary calculation of the net asset value of the banking business.

[70] Interviews with Nishimatsu descendants in Nishijō and Hashima, and with others in the polder, October 1984 and April & August 1985.

not alone in shifting his interests from land to other forms of investments. Jinnoemon 庄之右衛門, *shōya* of nearby Toyobami Shinden, nearly doubled his holdings between 1769 and 1844 from 108 to 211 koku, but then he added only 20 koku more in the following nineteen years.[71] Clearly not all members of the local elite were disillusioned in land as an investment. Yet also plainly, Gombei II was not alone in reducing the importance of land among his overall assets.

Conclusion

The Nishimatsu were wealthy and powerful peasants long before the Tempō era, and their status did not change with the crises of the time. Their crédit operations, and those of other rural financiers like them, both in the Nōbi lowlands and, making inferences from data gathered elsewhere, in other regions as well, had already been evolving to meet the pressures of an increasingly monetized, commercialized, and protoindustrial environment in the countryside. But in the Tempō era, growth in the money supply and secular inflation were combining with other long-term social and economic forces to accelerate a protoindustrial transition in Japan. This coincided with a generational transition in management of the Nishimatsu enterprises, and was the occasion for a major shift in the way that Gombei II deployed his considerable assets, a shift that addresses the complex nature of moneylending and banking in a late preindustrial society.

The pressures and opportunities of the Tempō era forced rural banks such as the Nishimatsu to make strategic decisions about the organization of their resources in land and money, decisions both conditioned and constrained by the need to adapt to the long-term trends noted above. The changes that Gombei II implemented starting in 1837 were to transform him from moneylender to banker, and from village landlord to rural entrepreneur. The beginning of an inflationary half-century around 1820, we have noted, is credited with catalyzing a favorable investment climate and an accelerated protoindustrial trend. By the time Gombei II took over management of the Nishimatsu enterprises in 1837, well-established inflationary expectations could naturally have increased people's inclination to borrow for investment purposes. Similarly, the expansion in protoindustrial entrepreneurship, increasingly requiring a market orientation in traditional production as well as in new forms of production, generated capital-hungry small enterprises, some of which turned to Gombei for funds.

Taking over the moneylending business at a time of apparently rising demand for credit, Gombei II made a series of decisions that enabled him both to expand the scale of his operations and to alter their nature. These changes tell us a great deal about the changing nature of rural credit in protoindustrial Japan. First, as we have seen, Gombei II began to participate regularly, and

[71] *Chōshi*, pp. 146 & 148. Landholding data for the Tanabashi and Jinnoemon are available for only isolated years, so these data must be used with care.

more heavily, in a regional network of interbank cross-lending, increasingly relying on borrowed capital to finance his own lending. As with many of the changes in the operation of the various Nishimatsu businesses, it is not clear from the records whether cross-borrowing was Gompei II's own idea, or originated with others. Gombei I had borrowed small amounts occasionally by the late 1820s, and the rapidity with which Gombei II moved from reliance on personal to borrowed loan capital makes it likely that the interbank lending network was operating even before 1837. He probably joined the network as a regular participant that very year, and by the early 1840s was borrowing nearly four-fifths of his loan capital through the network.

One can imagine Gombei II: although nearly forty years of age, he had been excluded from managing the family's businesses. But with almost twenty years' experience as village headman, he already had working relationships with most of the moneylender/bankers in the area, who were, like him, also headmen. As a newcomer to the network, he moved cautiously at first, going to the network for only about 10% or 20% of his funds; but by 1840 he was relying on borrowed funds for more than half his loan capital, and soon after was so heavily involved that he was borrowing sums equal to four-fifths of his outstanding loans.

Thus the Nishimatsu credit operation moved rapidly from simply moneylender to banker, developing a primitive capital account as well, while diversifying from land and lending to a more complex array of enterprises. It is difficult to be certain whether these changes were all as rapid as they appear from the record, or products of a long evolution catalyzed into visibility by recent events. But the appearance in the Nishimatsu records of numerous similar local capitalists who participated with Gombei II in a regional network strongly suggests the latter case. Similarly, if the inference drawn above of lender reliance on borrowed capital in Fukuoka, and later in the Osaka region,[72] is correct, then further research should find patterns of debt-financed lending to be characteristic not simply of the Nōbi lowlands but more generally around the country.

The reverse of this coin is a picture of entrepreneurship built more heavily on borrowed capital than we have yet recognized. The Nishimatsu ledgers do not reveal the uses that borrowers made of their loans, and so this must remain speculative. But it is clear from the ledgers that substantial numbers of rural and urban entrepreneurs, including the Nishimatsu, were supplementing their own capital by borrowing. And it is also clear from the Nishimatsu documents that this enabled them to increase their scale of operations in one area (banking), while reducing the amount of their own capital in the enterprise; at the same time this apparently freed capital for deployment in other projects.

The interbank network the Nishimatsu joined was situated in the Nōbi lowlands, the heart of protoindustrial Japan, and straddling the boundary

[72] Kalland, 'A Credit Institution'; 'Rural Credit Institutions'; Sakudō, *Kinsei Hōken Shakai*.

between the *shima-momen* region east of the Nagara and the more purely farming-oriented region west of the Nagara. With the advance of regional specialization and industrial production for the national market becoming more central to the economy and society of the manufacturing subregion, these subregions became increasingly interdependent. Mendel's model proposes not merely the industrialization of farming villages but the emergence of organically interdependent subregions of primarily industrializing and primarily agricultural production. As noted above, this model has developed up to now without concern for the role of credit.

The investigation of the Nishimatsu banking operations reveals an increasingly active network of interbank wholesale credit, straddling both primarily agricultural and more heavily industrial subregions of the Nōbi lowlands, while other scholarship also suggests the existence of other networks elsewhere. These findings support Mendel's initial formulation and offer a promising new way to elaborate the model still further, advancing our understanding of the place of credit in protoindustrialization and in late Tokugawa Japan.

Acknowledgments

Crawcour, E.S. and Kozo Yamamura. "The Tokugawa Monetary System: 1787–1868." *Economic Development and Cultural Change* 18 (1970): 489–518. Reprinted with the permission of the University of Chicago Press.

Furushima, Toshio. "The Village and Agriculture During the Edo Period." Translated by James L. McClain. In *The Cambridge History of Japan*, vol. 4, *Early Modern Japan*, edited by John Whitney Hall (New York: Cambridge University Press, 1991): 478–518. Reprinted with the permission of the Cambridge University Press.

Hayami, Akira. "Population Changes." In *Japan in Transition: From Tokugawa to Meiji*, edited by Marius B. Jansen and Gilbert Rozman (Princeton: Princeton University Press, 1986): 280–317. Reprinted with the permission of Princeton University Press.

Howell, David L. "Proto-Industrial Origins of Japanese Capitalism." *Journal of Asian Studies* 51 (1992): 269–86. Reprinted with the permission of the Association for Asian Studies, Inc.

Nakai, Nobuhiko and James L. McClain. "Commercial Change and Urban Growth in Early Modern Japan." In *The Cambridge History of Japan*, vol. 4, *Early Modern Japan*, edited by John Whitney Hall (New York: Cambridge University Press, 1991): 519–95. Reprinted with the permission of the Cambridge University Press.

Nishikawa, Shunsaku. "The Economy of Chōshū on the Eve of Industrialization." *Economic Studies Quarterly* 38 (1987): 323–37. Reprinted with the permission of the Japan Association of Economics and Econometrics.

Nishikawa, Shunsaku. "Productivity, Subsistence, and By-Employment in the Mid-Nineteenth Century Chōshū." *Explorations in Economic History* 15 (1978): 69–83. Copyright by Academic Press, Inc.

Ohkura, Takehiko and Hiroshi Shimbo. "The Tokugawa Monetary Policy in the Eighteenth and Nineteenth Centuries." *Explorations in Economic History* 15 (1978): 101–24. Copyright by Academic Press, Inc.

Saitō, Osamu. "The Labor Market in Tokugawa Japan: Wage Differentials and the Real Wage Level, 1727–1830." *Explorations in Economic History* 15 (1978): 84–100. Copyright by Academic Press, Inc.

Saitō, Osamu. "Scenes of Japan's Economic Development and the 'Longue Duree.'" *Bonner Zeitschrift für Japanologie* 8 (1986): 15–27.

Schaede, Ulrike. "Forwards and Futures in Tokugawa-Period Japan: A New Perspective on the Dōjima Rice Market." *Journal of Banking and Finance* 13 (1989): 487–513. Reprinted with the permission of North-Holland Publishers.

Toby, Ronald P. "Both a Borrower and a Lender Be: From Village Moneylender to Rural Banker in the Tempō Era." *Monumenta Nipponica* 46 (1991): 483–512. Reprinted with the permission of *Monumenta Nipponica*.